Photography: A Critical Introduction

This is the first introductory textbook to examine key debates in photographic theory and place them in their social and political contexts. Written especially for students in further education, higher education and introductory college courses, it provides a coherent introduction to the nature of photographic seeing.

Individual chapters cover principal debates and theorists; the documentary role of the camera; the popular and personal, including the family album; advertising and commodity culture; photography as fine art and photography and digital imaging.

Designed to direct students to key reading and to assist understanding of central concepts, this accessible textbook includes:

- principal references and notes in the margin
- a full glossary of terms
- comprehensive end-of-chapter bibliographies
- case studies demonstrating methods of analysis

The discussion of theories, case studies and developments is impressively illustrated throughout with photographs and images, their diversity reflecting the breadth of issues and practices covered. Work by Jacob Riis, Dorothea Lange and Lee Friedlander features in the discussion of documentary photography. Advertising and contemporary fashion photography are exemplified by images from early Kodak advertising and recent campaigns by Benetton. Photographers referenced in the discussion of photography as fine art include Bill Brandt, Alexander Rodchenko, Lee Miller and Ingrid Pollard. The significance of new image technologies in the 'post-photographic' era is illustrated with computer-generated images and a NASA satellite image of earth.

The Editor: Liz Wells is a senior lecturer in film, video and photographic studies at the School of Media, The London Institute, London College of Printing and Distributive Trades.

Contributors: Patricia Holland, Martin Lister, Derrick Price, Anandi Ramamurthy and Liz Wells.

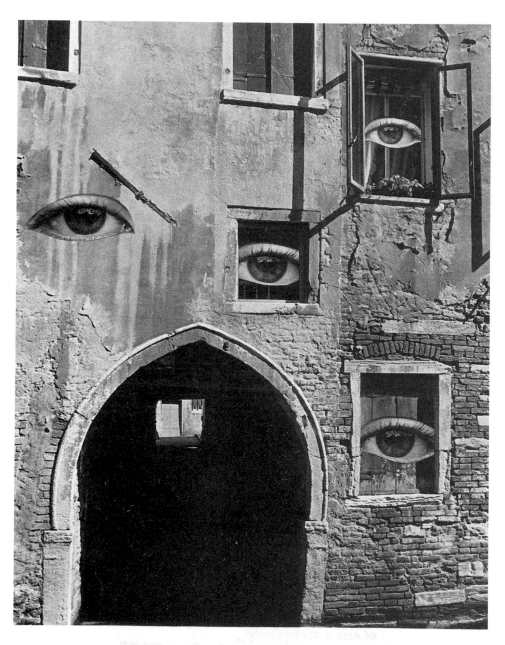

Photography:
A Critical Introduction

EDITED BY LIZ WELLS

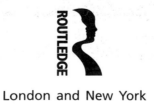

London and New York

First published 1997
by Routledge
11 New Fetter Lane, London EC4P 4EE

Simultaneously published in the USA and Canada
by Routledge
29 West 35th Street, New York, NY 10001

Typeset in Bembo by Florencetype Ltd, Stoodleigh,
Devon

Text design by *Secondary Modern*

Printed and bound in Great Britain by Butler and
Tanner Ltd, Frome and London

British Library Cataloguing in Publication Data
A catalogue record for this book is available from
the British Library

Library of Congress Cataloguing in Publication Data
A catalogue record for this book has been requested

ISBN 0–415–12558–8 (hbk)
ISBN 0–415–12559–6 (pbk)

Contents

Contributors

Patricia Holland is a writer, lecturer and film-maker. She has written about personal photography in *What is a Child* (Virago 1992), and *Family Snaps* (Virago 1991), co-edited with Jo Spence. She has contributed to several readers on photography, television and cultural studies and is the author of *The Television Handbook* (Routledge 1997). She is a visiting tutor at Goldsmiths' College, University of London.

Martin Lister is a senior lecturer in the School of Cultural Studies at the University of the West of England, Bristol. He is the editor of *The Photographic Image in Digital Culture* (Routledge 1995) and co-author of *Youth, Culture and Photography* (Macmillan 1988). He is a contributor and project director of the forthcoming Interactive CD Rom *From Silver to Silicon* (ARTEC, London).

Derrick Price has published articles on film, photography, literature and tourism. He is Associate Dean of the Faculty of Art, Media and Design at the University of the West of England, Bristol and directs a research group in media and cultural policy.

Anandi Ramamurthy lectures in the Department of Historical and Critical Studies, University of Central Lancashire. She is finishing PhD research on 'The representation of African and Asian people in British advertising (1881–1990)'. She curated the exhibition *Black Markets* (Manchester, Cornerhouse) and was guest editor for the *Museums Journal* special issue on Museums and Black History (October 1990). Forthcoming publications include 'Orientalism and the "Paisley" Pattern', in Boydell and Schoeser (eds), *Disentangling Textiles* (1996).

Liz Wells is a senior lecturer, contextual studies in film, video and photography, at the School of Media, The London Institute: LCPDT, and course leader, MA Independent Film and Video. She has researched and published widely, was editor of *Camerawork* (Issues 31 and 32), and contributes to *Creative Camera*, *Portfolio* and *Women's Art*. She edited *Viewfindings, Women Photographers: 'Landscape' and Environment* (1994) and curated the related exhibition (toured by Newlyn Art Gallery).

Editor's preface

This book sets out to remedy the absence of a good, coherent introduction to issues in photography theory, and results from the frustrations of teaching without the benefit of a succinct introductory textbook. There are a number of published histories of photography which define the field according to various agendas, although almost invariably with an emphasis upon great photographers, historically and now. Fewer publications critically engage with debates about the nature of photographic seeing. Most are collections of essays pitched at a level which assumes familiarity with contemporary cultural issues and debates which students new to this field of enquiry may not yet have.

The genesis of this book has been complex. It results initially from a discussion between myself and Rebecca Barden, of Routledge, in which she solicited suggestions for publications which would support the current curriculum. Responding subsequently to her invitation to put forward a developed book proposal, two factors were immediately clear: first, that the attempt to be relatively comprehensive could be tackled best through a collective approach. Thus, a team of writers was assembled right from the start of the project. Second, it quickly became apparent that the project was, in effect, impossible. Photography is ubiquitous. As a result, there are no clear boundaries. It follows that there cannot be precise agreement as to what a 'comprehensive' introduction and overview should encompass, prioritise or exclude. After much consideration, we have focused on issues and areas of practice which, given our experience as lecturers in a number of different university institutions, we know crop up frequently. That we have worked to a large extent in relation to an established curriculum does not mean that the project has been either straightforward or easy. On the contrary, the intention to introduce and explore issues reasonably fully, taking account of what critics have had to say on various aspects of photographic practices, has involved investigating and drawing upon a wide and diverse range of resources. Speaking personally, researching this book has led to further questions, as well as to engaging discoveries. The tension between looking, thinking, investigation and discovery is one of the pleasures of academic research.

This book aims to be relevant, and of interest, to students of photography, graphics, fine art, art and design history, journalism, media studies, communication and cultural studies. We hope that it proves both useful and enjoyable.

Acknowledgements

This book could not have been produced without the support of a number of people. First and foremost I should like to thank Patricia Holland, Martin Lister, Derrick Price, Anandi Ramamurthy, without whom the book would not have been possible. The project has been a difficult one but nonetheless a happy one, due to the quality of the team which I have had the good fortune to be in a position to assemble. I should like to thank Rebecca Barden, Moira Taylor and others at Routledge for their support.

I should like to thank Deborah Roland, Department of Learning Resources, The London Institute: LCPDT, for support as librarian, and for access to her postgraduate diploma dissertation on histories of photography; also Anne Braybon, for discussion of her research on photography exhibitions in London in 1969–1971. I should also like to thank my colleagues Janice Hart, Patrick Sutherland, Anne Williams, each of whom has, maybe without realising, contributed to the final shaping of this book.

Patricia Holland would like to thank Sue Isherwood; also Barry Lane, Pam Roberts, Kate Rousse and Debbie Ireland at the Royal Photographic Society; Guillermo Mari, and Arthur Lockwood for bringing her albums and other material and for his help in rephotographing the albums; Jenny Ransom for discussing her work at Kodak; Marian and Jeanette Covington, Paula Fascht and Ursula Kocharian for lending her their photographs and discussing their family histories with her, and many other people who showed and lent her personal pictures.

Liz Wells
November 1995

Illustration acknowledgements

We are indebted to the people and archives below for permission to reproduce photographs. Every effort has been made to trace copyright-holders but in a few cases this has not been possible. Any omissions brought to our attention will be remedied in future editions.

Frontispiece: Patricia Townsend, *Critical Observations*, 1988, courtesy of the artist

2.1 **Dorothea Lange**, *Migrant Mother*, 1936, courtesy of the Library of Congress, Washington, LCUSF341-9058C

2.2 **William Thomas**, *Mrs Lewis Waller with a Kaffir Boy*, 1903, courtesy of the Public Record Office, London, 517 Copy 1 464

2.3 **Thomas Annan**, *Close No 118 High Street*, 1868, courtesy of the Glasgow City Council Libraries Department

2.4 **Jacob Riis**, *Lodgers in a Crowded Tenement – 'five cents a spot'*, 1880s, courtesy of the Museum of the City of New York

2.5 **John Thomson**, *Covent Garden Labourers*, c. 1877, courtesy of the Royal Photographic Society

2.6 **Frank Meadow Sutcliffe**, *A Fish Stall*, c. 1882, courtesy of the Royal Photographic Society

2.7 **Russell Lee**, *Wife of a Homesteader*, 1936, courtesy of the Library of Congress, Washington, LCUSF341-10435B

2.8 **Humphrey Spender**, *Men Greeting in a Pub*, Worktown Series, 1937, courtesy of the Mass Observation Archive, Bolton Museum and Art Gallery

2.9a; 2.9b **Bert Hardy**, *Fire-Fighters*, in *Picture Post*, 1941, courtesy of the Hulton Deutsch Picture Library, London

2.10 **Edith Tudor Hart**, *Piano Player in the Street*, c. 1934, courtesy of Wolfgang Suschitzky

2.11 **Helen Levitt**, *New York*, 1942, courtesy of the Spencer Museum of Art, University of Kansas

2.12 **Lee Friedlander**, *1 Lafayette, Louisiana*, 1970, courtesy of Fraenkel Gallery, San Francisco

2.13 **Roshini Kempadoo**, *Women of the UK Asian Women's Centre, Handsworth, Birmingham*, 1990, courtesy of the artist

2.14 **Nick Hedges**, *Packing Department, Lock Factory, Willenhall*, from *Born to Work*, 1982, courtesy of the artist

3.1 Studio photograph of Lily Peapell in peasant dress on roller skates, USA Studios, Peckham, South London, *c.* 1912, courtesy of her grandson, Colin Aggett

3.2a Page from the album of Sir Arnold Wilson (No. 3 Persian scenes), 1909, courtesy of the Royal Photographic Society
3.2b Page from the album of Sir Arnold Wilson (No. 7), 1900, also courtesy of the Royal Photographic Society

3.3 'The photographic craze', *Amateur Photographer*, 10 June 1887

3.4 Stereoscopic slide from the late nineteenth century, courtesy of the National Museum of Photography, Film and Television, Bradford, uncatalogued

3.5 Earliest known daguerrotype of a photographer at work. Jabez Hogg photographs Mr Johnson, *c.* 1843, courtesy of the National Museum of Photography, Film and Television, Bradford

3.6 A page from the album of R. Foley Onslow, *c.* 1860, courtesy of Arthur Lockwood

3.7 Illustration from Cuthbert Bede, *Photographic Pleasures*, 1855

3.8 Pupils at St Mary's School, Moss Lane, Manchester, *c.* 1910, courtesy of the Manchester Documentary Photography Archive

3.9 Studio photograph of Edward and May Bond, *c.* 1910, courtesy of the Manchester Documentary Photography Archive

3.10 Edward and May Bond taken by a street photographer outside their home in Manchester, 1910, courtesy of the Manchester Documentary Photography Archive

3.11 Holiday postcard from a Blackpool studio, 1910, courtesy of Martin Parr

3.12 Mobile sales tent for Bailey's photographers, Bournemouth, *c.* 1910, courtesy of Martin Parr

3.13 Black Country chain-makers, postcard, 7 August 1911, courtesy of Jack Stasiak

3.14 Kodak advertisement, 1920, courtesy of the Punch Picture Library, London

3.15 A page from a Kodak 'Brownie' album, *c.* 1900, courtesy of Guillermo Marin Martinez

3.16 A page from the album of Frank Lockwood, 1927, courtesy of his son, water-colourist and designer Arthur Lockwood

3.17 From the album of Ursula Kocharian, courtesy of Ursula Kocharian

3.18 **Jo Spence/Dr Tim Sheard**, *Greedy – I recreate my journey into emotional eating, a rebellion against parental disapproval*, 1989, courtesy of Terry Dennett, the Jo Spence Archive

3.19 Valerie Walkerdine as the Bluebell Fairy, courtesy of Valerie Walkerdine

4.1 **Victor Burgin**, *What does Possession mean to you*?, 1974, courtesy of the artist

4.2 Elizabeth Taylor's Passion Perfume ad, 1988, courtesy of Elizabeth Taylor

4.3 South African miners demonstrating. Photograph from the *Independent*, 26 August 1987, and used in the Anglo-American Corporation of South Africa advertisement published in the *Guardian*, 2 April 1990

4.4 Illustration from Mrs Christine Frederick's *The New Housekeeping*, 1913

4.5 'Billy Durm', Jack Daniel's Tennessee Whiskey, as it appeared in *FHM* magazine, August 1995

4.6 Ronson Lighters, 1951

4.7 'Make it up as you go', Maxi make-up ad, *Cosmopolitan*, October 1989, courtesy Procter & Gamble

4.8 French colonial postcard, c. 1910 from Malek Alloula (1985), *The Colonial Harem*, Manchester: Manchester University Press, p. 26, courtesy of Malek Alloula

4.9 'Morocco', 1990, courtesy of the Moroccan National Tourist Office, London

4.10a; 4.10b **Paul Wombell**, Montage, 1979, courtesy of the artist, The Photographers' Gallery, London

4.11 Tourist photograph, courtesy of Sita Ramamurthy

4.12 'Arabia Behind the Veil', *Marie Claire*, September 1988, no. 1, pp. 14–15. Photographers: Pascal and Maria Maréchaux

4.13 French colonial postcard, c. 1910 from Malek Alloula (1985), *The Colonial Harem*, p. 82, courtesy of Malek Alloula

4.14 'Afternoon Dream' from 'Indian Summer', *Marie Claire*, June 1994, pp. 156–157. Photographer: Christian Moser

4.15 From 'The Golden Age of Hollywood', *Marie Claire*, June 1994, pp. 160–161. Photographer: Matthew Ralston

4.16 From 'Weave a Winter's Tale', *Elle*, November 1987, pp. 136–137. Photographers: Eddy Cohli for 'Salsa style' and Susan Griggs agency for 'Modern folk'

4.17 *Schenectady Works News*, General Electric, 2 November 1923, courtesy of the Hall of History Foundation, Schenectady, New York

4.18 Benetton advertisement, 1987, courtesy of Modus Publicity, London

4.19 USSR, Benetton, 1987, courtesy of Modus Publicity, London

4.20 USA, Benetton, 1987, courtesy of Modus Publicity, London

4.21   'Black Mama', Benetton, 1989, courtesy of Modus Publicity, London

4.22   *David Kirby*, Benetton, 1992, courtesy of Modus Publicity, London

4.23   From *Colors* 13, Benetton, 1995, courtesy of Modus Publicity, London

5.1   **Karen Knorr**, from *Country Life*, courtesy of the artist

5.2   **Camille Silvy**, *River Scene, France*, 1858, courtesy of the Victoria and Albert Picture Library, London

5.3   **Henry Peach Robinson**, *The Lady of Shallot*, 1860–1861, courtesy of the Royal Photographic Society, Bath

5.4   **Thurston Thompson**, *Exhibition Installation*, 1858, courtesy of the Victoria and Albert Picture Library, London

5.5   **Bill Brandt**, *Prior Park, near Bath*, 1936, copyright Bill Brandt, courtesy of John-Paul Kernot, London

5.6   **Alexander Rodchenko**, *White Sea Canal*, from *USSR in Construction* 12, 1933, copyright A. Lavrentiev/Rodchenko Family Archive, courtesy of the Slavic and Baltic Division, The New York Public Library, Astor, Lenox and Tilden Foundation

5.7   **Edward Weston**, *Dunes, Oceano*, courtesy of the Victoria and Albert Picture Library, London

5.8   **Lee Miller**, *Portrait of Space, near Siwa, Egypt*, 1937, courtesy of the Lee Miller Archive, Chiddingly, East Sussex

5.9   **Keith Arnatt**, *Self Burial*, TV Interference Project, 1969, copyright Keith Arnatt, courtesy of Tate Publishing

5.10   **Ingrid Pollard**, from *Pastoral Interludes*, 1987, courtesy of the artist

5.11   **John Kippin**, *Pilgrims*, 1994, courtesy of the artist

6.1   **David Bate**, *The Travellers*, 1995, from the series *Strangers*, courtesy of the artist

6.2   **Pedro Meyer**'s image *El Asombrado*, electronically enhanced print exhibited at *PhotoVideo* exhibition, The Photographers' Gallery, London, 1991, courtesy of the artist

6.3   A three-stage illustration of the principle of digitising a photograph. Richard Mark Friedhoff and William Benzon (1989), *The Second Computer Revolution: Visualisation*, New York: Harry N. Abrams Inc., p. 49

6.4   Diagrammatic representation of the concept of a 'virtual camera'. From T. Binkley (1993), 'Refiguring Culture' in B. Hayward and T. Wollen (eds), *Future Visions: New Technologies of the Screen*, London: BFI, p. 104

6.5   Computer-generated image of billiard balls. From Richard Mark Friedhoff and William Benzon (1989), *The Second Computer Revolution: Visualisation* (1989), New York: Harry N. Abrams Inc., p. 102. Copyright: 1984, Thomas Porter, Pixar

xii

6.6 Albrecht Dürer, *Draughtsman Drawing a Nude*, 1538, courtesy of The Trustees of the British Museum

6.7 Front page of the *Daily Mirror*, 20 April 1912, Historic Newspapers, Wigtownshire, Scotland

6.8 Nadar (Gaspard Felix Tournachon), *The Arc de Triomphe and the Grand Boulevards, Paris, from a balloon*, 1868, courtesy of Caisse Nationale des Monuments Historiques et des Sites, Paris

6.9 NASA, Johnson Space Center, Houston, Texas, *Earth View (Sinai Peninsular)*, no. 93-HC-232 STS-052, courtesy of NASA

6.10 Press photographer photographing a Gulf War briefing, from *Ten. 8*: 2, p. 18

6.11 Sophie Ristelhueber, *Fait*, 1992, courtesy of the artist

6.12 Viewers at a panorama, from Buck Morss (1991), *The Dialectics of Seeing: Walter Benjamin and the Arcades Project* (1991), Cambridge, MA: MIT Press, p. 82

6.13 A contemporary games arcade, courtesy of the Last Resort Picture Library, Tuxford, Nottingham

6.14 Esther Parada, *2-3-4-D: Digital Revisions in Time and Space*, 1991–1992, *At the Margin*, from *Digital Photography*, catalogue of the exhibition of the same name, Paris, Palais de Tokyo, Centre National de la Photographie, 1992, ART-EL, 25 rue de Washington, 75008 Paris, p. 15

Introduction

LIZ WELLS

Introduction

THE PURPOSE OF THIS BOOK

The purpose of this book is to introduce and offer an overview of conceptual issues relating to photography and to ways of thinking about photographs. It considers the photograph as an artefact used in a range of different ways and circumstances, and photography as a set of practices which take place in particular contexts. Thus it is essentially about *reading* photographic images rather than about their making. The primary purpose is to introduce key debates, and to indicate sources and resources so students (and other readers) can further develop particular lines of enquiry. The book centrally examines British debates and developments. We also refer to developments in other parts of Europe and in North America. There is no chronological history. Rather, we discuss past attitudes and understandings, technological limitations, and sociopolitical contexts through focus on issues pertinent to contemporary practices. In other words, we consider how ideas about photography have developed in relation to the specific field of practice which forms the theme of each chapter. We cannot render theory easy, but we can contribute to clarifying key issues by pointing to ways in which debates have been framed.

Why study theory? As will become clear, theory informs practice. Essentially there are two choices. You can disregard theoretical debates, taking no account of ways in which images become meaningful, thereby limiting critical understanding and, if you are a photographer, restricting the depth of understanding supporting your own work. The alternative is to engage consciously with questions of photographic meaning in order to develop critical perceptions which can be brought to bear upon photographic practices, historically and now, or upon your own photography.

HOW TO USE THIS BOOK

This book introduces a range of debates pertaining to specific fields of photographic practice. We identify key reading, and other resources, in order to illuminate critical debates about photography itself, and to place such debates in relation to broader theoretical and critical discussions. Our aim is to mediate such discussions, indicating key positions adopted within the debates and alerting you to core reading and other resources. In some instances, our recommendations are highly directive. Thus, we summarise and appraise different critical positions, and point to books and articles in which these positions have been outlined. In most cases the literature which we discuss offers clear priorities and quite explicit positions in relation to photographic cultures. In a few instances, our task is to draw attention to implicit, underlying assumptions which inform the theoretical stances adopted.

Since the purpose of the book is to introduce issues and ideas which may not yet be familiar, design elements have been incorporated to help. Some chapters include specific case studies, and summary diagrams, which are separated from the main flow of text. This is so that they can be seen in relation to the main argument, but also considered relatively autonomously. Likewise, photographs are sometimes used to illustrate points of discussion. However, they may also be viewed as a specific line of development within each chapter. In order to facilitate visual connections we have limited the range of topics or genres in each chapter. Thus, for instance, in chapter 2, on documentary practices, we concentrate primarily upon street photography. Comparison of images of similar content should help you to see some of the ways in which forms and styles of documentary have changed over time. It should be added that, in order to keep the size (and price) of the book reasonably manageable, we have used fewer photographs than is really desirable in a book about photography. Furthermore, the book has no colour which means that we have been limited to black and white images. On occasions, especially in examples of advertising in chapter 4, when the original was in colour, we have offered a brief description. However, you will need to use other visual sources, books and archives, alongside this book, in order to pursue visual analysis in proper detail.

Throughout the book there is a margin for notes. Key references to core reading, and also to archive sources, appear in the margin so you can follow up the issues and ideas which have been introduced. All references are summarised in a consolidated bibliography at the end of each of the six chapters. We include a list of the principal archives in Britain open to the public and glossary at the end of the book. Terms which may be new to you are printed in bold on their first occurrence in each chapter to remind you that a glossary definition is available.

The book is divided into six chapters, each of which may be read separately, although there are points of connection between them. We have indicated some of these linkages between chapters, but it is up to you to think them through in detail. A summary of the principal content of each chapter follows at the end of this introduction. This will help you to map your route through the book.

The book cannot be fully comprehensive. Photographic practices are diverse, and it is not possible to focus upon every possible issue and field of activity of interest, historically and now. Furthermore, since the book is reliant on the existence of other source material to which it acts as a guide, it is largely restricted to issues and debates which have been already documented and discussed. Some areas of practice have not had the full focus they might be deemed to deserve. For example, there are many collections of fashion photographs, and there have been numerous articles and books written in recent years on questions of gender, representation, fashion, style and popular culture. But there has been relatively little *critical* writing on fashion photography. This is a major omission which we could not rectify here. Thus, fashion photography forms one section of the more general chapter on commodity culture rather than attracting a chapter to itself. Likewise, a number of more technical practices within medical and scientific imaging fall beyond the scope of this book because relevant philosophical and critical writing to date is insufficiently developed.

To some extent the chapters seem quite different from one another. There are a number of reasons for this of which the first – and most obvious – is that each is written by a different author, and writers each have their own style. The specific tasks allotted to each chapter, and the material included, also lead to different approaches. Two chapters, concerning photography in relation to commodity culture and to digital imaging, both broadly concentrate upon the contemporary. Three chapters, in appraising the specific fields of documentary, photography as Art, and personal photography, are more obviously historical in their approach. Each takes it as axiomatic that the exploration of the history of debates and practices is a means to better understanding how we have arrived at present ways of thinking and operating.

Finally, of course, writing is not interest-free. You should not take the discussion in any of the chapters as representing everything that could be said on its subject. Aside from the limitations of length, authors have their own priorities. Each chapter is written from a considered viewpoint, and each of the authors has studied their subject in depth over many years. As a result of their expertise, and their broader political and social affiliations, they have arrived at particular conclusions. These contribute to determining which issues and examples they have selected for central focus and, indeed, the way they have structured the exposition and argument in their chapter.

Whilst each offers you the opportunity to consider key issues and debates, you should not view them as either comprehensive or objectively 'true'. Rather, you should see the book as a guide to what is at stake within particular debates, bearing in mind that the writer, too, has something at stake. You should also remember that this is essentially only an introduction to issues and ideas.

CHAPTER BY CHAPTER

● Chapter 1 introduces key debates relating to photography and, most particularly, identifies some of the positions within these debates taken by established theorists. The chapter focuses initially on historical accounts, taking the interrelation between aesthetics and technologies into consideration. We then outline a number of debates which have characterised theoretical and critical discussions of the photograph and of photographic practices. Finally we consider sites of practice, institutions and the audience for photography. The chapter is designed as a foundation for discussions, many of which will be picked up again for more detailed examination later in the book.

● Chapter 2 focuses upon the documentary role of the camera, especially in relation to recording everyday life. There is also some discussion of travel photography and of photojournalism, especially the expanding journalistic role for photography in the early twentieth century. Claims have been made for the authenticity or 'truth' of photography used within surveys or viewed as evidence. The chapter considers disputes that have arisen in relation to such claims in the nineteenth century, in the early twentieth century – especially in the 1920s and 1930s when the term 'documentary' was coined – and, finally, in relation to contemporary practices in documentary and reportage. A case study of the American Farm Securities Administration (FSA) project is included. This is designed not only as illustration of the debates examined in the chapter but also as a model of how particular discussions can be illuminated through considering a specific example.

The chapter is concerned throughout with the multiple discourses through which the nature of photography and its social project has been constructed and understood. By concentrating on particular periods it offers a critical history of documentary which problematises and clarifies the relationship of a specific form of representation to other debates and movements.

● Chapter 3 focuses upon the popular and the personal, developing an historical overview of leisure and domestic uses of photography as a medium through which individual lives and fantasies have been recorded. Particular attention is paid to the family album, which both documents social histories and stands as a talisman of personal experience. The chapter also considers the strategies by which a mass market for photography was constructed, in particular by Kodak. Finally the chapter comments upon recent research on the family photograph, considering what is concealed, as much as what is revealed, in family relationships, gender and sexuality. Attention throughout is drawn to the role of women as photographers and keepers of the photograph album.

In keeping with the style of this book, this chapter signals key texts and further reading. However, the history of popular photography to date has attracted less critical attention than has been directed to other fields of photographic practice; for instance, documentary. In contrast to other parts of the book, this chapter draws upon original research and little-known materials.

● Chapter 4 continues the focus upon everyday uses of photography through considering advertising and commodity culture. Photography is a cultural tool which is itself a commodity as well as a key expressive medium used to promote commercial interests. These links are examined through a series of case studies offering examples of analysis of the single image; tourism, fashion and the exotic; and Benetton as an example of strategic self-publicity. Within commodity culture, that which is specific to photography interacts extensively with broader political and cultural issues. Thus we note references both to commercial photography and, more generally, to questions of the politics of representation, paying particular attention to gender and ethnicity. The chapter employs semiotics within the context of socio-economic analysis to point to ways in which photography is implicated in the concealing of international social and economic relations.

● By contrast, chapter 5 considers photographic practices in relation to Art, discussing claims made for the status of photography as a fine art practice, historically and now. The chapter is organised chronologically in three historical sections: the nineteenth century, modern art movements, and the contemporary. This historical division is intended not as a sort of chart of progress so much as a method of identifying different moments and shifting terms of reference relating to photography as an Art practice. Attention is paid to current forms of work and to themes which feature frequently in contemporary practice including questions of gender, ethnicity and identity. The principal concern is to trace the shifting terms of debate as to the status of the photograph as Art and to map historical changes in the situation of the photographic within the museum and art gallery.

● Chapter 6 explores photography and digital imaging. New means of electronic and digital imaging are emerging within societies that are undergoing significant economic, technological and political change. How can these developments be understood? How are these technologies being used? What effect will they have on the historically established practices of photography? The chapter is based on two key ideas. First, amidst dramatic developments in electronic communications and digital image technologies, it no longer seems possible to take the cultural dominance of the photographic for granted. Second, given that the photographic image has shaped the way the world is seen and represented, that the history of photographic codes, practices and uses will contribute to shaping new media.

Given the very contemporary nature of this chapter it is, inevitably, more speculative than other sections of this book. The range of relevant further reading references is also more restricted, certainly in relation to cultural theory and digitalisation. However, as is clearly argued in the chapter, old debates persist through new technological developments. The unease associated with the idea of manipulation of the image indicates the extent to which, in terms of commonsense ideologies, the photograph is viewed as relating directly and unproblematically to (what is conceptualised as) external reality. It is suggested that the introduction of (relatively) cheap and accessible photo-manipulation software programs has brought discussion of realism once again into central focus.

CHAPTER 1

Thinking about photography

Debates, historically and now

DERRICK PRICE

LIZ WELLS

A knowledge of photography is just as important as that of the alphabet. The illiterate of the future will be ignorant of the use of camera and pen alike.

László Moholy-Nagy 1923

Thinking about photography
Debates, historically and now

INTRODUCTION

This chapter introduces and discusses key writings on photography. The references are to relatively recent publications, and to current debates about photography; however, these books often refer back to earlier writings, so a history of changing ideas relating to photography can be discerned. This history focuses on photography itself as well as considering photography alongside art history and theory, and cultural history and theory more generally.

The chapter is in four sections: Histories of photography, Aesthetics and technologies, Photography and social history, and Contemporary debates. All writing about photography is founded upon a set of assumptions about the nature of the photographic, although such assumptions may be taken for granted, rather than explicit. The principal aim is to locate writings about photography both in terms of its own history, as a specific medium and set of practices, and in relation to broader historical, theoretical and political considerations. The final section introduces and considers some of the different approaches – and difficulties – which emerge in relation to the project of theorising photography.

HISTORIES OF PHOTOGRAPHY

Considering history

E.H. Carr has observed that history is a construct consequent upon the questions asked by the historian (Carr 1964). Thus, he suggests, histories tell us as much about the historian as about the period or subject under interrogation. Furthermore, the historian's selection and organisation of material is to some extent predetermined by the purpose and intellectual parameters of any particular project. Such parameters reflect the interests of the historian, who nearly always has to take account of institutional constraints (for instance, the expectation that a publication will be made from research findings within a set period of time). Projects are also framed by underpinning ideological and political assumptions and priorities.

Such observations are obviously pertinent when considering the history of photography. They are also relevant to investigating ways in which photography has been implicated in the construction of history. As the French cultural critic, Roland Barthes, has pointed out, the nineteenth century gave us both History and Photography. He distinguishes between *history* which he describes as 'memory fabricated according to positive formulas', and *the photograph* defined as 'but fugitive testimony' (Barthes 1984: 93). It is attitudes to photography, its contexts, usages and critiques of its nature that we explore in this chapter.

Histories of photography

> Inventions – the name by which we call devices that seem fundamentally new – are almost always born out of a process that is more like farming than magic. From a complex ecology of ideas and circumstance that includes the condition of the intellectual soil, the political climate, the state of technical competence, and the sophistication of the seed, the suggestion of new possibilities arises.
>
> (Szarkowski 1989: 11)

Typically, histories of photography offer a series of histories of photographers illustrated with examples from their work. In the twentieth century, in common with other areas of the arts, such as painting or the novel, there has been a tendency to conflate the history of the subject with the work of particular practitioners. The central purpose of this opening section is to compare key books, published in English in recent years, most variously titled *The History* . . . or *A Concise History.* . . .

What is the story of photography? It was invented in 1939, or so we have commonly been led to believe, but this apparently simple statement masks a complex set of factors. It is true that it was in 1939 that both Fox Talbot in England and Daguerre in France announced the processes whereby they had succeeded in making and fixing a photo-graphic image. But the idea of photo-graphy long precedes that date.

12

To a large extent the history of photography prior to 1938, when **Beaumont Newhall** first published his commentary, then entitled *Photography, A Short Critical History*, has been represented as a history of techniques. The focus was not on what sort of images were made, but on *how* they were made. This approach is to some extent reflected in museum collections wherein it is the instruments of photography which are prioritised for display, with photographs acting as examples of particular printing methods, detailed in accompanying descriptions. The subject-matter of such photographs (and associated aesthetic and social implications), if acknowledged at all, is presented as being of secondary importance.

So, was the story of photography always an account of changing technologies? Martin Gasser suggests that this history is more complicated (Gasser 1992). Considering German, French, British and American publications written between 1839 and 1939, he identifies three emphases: first, what is termed 'the priority debate'; second, histories of the development of photography written primarily as handbooks detailing methods and techniques and also potential uses for photography; third, histories of the photograph as image. It is worth noting that it is the proliferation of material in the second of these categories which has led to the false assumption that the first hundred years of publication were largely devoted to technologies and techniques. Aside from any other consideration, a number of the papers published in the early years of photography made assertions about the intrinsic nature of the medium and speculated on its potential uses.

Which founding father?

Before turning to consider histories of the photograph as *image*, the priority debate deserves brief comment. This debate is concerned with who first achieved the fixing of the photographic image. A number of historical accounts exist whose primary purpose is to argue – usually through a combination of biography and discussion of photographic techiques – that someone other than Fox Talbot in Britain or Daguerre in France 'invented' photography. These two men were the first to announce their findings publicly (in the appropriate scientific journals of the time, in Britain and France) in 1939. But it is also clear, from contemporary correspondence, that Fox Talbot was not alone in Britain in his experimentation. Similarly, in France, Nicephore Nièpce was responsible in the early 1820s for key discoveries leading up to the **daguerreotype**. As every history of early photography emphasises, the challenge did not lie with the development of camera and lens technology. The principle of concentrating light through a small hole in order to create reflection on the wall of a dark chamber was known to Aristotle (384–322 BC). The photographic camera was based on the camera obscura, described as early as the tenth century AD, of which the first illustration was published in 1545. The problem which preoccupied experimentation in the late

BEAUMONT NEWHALL (1982) **The History of Photography**, New York: MOMA, fifth edition, revised and enlarged

Key Archives: The National Centre for Photography, Bath
The National Museum of Photography, Film and Television, Bradford

13

eighteenth and early nineteenth centuries was how to fix the image once it had been obtained.

The credit for discovering practical chemical processes lies with no single person. As historian, Helmut Gernsheim, remarks in relation to the daguerreotype, 'though to Nièpce goes the credit of having devised the first photographic process, and of having invented the earliest photo-engraving method, it was left to his partner Daguerre to make photography practicable as distinct from possible' (**Gernsheim and Gernsheim 1969: 41**).

Nor, indeed, does the credit lie with any particular nation, although, as Gasser reminds us, the ascription of credit has always had nationalistic over-tones with the French, keen to downgrade British claims. (1839 was within a generation of the Battle of Trafalgar.) Likewise, strenuous rewritings of history allowed the German photo-historian, Stenger, writing in the 1930s during the ascendance of Hitler, to claim German experiments of the eighteenth century as fundamental for photography. Re-examining the prehistory, Mary Warner Marien urges caution in two respects: first, she warns against too uncritical an acceptance of the work of early photo-historians (Warner Marien 1991). She notes the extent to which the burgeoning of research in the field since the Second World War has both uncovered new findings and suggested new ways of thinking about previously known facts within the history of photography; recent research represents only the beginning of a much needed archaeology of early photography. In addition, she emphasises the broader historical context of political, technological and cultural change within which photography developed. The overall point is that, in considering the origins of photography, a stance which is both cautious and critical should be adopted.

The photograph as image

While earlier writing on photography by no means exclusively focused on technology and techniques, since the Second World War art-historical concerns have become more central, together with stress on connoisseurship of the photograph as a privileged object. A number of the books which we now take as key texts on the history of photography were first written as exhibition catalogues for works collected and shown in institutions. For instance, Beaumont Newhall's *The History of Photography* stems from a catalogue written to accompany 'Photography 1839–1937' at the Museum of Modern Art (MOMA) in New York in 1937. The broader context for the introduction of art historical methods and concerns into photography collection and exhibition includes the development of art history as an academic discipline and, more particularly, the increasing influence of art criticism within modern art in the first half of the twentieth century. Here it is relevant to remember the emphasis upon **Art** as a set of special sort of practices which informed **modernist** thinking. A central feature of modernist criticism was that of maintaining a clear distinction between high and low

HELMUT AND ALISON GERNSHEIM (1969) **The History of Photography from the Earliest Use of the Camera Obscura in the Eleventh Century up to 1914**, 2 vols, London/New York (first edition, 1955)

culture, a differentiation which was equally evident in the writings of some Marxist critics as it was among conservative critics. If photographs were to take their place in the gallery, then inevitably they became caught up within more general intellectual trends and discourses.

Since the Second World War, then, the predominant approach to writing the history of photography has been to focus on the photograph as image. Two classic histories, still consulted, are Beaumont Newhall's *The History of Photography* (now in its fifth, revised edition); and Helmut and Alison Gernsheim's *History of Photography*, which, as we have seen, was organised in its earliest form in relation to developing technologies but has subsequently been rewritten to take fuller account of photographs as specific types of image. It is worth pausing to consider and compare these two publications; together they established a specific canon for the history of photography which has been the basis for further development – or taken as a starting point for challenge – ever since.[1]

Educated as an art historian, and appointed on to the library staff at New York's Museum of Modern Art, Newhall was invited to research their first major photography exhibition. His historical overview, which formed the principal essay in the exhibition catalogue, described changing techniques, but also included comments on specific photographers and particular periods of aesthetic development. Newhall was one of the first to introduce aesthetic judgements into the discussion of photographs, but, at this stage, as he has noted himself, he avoided the identification of artists, thereby refusing MOMA's expectations of what an exhibition catalogue should be. It was only in the third edition of his *History of Photography* that emphasis on photographers and account of the work of practitioners emerges. In this edition he also, for the first time, introduced chapters on **straight photography**, documentary and 'instant vision', thereby acknowledging characteristics specific to photography. The third edition thus represents the beginning of an engagement with the idea of photography theory as distinct from art theory.[2]

Similarly, it is only in later editions that Helmut Gernsheim refocuses the history to comment more extensively upon particular practitioners. His contribution to the history, developed in collaboration with Alison Gernsheim, was founded in the study of their collection of nineteenth-century photographs.[3] The full title of their research, first published in 1955 and dedicated to Beaumont Newhall, is *The History of Photography from the Earliest Use of the Camera Obscura in the Eleventh Century up to 1914*. The second edition, in 1969, was divided into two volumes, with considerably more emphasis on illustration than previously. The third, revised, edition appeared in the 1980s, by then under the single authorship of Helmut Gernsheim (since the death of his wife). The first volume of *The History of Photography* focuses on the origins of photography in France, America, Great Britain and Germany.[4] A chapter on Italy was added later, in the third edition, which was published in 1982. A summary version of the research was

1 We are indebted to insights and observations offered by Deborah Roland in her unpublished postgraduate diploma dissertation on *Two Histories of Photography*, London Institute, 1995.

2 All editions are credited to Newhall, but a number of commentators have noted the research contribution of his wife, Nancy Newhall.
3 The Gernsheim collection is now at the University of Texas in Austin.
4 The chapter is in fact entitled 'The Daguerreotype in German-Speaking Countries'. He refers to what is now known as Germany and Austria, although in the mid-nineteenth century Germany had not yet been united so, technically, these were developments in Prussia, Bavaria, and elsewhere.

published in 1965 as *A Concise History of Photography*, offering a shorter, and thus easier, entry into his work. This version includes a brief, and highly selective, discussion of modern photography up to the 1950s. For purposes of studying the nineteenth century, the two-volume edition (which is in large format, with good quality picture reproduction) is recommended for the detail of observation and the range of imagery.

Both Newhall and Gernsheim focus upon Western Europe and the United States (with no comment, for instance, on Soviet Russia or on South America). The key difference between Newhall and Gernsheim lies in Gernsheim's relative concentrations on the nineteenth century, and his greater emphasis on technical aspects of photography. His study is more lengthy and less literary in approach than Newhall's. This may reflect the origins of Newhall's essay as an exhibition catalogue which meant that he had to take account of the problem of succinct communication to a diverse audience. Further differences may stem from nationality: Newhall was American; Gernsheim was born in Germany but was naturalised English. As has already been noted, they were working in relation to particular archive collections, the former drawing upon the collection at MOMA with, inevitably, a central focus upon developments in America, as well as upon the research in Europe conducted prior to the 1937 exhibition. The Gernsheim collection focused on the nineteenth century, and was centred upon British photography.

Both historians proceed to a greater or lesser extent by way of discussion of great photographers. Gernsheim notes that their collection was organised not only in files about photographic processes, apparatus, exhibitions, but also folders on important photographers (see **Hill and Cooper 1992**). Newhall, as an art historian, was accustomed to emphasis on the contribution of the individual artist, and by the fifth edition of his work, the contribution of individual photographers and the authority of their work is clearly a priority. This has the effect of raising the profile of certain 'masters' of photography, thereby defining a canon, or authoritative list, of great practitioners. To quote lecturer and critic, Stevie Bezencenet:

> The complex detail of Gernsheim's history and the simple linear progression that Newhall presents do not allow us to comprehend just how these histories have been constructed. We are locked into a limited and traditional perception of a medium developing from one *Master* to another, marginally influenced by technical factors and with a minimal relation to anything else: the key site of analysis becomes the qualities of the individual photograph.
>
> (Bezencenet 1982a: 485)

The canonisation of photographers as artists, in line with the emphasis on individual practitioners in other art fields in the Modern period, characterises many contemporary histories of photography. For instance, Photo Poche publish a three-part history organised around brief biographies and

VICKI GOLDBERG (ed.) (1981) **Photography in Print**, Albuquerque: University of New Mexico Press

PAUL HILL AND THOMAS COOPER (1992) **Dialogue with Photography**, Manchester: Cornerhouse Publications

NATHAN LYONS (1966) **Photographers on Photography**, Englewood Cliffs: Prentice-Hall

CHRISTOPHER PHILLIPS (ed.) (1989) **Photography in the Modern Era**, New York: Metropolitan Museum/Aperture

comments on photographers, accompanied by one image selected from their lifetime's work. This approach is also reflected in a number of publications focusing upon interviews with photographers or on extracts from their writings. Such publications offer insights into the philosophical starting points, contexts and technical methods employed by individual photographers or researchers to achieve particular results. They explicitly acknowledge the contribution of individual photographers in shaping ideas and photographic practices, and also the fact that authorship of the picture lies with the photographer, not with the camera, thereby denying any oversimplified notion that the photograph straightforwardly records that which was in front of the lens. But, by selecting known practitioners as their starting point, rather than sets of ideas or types of practice, such books have the effect of reinforcing the canon of acclaimed photographers and marginalising practices which cannot be acknowledged in relation to named photographers.

History in focus

There are several consequences of canonisation: first, changing attitudes to photography as a set of practices have tended to become obscured behind the eulogisation of particular photographers, their photographs and their contribution. Second, the focus (led by male historians) has been upon male photographers, with the consequence that the participation of women has been overlooked or obscured. Third, there has been relatively extensive discussion of professional and serious commercial practices, but relatively few accounts of popular photography or of more specialist areas of practice, such as architecture or medicine. Fourth, as has already been mentioned, photography history has tended to prioritise aesthetic concerns over broader and more diverse forms of involvement of photography in all aspects of social experience, including personal photography, publishing and everyday portraiture.

Other contemporary histories, published in English and selected for comment here, reflect or engage with these problems to a greater or lesser degree. **Peter Turner**'s *History of Photography* is perhaps the most aware of the limitations of the brief, and most explicitly sets out to transcend it. His focus is broader than the other histories, and includes fashion photography and advertising within its compass. Sections are organised primarily in terms of discussion of particular practices rather than technologies or practitioners, although, perhaps inevitably, there is some focus on particular photographers, through the selection of photographs as illustration and through identification of leading exponents. This book, with reasonable size reproductions of photographs (including some colour reproduction) makes pleasurable reading.

PETER TURNER (1987) **History of Photography**, London: Hamlyn

Likewise, **Ian Jeffrey**'s account *Photography, A Concise History* is purposeful and generally clearly written. This book set out to be a radical reappraisal of the history of photography as written to date, although Stevie Bezencenet

IAN JEFFREY (1981) **Photography, A Concise History**, London: Thames and Hudson

17

has argued that it was less than successful in its re-evaluation on the grounds that to produce a history of photography now requires a diversity of academic approaches (Bezencenet 1982b). She also notes that Jeffrey offers another history overwhelmingly concerned with male practitioners, making the point that, however radical his declared intentions, his work mirrors the established formula of a chronological account of changes and focuses on dominant modes of photography and particular practitioners.

JEAN-CLAUDE LEMAGNY AND
ANDRÉ ROUILLE (1987) **A
History of Photography**,
Cambridge: Cambridge
University Press

Lamagny and Rouille's account is of interest to the English reader for its central starting point is within French culture which, in effect, recentres Europe. Whilst discussion of photography in Britain is more limited than in some of the other accounts, the references to Europe as a whole are more comprehensive. This book is an edited collection. Despite the editors' stated intention of holding a balance between discussion of photography as a field in itself, and discussion of the broader context within which it functions, some chapters succeed in being more analytic than others. While expressing strong criticisms, in reviewing the book, Warner Marien suggests that its strengths lie in two chapters on photography as art, and she adds that in general this collection takes more account of contemporary theoretical ideas than do most works of this kind (Warner Marien 1988).

1989 saw the publication of two major historical overviews, both designed to accompany retrospective exhibitions celebrating 150 years of photography. The title of Mike Weaver's *The Art of Photography* (1989) reflects the location of this exhibition at the Royal Academy in Piccadilly, London. This was the first ever exhibition of photographs held there and, as such, both the show and the accompanying publication emphasise the image as art and the status of the photographer as artist. Similarly, **John Szarkowski**'s

JOHN SZARKOWSKI (1989)
Photography Until Now,
New York: MOMA

Photography Until Now (1989) – which accompanied the MOMA celebration of 150 years of photography – in relying primarily on the MOMA collection reinforces the American canon (which includes a number of European photographers). Szarkowski trained both as an art historian and as a photographer before working in the MOMA collection for thirty years. His interests centred upon the formal and technical properties which distinguish photographs from other visual media, and in the status of the unauthored or vernacular photograph. However, the production values of both these publications are high, which makes each a useful source for visual reference and research.

Coming to the story of photography for the first time, it is perhaps worth remarking that the combination of Szarkowski and Jeffrey offers a good starting point for engaging with the history as it has been written to date. Each is clearly written, and they complement one another in taking America, or Europe, as central starting points. Indeed, Szarkowski specifically comments on the difference in the situation of photography in the States, as opposed to Europe, at the turn of the century. He suggests that American (he specifies 'Yankee') photographers were more inclined toward reportage than their European counterparts, having invested less in claims for the status of the photograph as art, since America lacked the depth of artistic tradition that was central to post-Renaissance Europe.

Each of the histories reviewed above reflects, to a greater or lesser degree, an established selection of photographers and their images. The 'great masters' approach has been challenged variously. Anne Tucker, in *The Woman's Eye* (1973) was among the first to draw attention to the considerable participation of women as photographers historically. As the title implies, she suggests that what we see photographically – that is, subject-matter and treatment – to some extent reflects gender. This question of gender has been pursued by **Val Williams** in her discussion of British women's participation in a range of practices, including the local (studio) and the domestic (the family album), and like Peter Turner, her historical account takes account of commercial practices. Likewise Jeanne Montoussamy-Ashe (1985) reinstates black women into the history of American photography noting, for instance, documentation for the 1866 Houston city directory which lists 'col' against the name of a female photographic printer. (Some women are also listed in D. Willis Thomas' *Black Photographers* bio-bibliography (1985), again American.) In all instances what is at stake is to note the presence of women within a particular field and to consider ways in which gender, positively or negatively, contributed to constructing or limiting the roles played. By contrast, Constance Sullivan's *Woman Photographers* (1990), considering European (including British) and American examples, has stressed women's participation as Artists, arguing that women's work historically has demonstrated equivalent aesthetic values to those which characterise the work of their better-known male contemporaries, while often bringing different subject-matter into focus. This book is particularly useful for its quality reproduction of images. But the fundamental point is that each author focuses on putting women back into the picture even if, ultimately, they challenge the canon rather than challenging canonisation.

VAL WILLIAMS (1986) **Women Photographers: The Other Observers, 1900 to the Present**, London: Virago. Revised edition (1991) **The Other Observers: Women Photographers from 1900 to the Present**

AESTHETICS AND TECHNOLOGIES

The impact of new technologies

Photography emerged as part of a cluster of technical inventions and innovations around the middle of the nineteenth century (including inventions in the electrical industries and new discoveries in optics and chemistry). Hailed as a great technological invention it immediately became the subject of debates concerning its aesthetic status and social uses.

The excitement generated by the announcement, or marketing, of technological innovations tends to distract us from the fact that technologies are researched and developed by human societies. New machinery is normally presented as the agent of social change, not as the outcome of a desire for such change, i.e. as a cause rather than a consequence of culture. However,

19

it can be argued that particular cultures invest in and develop new machines and technologies in order to satisfy previously foreseen social needs. Photography is one such example. A number of theorists have identified precursors of photography in the late eighteenth century. For instance, an expanding middle-class demand for portraiture which outstripped available (painted) means led to the development of the mechanical Physiognotrace and to the practice of silhouette cutting (Freund 1980). Geoffrey Batchen also points out that photography had been a 'widespread social imperative' long before Daguerre and Fox Talbot's official announcements in 1839. He lists twenty-four names of people who had 'felt the hitherto strange and unfamiliar desire to have images formed by light spontaneously fix themselves' from as early as 1782 (Batchen 1990: 9). Since most of the necessary elements of technological knowledge were in place well before 1839, the significant question is not so much who invented photography but rather why it became an active field of research and discovery at that particular point in time (see Punt 1995).

Once a technology exists it may become adapted and introduced into social use in a variety of both foreseen and unforeseen ways. As cultural theorist Raymond Williams has argued, there is nothing in the technology itself which determines its cultural location or usages (Williams 1974). If technology is viewed as determining consequent cultural uses, much remains to be explained. Not the least of this is the extent to which people subvert technologies, resist or invent new uses which had never originally been intended or envisaged. In addition, new technologies become incorporated within established relations of production and consumption contributing to articulating – but not causing – shifts and changes in such relations and patterns of behaviour.

Art or technology?

Central to the nineteenth-century debate about the nature of photography as a new technology was the question as to how far it could be considered as Art. It was celebrated for its putative ability to produce accurate images of what was in front of its lens; images which were seen as being mechanically produced and thus free of the selective discriminations of the human eye and hand. On precisely the same grounds, the medium was often regarded as falling outside the realm of art, as its assumed power of accurate, dispassionate recording appeared to displace the artist's compositional creativity.

Writing on the Salon of 1859, the French poet Charles Baudelaire attacked those who confused photography with art and were excited by the new discovery, seeing in it the possibility of the exact delineation of nature. Fox Talbot had defined photography as 'the pencil of nature'. Indeed, in referring to his images as photogenic *drawing*, he seems to have been claiming photography to be just as much a useful art as it was a chemistry. But some caution is appropriate, as it is probable that drawing was perceived differently then.

If drawing was viewed as primarily functional, rather than creative, then Talbot was welcoming the photograph as a substitute for the informational sketch. The French journal, *La Lumière*, encompassed writings on photography both as a science and as an art.[5] Indeed, debates concerning the status of photography as art took place in periodicals throughout the nineteenth century. Baudelaire linked 'the invasion of photography and the great industrial madness of today' and asserted that 'if photography is allowed to deputize for art in some of art's activities, it will not be long before it has supplanted or corrupted art altogether' (Baudelaire 1859: 297). Its only function was that of a support system to the arts and the sciences:

> Photography must, therefore, return to its true duty which is that of handmaid of the arts and sciences, but their very humble handmaid, like printing and shorthand, which have neither created nor supplemented literature. Let photography quickly enrich the traveller's album and restore to his eyes the precision his memory may lack; let it adorn the library of the naturalist, magnify microscopic insects, even strengthen, with a few facts, the hypotheses of the astronomer; let it, in short, be the secretary and record-keeper of whomsoever needs absolute material accuracy for professional reasons.
>
> (Baudelaire 1859: 297)

'Absolute material accuracy' was seen as the hallmark of photography because most people at the time accepted that the medium rendered a complete and faithful image of its subjects. Moreover, the nineteenth-century desire to explore, record and catalogue human experience, both home and abroad, encouraged people to emphasise photography as a method of naturalistic documentation. Baudelaire not only accepts its veracity but adds that: 'if once it be allowed to impinge on the sphere of the intangible and the imaginary, on anything that has value solely because man adds something to it from his soul, then woe betide us!' (1859: 297). Here he is opposing industry (seen as mechanical, soulless and repetitive) with art, which he considered to be the most important sphere of existential life. Thus Baudelaire is evoking the irrational, the spiritual and the imaginary as an antidote to the positivist interest in measurement and statistical accuracy which, as we have noted, characterised much nineteenth-century investigation. From this point of view the mechanical nature of the camera militated against its use for anything other than mundane purposes.

Photographers responded to criticisms of this kind in two main ways: either they accepted that photography was something different from Art and sought to discover what the intrinsic properties of the medium were; or they pointed out that photography was more than a mechanical form of image-making, that it could be worked on and contrived so as to produce pictures which in some ways resembled paintings. 'Pictorial' photography, from the 1850s onwards, sought to overcome the problems of photography by careful

5 Lamagny and Rouille (1987: 44) point out that the subtitle for the journal was 'Review of photography: fine arts-heliography-sciences, non-political magazine published every Saturday'.

21

arrangement of all the elements of the composition and by reducing the signifiers of technological production within the photograph (see chapter 5 for discussion of Pictorialism as a specific photographic movement towards the end of the nineteenth century). For example, they ensured that the image was out of focus, slightly blurred and fuzzy; they made pictures of allegorical subjects, including religious scenes; and those who worked with the gum bichromate process scratched and marked their prints in an effort to imitate something of the appearance of a canvas.

In the other camp were those photographers who celebrated the qualities of straight photography and did not want to treat the medium as a kind of monochrome painting. They were interested in photography's ability to provide apparently accurate records of the visual world and tried to give their images the formal status and finish of paintings while concentrating their attention on its intrinsic qualities.

Most of these photographs were displayed on gallery walls – this was a world of exhibition salons, juries, competitions and medals. In the journals of the time (which already included the *British Journal of Photography*), tips about technique coexisted with articles on the rules of composition. If the photographs aspired to be Art, their makers aspired to be artists and they emulated the characteristic institutions of the art world. However, away from the salon, in the high streets of most towns, jobbing photographers earned a living by making simple photographic portraits of people, many of whom could not have afforded any other record of their own appearance. This did not please the painters:

> The cheap portrait painter, whose efforts were principally devoted to giving a strongly marked diagram of the face, in the shortest possible time and at the lowest possible price, has been to a great extent superseded. Even those who are better entitled to take the rank of artists have been greatly interfered with. The rapidity of execution, dispensing with the fatigue and trouble of rigorous sittings, together with the supposed certainty of accuracy in likeness in photography, incline many persons to try their luck in Daguerreotype, a Talbotype, Heliotype, or some method of sun or light-painting, instead of trusting to what is considered the greater uncertainty of artistic skill.
>
> (Howard 1853: 154)

The industrial process, so despised by Baudelaire and other like-minded critics, is here seen as offering mechanical accuracy combined with a degree of quality control. Photography begins, then, to emerge as the most commonly used and important means of communication for the industrial age.

Writing at about the same time as Baudelaire, Lady Elizabeth Eastlake agreed that photography was not an art but emphasised this as its strength. She argued that:

She is made for the present age, in which the desire for art resides in a small minority, but the craving, or rather the necessity for cheap, prompt, and correct facts in the public at large. Photography is the purveyor of such knowledge to the world. She is the sworn witness of everything presented to her view . . . (her studies are 'facts') . . . facts which are neither the province of art nor of description, but of that new form of communication between man and man – neither letter, message, nor picture – which now happily fills the space between them.

(Eastlake 1857: 93)

In this account, photography is not so much concerned with the development of a new aesthetic, as with the construction of new kinds of knowledge as the carrier of 'facts'. These facts are connected to new forms of communication for which there is a demand amongst all social groups; they are neither arcane nor specialist, but belong in the sphere of everyday life. In this respect, Eastlake is one of the first writers to argue that photography is a democratic means of representation and that the new facts will be available to everyone.

Photography does not merely transmit these facts, it creates them, but Eastlake sees photography as the 'sworn witness' of the appearance of things. This juridical phrase strikingly captures what, for many years, was considered to be the inevitable function of photography – that it showed the world without selection, contrivance or prejudice. For Eastlake, such facts came from the recording without selection of whatever was before the lens. It is photography's inability to choose and select the objects within the frame that locates it in a factual world and prevents it from becoming Art.

Every form which is traced by light is the impress of one great moment, or one hour, or one age in the great passage of time. Though the faces of our children may not be modelled and rounded with that truth and beauty which art attains, yet *minor* things – the very shoes of the one, the inseparable toy of the other – are given with a strength of identity which art does not even seek.

(Eastlake 1857: 94; emphasis in original)

The old hierarchies of Art have broken down. Photography bears witness to the passage of time, but it cannot make statements as to the importance of things at any time nor is it concerned with 'truth and beauty' or with teasing out what underlies appearances. Rather, it voraciously records anything in view, in other words is firmly in the realm of the contingent.

Photography, then, is concerned with facts that are 'necessary', but may also be contingent, may draw our attention to what formerly went unnoticed or ignored. Writing within fifteen years of its invention Eastlake points to the many social uses to which photography has already been put:

. . . photography has become a household word and a household want; it is used alike by art and science, by love, business and justice; is found in the most sumptuous saloon and the dingiest attic – in the solitude of the Highland cottage, and in the glare of the London gin palace – in the pocket of the detective, in the cell of the convict, in the folio of the painter and architect, among the papers and patterns of the mill owner and manufacturer and on the cold breast of the battle field.

(Eastlake 1857: 81)

For Eastlake, photography is ubiquitous and classless; it is a popular means of communication. Of course, it was not true that people of all classes and condition could commission photographs as a necessary 'household want' – she anticipates that state by several decades, during which time use of photography was also spreading from its original practitioners (relatively affluent people who saw themselves as experimenters or hobbyists) to those who undertook it as a business and began to extend the repertoire of conventions of the 'correct' way to photograph people and scenes.

Eastlake's facts are produced, she claims, by a new form of communication, which she is unable to define very clearly. But for all her vagueness, she identifies an important constituent in the making of modernity: the rise of previously unknown forms of communication which have a dislocating effect on traditional technologies and practices. She is writing at an historical moment marked by a cluster of technical inventions and changes and she places photography at the centre of them. The notion that the camera should aspire to the status of the printing press – a mechanical tool which exercises no effect upon the medium which it supports – is here seriously challenged. For Eastlake calmly accepts that photography is not Art, but hints at the displacing effect the medium will have on the old structures of Art. Photography, she says, bears witness to the passage of time, but it cannot select or order the relative importance of things at any time. Nor is it concerned to tease out what underlies appearances, but to record voraciously whatever is in its view. Nor were the attempts to convert it into a craft and provide it with the markers of human artifice to prove successful. By the first decade of the twentieth century the Pictorialists had all but retreated from the field and it was the qualities of straight photography that were subsequently to be prized. Moreover, modernism, with its celebration of a machine ethic and its contempt for the art of the past, argued for a photography that was in opposition to the traditional claims of Art.

The photograph as document

In Britain, as elsewhere, the idea of documentary has underpinned most photographic practices since the 1930s (see chapter 2). The terminology is indicative: the *Oxford English Dictionary* definition of 'documentary' is 'to document or record'. The simultaneous 'it was there' (the pro-photographic event) and 'I was there' (the photographer) effect of the photographic record of people and circumstances contributes to the authority of the photographic image. Furthermore, especially in the case of images made for the gallery or for book publication, the fact that the artist thought a scene or event worth observing is of significance. Photographic aesthetics commonly accord with the dominant modes and traditions of Western two-dimensional art, including perspective and the idea of a vanishing point. Indeed, as a number of critics have suggested, photography not only echoes post-Renaissance painterly conventions, but also achieves visual renderings of scenes and situations with what seems to be a higher degree of accuracy that was possible in painting. Photography can, in this respect, be seen as effectively substituting for the **representational** task previously accorded to painting. In addition, as Walter Benjamin argued in 1936, changes brought about by the introduction of mechanical means of reproduction which produced and circulated multiple copies of an image shifted attitudes to Art (Benjamin 1973). Formerly unique objects, located in a particular place, lost their singularity as they became accessible to many people in diverse places. Lost too was the 'aura' that was attached to a work of Art which was now open to many different readings and interpretations. For Benjamin, photography was therefore inherently more democratic. Yet established attitudes persist. In Western art the artist is accorded the status of someone endowed with particular sensitivities and vision. That the photographer as artist, viewed as a special kind of seer, chose to make a particular photograph lends extra authority and credibility to the picture.

The photograph, technically and aesthetically, has a unique and distinctive relation with that which is/was in front of the camera. Analogical theories of the photograph have been abandoned; we no longer believe that the photograph directly replicates circumstances. But it remains the case that, technologically, the chemically produced image is an indexical effect caused by a particular conjuncture of circumstances (including subject-matter, framing, light, characteristics of the lens, chemical properties and darkroom decisions). This basis in the observable lends a sense of authenticity to the photograph. Italian **semiotician**, Umberto Eco, has commented that the photograph reproduces the conditions of optical perception, but only some of them (see Eco in Burgin 1982). That the photograph appears iconic not only contributes an aura of authenticity, it also seems reassuringly familiar. The articulation of familiar-looking subjects through established aesthetic conventions further fuels realist notions associated with photography. Thus philosophical, technical and aesthetic issues − along with the role accorded to the artist − all feature within **ontological** debates relating to the photograph.

In recent years, developments in computer-based image production and the possibilities of digitalisation and reworking of the photographic image have increasingly called into question the idea of documentary realism. The authority attributed to the photograph is at stake. That this has led to a reopening of debates about 'photographic truth' in itself shows that, in everyday parlance, photographs are still viewed as realistic (see chapter 6 for a full discussion of recent positions on this).

Photography and the modern

Photography was born into a critical age and much of the discussion of the medium has been concerned to define it and to distinguish it from other practices. We should remember, though, that there has never been a single object, practice or form that is *photography* at any one time. Rather 'photography' has always been made from a plethora of kinds of work and types of image, which often served different material and social uses. Discussion of the nature of the medium has, in consequence, often been either reductionist – looking for the *essence* of the medium which transcends its social or aesthetic forms – or highly descriptive and not theorised. Photography was a major carrier and shaper of modernism. Not only did it dislocate time and space but it also undermined the structure of conventional narrative. Its relationship to the contingent destroyed traditional hierarchies of meaning and it was central to the creation of particular forms of, and to inscribing desire into our relationship with, the world of goods. As we have seen, the Victorians invested considerable faith in the power of the camera to record, classify and witness. This meant that the camera was also entrusted with delineating social appearance, classifying the face of criminality and lunacy, offering racial and social stereotypes.

Modern photography, in the first half of the twentieth century, embodies a particular *way of seeing*. To some extent this idea is as old as the medium itself. But it took on a particular form in the 1920s and 1930s when both the putative political power of photography and its status as the most important modern form of communication were at their height. Modernism aimed to produce a new kind of world and new kinds of human beings to people it. The old world would be put under the spotlight of modern technology and the old evasions and concealments revealed. The photo-eye was seen as revelatory, dragging 'facts', however distasteful or deleterious to those in power, into the light of day. As a number of photographers in Europe and North America stressed, another of its functions was to show us the world as it had never been seen before. Here, the stress on form in *photographic seeing* typical of American modern photography parallels the stress on photography as a particular kind of vision in European movements of the 1920s. Our vision will be changed because we will see the world through a microscope: from the top of high buildings, under the sea, etc. Moreover, photography validated our experience of 'being there', which is not merely one of visiting an unfamiliar place, but of capturing the authentic experience *of* a strange place. Photographs are records and documents which pin down the changing world of appearance.

European modernism, with its contempt for the aesthetic forms of the past and its celebration of the machine, endorsed photography's claim to be the most important form of representation. Now, says Moholy-Nagy, writing in the 1920s, our vision will be corrected and the weight of the old cultural forms will be removed from our shoulders:

> Everyone will be compelled to see that which is optically true, is explicable in its own terms, is objective, before he can arrive at any possible subjective position. This will abolish that pictorial and imaginative association pattern which has remained unsuperseded for centuries and which has been stamped upon our vision by great individual painters.
>
> (Moholy-Nagy 1967: 28)

A world cleansed of traditional forms and hierarchies of values would be established, one in which we would be free to see clearly without the distorting aesthetics of the past. This new world has already been named by Paul Strand in describing American photographic practice, which he saw as indigenous, and viewed as being as revolutionary as the skyscraper. As he put it in a famous article in the last issue of Alfred Stieglitz's *Camera Work*:

> . . . America has been expressed in terms of America without the outside influence of Paris art schools or their dilute offspring here . . . [photography] found its highest esthetic achievement in America, where a small group of men and women worked with honest and sincere purpose, some instinctively and a few consciously, but without any background of photographic or graphic formulae much less any cut and dried ideas of what is Art and what isn't: this innocence was their real strength. Everything they wanted to say had to be worked out by their own experiments: it was born of actual living. In the same way the creators of our skyscrapers had to face the similar circum- stances of no precedent and it was through that very necessity of evolving a new form, both in architecture and photography that the resulting expression was vitalised.
>
> (Strand 1917)

Here, the aesthetic of photography is seen as having been created outside history. A new frontier of vision is established by hard work and innocence: a product of human experience rather than cultural inheritance.

The postmodern

There are several strands within the notion of the **postmodern** which are pertinent to photography. First, there is a philosophical argument that defines postmodernism as marking the collapse of overarching narratives and witnessing the end of history. Then there is the notion of the centrality of the simulacrum in which the endless production, reproduction and circula- tion of signs has rendered trivial the distinction between 'original' and 'copy', thereby, some fifty years later, achieving the democratisation and loss of 'aura' that Benjamin had advocated. The camera has, of course, been centrally implicated in this. Finally, there is the idea that what marks this period is the endless creation, circulation, distribution and exchange of signs.

In a world overwhelmed by signs, what status is there for photography's celebrated ability to reproduce the real appearance of things? Fredric Jameson argues that photography is:

> . . . renouncing reference as such in order to elaborate an autonomous vision which has no external equivalent. Internal differentiation now stands as the mark and moment of a decisive displacement in which the older relationship of image to reference is superseded by an inner or interiorized one . . . the attention of the viewer is now engaged by a differential opposition within the image itself, so that he or she has little energy left over for intentness to that older 'likeness' or 'matching' operation which compared the image to some putative thing outside.
>
> (Jameson 1991: 179)

Photography, then, has given up attempting to provide depictions of things which have an autonomous existence outside the image; nor do we spectators possess the psychic energy needed to compare the photograph with objects, persons or events in the world external to the frame of the camera. Roland Barthes argued that the photograph is always *of* something (Barthes 1984: 28). Writing as early as 1859 the American jurist and writer, Oliver Wendell Holmes, considered the power of photography to change our relationship to original, single and remarkable works:

> There is only one Coliseum or Pantheon; but how many millions of potential negatives have they shed – representatives of billions of pictures – since they were erected! Matter in large masses must always be fixed and dear; form is cheap and transportable. We have got the fruit of creation now and need not trouble ourselves with the core. Every conceivable object of Nature and Art will soon scale off its surface for us. We will hunt all curious, beautiful grand objects, as they hunt the cattle in South America, for their *skins*, and leave the carcasses as of little worth.
>
> (Holmes 1859: 60)

While this is a percipient remark, Holmes has not gone far enough. He realises that the mass trade in images will change our relationship to originals; making them, indeed, little more than the source of representation. Nevertheless, he does conceive of some essential difference between originals and copies. A simulacrum is a copy for which there is no original; it is, as it were, a copy in its own right. In postmodernity it may be that the photograph has no referent in the wider world and can be understood or critiqued only in terms of its own internal aesthetic organisation.

So what are we to make of a photography which does not traffic in multiple images but, rather, is constructed for the gallery? Cultural theorist, Rosalind Krauss, has described photography's relationship to the world of aesthetic distinction and judgement in the following terms:

> Within the aesthetic universe of differentiation – which is to say; 'this is good, this is bad, this, in its absolute originality, is different from that' – within this universe photography raises the specter of nondifferentiation at the level of qualitative difference and introduces instead the condition of a merely quantitative array of difference, as in series. The possibility of aesthetic difference is collapsed from within and the originality that is dependent on this idea of difference collapses with it.
>
> (Krauss 1981: 21)

This 'collapse of difference', however, has had an enormous effect on painting and sculpture, for photography's failure of singularity undermined the very ground on which the aesthetic rules that validated originality was established. Multiple, reproducible, repetitive images destabilised the very notion of 'originality' and blurred the difference between original and copy. The 'great masters' approach to the analysis of images becomes increasingly irrelevant, for in the world of the simulacrum what is called into question is the originality of authorship, the uniqueness of the art object and the nature of self-expression.

PHOTOGRAPHY AND SOCIAL HISTORY

Social history and photography

Further challenge to the dominance of the 'great masters' history of photography has been a re-interrogation of the status and significance of popular photography. By 'popular' we refer to personal photography, or to photographs which may have been commissioned from professional photographers, but were intended for personal use.[6] The term also extends to include postcards exchanged between individuals, and pictures made to record events or membership of clubs and societies. The high-street portrait studio is also a legacy of Victorian photography, and was by no means confined to major cities. Such studios were often family enterprises, or were run by women photographers.

The contribution of particular photographers, and the economic circumstances within which Victorian and Edwardian photography was pursued, has become a focus of much recent research. But one of the points about reviewing popular photography and rethinking its significance is that concern with the authoring of images is related to questions of provenance (establishing where and when a photograph was taken) rather than to questions of artistic significance. This is because popular photography is increasingly

6 Travelling photographers were common prior to Kodak's introduction of the Box Brownie and the consequent more widespread ownership of cameras.

29

used as social-historical evidence. Personal albums, and other materials, are viewed as a form of visual anthropology and are catalogued within a number of archives, of differing scale and thematic concern. Public museums and libraries may have photographic collections within their local or regional archive; and there are many independent collections.[7] Such rich collections offer myriad research possibilities. They also contribute to the fast-expanding 'Heritage' industry in Britain wherein photographs play a high profile as 'evidence' from the past. As such, they are displayed, or used as reference for the design of reconstructions of buildings or machinery, or republished as postcards.

7 See the Royal Photographic Society *Directory of British Photographic Collections*, London: Heinemann, 1977.

The photograph as testament

Photographs are commonly used as evidence. They are among the material marshalled by the historian in order to investigate the past. Over the last thirty years, they have become a major source of information by which we picture or imagine the nineteenth century. Historians have for the most part had an uneasy relationship with the medium, as their professional training did not introduce them to the analysis of visual images. It was television that first raided the many photographic archives for images of historical interest; this necessarily led to some difficulties, not least of which was that of an archive used in a general way to illustrate commentary, with scant regard for the purposes for which the photographs were made. The social historian may be interested in changing modes of dress, or agricultural and industrial machinery. Photographs are used as evidence of such changes, which means that the detailing of the source and date of the photograph – that is, its *provenance* – becomes especially important. Hence, we come across titles of publications such as 'The Camera as Historian' or 'The Camera as Witness'.[8]

Popular education also led to a growth in the use of photographs for the analysis of local or community history. There are a number of reasons why people are interested in using old photographs: some have an ethnographic curiosity about the kinds of clothes or tools that were common at a particular period, while others are fascinated by the characteristic stance and gait of workers in particular trades. Social and labour historians who wanted to gain some idea of ordinary life and work in the Victorian era have also been drawn to the examination of visual material; not merely for the information provided by photographs, but also to begin to recognise in the lineaments of the subjects something of the real human beings who peopled the scenes that have been the subject of so many accounts and narratives.

Photography was used throughout the nineteenth century in the service of political and industrial change. One motivation for early landscape photography was governmental employment of photographers for civil and military mapping purposes. For instance, the British government employed photographers for a military survey of the Highlands of Scotland in order

8 Tagg remarks on the publication in London in 1916 of a handbook entitled *The Camera as Historian* aimed at those who used the camera for survey and record societies. See 'The Pencil of History' in Patrice Petro (ed.) *Fugitive Images* Bloomington: Indiana University Press, 1995.

to help quell anti-English rebellion (see Christian 1990). Similarly, in America, early landscape photography in the West was often commercial in origin: Carleton Watkins' employers included the California State Geological Survey and the Pacific railroads (see Snyder 1994). These photographs, along with others made for less systematic purposes, remain used as a form of social-historical evidence. Examples range widely: for instance, Alison Gernsheim uses photographs as a basis for a survey of changing fashions (A. Gernsheim 1981). The status of the photograph as evidence is not questioned. Likewise, books based on past photojournalism are common.[9] Such books purport to present the past 'as it was', taking for granted that this is what photographs do. As is asserted on the inside cover of one such book presenting pictures of Britain and Ireland, 'More than words, more than paintings or prints, old photographs convey an immediate, undistorted impression of the past' (Minto 1970).

Such use of photographs reflects a broader set of academic assumptions. Until recently, British historical, scientific and social scientific method was characterised by positivism. As is implied in the roots of the term itself, positivism stresses that which is definite or positive, i.e. factually based. Positivism, with its associated emphasis upon logical deduction and empirical research methods, including the social survey, is associated with the Victorian period in Britain, although its roots lie in earlier, eighteenth-century philosophy. The nineteenth century was a period of extensive technological and social change, characterised by a faith in 'Modernity'. Modernity refers to a complex set of developments relating to industrial change, which include the increasing concentration of people in towns and cities, geographical mobility consequent upon the invention of the steam engine and the spread of railway networks, and economic faith in technological progress. In Britain, France and elsewhere, such changes were underpinned economically through imperialism (which made available raw materials and cheap labour from other parts of the world) and through the low pay and bad working conditions experienced by industrial and agrarian labour at home. All these factors contributed to the increasingly public and urban nature of modern life, with the increasing separation of the aristocracy (in Britain), the professional and entrepreneurial middle class, and the workers.

Photography not only developed in the Victorian era but was also implicitly caught up in nineteenth-century interests and attitudes. In one of few histories to investigate the photograph neither primarily as image nor as technology, **Alan Thomas** in *The Expanding Eye* considers ways in which early uses of photography reflect and reinforce nineteenth-century concerns. Centred upon Victorian Britain, his account focuses on the popularisation of photography and upon the everyday both in terms of everyday *uses* of photographs (it is one of the first accounts to give a whole chapter to photography as family chronicler) and in terms of **representation** of the everyday. Thus he includes discussion of personal uses of photography in, for instance, the family

9 There are too many examples to enumerate, but many draw upon pictures from the *Illustrated London News* or the *Picture Post*.

ALAN THOMAS (1978) **The Expanding Eye**, London: Croom Helm

album; portraiture (including theatre portraits); and early uses of photographs to investigate rural and urban working and living conditions.

One of the consequences of extensive social change was a series of social surveys, which were designed to try to understand further how different social groups responded to the changing times and sought explanation through the quantitative assembly of information. The British Census of 1851 recorded differences in living circumstances; it is interesting to note that in 1851, 51 people recorded themselves by occupation as photographers, and in 1961 there were 2879 (Gernsheim 1969: 234). However, the motivation for the Victorian survey was not simply academic. In the same year the Great Exhibition celebrated industrial and technological achievement and Henry Mayhew published his *London Labour and London Poor*. This was the first survey account to focus on working-class living conditions. It was illustrated with wood engravings based upon photographs and therefore stands as an early example of the photograph being used as documentation. It became common for authenticity to be stressed through using such phrases as 'drawn from an original photograph'. The photographic image was already being mobilised as witness.

Categorical photography

JOHN TAGG (1988) **The Burden of Representation: Essays on Photographies and Histories**, London: Macmillan

John Tagg has written extensively on the uses of photography within power relations, noting that photographs very early on became implicated in surveillance. He employs the geneological method typical of the work of French philosopher, Michel Foucault, to trace intersecting ways in which photography was involved in maintaining social class hierarchies through delineation of, for instance, prisoners or the poor.

ELIZABETH EDWARDS (ed.) (1992) **Photography and Anthropology**, New Haven: Yale University Press

Likewise, recent reappraisals of uses of photography within social anthropology, and within the records of colonial travellers implicated in European imperialisms, have drawn attention to the political and ideological implications of using photography to define social types viewed as different or **Other**. As a number of critics have variously observed, such definitional uses of the image contribute to legitimating colonial rule (see **Edwards 1992**). Furthermore, as Sarah Graham-Brown has argued, there is a complex interplay between imperialism and patriarchy, within which women become particular sorts of exoticised victims of the stereotyping of the colonial Other (Graham-Brown 1988).

Discussing his 'The Archive and the Body' (1986), photographer and critic Alan Sekula traces the attempts of Victorian men of science to delineate, record and classify particular 'types' of human being (Sekula 1991). They used physiognomy and phrenology to show that it was possible to read from the surface of the body the inner delineation and moral character of the subject being studied. They employed the developing science of statistics within a positivist framework, and set out to demonstrate that science – aided by one of its new tools, the seemingly impartial eye of the camera – would reveal and systematically record the varieties of criminal faces.

Sekula is, in this complex article, particularly interested in photography's relation to police procedures, but mad and native peoples from other cultures were similarly subjected to processes of measurement and scentific appraisal. In 1869 T.H. Huxley was asked to make a photographic record of people from a number of races:

> Huxley . . . was asked . . . by the Colonial Office to devise instructions for the 'formation of a series of photographs of the various races of men comprehended within the British Empire'. The system he conceived called for unclothed subjects to be photographed full- and half-length, frontally and in profile, standing in each exposure beside a clearly marked measuring stick. Such photographs reproduced the hierarchical structures of domination and subordination inherent in the institutions of colonialism.
>
> (Pultz 1995: 25)

But a number of further issues beg attention in considering surveillance, social survey and other 'mapping' usages of photography. In referring to the photograph as 'fugitive testimony', Barthes draws our attention to the fleeting nature of the moment captured in the photograph and the extent to which contemporary experience (we are looking back with eyes informed by circumstances and ways of thinking of the 1990s), along with limited knowledge of the specific context within which – and purpose for which – the photograph was taken, make the image an unreliable witness. Photography is implicated in the construction of history. But when photographs are presented as 'evidence' of past events and circumstances, a set of assumptions about their accuracy as documents are being made. Such assumptions are usually acknowledged through statements of provenance: dates, sources, and so on. But this is to ignore wider questions relating to visual communication and ways in which we interpret photographs.

In recent years photography has been used by those who want to construct history around the notion of 'popular memory'. Here the photographs are often family albums or other kinds of personal photograph, through which communities might begin the process of establishing the grounds of their own non-formal history; accounts which might well challenge or be oppositional to more official versions. One problem with this is that photographs have often been treated as though they really were a source of disinterested facts, rather than as densely coded cultural objects:

> Ultimately, then, when photographs are uncritically presented as historical documents, they are transformed into aesthetic objects. Accordingly, the pretence to historical understanding remains although that understanding has been replaced by aesthetic experience.
>
> (Sekula 1991: 123)

Photography history is to a large extent shaped by the characteristic ways in which photographs have been collected, stored, used and displayed. With the passage of time the original motive for the making of a photograph may disappear, leaving it accessible to being framed by new contexts.

Institutions and contexts

A photograph of a homeless, unemployed man, published in a 1930s magazine to advance some philanthropic cause, is shown, massively enlarged, on the walls of a gallery fifty years after it was first made. Originally tied to the page with a caption and an explanatory text, it now stands alone as some kind of Art object. How are we to read such an image? As an example of a genre, for its technical qualities? As part of the *oeuvre* of a distinguished practitioner? As a work of Art, or as an historical object which conveys specific information or exemplifies 'pastness'? Do we try to make sense of it in terms of its distance from our own lives, or because there are many similarities to prevailing conditions? Do we try to read through the image some notion of human nature, of how, regardless of political context or the specificity of time, it would feel to be destitute and suffering? Or do we see it merely as a *photograph*, one among many and to be distinguished in terms of its formal, aesthetic qualities rather than its relationship to a world outside itself?

The very ubiquity of the medium has meant that photographs have always circulated in contexts for which they were not made. Also, it is important to remember that there is no single, intrinsic, aboriginal meaning locked up within them. Rather, there are many ways in which photographs can be read and understood, but in 'reading' photographs we rely on many contextual clues which lie outside the photography itself. We rarely encounter photographs in their original state, for we normally see them on hoardings, in magazines and newspapers, as book covers, on the walls of galleries or on the sides of buses. Their social meanings are already indicated to us and they are designed into a space, often accompanied by a text that gives us the preferred readings of their producers and allows us to make sense of what might otherwise be puzzling or ambiguous images. Indeed, commercial uses of photography, especially in advertising, often play on the multiple possible connotations that are provoked by the image.

One determinant of the way in which we understand photographs, then, is the context within which we view them, and key institutions shape the nature of photography by the way they provide this context. As we have seen, photographs are weak at the level of imminent meaning and depend for their decoding on text, surrounding, organisation, and so on. Although collections of photographs have always been assembled, photography's ambiguous status with respect to Art has often meant that they were not displayed in museums as objects in themselves, but, rather, used as a source of supplementary information to some more valued objects.

The Museum

Douglas Crimp has argued that the entry of photographs into the privileged space of the museum stripped them of the multiple potential meanings with which they are invested. They were removed from the many realms within which they made sense, in order to stress their status as separate objects – as *photographs*. Crimp is particularly interested in the work of the Museum of Modern Art, New York, in transforming photographs into objects of merely aesthetic attention. He is not alone in drawing attention to the way in which MOMA embraced photographs as art objects, brought them into the privileged space of the gallery and surrounded them with the apparatus of scholarship, appreciation and connoisseurship formerly reserved for paintings and sculptures.

But Crimp also examined the practice of the New York Public Library which, becoming aware of the number of photographs it possessed and of their historic and financial value, created a Department of Photography. They scoured all sections of the huge library for a trawl of photographs, which were removed from multitudinous subject areas and reclassified as photographs often under the individual photographer.[10] Crimp comments of photography that:

> Thus ghettoized it will no longer primarily be *useful* within other discursive practices; it will no longer serve the purposes of information, documentation, evidence, illustration, reportage. The formerly plural field of photography will henceforth be reduced to the single, all-encompassing *aesthetic*.
>
> (Crimp 1995: 75)

What is lost in this process is the ability of photography to create information and knowledge through its interaction with other discourses. Photographs, doomed to the visual solitude of the art object, will lose their plurality and their ability to traverse fields of meaning. They will be treated as though they are unique and singular, rather than as the kind of industrial object – capable of being multiply reproduced – that constitutes their real existence.

The archive

Alan Sekula, in his article 'Reading an Archive' (1991), draws our attention to the power of the photographic archive. There are, of course, many different kinds of archive, from those held in museums to commercial or historical collections or family albums. They are found, then, in libraries, commercial firms, museums and private collections. What they have in common is the fact that they heap together images of very different kinds and impose upon them a homogeneity that is a product of their very existence within an archive. The unity of an archive, he argues, is imposed by ownership of the objects themselves and of the principles of classification and organisation by which they are structured.

DOUGLAS CRIMP (1995) **On the Museum's Ruins**, Cambridge, MA: MIT Press

10 Likewise, the V&A collection of photographs was established through bringing together photographs from a number of different sections of the museum.

Photographs of many kinds, which may have been taken for different – perhaps even antagonistic – purposes, are brought together: 'in an archive, the possibility of meaning is "liberated" from the actual contingencies of use. But this liberation is also a loss, an *abstraction* from the complexity and richness of use, a loss of context' (Sekula 1991: 116). But archives play an important function in the creation of knowledge. Characteristically, an archive seeks to grow; it aspires to completeness and through this process of mass acquisition a kind of knowledge emerges:

> And so archives are contradictory in character. Within their confines meaning is liberated from use, and yet at a more general level an empiricist model of truth prevails. Pictures are atomised, isolated in one way and homogenized in another.
>
> (Sekula 1991: 118)

But if serious historians have sometimes neglected to read photographs in the complex way they deserve, the heritage industry has used photography as a central tool in its attempt to reconstruct the past as a site of tourist pleasure. Here, photography becomes a direct way through which our experience of the past is structured.

Many critics have been worried by, or contemptuous of, the touristic use of historical materials and of the function of the visual. For example, Donald Horne claims that photography is an essential part of the tourist experience because it allows us to convert the places we visit into signs which we can then possess. Photography, he suggests:

> offers us the joys of possession: by taking photographs of famous sites and then, at home, putting them into albums or showing them as slides, we gain some kind of possession of them. For some of us this can be the main reason for our tourism. Between them, the camera and tourism are two of the uniquely modern ways of defining reality.
>
> (Horne 1984: 12)

Similarly, Robert Hewison argues:

> Heritage is gradually effacing history, by substituting an image of the past for its reality. At a time when Britain is obsessed by the past, we have a fading sense of continuity and change, which is being replaced by a fragmented and piecemeal idea of the past constructed out of costume drama on television, re-enactments of civil war battles and mendacious celebrations of events such as the Glorious Revolution, which was neither glorious nor a revolution.
>
> (Hewison, in Corner and Harvey 1991: 175)

Now the archive is raided not for photographs as aesthetic objects, but for photographs as signifiers of past times. Blown up from their original proportions, sepia-toned and mounted on walls, photographs retain their implicit claim to authenticity. As cultural critics, including **John Corner** and **Sylvia Harvey**, have argued, we are now looking at the past in new ways and this kind of commodification of the image raises complex questions about how history is constructed and photographs employed to visualise the past.

JOHN CORNER AND SYLVIA HARVEY (1990) 'Heritage in Britain', **Ten/8** 36

JOHN TAYLOR (1994) **A Dream of England: Landscape, Photography and the Tourist's Imagination**, Manchester: Manchester University Press

CONTEMPORARY DEBATES

What is theory?

> The role of any theory is to explain. But as recent critical debate has taught us, systems of discourse are themselves implicated in real social and political relationships of power. Explanations inevitably privilege one set of interests over others, and today few of those engaged in critical work would claim to speak from a neutral or objective place. Theoreticians now aspire less to the erection of alternative global systems and more to the questioning and challenging of existing patterns of cultural power. In the current climate, any smooth and unambiguous unity of theory is likely to arouse suspicion. The most insidious explanations are those which see no need to explain themselves.
>
> (Ferguson 1992: 5)

All discussions of photographs rest upon some notion of the nature of the photograph and how it acquires meaning. The issue is not whether theory is in play but, rather, whether it is acknowledged. Two strands of theoretical discussion have featured in recent debates about photography: first, theoretical approaches premised on the relationship of the image to reality; second, theoretical approaches which stress the act of interpretation of the image through focusing upon the reading, rather than the taking, of photographic representations. In so far as there has been crossover between these two strands, this is found in recent increasing interest in the contexts and uses of photographs.

Theory refers to a coherent set of understandings about a particular issue which have been, or potentially can be, *appropriately* verified. It emerges from the quest for explanation, offers a system of explanation and reflects specific intellectual and cultural circumstances. Theoretical developments occur within established paradigms, or manners of thinking, which frame and structure the academic imagination. On the whole, modern Western philosophy, from the eighteenth century onwards, has stressed rational thought and posited a distinction between subjective experience and the objective, observable or external. This has led to positivist approaches to research both in the sciences and the social sciences. As we have already indicated, photography has been centrally implicated within the empirical as a recording tool.

Positivism has not only influenced uses of photography; it has also framed attitudes towards the status of the photograph.

Academic interrogation of photography implicates a range of different types of theoretical understandings: scientific, social scientific and aesthetic. Historically, there has been a marked difference between scientific expectations of theory, and the role of theory within the humanities. Debates within the social sciences have occupied an intellectual space which has drawn upon both scientific models *and* the humanities. In the early/mid-twentieth century, literary criticism centred upon a canon of key texts deemed worthy of study. Similarly, art history was devoted to a core line of works of 'great' artists, and much time was given to discussion of their subject-matter, techniques, the provenance of the image, and so on. The academic framework was one of maintaining a particular set of critical standards and, perhaps, extending the canon through advocating the inclusion of new or newly rediscovered works. A number of major exhibitions and publications on photography take this as their model, offering exposition of the work of selected photographers as 'masters' in the field. This approach, in literature, art history and aesthetic philosophy, has been criticised for its esoteric basis. It has also been criticised for reflecting white, male interests and, indeed, for blinkering the academic from a range of potential alternative visual and other pleasures. For instance, within photography the fascination of domestic or popular imagery, in its own right as well as within social history, was long overlooked, largely because such images do not necessarily accord with the aesthetic expectations of the medium and because they tend to be anonymous.

A more systematic critical approach, associated with mainland European intellectual debates, penetrated the Anglo-American tradition in some areas of the humanities, especially philosophy and literary studies, in the 1970s. The parallel influence on visual studies came slightly later. This impact was most pronounced in the relatively new – and therefore receptive – discipline of film studies. But there was also a significant displacement of older, established preoccupations and methods within art history and criticism, from which emerged what has come to be termed *new art history*. Increasingly, methodologically more eclectic visual cultural studies have superseded the more limited focus of traditional art history and aesthetic philosophy.

Photography theory

One of the central difficulties in the establishment of photography theory, and of priorities within debates relating to the photographic image, is that photography lies at the cusp of the scientific, the social scientific and the humanities. Thus, contemporary ontological debates relating to the photograph are divergent. One approach centres on analysis of the rhetoric of the image in relation to looking, and the desire to look. This is premised on models of visual communication which draw upon linguistics and, in particular,

psychoanalysis. This approach locates photographic imagery within broader **poststructuralist** concerns to understand meaning-producing processes.

In introducing the collection of essays, *Thinking Photography*, artist/critic Victor Burgin distinguishes between photography theory, and criticism (**Burgin 1982**). This distinction is crucial. Up until the 1980s 'photography theory' within education had been taken to refer to technologies and techniques as in optics, colour temperature, optimum developer heat, etc. 'Theory' related to the craft base of photography. Burgin argues that photography theory must be interdisciplinary and must engage not only with techniques but, more particularly, with processes of signification. He also comments that, as yet, photography theory does not exist in any adequately developed form. Rather, we have photography criticism which, as currently practised, is evaluative and normative, authoritative and opinionated, reflecting what he terms an 'uneasy and contradictory amalgam' of Romantic, Realist and Modernist aesthetic theories and traditions. He suggests that photography history, as written up until the 1980s, reflects the same ideological positions and assumptions; that is to say, it uncritically accepts the dominant paradigms of aesthetic theory. As we shall see, his book set out to posit alternative ways of thinking about photography, ones which reflect broader trends in cultural theory, including taking account of ideological processes. Burgin warns against confusing photography theory with a general theory of culture, arguing for the specificity of the still, photographic image. He does not make exaggerated claims for the book, suggesting that photography theory has yet to be developed in any comprehensive way.

In relation to this, as we have already seen, a number of critics have focused on the realist properties of the image. Film critic, André Bazin, in the 1950s, in his key essay on the subject, emphasised the truth-to-appearances characteristics of the photographic (Bazin 1967). Albeit within wider-ranging terms, **Susan Sontag**, in her 1970s series of essays collected as *On Photography*, also discussed photographs as traces of reality and interrogated photography in terms of the extent to which the image reproduces reality. Similarly, Roland Barthes emphasised the referential characteristics of the photograph in his final book *Camera Lucida* (**Barthes 1984**). As we shall see, this contrasts with the emphasis upon cultural coding, meaning and usage posited as central by a number of more recent theorists.

In order to explore a number of different theoretical positions, we proceed by reviewing the three books mentioned above, each of which takes a particular approach to the problem of theoretical understanding.

Critical reflections on realism

> Photographing is essentially an act of non-intervention.
>
> (Sontag 1979: 11)

VICTOR BURGIN (ed.) (1982) **Thinking Photography**, London: Macmillan

SUSAN SONTAG (1979) **On Photography**, Harmondsworth: Penguin

ROLAND BARTHES (1984) **Camera Lucida**, London: Fontana. First published in French in 1980 as La Chambre Claire

39

Because of the disjunction between the thinking, seeing photographer and the camera that is the instrument of recording, the viewer finds it more difficult than with other visual artifacts to attribute creativity to any photographer.

(Price 1994: 4)

In philosophical terms, any concern with truth-to-appearances or traces of reality presupposes 'reality' as a given, external entity. Notions of the photograph as empirical proof, or the photograph as witness offering descriptive testimony, ultimately rest upon the view of reality as external to the human individual and objectively appraisable. If reality is somehow there, present, external, and available for objective recording, then the extent to which the photograph offers accurate reference, and the significance of the desire to take photographs or to look at images of particular places or events, become pertinent.

Susan Sontag defines the photograph as a 'trace' directly stencilled off reality, like the footprint or the death mask. *On Photography* offers a series of interconnected essays, essentially based on a realist view of photography. Her concern is with the extent to which the image adequately represents the moment of actuality from which it is taken. She emphasises the idea of the photograph as a means of freezing a moment in time. If the photograph misleads the viewer, it is because the photographer has not found an adequate means of conveying what he or she wishes to communicate about a particular set of circumstances. Her concern is with the photograph as document, as a report, or as evidence of activities such as tourism, adding that the use of a camera satisfies the work ethic and stands in when unsure of other responses to unfamiliar circumstances, but can also limit travel and other experiences to the search for the photogenic. Sontag is also concerned to point out the ethics of the relationship between the photographer as reporter and the person, place or circumstances recorded. The photographer, especially the photojournalist, is relatively powerful within this relationship and, thus, may be seen as predatory. She points out that the language of military manoeuvre – 'load', 'shoot' – is central to photographic practices. Given this relative power, in her view it is even more important to emphasise the necessity of accurate reporting or relating of events. Photographs are not necessarily sentimental, or candid; they may be used for policing or incrimination.

Her discussion veers between purposes of taking photographs and the uses to which they are put. It is marked by a sense of the elusiveness of the photo-image itself. She notes our reluctance to tear up photos of relatives, or the symbolic rejection of politicians through burning their image, for example. She describes photographs as relics of people as they once were, suggesting that the still camera embalms (by contrast with the movie camera, which savours mobility). Thus she draws attention to the fascination of looking at photographs in terms of what we think they might reveal of that which we cannot otherwise have any sense of knowing, characterising photographs as a catalogue of acquired images which stand in for memories. Photographs can also, she suggests, give us an unearned sense of understanding things, past and present, having both the potential to move us emotionally, but also the possibility of holding us at a distance through aestheticising images of events. Photographs can also exhaust experiences, using up the beautiful through rendering it into cliché. For instance, she notes that sunsets may now look corny, too much like photographs of sunsets. Throughout, however, we have the sense that meaning may be sought within the photograph, providing it has been well-composed and therefore accurately traces, and becomes, a relic of a person, place or event.

In her recent book *The Photograph* (1994), American critic Mary Price argues that the meaning of the photographic image is primarily determined through associated verbal description and through the context in which the photograph is *used*. By contrast with Sontag's emphasis on the relation between the image and its source in the actual historical world, Price starts from questions of viewing and the context of reception. Thus, she suggests, in principle there is no single meaning for the photograph, but rather an emergent meaning, within which the subject-matter of the image is but one element. Her analysis is practical in its approach. She takes a number of specific examples, aiming to demonstrate the extent to which usage and contextualisation determine meaning.

Realist theories of photography can take a number of different starting points: first, the photograph itself as an aesthetic artefact; second, the institutions of photography and the position and behaviour of photographers; third, the viewer or audience and the context in which the image is used, encountered, consumed. The particular starting point organises investigative priorities. For instance, ethical questions relating to who has the right to represent whom are central when considering the photographer and institutions such as the press.

Sontag takes a particular position within debates about realism, stressing the referential nature of the photographic image both in terms of its iconic properties and in terms of its **indexical** nature. For Sontag, the fact that a photograph exists testifies to the actuality of how something, someone or somewhere once appeared. Max Kozloff has challenged Sontag's conceptual model, criticising her proposition that the photograph 'traces' reality, and arguing instead for a view of the photograph as 'witness' with all the possibilities of misunderstanding, partial information or false testament that the term 'witness' may be taken to imply (Kozloff 1987: 237). In his collection of essays, *Photography and Fascination*, Kozloff starts from the question of the enticement of the photograph. He concludes that:

> Though infested with many bewildering anomalies, photographs are considered our best arbiters between our visual perceptions and the

memory of them. It is not only their apparent 'objectivity' that grants photographs their high status in this regard, but our belief that in them, fugitive sensation has been laid to rest. The presence of photographs reveals how circumscribed we are in the throes of sensing. We perceive and interpret the outer world through a set of incredibly fine internal receptors. But we are incapable, by ourselves, of grasping or tweezing out any permanent, sharable figment of it. Practically speaking, we ritually verify what is there, and are disposed to call it reality. But, with photographs, we have concrete proof that we have not been hallucinating all our lives.

(Kozloff 1979: 101)

However the relation between the image and the social world is conceptualised, it is worth noting that the authority which emanates from the sense of authenticity or 'truth to actuality' conferred by photography is a fundamental element within photographic language and aesthetics. This authority, founded in realism, has come to be taken for granted in the interpretation of images made through the lens. However, it is precisely this which sets lens-based imagery apart from other media of visual communication. Again, to quote Kozloff, 'A main distinction between a painting and a photograph is that the painting alludes to its content, whereas the photograph summons it, from wherever and whenever, to us' (1987: 236). The photographic is distinct from the **autographic**, or from the digital, in that it seems to emanate directly from the external. Inherent within the photographic is the particular requirement for the physical presence of the referent. This has led to photographs (along with film and video) being viewed as realist in ways that, say, technical drawing or portrait painting are not (although they are also based upon observation). That this is the case needs to be clearly acknowledged and addressed, in order to develop theory adequate and specific to photography.

The essential image

It is seeing which establishes our place in the surrounding world, we explain that world with words, but words can never undo the fact that we are surrounded by it. The relationship between what we see and what we know is never settled.

(Berger 1972: 7)

Two key theoretical developments, semiotics and psychoanalysis, have significantly contributed to changes within the humanities and both have figured in recent debates relating to the constitution of photographic meaning. **Semiology**, or semiotics, the idea of a science of signs, originates from comments in Ferdinand de Saussure's *General Theory of Linguistics* (1916) but was not further developed until after the Second World War. Essentially, semiology proposed the systematic analysis of cultural behaviour. At its extremes it aimed at establishing an empirically verifiable method of analysis of human communication systems. Thus, **codes** of dress, music, advertising – and other forms of communication – are conceptualised as logical systems. The focus is upon clues which together constitute a *text* ready for reading and interpretation. The key limitation of semiology as first proposed, with its focus upon systems of signification, was that it failed to address how particular *readers* of signs interpreted communications, made them meaningful to themselves within their specific context of experience. It has now become common to use the term 'semiology' to refer to the earlier, relatively inflexible, approach based upon structuralist linguistics, and to use 'semiotics' to indicate later, more fluid models, incorporating psychoanalysis, wherein the focus is more upon meaning-producing processes than upon textual systems. Social semiotics, taking account of questions of interpretation and context, inflects the emphasis specifically towards cultural artefacts and social behaviour.

French semiotician Roland Barthes is known for his contribution to the analysis of visual culture, in particular from his early work, *Mythologies*.[11] Working inductively from his observations of differing cultural phenomena, he proposed that everyday culture can be analysed in terms of language of communication (visual and verbal) and integrally associated myths or culturally specific discourses. Cultural phenomena discussed include the iconography of 'Roman-ness' as conventionally depicted on film, the politician's electoral portrait, French symbolic attitudes to wine by contrast with milk, the representation of the Alps in the *Blue Guide*, the advertising of soap powders and detergents, and the photography exhibition 'The Family of Man'. As these titles indicate, his interests at that time encompassed a range of visual and other phenomena. Central to his early work is a general explanatory concern with cultural processes. At this point his primary focus was upon the development of all-encompassing models of analysis of meaning-production processes conceptualised both in general terms and in terms which could take account of particular cultural characteristics. Thus, for example, his analysis of the codification of a short story *S/Z* (1970) was intended to identify, test and demonstrate the explanatory potential of a set of five codes which, he was then suggesting, were potentially applicable to a range of storytelling media (the novel, film, oral narratives). This is the point at which his work is most characterised by strict **structuralist** methodology. Later works, including *The Pleasure of the Text* (1973) and *Camera Lucida* (1984), are no longer primarily text-focused and less strictly 'scientific' (i.e. seeking to objectively classify significatory phenomena) in their approach. These works take more account of the individual reader, of processes of interpretation, of psychoanalytic factors, and of what we might term cultural 'slippages' – thereby implicitly accepting a degree of unpredictability in human agency or response.

11 Roland Barthes (1915–1980) Studied French Literature and Classics at the University of Paris, and taught French abroad in Romania and Egypt before returning to Paris for a research post in Sociology and Semiotics. He taught a course on the sociology of signs, symbols and collective representations at the *École Pratique des Hautes Études*, and became known for his contribution to the development of semiology, the science of signs, first proposed by linguist Ferdinand de Saussure in 1916 but not fully explored until after the Second World War. Barthes' publications include *Mythologies* (1957), *Elements of Semiology* (1964), *The Empire of Signs* (1970) and *Image, Music, Text* (1977), which includes his well-known essay on 'The Rhetoric of the Image'. *Camera Lucida*, originally titled *La Chambre Claire* (1980), was his last work, and the only publication devoted entirely to photography.

Camera Lucida is motivated by an ontological desire to understand the nature of the photograph 'in itself'. In semiotic terms, the photograph is disorderly because its ubiquity renders it unclassifiable: 'photography evades us' (Barthes 1984: 4). The style of writing is narrative and rhetorical, the tone is personal: he starts from discussion of himself as reader of the photographic image, asking why photos move him emotionally. In Part One he develops a commentary upon the nature and impact of the photograph using examples from documentary and photojournalism. In Part Two he focuses upon his own family photographs, particularly images of his mother – some of which date from 'history'; that is, a time before his birth – in order to contemplate more subjective meanings. There is no discussion of commercial imagery; nor of fine art uses of the medium. However, the objective is not to do with specific genres. His purpose is essentialist in that he seeks to define that which is specific to the photograph as a means of representation. He is not concerned with the taker of a photograph (the photographer or, as he terms it, 'operator') and the act of taking but, rather, with the act of looking (the spectator) and with the 'target' of the photograph; that is, the object or person represented within the 'spectrum' of the photograph. Thus he observes that the knowing portraitee adopts a pose which anticipates the representational image, and takes account of the fact that this piece of paper will outlast the actual person who is the subject of the portrait becoming the 'flat death', which both exposes that which has been and precedes actual death.

He concludes that it is 'reference' rather than Art, or communication, which is fundamental to photography. Central to his exploration is the contention that, unlike in any other medium, in photography the referent uniquely sticks to the image. In painting, for instance, it is not necessary for the referent to be present. Painting can be achieved from memory, photography cannot. From this emerges the time-specific characteristic of the photograph. It deals with *what was*, regardless of whether the terms or conditions continue to obtain. For Barthes photography is never about the present, although the act of looking occurs in the present. Also, the photograph is indescribable: words cannot substitute for the weight or impact of the resemblance of the image. The photograph is always about looking, and seeing. Furthermore, the photograph itself – that is, the chemically treated and processed paper – is invisible. It is not *it* that we see. Rather we see that which is represented. (This, he suggests, is one source of the difficulty in analysing photography ontologically.)

What, then, is the attraction of certain (but never all) photographs for the spectator? As writer-lecturer Philip Stokes has pointed out in relation to the potentially boring experience of looking at other people's family albums, 'in every dreary litany there is an instant when a window opens onto a scene of fascination that stops the eye and seizes the mind, filling it with questions or simply joy' (Stokes 1992: 194). Why do some images arrest

attention, animating the viewer, while others fail to 'speak' to the particular
spectator? Barthes proposes that photographs arrest attention when they
encompass a duality of elements – two (or more) discontinuous, and not
logically connected, elements which form the 'puzzle' (our term, not his)
of the image. Here he distinguishes between *studium*, general enthusiasm for
images and, indeed, the polite interest which may be expressed when
confronted with any particular photograph, and the *punctum* (prick, sting or
wound) which arrests attention. Previously, in an essay entitled 'The Third
Meaning', he has suggested that photographs encompass the obvious and the
obtuse, implying play of meaning within the photograph as text (Barthes
1977). This leads him to explore why, when so many images are noted as
a matter of routine, only some images make an impact on us. Here, again,
he makes a detailed distinction between the photograph which captures
attention through 'shouting' or because of the *shock* of revelation of subject-
matter (for instance, a particularly startling photojournalistic image), and the
punctum of recognition which transcends mere surprise, or rarity value, to
inflict a poignancy of recognition for the particular spectator. This, he
proposes, emanates more often from some detail within the image which
stands out, rather than from the unity of the content as a whole. He sees
this effect as essentially a product of the photograph itself. This, we would
suggest, limits his discussion. Surely the noticing of any particular detail is
as much a consequence of the particular spectator's history and interests. In
other words, the poignancy or joy of recognition is founded in the act of
engagement, the act of looking at a particular image, the relation between
the spectator and the photograph.

Barthes goes on to suggest that the photograph, through being contingent upon its referent, is outside meaning. In this sense he views it as 'a
message without a code' (to use a phrase drawn from his earlier essay on
the rhetoric of the image). He suggests that it is the fact of social observation
(in the portrait, for instance) which is the intermediacy rather than the
photograph, and that meaning does not, therefore, reside in photography
but in its contingency. For Barthes photography is at its most powerful not
because of what it can reveal, but because it is, as he terms it, 'pensive'. It
thinks. Of course Barthes knows that a photograph is not a thinking subject:
the photographer may think, the portraitee may pose, and the spectator may
respond reflectively. The photograph itself is an inanimate piece of paper.
Animation occurs through the act of looking.

Barthes' precise use of words (which, in the French, offers careful nuancing
but, in translation, may seem over-precious), and the personal tone, to some
extent obscure the general argument which is more phenomenological than
semiotic in its method. His discussion is useful in reminding us of the essential
contingency of the photograph. Like Sontag, he draws attention to its
referential characteristics; unlike Sontag, who relates this to a range of practices, he defines this as that which characterises the medium, but it does not

necessarily follow from this that it is a representation without a code. On the contrary, it is impossible to contemplate the image without operationalising a range of aesthetic and cultural codes. Ultimately, he also takes relatively little account of the specificity of the spectator and the reasons and context of looking. His discussion of his search for the representation of his mother which accords with his memory of her acknowledges his particular position as the spectator who is also her son. However, he does not attempt to move towards more general conclusions about spectatorship. Despite his emphasis upon looking, and seeing, he focuses centrally on the image as text rather than upon the relation between image and spectator. This does limit his ontological conclusions.

Photography reconsidered

The individual as spectator, the reception and usage of photographs, and the nature of processes whereby photographs become meaningful subjectively and collectively have remained central to contemporary debates. Here the influence of psychoanalysis has to be taken into account alongside semiotics, and also the concerns of **social history**.

Psychoanalysis, founded in Freud's investigations of the human psyche (from the 1880s onwards), centres upon the individual in ways which are now taken for granted but which, at the time, reflected certain revolutionary strands of political and philosophical thought.[12] For political theorists the individual became viewed as the basic social unit; also, someone expected to take personal responsibility for social and economic survival. Philosophers such as Nietzsche, regarded by many as the father figure of individualism, emphasised personal moral responsibility, engaging, in particular, with what he conceptualised as the enslaving influence of Christianity. Individualism is a taken-for-granted feature of twentieth-century Western experience. We talk of the individual consumer, individual professional responsibilities, individual responsibilities within the family, and so on. Yet this emphasis is relatively new. Psychoanalytic understandings of individual subjective responses to social experience have offered new models of insight into human behaviour in ways which have been challenging academically (as well as offering therapeutic means of coming to terms with personal trauma).

Published in the context of a series on communications and culture, Victor Burgin's *Thinking Photography* (1982) focuses on debates within the theory and practice of photography and photography criticism. The book sets out to challenge the notion of the autonomous creative artist, to question the idea of documentary 'truth' and to interrogate the notion of purely visual languages. The intention is to situate photography within broader theoretical debates and understandings pertaining to meaning and communication, visual culture and the politicals of representation.[13] The history of theories of art as they pertain to – or 'position' – photography is also a key theme. The eight essays (including three by Burgin himself), while they vary in

12 Sigmund Freud (1856–1939) Freud's copious writings and his work with patients form the basis of the discipline of psychoanalysis, used both as a therapeutic method and as a tool to understand interpersonal relations and cultural activities. Psychoanalysis has irrevocably changed the way we understand the world and ourselves. Possibly Freud's most important contribution to modern thought is the concept of the unconscious, which insists that human action always derives from mental processes of which we cannot be aware. Many photographers have used the ideas of Freud as the basis of their work.
13 At this time Burgin lectured in photography at the Polytechnic of Central London (now the University of Westminster). His other publications include *Between* (1986), *The End of Art Theory* (1986), *Formations of Fantasy* (coedited 1989). He is now based at the University of California.

their theoretical stance and critical style, share 'the project of developing a materialist analysis of photography'. What Burgin is concerned with is photography 'considered as a practice of *signification*'; that is, specific materials worked on for specified purposes within a particular social and historical context. Semiotics is one starting point for this theoretical project, but, as Burgin states, semiotics is not sufficient to account for 'the complex articulations of the moments of institution, text, distribution and consumption of photography' (Burgin 1982: 2).

In effect, through its selection of contributors, the book traces a particular trajectory through Left debates, from centralising questions of class, revolutionary struggle and the role of the artist, through semiotics, to questions of realism, to psychoanalysis and spectatorship. (Questions of gender are addressed, although, notably, no essays by women theorists are included.) The book posits two key theoretical starting points: materialist analysis, as represented in the reprinting of Frankfurt School theorist Walter Benjamin's essay on 'The Author as Producer' (first published in German in 1966) and the semiotic, represented in Italian semiotician Umberto Eco's essay, 'Critique of the Image'. The other central historical reference is that of Russian Futurism and the **Formalist–Constructivist** theoretical debates which followed. Touched upon by Benjamin in the first article, the Russian reference is taken up by Burgin and by Simon Watney in his discussion of 'Making Strange: The Shattered Mirror'.

In locating Benjamin's 'The Author as Producer' first, Burgin is both anchoring the book within traditional Marxist debates on the role of the artist and reminding us of the contribution of the Frankfurt School theorists to debates about the function and status of art. It reflects a traditional Left position in relation to modern art movements; namely, that the artist wittingly or unwittingly is caught up in the reproduction of the dominant ideology of Capitalism. Benjamin is thus interested in discussing the function of a work within the dominant relations of production and, in order to approach this, argues for a central focus on questions of technique within any social or materialist analysis. For instance, he notes **photomontage**, and the use of everyday items by the Dadaists to challenge the status and justification of High Art. Since the essay was written within the context of *Understanding Brecht* some space is given to advocating Epic Theatre, that is, the non-naturalistic. In conclusion he restates the classic Marxist premise that the revolutionary struggle is fought between capitalism and the proletariat.

Classic Marxist models of artistic production are addressed, critically, in the penultimate essay of the book, 'Making Strange: The Shattered Mirror', by Simon Watney. Focusing on seeing, vision and the social nature of perception, Watney discusses various 1920s/1930s manifestations – in Russian aesthetic debates and in Brecht – of the proposal that through alienation, or 'making strange', new ways of 'seeing', politically and aesthetically, may be forged. The subtitle, 'The Shattered Mirror', refers to the rupturing of any notion of the photograph as a mirror or transparent recorder of reality. (It does not carry the psychoanalytic implications which, as we shall see, characterise Burgin's contributions.) The essay situates ideas of defamiliarisation in relation to past practices in order to reflect upon modern European and American work which he exemplifies, briefly, through reference to French photographer Atget, Bauhaus theorist-photographer Moholy-Nagy, and American documentarian Berenice Abbott. He argues that the project of defamiliarisation in photography rested upon acceptance of the fallacy of the transparency of the photograph. In other words, if we relinquish realist theories of the photograph, then the problem of employing effective techniques for defamiliarisation dissolves.

By contrast with Benjamin's concern with the context and purpose of production, Eco's 'Critique of the Image' centres upon the codification of the photograph as text. In terms of the organisation of the book, this is intended as the second key theoretical anchoring-piece. As we have already seen, Eco argues that, despite the appearance of resemblance between the image and its referent, the iconic sign is, nonetheless, like other sign systems, 'completely arbitrary, conventional and unmotivated'. Thus he focuses on the conventions of perception and the cultural understandings which inform interpretation. The essay offers a ten-point summary of the range of codes implicated in photographic communication. The codes are presented with relatively little elaboration, and with no ascription of hierarchy or relative importance within the overall analytic model. Therefore, this represents a starting point for exploring the potential of this model rather than a fully fledged, illustrated argument for complex semiotics.

Semiotics, in conjunction with psychoanalysis, informs Burgin's own three essays which, respectively, develop a series of related points about: the nature of the photograph as conceptualised in the context of new art theory; the experience of 'looking at photographs' from the point of view of the spectator; and exploring the psychological nature of the pleasurable response to the image. Thus he is concerned to trace links between the image, interpretation and ideological discourses. The model is most fully developed in 'Photography, Phantasy, Function', wherein the main part of the essay draws upon Freud to discuss the psychological investment in the act of looking, noting that looking is not indifferent. Thus, he draws our attention to the voyeuristic and fetishistic *investment* in looking, arguing that to look is to become sutured within ideological discourse(s). He further argues that the photograph, like the fetish, is the result of an isolated fragment or frozen moment, and describes the fetishistic nature of the photograph as one source of its fascination.

While the focus on realism which constitutes Sontag's starting point tends to distract from discussion of meaning-production, semiologically informed models of meaning analysis have tended to take relatively little account of the question of realism, thereby marginalising discussion of the realist coding of the photograph and ways in which this informs interpretation.

Arguably the cultural effect of the realist characteristics attributed to the photograph must be taken into account if *photography* theory is to be more fully developed.

Realism is addressed in the remaining two essays, albeit social-historically as much as semiotically. Starting with the work of Berenice Abbott, John Tagg focuses on what he terms 'the prerequisites of realism'. The title, 'The Currency of the Photograph', metaphorically references the idea of the photograph as symbolic exchange, while simultaneously referring to the values implicated in such an exchange. Thus he discusses the relationship of the photograph to reality, the constitution of photographic meaning, the social utility of photographs, and the institutional frameworks within which they are produced and consumed. Arguing that photography cannot exist outside of the material operation of ideological apparatuses, he insists on the need to trace the complex relations between representation, knowledge and ideology in terms which take account of the fundamental class interests at stake. The argument is developed in some detail in relation to the example of the American 'New Deal' Farm Security Administration project.

Remarking 'On the Invention of Photographic Meaning', Alan Sekula likewise considers the complexity of values articulated in relation to the photograph through exploring the notional opposition between the realist (Lewis Hine's *Immigrants going down a gangplank*) and the expressive (Stieglitz's *The Steerage*). Taking account of the context of making and publication of the images, as well as the connotative and aesthetic characteristics attributed to the photographs themselves, he identifies a series of what he terms 'folkloric' binary oppositions within which photographic communications occur: the symbolist vs the realist, often misleadingly viewed as the opposition between art and documentary; photographer as seer vs witness; photography as expression vs reportage; imagination vs empirical truth; affective vs informative value; metaphoric vs metonymic signification. In conclusion, he suggests that the complexity of relatively abstract values within which the photograph is articulated contributes to the possibility of political reappropriation.

At the time of its publication this collection of essays provoked markedly differing critical responses. For instance, writing in *Creative Camera* (1982), excepting Sekula's contribution, Ian Jeffrey dismissed what he described as an unfortunate new line of development in photography analysis on the grounds that:

> History, dialectical or otherwise, is a department in which the Burgin squad is under-rehearsed. History is often invoked but not much practiced, and I am left with the sense here of an endless drawing up of rules for a game which is never played.
>
> (Jeffrey 1982: 724)

Conversely, Stevie Bezencenet in the same issue of *Creative Camera* welcomed the attempt to move beyond the traditional analysis of photography – from the three standpoints of the technical, artistic and social – towards a more complex theoretical comprehension of the medium, noting that, as a publication, it had emerged from contemporary debates and suggesting that:

> The practising of theory and theorising of practice are becoming united in the development of a materialist analysis of photography. This is a process which will lead us into the disciplines of linguistics, sociology, Marxism, art history and psychoanalysis, so that we may return to a study of the production of images, with a better understanding of their social operations.
>
> (Bezencenet 1982b: 727)

Theory, criticism, practice

What has all this got to do with making photographs? Visual methods of communication are, of course, embedded in particular cultural circumstances and therefore reflect specific assumptions and expectations. For instance, as has been argued, given the nineteenth-century desire for empirical evidence, photography was hailed for its apparent ability to represent events accurately. This desire or expectation persists in fields such as photojournalism. Furthermore, theoretical concepts interact. For instance, criteria based upon established visual aesthetics inform the assessment of what makes a 'good' photograph, photojournalistic or otherwise. Similarly, questions of representation pertaining to, for example, gender or race, which have contributed to the challenge to the canon within literary studies and art history, are relevant to photography.

The key point is that theoretical presumptions founded in varying academic fields, from the scientific to the philosophic and the aesthetic, intersect to inform both the making and the interpretation of visual imagery. One consequence of the postmodern is a change in type of theoretical endeavour and, consequently, a change in style of publications concerning photography which, in recent years, have become more eclectic in their theoretical sources and less all-embracing in terms of questions posed and projects pursued. Books of essays on a diversity of subjects, adopting a range of differing theoretical concerns and conjunctions, are increasingly common.

Yet, in common with other fields of the arts, photography criticism still tends to be normative, evaluating work in relation to established and accepted traditions and practices. At its worst, criticism masks personal opinion, dressed up as objective or authoritative with the aim of impressing, for example, the readers of review articles in order to generate their respect and support for the reviewer. At its best, criticism helps to locate particular work in relation to specific debates about practice through elucidating appreciation of the effect, meaning, context and import of the imagery under question.

In order to think about photographic communication, we need to take account of communications theory in broad terms as well as focusing specifically on photographs as a particular type of visual sign, produced and used in particular, but differing, contexts. The photograph, therefore, might be conceptualised as a site of intersection of various orders of theoretical understanding relating to its production, publication and consumption or reading. Central to the project of theorising photography is the issue of the relation between that which particularly characterises the photographic (which, as we have seen, is its referential qualities), and theoretical discourses which pertain to the making and reading of the image but whose purchase is broader, for instance, aesthetic theory or sexual politics. What is crucially at stake is how we think about the tension between the referential characteristics of the photograph and the contexts of usage and interpretation.

The key characteristic of photography – as opposed to digital imaging – is its ultimate dependence upon, and therefore reference to, a physical person or object present at the moment of making the original exposure. This physical presence is the origin or source of the possibility of an image and, consequently, the image stands as an index of the once physical presence. It is this indexical status which is the source of the authority of the image and, thus, of central theoretical debates relating to realism and 'truth'. Photography theory cannot rest simply on optics and chemistry (or, indeed, the binary mathematical systems which underpin digital imaging). Given the ubiquity of photographic practices, a twofold problem emerges: first, to analyse ways in which clusters of theoretical discourses intersect, or acquire priority, in particular fields of practice; and second, to define and analyse that which is peculiar to photography. If we take Barthes' final words on the subject, it is, primarily, its referential characteristic which, variously, lends it particular credibility, force or significance. If we start from the greater diversity of positions – semiotic, psychoanalytic and social-historical – outlined in Burgin's edited collection, then the focus must be upon the political and **ideological**. The project of theorising photography thus relies upon the development of complex models of analysis which can take account of these rather different starting points.

Within this conceptual approach it is not the objective presence of the image which is at stake, but rather the force field within which it generates meaning. This contrasts with semiological stress on systems of signification. In effect we are invited to consider not only the text, its production and its reading, but also to take account of the social relations within which meaning is produced and operates. Here, the semblance of the real underpins processes of interpretation. Photography is reassuringly familiar, not least because it seems to reproduce that which we see, or might see. In so far as visual representations contribute to constructing and reaffirming our sense of identity, this familiarity, and the apparent realism of the photographic image, render it a particularly powerful discursive force.

BIBLIOGRAPHY

KEY TEXTS

Barthes, Roland (1984) *Camera Lucida*, London: Fontana
Burgin, Victor (ed.) (1982) *Thinking Photography*, London: Macmillan
Corner, John and Harvey, Sylvia (1990) 'Heritage in Britain', *Ten/8* 36
Crimp, Douglas (1995) *On the Museum's Ruins*, Cambridge, MA: MIT Press
Edwards, Elizabeth (ed.) (1992) *Photography and Anthropology*, New Haven: Yale University Press
Gernsheim, Helmut and Gernsheim, Alison (1969) *The History of Photography from the Earliest Use of the Camera Obscura in the Eleventh Century up to 1914*, 2 vols, London and New York: MacGraw Hill (first edition, 1955)
Goldberg, Vicki (ed.) (1981) *Photography in Print*, Albuquerque: University of New Mexico
Hill, Paul and Cooper, Thomas (1992) *Dialogue with Photography*, Manchester: Cornerhouse Publications
Jeffrey, Ian (1981) *Photography, A Concise History*, London: Thames and Hudson
Lemagny, Jean-Claude and Rouille, André (1987) *A History of Photography*, Cambridge: Cambridge University Press
Lyons, Nathan (1966) *Photographers on Photography*, Englewood Cliffs: Prentice Hall
Newhall, Beaumont (1982) *The History of Photography*, New York: MOMA, fifth edition, revised and enlarged
Phillips, Christopher (ed.) (1989) *Photography in the Modern Era*, New York: Metropolitan Museum/Aperture
Sontag, Susan (1979) *On Photography*, Harmondsworth: Penguin
Szarkowski, John (1989) *Photography Until Now*, New York: MOMA
Tagg, John (1988) *The Burden of Representation: Essays on Photographies and Histories*, London: Macmillan
Taylor, John (1994) *A Dream of England: Landscape, Photography and the Tourist's Imagination*, Manchester: Manchester University Press
Thomas, Alan (1978) *The Expanding Eye*, London: Croom Helm
Turner, Peter (1987) *History of Photography*, London: Hamlyn
Williams, Val (1986) *Women Photographers: The Other Observers, 1900 to the Present*, London: Virago (revised edition 1991, *The Other Observers: Women Photographers from 1900 to the Present*)

OTHER REFERENCES

Montoussamy-Ashe, Jeanne (1985) *Viewfinders: Black Women Photographers*, New York: Dodd, Mead
Barthes, Roland (1977) 'The Rhetoric of the Image' and 'The Third Meaning' in *Image, Music, Text*, London: Fontana
Batchen, Geoffrey (1990) 'Burning with Desire: The Birth and Death of Photography', *Afterimage*, January
Baudelaire, Charles (1859) 'The Salon of 1859', reprinted in P.E. Charvet (1992) (ed.) *Baudelaire, Selected Writings on Art and Artists*, Harmondsworth: Penguin
Benjamin, Walter (1931) 'A Small History of Photography' in (1979) *One Way Street*, London: New Left Books
Benjamin, Walter (1973) 'The Work of Art in an Age of Mechanical Reproduction' in Hannah Arendt (ed.) *Illuminations*, London: Fontana (first published 1936)
Beloff, Halla (1985) *Camera Culture*, Oxford: Basil Blackwell
Berger, John (1972) *Ways of Seeing*, Harmondsworth: Penguin

Bezencenet, Stevie (1982a) 'What is a History of Photography?', *Creative Camera* 208, April
—— (1982b) 'Thinking Photography', *Creative Camera* 215, November
Bolton, Richard (ed.) (1989) *The Contest of Meaning*, Cambridge, MA: MIT Press
Burgin, Victor (1986) 'Re-Reading Camera Lucida' in *The End of Art Theory*, London: Macmillan
Carr, E.H. (1964) *What is History?*, Harmondsworth: Penguin
Christian, J. (1990) 'Paul Sandby and the Military Survey of Scotland' in N. Alfrey and J. Daniels (eds) *Mapping the Landscape*, University of Nottingham
Corner, John and Harvey, Sylvia (eds) (1991) *Enterprise and Heritage*, London: Routledge
Delpire, Robert and Frizot, Michel (1989) *Histoire de Voir*, Paris: Photo Poche
Eastlake, Lady Elizabeth (1857) 'Photography', *Quarterly Review*, April, reprinted in B. Newhall (ed.) (1980) *Photography: Essays and Images*, London: Secker and Warburg
Ferguson, Russell (1992) 'A Box of Tools: Theory and Practice' in R. Ferguson *et al.* (eds) *Discourses: Conversations in Postmodernism, Art and Culture*, Cambridge, MA: MIT Press
Freund, Gisele (1980) *Photography and Society*, London: Gordon Fraser
Gasser, Martin (1992) 'Histories of Photography 1839–1939', *History of Photography* 16(1), Spring
Gernsheim, Alison (1981) *Victorian and Edwardian Fashion, A Photographic Survey*, New York: Dover (originally published 1963, revised edition)
Graham-Brown, Sarah (1988) *Images of Women: The Portrayal of Women in Photography of the Middle East 1860–1950*, London: Quartet Books
Heron, Liz and Williams, Val (1996) *Illuminations: Women Writing on Photography from the 1850s to the Present*, London and New York: I.B. Tauris
Hewison, Robert (1987) *The Heritage Industry*, London: Methuen
Holmes, Oliver Wendell (1859) 'The Stereoscope and the Stereograph', *Atlantic Monthly* 3, reprinted in B. Newhall (ed.) (1980) *Photography: Essays and Images*, London: Secker and Warburg
Horne, Donald (1984) *The Great Museum: The Re-presentation of History*, London: Verso
Howard, F. (1853) 'Photography Applied to Fine Art', *Journal of the Photographic Society*, London
Jameson, Fredric (1991) *Postmodernism, Or, the Cultural Logic of Late Capitalism*, London: Verso
Jeffrey, Ian (1982) 'Some Sacred Sites', *Creative Camera* 215, November
Krauss, Rosalind (1981)'A Note on Photography and the Simulacral', *October*, Winter, reprinted in Carol Squiers (ed.) (1991) *The Critical Image*, Seattle: Bay Press/London: Lawrence and Wishart
Kozloff, Max (1979) *Photography and Fascination*, USA New Hampshire: Addison House
Kozloff, Max (1987) *The Privileged Eye*, Albuquerque: University of New Mexico Press
Moholy-Nagy, Lazlo (1967) *Painting, Photography, Film*, London: Lund Humphries
Minto, C.S. (1970) *Victorian and Edwardian Scotland from Old Photographs*, London: Batsford
Price, Mary (1994) *The Photograph: A Strange, Confined Space*, Stanford, CA: Stanford University Press
Pultz, John (1995) *The Body and the Lens: Photography 1839 to the Present*, New York: Harry N. Abrams, Inc.
Punt, Michael (1995) 'The Elephant, the Spaceship and the White Cockatoo: An Archeology of Digital Photography' in Martin Lister (ed.) *The Photographic Image in Digital Culture*, London: Routledge
Sekula, Alan (1986) 'The Archive and the Body', *October* 39, reprinted in Richard Bolton (ed.) (1989) *The Contest of Meaning*, Cambridge, MA: MIT Press
—— (1991) 'Reading an Archive' in Brian Wallis and Marcia Tucker (eds) *Blasted Allegories*, Cambridge, MA: MIT Press
Snyder, Joel (1994) 'Territorial Photography' in W.J.T. Mitchell (ed.) *Landscape and Power*, London: University of Chicago Press

Squiers, Carol (ed.) (1990) *The Critical Image*, London: Lawrence and Wishart

Stokes, Philip (1992) 'The Family Photograph Album: So Great a Cloud of Witnesses' in Graham Clarke (ed.) *The Portrait in Photography*, London: Reaktion Books

Strand, Paul (1917) 'Photography', *Camera Work* 49/50, reprinted in B. Newhall (1982)

—— (1980) *Photography: Essays and Images*, London: Secker and Warburg

Sullivan, Constance (1990) *Woman Photographers*, London: Virago

Thomas, Deborah Willis (1985) *Black Photographers 1840–1940: An Illustrated Bio-Bibliography*, New York: Garland

Tucker, Anne (1973) *The Woman's Eye*, New York: Knopf

Warner Marien, Mary (1988) 'Another History of Photography', *Afterimage*, October: 4–5

—— (1991) 'Toward a New Prehistory of Photography' in Daniel P. Younger (ed.) *Multiple Views*, Albuquerque: University of New Mexico Press

Weaver, Mike (1989) *The Art of Photography*, London: Royal Academy of Art

Williams, Raymond (1974) *Television, Technology and Cultural Form*, London: Fontana

CHAPTER 2

Surveyors and surveyed

Photography out and about

DERRICK PRICE

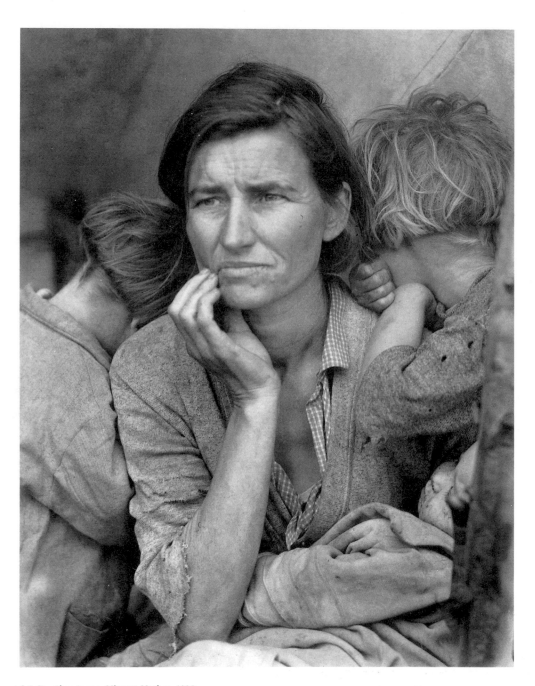

2.1 Dorothea Lange, Migrant Mother, 1936
This picture of an itinerant agricultural worker is among the most frequently reproduced in the history of photography

Surveyors and surveyed
Photography out and about

INTRODUCTION

Within a decade or two of its invention, photography was used to chronicle wars, to survey remote regions of the world and to make scientific observations. Life on the streets of great cities was recorded, but so were the monuments of Egypt and Syria, the vast ranges of the Himalayas, the USA railroad as it moved West, the fishing village of Whitby and the architecture of Paris. Pornographic images were soon in circulation, as were charity shots of the poor and homeless. **Montage** techniques were used to produce pictures of fairies, ghosts and elves. Less sensationally, the dead were recorded as they lay in their coffins (photography was hailed as an excellent substitute for the death mask), while all the living seemed appropriate subjects for the camera's **gaze**.

In this chapter we examine some of the ways photography has been used in order to bring us images of the wider world. Although we look briefly at some aspects of travel and war photography, we are essentially concerned with documentary photographs and with the history through which 'documentary' was shaped and developed. It was to grow into a movement with many practitioners throughout the world but, in order to look closely at the nature of its origins and development, we have concentrated on the British experience. So closely is that related to documentary projects in the USA, however, that we have also taken examples from that country. Documentary realism as expressed in film, photography and literature was of importance in the development of cultural politics and social investigation in both countries.

This approach allows us to explore the connections between documentary, social investigation, modes of **representation** and forms of reportage at particular times. In this sense the chapter is centrally concerned with questions of history, but it does not offer a chronicle of the great practitioners of documentary photography. Indeed, so all-pervasive has been documentary, and its associated forms, that such a chronicle would need to include many of the major figures in the history of photography. Particular photographers are discussed in order to illustrate some aspect of the documentary project, rather than to provide a description of the nature of their work.

We begin by noting photography's inexhaustible ability to provide us with pictures of the world; images which we are asked to accept as faithful to the real appearance of things. We want to examine the medium's putative capability to furnish us with accurate transcription of reality; an ability once thought to be guaranteed by the technology itself. Later this naive view was challenged and, as we shall see, the relationship of photography to reality was problematised and contested.

More recent critical work has rejected the notion that acts of looking and recording can ever be neutral, disinterested or innocent, but has seen them as containing and expressing relations of power and control. To examine this we need to consider why, and under what conditions, certain groups became the object of the camera's gaze, as well as to investigate the ways in which they were represented.

SURVEYS AND SOCIAL FACTS

Photography and imperialism

Despite the physical difficulties of transporting large, unwieldy cameras and portable darkrooms, photographers covered the world in search of images of historic sites, sacred places and curious peoples. Photography grew up in the days of Empire and became an important adjunct of imperialism, for it returned to the Western spectator images of native peoples which frequently confirmed prevailing views of them as primitive, bizarre, barbaric or simply picturesque.

As Robert Hershkowitz has put it:

> Photographic images, particularly from the late 1850s onward, reinforced the attitude(s) of mind which lay behind the imperialist approach to international politics, the positivist, materialist approach to the natural world and a belief in progress through advancing technological development.
>
> (Hershkowitz 1980: 7)

These photographs were often regarded as offering amusing or fascinating glimpses of other societies, but they were also considered to be instructive or educative for, within the evolutionary theories of the day, they were considered to reveal something of people at an earlier stage of development. In consequence, the images were also invested with a certain kind of poignancy for, at the height of industrialism in the USA and Europe, it seemed clear that many of the communities recorded by the photographers of Empire were doomed to disappear.

The Victorian passion for classification extended to whole peoples, who were categorised and ranked according to 'anthropological type'. Those who were subjected to the coloniser's gaze were often seen as merely representative of racial or social groups, and were usually posed so as to embody particular kinds of dress, social roles and material cultures.

Peter Quartermaine, in his discussion of the photographs of Johannes Lindt of the native peoples of Australia and New Guinea, comments that:

> These people were photographed as 'other': the white settler population was interested in learning *about* them, a quasi-scientific attitude which presupposed a controlling position. The photographic images produced by Australian photographers sold to a metropolitan and international consumer market. Such prints doubly privileged the purchasers since, although reflecting their own aesthetic (natives clothed and posed with decorative artefacts), they also supposedly granted direct access to the culture depicted; their use as raw evidence by anthropologists and ethnographers certainly assumed this.
>
> (Quartermaine 1992: 85)

The concept of **the Other** is of central importance to this argument. The phrase is used in feminist, **psychoanalytic** theory to indicate that men construct women as 'the Other'; that is, as an opposite, in reaction to which their own maleness can be defined. Similarly, European culture was defined *against* 'the Other' of colonised peoples: 'Photography is here no mere handmaid of empire, but a shaping dimension of it: formal imperial power structures institutionalised the attitudes and assumptions necessarily entailed in viewing another individual as a subject for photography' (Quartermaine 1992: 85).

We must remember that, unlike the body of painting and engravings of 'exotic' peoples that had been popular Victorian subjects, photography claimed to be able to create objective, 'scientific' records which were free from the bias of human imagination. Carefully contrived and constructed photographs were consumed as though they were unmediated images and offered a neutral reflection of the world. They were, however, far from being transparent and dispassionate images of the world for, as Jill Lloyd puts it: 'both photography as a medium and anthropology as a discipline masked their ideological standpoints and connotative potential with the appearance of scientific objectivity' (Lloyd 1985: 13).

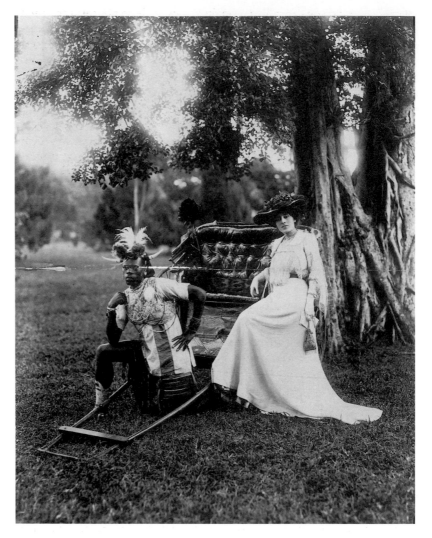

2.2 William Thomas, Mrs Lewis Waller with a Kaffir Boy, 1903
The relationship between coloniser and colonised is sharply focused in this portrait of Mrs. Waller and her African servant

The public appetite for images of native peoples was accompanied by a demand for photographs of historic sites, many of which were familiar from paintings and engravings, but which were given a new authenticity by the camera. It is difficult now to gain any idea of just how many travel photographs were made and sold, but the market in them was certainly vast. In addition to the beautifully mounted and bound albums that are now preserved in archives and museums, the new commercial photography firms that were

60

established in the years after 1850 sold thousands of cheap postcards and single prints. For example, in 1865 the London Stereoscopic Company sold half a million pictures, many of them scenes from foreign places. At the same time we see the emergence of the professional travel photographer of whom Francis Frith is probably the best known. In addition to his own work he established a company bearing his name that was to become the largest publisher of photographs in its time. The camera and travel became linked together and, as tourism slowly developed into a mass industry, photography functioned both to set the scene in advance of a trip and to provide a record of the journey when it was over. Soon there were few places in the world that had not been surveyed by the camera and few people who had not been subjected to the photo-eye; wildernesses gave up their seclusion as surely as cities yielded their secret places to the new image-makers.

It has frequently been argued that photography has been used as a way of consuming the world in a manner that gives us power over it; a way that allows us to discipline and naturalise what might otherwise seem strange or frightening:

> To photograph is in some ways to appropriate the object being photographed. It is a power/knowledge relationship. To have visual knowledge of an object is in part to have power, even if only momentarily over it. Photography tames the object of the gaze, the most striking examples being of exotic cultures. In the USA the railway companies did much to create 'Indian' attractions to be photographed, carefully selecting those tribes with a particularly 'picturesque and ancient' appearance.
>
> (Urry 1990: 139)

While photography produced a particular kind of knowledge it was also seen by many of its practitioners as a form of entertainment, and not all photographers went abroad with educational aims. Burton Holmes made his debut in 1890 with a slides and anecdote show, 'Through Europe with a Kodak', which he delivered to the Chicago Camera Club.

In order to distinguish his performance from lectures, Holmes invented the word 'travelogue'. In pursuit of material he went around the world six times and gave over 8,000 illustrated talks. Holmes was so successful an entertainer and entrepreneur of photography that he was said to have grossed $5 million in fifty-three years.

The camera at war

While Burton Holmes was coining a name for a new kind of photographic show, other people travelled with graver purposes. War plays an important part in the story of photography and today most people's understanding of the nature of war comes from photographic images rather than literary accounts. It was, however, the highly critical reports of the London *Times* reporter, William Russell, on the progress of the Crimean War that led to Roger Fenton being sent to take photographs that would reassure the public. Fenton used the newly invented wet collodion process to produce more than 350 photographs which did, indeed, show scenes of calm and disciplined order. He produced a number of handsome albums with original photographs 'tipped in', but his images were also used as the basis of illustrations in the *Illustrated London News*.

Fenton is usually considered to be the first person systematically to photograph soldiers at war, but he did not produce images which revealed much about the nature of war. That distinction is accorded to Mathew Brady who, in the 1860s, photographed the American Civil War. Within the technical limits of the time, Brady showed scenes of action, together with shots of the dead on the battlefield, and more tranquil views of soldiers relaxing at their camps. Since Brady's time, no war or violent conflict has lacked its photographic record and interpreters. For example, hundreds of thousands of images of the First World War were made, most of which have been rendered anonymous by the system of classification and archiving that was subsequently employed. Despite the sheer number of photographs of that conflict there is little work that really gives us a sense of the nature of trench warfare, and the poetry, films and paintings of the time are often more moving and revealing.

Photography was considerably more important as a means of depicting the Spanish Civil War (1936–1939). The many illustrated journals of the day carried photographs and these images were influential in shaping people's view of the war. The single most famous photograph was Robert Capa's 'Death of a Loyalist Soldier' which later became the subject of speculation as to its authenticity. Capa was also one of the photographers of the Second World War whose work became very familiar to the public, along with that of Bert Hardy, W. Eugene Smith, Carl Mydans and *Life* photographer David Douglas Duncan, who went on to produce heroic images of American soldiers in Korea and Vietnam.

The Second World War (1939–1945) blurred the distinction between combatant and civilian and, thereafter, war photographers concentrated as much attention on those caught up in conflict as on the soldiers themselves. This is, of course, also true for violent conflict which is not defined as a 'war', as in Cyprus or Northern Ireland.

Jorge Lewinski has commented that:

> It is only in the post-war period, starting with the Korean war, that the immediacy of war photographs begins to have a significant effect. Since then, a stream of authentic images has overwhelmed us with cumulative power. The images from Korea, Cyprus, Israel, the Congo, Biafra and Vietnam have left their indelible mark on our imaginations.
>
> (Lewinski 1978: 12)

Certainly, it is often said that the stream of images revealing the death, injury and sorrows of the people of Vietnam was a major factor in the public's eventual repugnance for that war. In the sophisticated photographic work of the time the themes of martial conflict and civilian anguish are intertwined. An excellent example is given in the work of Philip Jones Griffiths who produced one of the most important photographic records of the war (Griffiths 1971).

War has been seen as an important subject for photography for a number of reasons: the photographer might reveal scenes and actions which would not otherwise come to the attention of the public; war inevitably throws up scenes of great emotional force which can best be captured by the camera; it has a dark psychic fascination for us, which coexists with our feelings of revulsion. The person who has most mused on this ambivalence is the English photographer, Don McCullin, who has documented many wars and violent uprisings since the early 1960s.

Documentary photography

Photographs by travellers and scenes of war became photographic genres in their own right, and they are sometimes difficult to distinguish from the kind of photograph with which we are most interested in this chapter – the documentary.

Since documentary has been described as a form, a genre, a tradition, a style, a movement and a practice, it is not useful to try to offer a single definition of the word. John Grierson coined the word in 1926 to describe the kind of cinema that he wanted to replace what he saw as the dream factory of Hollywood, and it quickly gained currency within photography. The word had an imperialist tendency and soon rather different kinds of photography were being subsumed within it. Some nineteenth-century photographers had regarded their work as 'documents', but many more were innocent of the fact that they were documentary photographers. Indeed, **Abigail Solomon-Godeau** (1991) has pointed out that in the nineteenth century almost all photography was what would later be described as 'documentary'.

ABIGAIL SOLOMON-GODEAU (1991) **Photography at the Dock**, Minneapolis: University of Minnesota Press

But, if most photographs are a *kind* of documentary, how can we make distinctions between them? Historians and critics have frequently drawn attention to the difficulty of defining documentary which cannot be recognised as possessing a unique style, method or body of techniques. One answer to the question is to define documentary in terms of its connection with particular kinds of social investigation. Karin Becker Ohrn argues:

> The cluster of characteristics defining the documentary style
> incorporates all aspects of the making and use of photographs.
> Although not rigid, these characteristics serve as referents for
> comparing photographers working within . . . the documentary

tradition – a tradition that includes aspects of journalism, art, education, sociology and history. Primarily, documentary was thought of as having a goal beyond the production of a fine print. The photographer's goal was to bring the attention of an audience to the subject of his or her work and, in many cases, to pave the way for social change.

(Ohrn 1980: 36)

Our concern in this chapter will be to unpick some of the components of this tradition and examine ways in which we can distinguish documentary from other kinds of **straight photography**. Certainly the nature of an image itself is not enough to classify a particular photograph as in some essential way 'documentary'; rather we need to look at the contexts, practices, institutional forms, within which the work is set. Documentary work may be seen to belong to the history of a particular kind of social investigation although it employed its own forms, conventions and tropes. **Martha Rossler** (1989) tells us that to understand it we need to look to history and she characterises documentary as 'a practice with a past'. A past, we might add, which, despite changing technologies, practices and fashions, was always concerned to claim for documentary a special relationship to real life and a singular status with regard to notions of truth and authenticity. In looking at this past we will present an account of some of the theoretical, cultural and historical elements that are necessary in order to examine critically the history of documentary. The first of these is its implicit claim that it offers us a disinterested and true picture of the world.

MARTHA ROSSLER (1989) 'In, Around and Afterthoughts (on Documentary Photography)' in R. Bolton (ed.) **The Contest of Meaning: Critical Histories of Photography,** Cambridge, MA: MIT Press

Documentary and authenticity

Perhaps the simplest and most obvious test of authenticity in the kind of photography that claims to be an unmediated transcription of reality is to ask whether what is in front of the lens to be photographed has been tampered with, set up or altered by the photographer.

Early in its history photography had been presented with many cases of fraud as, for example, when the French photographer E. Appert published his book *Les Crimes de la Commune* in 1871. This purported to be a record of the vile behaviour of those who took part in the rising of the Paris Commune and was received with relish by many bourgeois commentators of the time. It consists, for the most part, of crudely montaged and retouched photographs, but was convincing enough for a public who were confident that the camera could not lie. It would, however, be incorrect to deduce that in the nineteenth century only outright deception was commented upon. Many more sophisticated arguments about the ability of photographs to be true to appearances were rehearsed at that time. Indeed the Victorians were to stage a dramatic debate on the relationship between truth and representation in the public trial of Dr Barnardo.

In 1876 the philanthropist Dr J.T. Barnardo appeared at a public hearing charged with deceiving the public. His detractors claimed, and Barnardo finally conceded, that he had misled the public in his use of 'before and after' photographs of the orphans in his care. He had produced a series of cards which purported to reveal the transformative power of his project: one card was of dirty, ragged children lounging about against a background of urban decay; a second card showed one of these children cleaned up and neatly dressed, undertaking some useful task. Dr Barnardo used child models for these cards and one, Katie Smith, is pictured in several of them, posing as a crossing-sweeper or a match-seller. At the hearing Barnardo agreed that Katie had never sold matches, but he pointed out that she was a child of the streets who might well have ended up as a beggar and that, in any case, she represented the appearance and state of a match-girl in an honest manner. Moreover, Katie could easily have stumbled into that kind of life had she not been saved by his mission.

As a result of the public hearing Barnardo gave up using photographs in this way, but his case raises questions that were to recur throughout the next century. Why should we trust the camera to be true-to-appearances? What is the relationship between the accurate portrayal of a single case and a general truth about the nature of things? Cannot something arranged or set up offer us an authentic insight into the nature of things? It was questions of this kind that were rehearsed, long after Barnardo, in the furore that broke out over a photograph made in the USA.

In 1936 the American photographer Arthur Rothstein photographed a steer's skull that had been bleached by the sun and left lying on the earth. A simple still life, then, but one that was clearly intended to exemplify the contemporary crisis in agriculture. Rothstein took two photographs of this object, the most famous of which shows it resting on cracked, baked, waterless earth. The second, however, revealed it as resting on the less symbolically charged ground of a stretch of grass. The photographer acknowledged that he had moved the skull a few metres in order to obtain a more dramatic pictorial effect. When the presence of these two rather different images was discovered there was an outcry from Republican politicians who claimed that the public had a right to see photographs that were objectively true rather than those that had been manipulated for purposes of rhetoric or propaganda. Two kinds of truth were in play; for, while the right-wing politicians demanded a truth at the denotative level, the photographer, like Dr Barnardo, laid claim to a greater truth at the connotative level. Nevertheless, Rothstein was at pains to draw attention to the smallness of his intervention in the 'real' state of things and would certainly have subscribed to the view that the authentic could only be guaranteed by a relatively unmediated representation of things as they are.

When it became plain that the technologies of photography were not automatic transcribers of the world, other questions about the nature of authenticity began to be raised and other guarantors of photography's fidelity were advanced. Among these was the notion that we need to trust, not the mechanical properties of the camera, but the personal integrity of the photographer. Increasingly the 'reality' revealed by the camera's lens was regarded as being to some extent a product of the personality, sensitivity or creativity of the photographer. The camera would provide not the objective facts that were craved by positivism, but accounts of the world in which 'truth' was achieved through the power of the image-maker. Thus, Tim Gidal sums up the qualities needed by a photojournalist:

> The genuine reporter – and by this we mean the rare phenomenon of the passionately committed photojournalist – personally experiences what he captures on film: laughter and tears, joy and sorrow, tragedy and comedy. It is only through his subjective experience of the objective facts that the photoreporter can become a witness to his time. His alertness and his gift of observation distinguish his work from that of others – not as an artist, but related to the artist by virtue of this talent of creative observation.
>
> (Gidal 1973: 6)

The photographer, on this account, is both gifted with a particular acuity of vision and acts as a kind of 'exemplary sufferer' on our behalf; an artist who, in his or her person, becomes a guarantor of the accuracy of the image. It is, of course, a major step to argue that authenticity is not certified by the medium itself, but is only validated through the personal qualities and professional practices of the photographer.

Victorian surveys and investigations

One reason why the veracity of the camera was readily accepted in the nineteenth century was that photographs appeared to confirm ideas about the world that had been the subject of other artistic and cultural forms. The camera reinforced journalistic and literary accounts of aspects of social life which had rarely been seen or experienced by middle-class people. Moreover, we may argue that Victorian actuality photographs were regarded as 'authentic' precisely because they were images of the poor and the dispossessed; people whose lives had about them (to the middle-class spectator) an air of being simple, real and untrammelled by the overt complexity of middle-class existence. 'Real', here, takes on a class inflection which it was not to lose in documentary work for many years as photography established itself as an important component in an extensive series of projects to investigate and record the lives of the poor. Photography's subjects were those that had already been the topic of examination in reports, surveys, philanthropy and literature. It established itself as part of a tradition of enquiry into the health, housing, education, economic condition and moral state of the poor. Enquiries emanated from government departments, newspapers, independent scholars, medical practitioners, religious leaders and philanthropic bodies. The discourses of these enquiries overlapped, from popular newspapers through statistical surveys and scholarly works to official boards of enquiry. The apparently impartial eye of the camera added to the Victorian passion for the accumulation of statistical detail, painstaking observation and careful classification.

Photography also became a mode of surveying the unknown. Gradually those mysterious and threatening city streets were being visually inspected and hauled into the light of day in much the same way as the wild places

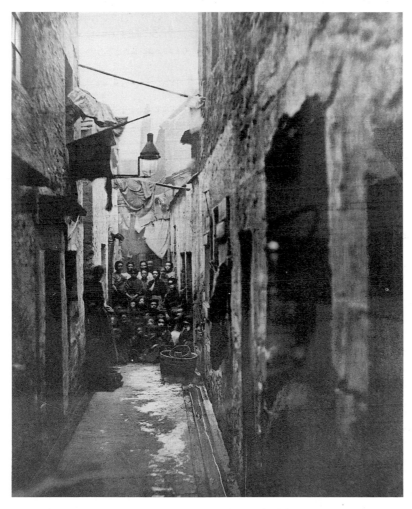

2.3 Thomas Annan, Close No 118 High Street, 1868
One of Annan's evocative studies of the Glasgow slums. The inhabitants of Close No 118 huddle together as they are recorded for posterity

ALAN THOMAS (1978) **The Expanding Eye: Photography and the Nineteenth Century Mind**, London: Croom Helm

and strange peoples of the earth were being recorded by map-makers, artists, scientists and photographers. Describing the anonymous photographers of the day, **Alan Thomas** comments that:

> They entered the back streets, it appears, in the same spirit as expeditionary cameramen journeying in strange lands, for one of the commonest documentary photographs of the century shows a line of back street dwellers, generally women and children, with perhaps a man lurking in the rear, who are ranged across the middle of the composition, gazing expectantly into the camera. From the 1860s to the end of the century, and from every great city comes this photograph; it always seems worth looking at because of the candid directness with which the subjects give themselves to the camera – like those foreign aboriginals photographed for the first time by expeditionary photographers.
>
> (Thomas 1978: 136)

The city was seen as dangerous, but also as obscure, crowded with secrets and containing districts that were inaccessible to respectable folk. It was to such areas that the inspectors of city life and labour had to journey in order to illuminate them.

In the United States the new newspapers consciously elevated the reporter to the position of adventurer in the obscure areas of the city. Alan Trachtenberg comments that:

> Exploration of forbidden and menacing spaces emerged in the 1890s as a leading mode of the dailies, making spectacles of the 'nether side of New York' or 'the other half'. The reporter appeared now often as a performer, one who had ventured into alien streets and habitations, perhaps in disguise, and returned with a tale, a personal story of the dark underside of the city.
>
> (Trachtenberg 1982: 126)

If the professional reporter journeyed to the dark places of the city an army of amateur photographers snapped away in the more salubrious areas. But here the all-pervading quality of photography began to be seen as undesirable, and by the 1880s the takers of snapshots had been defined as a public nuisance. In London, licenses were required to film in many places, while the photographic press carried articles deploring the activities of those who photographed respectable people without their specific consent.

Codes of conduct were beginning to emerge and a range of permissible and impermissible subjects was being informally drawn up. If the photographers were middle class the posed *anonymous* subjects were likely to be poor or working class. What distinguished documentary photographers within this ferment of picture-making was that they worked with some notion of improving or ameliorating the lot of their subjects. But this, in

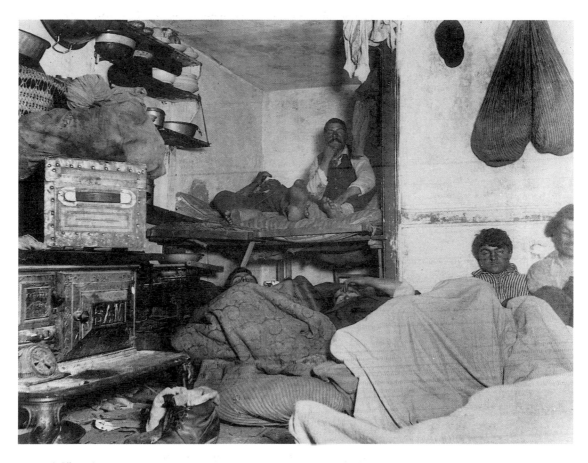

2.4 Jacob Riis, Lodgers in a Crowded Tenement – 'five cents a spot', 1880s
A typical scene of poverty and overcrowding is revealed in the harsh light of Riis's flash gun

turn, led to some curious social interactions. To illustrate this point it is worth looking at the work of the photographer who is generally taken to be the first of the American documentary photographers, Jacob Riis.

Riis in the New York slums

Danish-born Jacob Riis emigrated to the USA in the 1860s. He worked as a police reporter firstly for *Tribune* and later for the *Evening Sun* and began to concentrate on reporting the conditions of life in the East Side slums of New York City. Like many philanthropists and reporters before him, Riis was frustrated by his inability to convince people of the nature of the poverty, overcrowding, sweated labour and sheer misery that existed at the heart of a prosperous city. When he read an advertisement for an early kind of flash gun which would enable photographs to be taken indoors, he decided to use photography as an 'objective' witness to the way of life he had already described in his prose pieces. He cooperated originally with jobbing photographers, none of whom proved satisfactory, so he reluctantly decided to undertake the task himself.

He produced a picture of social conditions in the area that is of considerable interest despite the lack of formal aesthetic qualities in his images. In a typical Riis picture a crude flash of light in an otherwise dark room illuminates a scene of woeful overcrowding, with ragged people huddled on wooden benches or asleep on the floor. Others show garment-workers at their trade and, of course, children sleeping in doorways or labouring alongside their parents in tiny rooms.

Riis worked at a time when the conventions of documentary photography had yet to be established and he certainly wasted no time by seeking the cooperation of his subjects. Not only was he anxious to reveal the appalling social conditions of the area, but he sometimes cooperated with the police to bring prosecutions against landlords. His way of working might be described as direct and muscular and, in his autobiography *The Making of an American*, Riis cheerfully describes how he set about obtaining his images of the dispossessed:

> It is not too much to say that our party carried terror wherever it went. The flashlight of those days was contained in cartridges fired from a revolver. The spectacle of half a dozen strange men invading a house in the midnight hour armed with big pistols which they shot off recklessly was hardly reassuring, however sugary our speech, and it was not to be wondered at if the tenants bolted through windows and down fire-escapes wherever we went.
>
> (Riis 1918: 268)

Twice he set houses on fire in pursuit of his vigorous art and there is surely something chilling about the notion of the poor leaping from windows to evade the philanthropic documentarist. Perhaps inevitably, his photographs provide us with ethnographic detail of material life and social conditions rather than more complex subjective readings of the nature of poverty and destitution. Work of that kind was left to his successors, but Riis is important as a forerunner, and as a figure who directly connected photography to the journalistic enterprise. He was in no doubt of the power of photography to be a witness to the true nature of things. Describing a case of gross overcrowding, he writes:

> When the report was submitted to the Health Board the next day, it did not make much of an impression — these things rarely do, put in mere words — until my negatives, still dripping from the dark-room, came to re-enforce them. From them there was no appeal. It was not the only instance of the kind by a good many.

Neither the landlord's protests nor the tenant's plea 'went' in the face of the camera's evidence, and I was satisfied.

(Riis 1918: 273)

'Mere words' were to give way, in Riis's opinion, to the irrefutable veracity of the camera, and he saw his contribution as being that of bringing evidence to bear on what might otherwise be problematic. But he would not have seen his own personal vision as being of importance: the facts would speak for themselves and the people of the slums had been converted, through the documentary gaze, into 'facts'.

Complex and difficult lives are simplified into iconic statements of social deprivation. Riis captured his photographs as if he were shooting game; he inscribed 'objectivity' into his images by refusing to allow his subjects to negotiate in any way the manner in which they might be recorded. Sally Stein has commented perceptively on this:

We can indeed marvel at the consistency of Riis's photography in which so few of the exposures presented a subject sufficiently composed to return the glance of the photographer. That he rejected those rare photographs in which the subject did happen to look back suggests how premeditated the effect was. . . . The averted gaze, the appearance of unconsciousness or stupefaction, were only a few of the recurring features which gave Riis's pictorial documents stylistic unity and ideological coherence in relation to the text.

(Stein 1983: 14)

A history of documentary could be structured around an account of the association between photographer and subject, and of the power relationships that are mediated between them. In the ostensible interest of revealing (and subsequently ameliorating) harsh conditions of life, photographers often rendered those they recorded into passive sufferers of poverty, rather than active agents in their own lives.

Social travels and disguises

In Britain, too, the new journalism encouraged forays into the underworld, connecting the poor with crime, delinquency and hopelessness. Reporters went in search of the nether region of the city; a place that was, of course, constituted as both a physical and a psychic space. Sometimes, they went in disguise, pretending to be identical to the subjects of their studies, as James Greenwood did in 1866 to report on homeless men for his 'night in the workhouse' which was serialised in the *Pall Mall Gazette*.

The overt purpose of such masquerades was to pass unnoticed by those they were examining, so that they might share a common experience and avoid being treated as outsiders. Inevitably, though, these disguises inspired in readers a sense of vicarious danger or disgust. Social reformers, philanthropists and statisticians had reported on the state of the poor on innumerable occasions, but their work did not have the immediacy of the new journalism.

The taste for first-hand accounts, and a journalism based around interviews with participants in events, was developed in the United States and took a rather different character in the more formal press of Victorian England. Nevertheless, it created a narrative form which was structured around descriptions of scenes and people: accounts which were relatively free of moralising and which depended for their authenticity on the testimony of an individual journalist. In other words, it created a literary form to which the camera was an ideal adjunct and many reports were carried in the new periodicals of the day.

The new journalism of the 1890s coexisted with a movement of writers who, drawing on the wider movement of naturalism, produced novels which took the lives of the poor as their subject-matter. Out of the popular novels and journalism of the time came accounts of low life, full of ostensibly authentic detail which was reinforced by the use of argot and slang. Other investigators concentrated on describing the conditions of work and housing and presented a picture of people enduring lives of great hardship with patience and docility.

Constituted as 'the Other', workers, poor, lumpen proletariat, criminals, all were often ill-distinguished in the middle-class mind, despite the efforts of people such as Henry Mayhew to provide detailed typologies of the 'labouring poor'. Mayhew's approach to his investigations – that mixture of interview, statistics and descriptive writing – was to be one of the dominant modes through which working people were surveyed. Nor is it any accident that his monumental work was illustrated by engravings that were based on photographs (Mayhew 1861).

Photographing workers

During the last decades of the nineteenth century a number of significant British photographers worked on the task of recording the life of the poor in great cities: John Thomson and Paul Martin in London, and Thomas Annan in Glasgow are three examples. This preoccupation with the poor was not matched by a similar concern with capturing images of the world of work. Photography came into existence at a dynamic period in the development of capitalism, a time of technical innovation and of major engineering feats. Little of this energy is represented in the photographic archives; nor is the sheer drudgery of work and the army of labourers who carried it out made visible. Where there are shots of workers they tend to be inadvertently caught in a corner of the frame, or deliberately placed so as to give a sense of scale to some major building or engineering scheme. Rob Powell has commented:

> Very few photographs of workers in the time of Brunel exist, and indeed the catalogue of the British worker in 19th century photo-

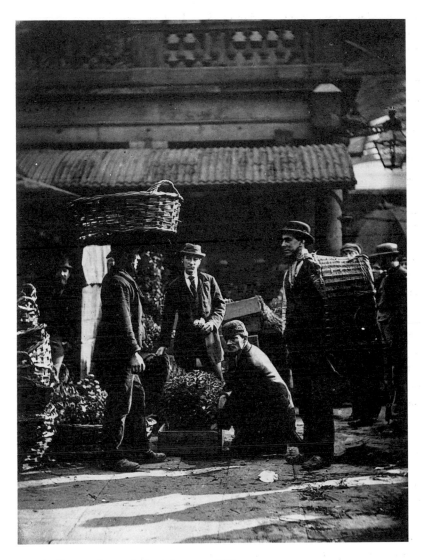

2.5 John Thomson, Covent Garden Labourers, *c.* 1877
Thomson was perhaps the first person to record systematically the street life, characters and traders of a great city

graphy – insofar as it can be gathered at all – is a history of exceptions. If real justice were to be done to this yawning absence, images of workers would be represented in the photographic history books by a long series of blank pages.

(Powell 1985: 32)

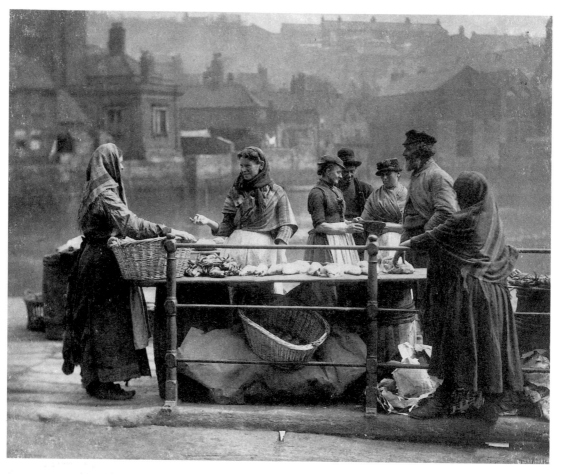

2.6 Frank Meadow Sutcliffe, A Fish Stall, c. 1882
Sutcliffe's long study of Whitby yielded hundreds of photographs that reveal the pattern of work and leisure in a Victorian fishing village

There are many reasons for the absence of portraits of workers, not least that photographers tended not to live in the sites where industrial work was carried out. Moreover, notions of what made a good subject for a photograph were determined by convention, and also by such factors as the subjects set by the juries of photographic competitions. In the 1890s many clubs established 'street characters' or 'city trades' as subjects for competition, but they would have been very unlikely to establish categories based on industrial labour or domestic work.

Once again one can trace some continuities of practice with older forms of representation. In the 1870s a group of British artists provided illustrations of scenes drawn from the life of the poor for the weekly magazine, *The Graphic*. These illustrations then acted as reference material for large oil paintings which were shown in galleries. Commenting on these artists, Julian Treuherz has noted that, throughout Victoria's reign, the poor were depicted within the sphere of social problems. He also draws our attention to the importance of literary sources in determining subject-matter for paintings – for example, Thomas Hood's poem *The Song of the Shirt* led to the seamstress becoming 'the most commonly depicted subject in Victorian painting' (Treuherz 1987: 26).

Photographers were deeply influenced by these conventional subjects and ways of treating the poor, and there are some examples of sustained and careful recording of working life. For example, Frank Meadow Sutcliffe diligently documented the village of Whitby both as a fishing village and as a holiday resort over a long period of time. This work drew on the picturesque qualities of much of the labour involved, but also added new qualities of directness and close observation.

But such detailed, long studies were rare, and confined to one or two trades. Other workers passed without any great notice; of the vast army of clerks and domestic workers there is scarcely a sign, and those photographs of workers that do exist are usually of male labourers engaged in heavy, manual tasks. There are few images of women carrying out any kind of work and they are absent from the ranks of manual labourers. Indeed, if it were not for the curious obsession of Arthur Munby, women manual workers would have disappeared with scarcely a trace (Hudson 1972). Of course, some documentary photographers were able to undertake sustained studies of labour as Lewis Hine did in the United States from the turn of the century. Hine was a most committed and subtle photographer of people at work and was dedicated to the cause of using his images in the service of social reform. His output spans the time from Jacob Riis to the Farm Security Administration project of the 1930s. An excellent account of the work of Lewis Hine is given in **Trachtenberg**'s *Reading American Photographs* (1989).

ALAN TRACHTENBERG (1989) **Reading American Photographs**, New York: Hill and Wang

DISCUSSION: ILLUSTRATED MAGAZINES

In the nineteenth century, magazines that told stories with the help of pictures were extremely popular. The *Illustrated London News* sold 26,000 copies of its first issue in 1842, and by 1863 had a weekly print run of 310,000. The illustrations were in the form of wood engravings which were produced with machine-like speed and precision through the use of a complex division of technical and artistic labour. The magazine claimed for itself a civilising mission rather than a concern for profit, but not all its competitors took such a high tone. *The Pictorial Times*, for example, was considerably less staid, but its general standards of drawing and of production were low. Of more interest was *The Graphic* which was founded in 1869 with the intention of using professional artists as illustrators of its copy, and it aimed for greater frankness and a more realist approach than its competitors.

Nor was this a particularly British movement, for these magazines had their counterparts in Germany, France and the United States. These illustrated magazines were to be radically changed by the coming of photography, but the photographic revolution was not immediately matched with a transformation in the means of reproduction. Not until 1880 was the half-tone process used to reproduce a photograph directly in the *Daily Graphic*, and it took decades for the process to be refined and widely accepted. Photography in this period celebrated its ability to scour the world for images, but it was powerless to put these images into general circulation. However, so potent was the idea that photography was an objectively true medium that publishers made it clear that particular illustrations (albeit copied and possibly edited by an artist) were based on photographs.

The development of documentary photography in the 1930s also owed much to the fact that there were many outlets through which such work could be shown. These magazines, which were based on the extensive use of photographs to tell stories, constitute the start of the modern movement of photojournalism. They include *Look* and *Life* in the USA, *Vu* in France, and *Illustrated* and *Picture Post* in Britain. There was also a host of new or revitalised publications in Germany where the movement began and most of the rhetorical devices of presentation were established; devices which emphasised the role of picture editors and designers in creating powerful stories through the juxtaposition of image and text. Many of the German *Illustrierte* disappeared after Hitler came to power in 1933 and the editors and photographers who had worked for them went into exile, taking their skills with them to their adopted countries. Stefan Lorant moved to Britain where he persuaded Edward Hulton to found a new magazine, *Picture Post*, which was to become (under the editorship of Tom Hopkinson, who succeeded Lorant) the most important publication of its kind in Britain.

In 1936 a new kind of illustrated magazine began in the USA. *Life* spread large format pictures over several pages, condoned flash, but would not at first allow the use of the newly developed 35mm cameras. *Life* was important for its size, technical slickness and for the fact that it routinised the production of photo-essays in a sophisticated way. The magazine was distant from the prevailing political ferment of the day and saw its mission in a soft-centred concern to capture images from around the world. Henry Luce had introduced *Fortune* in 1930, but *Life* was quickly to outstrip it in sales and income. Financially successful and technically resourceful, it was the most influential magazine of its day and, together with *Look*, dominated the market well into the 1950s.

During the next decade, though, the world of the illustrated magazine slowly crumbled. *Picture Post* ceased publication in 1958, *Look* and *Life* in 1972. Many people have offered explanations for the decline of these periodicals, citing, for example, the influence of television on sales and advertising revenue. The latter was also under threat from the free colour supplements that were introduced by newspapers. These were crowded with photographs, but were primarily designed to increase advertising revenue. Although interesting documentary photographs continued to be made, they were no longer part of a coherent movement of photojournalism.

THE CONSTRUCTION OF DOCUMENTARY

During the 1930s the paradigmatic form of documentary was produced: one which cast its subjects within a 'social problem' framework, and which argued for a politics of reform, and social education. Treating photographs produced much earlier as 'documentary' was not a simple act of labelling, but meant that we were invited to reconsider this work within the framework of the 1930s documentary project.

Photography in the 1930s was influenced by a number of factors. Technically the development of new, lightweight 35mm cameras made new camera angles possible. There was a growth in the number of illustrated magazines and, within these, an increasingly sophisticated approach to the role of photo editors and the construction of photo-essays. Not least, there was a new and vast public with a hunger to see images drawn from real life. The documentary movement was, of course, largely discussed in relation to the cinema and there is no doubt that John Grierson was an important figure in determining the nature of its aesthetic and political project. Grierson wanted to see a society of people who had received an appropriate education for citizenship; they would not aspire to be intellectuals, but would be trained so that they could make rational decisions about the society in which they lived, on the basis of the available information. Documentary was a tool of education which would militate against the foolish distractions offered by Hollywood and anchor people in a rational world of work and social obligation. It would offer, in an exciting form, facts about the social order which everyone would need in order to play a part in modern society. But how would documentary function in order to achieve these objects? In an influential book on documentary, **William Stott** (1973) writes:

> This is how documentary works. . . . It defies comment; it imposes its meaning. It confronts us, the audience, with empirical evidence of such nature as to render dispute impossible and interpretation superfluous. All emphasis is on the evidence; the facts themselves speak . . . since just the fact matters, it can be transmitted in any plausible medium. . . . The heart of documentary is not form or style or medium, but always content.
>
> (Stott 1973: 14)

WILLIAM STOTT (1973)
Documentary Expression and Thirties America,
London: Oxford University Press

The putative power of the camera to be an unmediated form of communication is here applied to a genre which is now held to be able to transcend the discursive structures of any particular form: imposing rather than creating meaning; disempowering the reader or spectator from any acts of interpretation *vis-à vis* the text. Documentary, on this definition, becomes a kind of ideologically charged common sense which is inaccessible to critical engagement. It is a fascinating definition because it spells out, forty years after the time, what lies at the heart of 1930s notions of documentary. There was an assumption that the world was productive of facts and that those facts could be communicated to others in a transparent way, free of the complex codes through which narratives are structured. The main component of what we might think of as 'the documentary gaze' is precisely described in the notion that 'the facts . . . speak'. Workers and the poor were caught in the documentary gaze; a gaze that transformed them into facts, facts that precisely could not be challenged, but which imposed meaning at a single stroke.

Journeys, facts and workers

What is interesting about the 1930s is the plethora of conventional and novel means of investigation which were employed. In addition to formal reports based on statistical investigation, there were varieties of journalistic reportage, travel books, diaries, films, photographs and newsreels. All involved some way of entering into the life of the people, of trying to understand the nature of particular communities and of reporting back to an audience situated geographically and socially elsewhere. Those photographers, writers, film-makers and intellectuals who undertook the journey to meet the workers did so from a variety of motives and from different political standpoints, but most found it a difficult trip. Some gazed on the workers as though they were the inhabitants of a strange land; others sought to keep a 'proper' distance from the subjects of their research. Some went with cameras, and many of those who did not, went (as it were) with the metaphor of the camera – with the documentary gaze.

Writing, appropriately enough, in the magazine *Fact* in 1937, Storm Jameson urged writers to go 'without any sense of personal advantage' to see for themselves something of the life of the working class:

> He must go for the sake *of the fact*, as a medical student carries out a dissection, and to equip himself, not to satisfy his conscience or to see what effect it has on him. His mind must remain cool; he must be able to give an objective report, neither superficial nor slickly dramatic.
>
> (Jameson 1937: 13)

Here the world of facts (the working class) has to be approached like a cadaver by the new species of literary investigator. Social life is conceived as being beyond the resources of the imagination and inaccessible to literary accounts. The aim was to research conditions of life, and to give not a description, but an 'objective report' to some putative group to whom he or she would report back. In other words, the writer should go with the documentary gaze, and it comes as no surprise to discover that the model for such work is to be found in the use of the camera:

> Perhaps the nearest equivalent of what is wanted exists already in another form in the documentary film. As a photographer does, so must the writer keep himself out of the picture while working ceaselessly to present *the fact* from a striking (poignant, ironic, penetrating, significant) angle. The narrative must be sharp, compressed, concrete. Dialogue must be short – a seizing of the significant, the revealing word. The emotion should spring directly from the fact.
>
> (Jameson 1937: 13)

The writer's task is 'not to tell us what he felt, but to be coldly and industriously presenting, arranging, selecting, discarding from the mass of his material to get to the significant detail which leaves no more to be said, and implies everything' (Jameson 1937: 14).

'Facts', in this account, are not the accumulation of statistical detail beloved by the Victorians (although they, too, were charged with moral value), nor are they to be used in Gradgrind's way so as to constrain the imagination and determine our lives only by what can be measured and tabulated. Rather, they are complex icons which, once seized and organised, are revelatory of greater meaning which can be mapped out in narrative. Also, they are socially specific, for they offer up the keys to the understanding of working-class life. Workers are seen as subjects dominated by 'facts', their lives contingent upon the shaping reality of economic and political forces. It is a short step from this to regarding entire working-class communities as grounded in a real world of facts. The writer's job is to edit these facts so as to present a picture of reality which closes the text and 'leaves no more to be said'. Or, as Stott would have it, 'imposes meaning at a stroke'. This is seen as the aspiration of writers and the necessary condition of photographers: 'I am a camera', wrote Christopher Isherwood, in a work of carefully constructed fiction, 'with its shutter open, quite passive, recording, not thinking' (Isherwood 1939: 7).

This is a more languid version of 'the camera eye' than Jameson's concept of it as a way of selecting and highlighting significant facts. Nevertheless, Isherwood lays claim to the documentary gaze in order to validate the *authenticity* of his fiction. Both affirm the power of the camera (or, rather, the metaphor of the camera) as a way of revealing and recording the world that can be distinguished from the work of artists and writers. The idea of a journey to discover the hidden life of the working class is, then, supplemented with an apparently ideal technical form for recording the researcher's findings – the disinterested, but insatiable camera eye.

CASE STUDY: THE FARM SECURITY ADMINISTRATION PROJECT

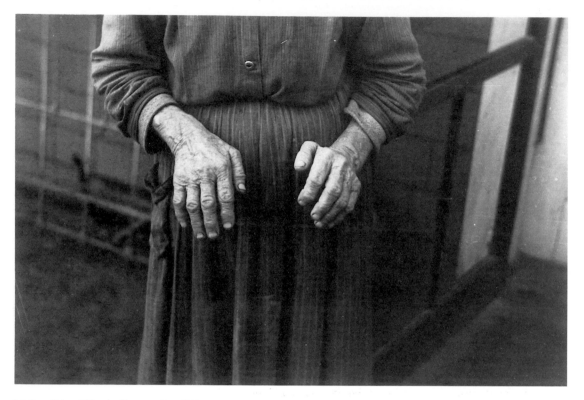

2.7 Russell Lee, Wife of a Homesteader, 1936
Russell Lee here crops his photograph so as to concentrate our attention on the work-worn hands of a woman who has clearly lived a life marked by labour and hardship

In 1936 Dorothea Lange took a photograph of a woman sitting in a rough shelter with her three children. Lange has recounted the story of how she stopped one night on the road – although she was already exhausted by the work of the day – to investigate a group of people who were employed to pick peas. In less than a quarter of an hour she was back on the road having taken several shots of the woman with her children. One of these photographs, 'Migrant Mother' (figure 2.1), became the most reproduced image in the history of photography and is known to many people who could not name its author.

At the time Lange was working for a government agency which had been established in 1935 as part of the Roosevelt administration's attempt to rebuild the economy of the United States. The Assistant Secretary of Agriculture, Rexford Guy Tugwell, was given responsibility for what quickly became called the Farm Security Administration (FSA). Tugwell appointed a young social scientist, Roy Stryker, to head the photography section, the function of which was to provide images to illustrate and support the written accounts of conditions in agriculture that would be given in official reports.

The FSA enterprise became the best example of a major state-funded documentary project in the world and many of its participants have entered into the pantheon of 'great photographers': Walker Evans, Dorothea Lange, Russell Lee, Arthur Rothstein, Ben Shahn, Marion Post Walcott. Photographs from the project have been extensively reproduced and shown on book jackets, as illustrations, on gallery walls, even in advertisements. They are often described in histories of photography as having revealed the human face of Depression day America.

Their initial task, however, was to show America at work; to collect visual facts which could illustrate the social surveys which lay at the heart of the FSA's work. Once on the road, though, the photographers were free from the constraints of Washington and often returned very different kinds of images to those which were expected. On some accounts their genius as visual artists allowed them to go beyond the mundane business of work and to penetrate to the secret heart of things. In fact, among the many thousands of negatives of the project there are very many which concern themselves with human labour.

But the archive has been used as a resource from which some photographs have been more often selected than others, so that our sense of the project is constructed from the editing that has taken place over the years. And this body of work does present us with an apparently coherent critique of American life. The most famous photographs are those of the sharecroppers of the Southwest and their migration west out of the 'dustbowl' to the orange groves and fruit farms of California in search of work as itinerant labourers. This is a familiar story and was the subject of one of the most celebrated 'social' novels and movies of the time, John Steinbeck's *The Grapes of Wrath*.

Through the interest shown in them by photographers, writers and painters, these people were to become emblematic of the US Depression. What we remember about them is that the winds eroded their fields, destroying their livelihood and that they were forced, though desperately poor, to travel long distances to try to find work in the low-wage fruit and cotton fields. The FSA photographs are almost always of individuals and families, and often show them as weary and defenceless. They evoke images of strain, of mental fatigue, but they also tease out the bonds of affection and connection between people; especially between mothers and children. And, of course, they show people on the road, moving out; their possessions packed away, their furniture roped to the tops of cars or heaped on to a rickety truck. In these images the solid elements of domestic life are often dissolved and relocated in strange, outdoor spaces. Objects do service as carriers of emotion; objects that are stranded, dislocated, treasured though cheap. For instance, Russell Lee shows us a harmonium upright, ready to be played, out in a field all by itself surrounded by mud. Walker Evans records a roughly piled grave of loose earth topped with the impermanent and unstable memorial of a dinner plate. Nothing appears to be anchored or solid, instead dust is everywhere; a friable earth is heaped against the walls of houses, has shawled over the gas pumps and the Coca-Cola signs, and is etched into the lines of faces and hands.

The FSA photographers used a variety of technical means to endow their subjects with particular qualities. For example, Dorothea Lange elaborated a complex repertoire of gestural forms through which to express their strength or their dignified response to suffering. She shot from low angles, framing her subjects against a wide sky to give them a monumental look. She used the newly available small cameras to go in very close, capturing the dust-encrusted lines of a hand or face. She cropped images very tightly so that, for example, the line of strain in a muscle is revealed. In one case she cropped off a woman's head so that we can better reflect on the fatigue of the body.

These documentary photographs, then, like all others, are densely constructed works which use certain techniques and forms to produce a desired response in the spectator. They do contain 'facts' in a simple sense: a woman wears a dress made from a flour sack, a family lives under a hastily constructed tent of twigs and tarpaulin. There is, in other words, plenty of evidence of poverty indicated by the traditional markers of lack of material prosperity. But, in their more complex versions, they are photographs of the (literally) dispossessed, carefully constructed to produce a meaning that transcends what is shown.

These people were not chosen merely for their 'representative' qualities: they are not simple icons of dispossession. Although they are anonymous subjects of the camera, their singularity is often stressed and their individual gestures carefully recorded. This is emphasised by the closeness of the camera and the informal stances people are allowed to take up in front of it. We feel that we are not in the presence of representatives of a class, but of ordinary people, much like us, who have fallen on hard times and are doing the best they can in the circumstances. Poverty and misery thus cease to be pos-sessions of particular social groups living at a particular time in determinate conditions, and become a kind of dislocation or breakdown into which any one of us might stumble. In other words, we are asked to accept that we can make immediate connections between this body of work and our own life and condition; but also that these are photographs that sum up the specific experience of the migrant workers in the USA; that these are 'honest' images drawn from life, but are also the product of extraordinarily gifted photographers. Some of the central contradictions of documentary photography are revealed here, for these photographs are seen as historical, but timeless; densely coded, but transparent; highly specific, but universal.

Thousands of these images exist in an archive that is constantly drawn on by historians and critics of photography. They are very frequently reproduced, torn now from the official reports which they were intended to illustrate, and presented as images that can stand without text or comment. At each re-presentation, in each new context, they need to be reappraised, but they are likely to remain as the single most important body of documentary photographs ever produced by a government agency.

In 1978, the 'Migrant Mother' herself, Florence Thompson, was tracked down to her trailer home in Modesto, California. One of documentary's most familiar and telling images was recuperated as an ordinary, aged woman who was poor in a humdrum way and no longer able to function as an icon of nobility and sadness in the face of destitution.

Her image had appeared in many forms and in many settings, and had been multiply copied millions of times. She was a most familiar figure, but not until fifty years after the event did she get to comment on it publicly. She told United Press that she was proud to be the subject of the photograph, but that she had never made a penny out of it and that it had done her no good (Rossler 1989: 315).

Forms of investigation

In issue 4 of *Fact* an editorial draws attention to the success of the previous issues and then informs its readers of a new venture:

> It is nothing less than to begin a social and anthropological survey of typical parts of Britain. You have read, no doubt, plenty of statistical and economic accounts of this or that area or this and that industry. But have you ever considered the place in which you live and the trade in which you work with the impartial and distant eye of an anthropologist?
>
> (*Fact* 1937: no page number)

There were several organisations which set out to undertake an anthropological survey of British life. The best known is *Mass Observation*, founded in 1936 by Tom Harrison and Charles Madge. Harrison was an anthropologist newly returned from Borneo, and Madge a poet. What these projects have in common with the documentary movement is the sense that the world could no longer be taken for granted and understood. That ordinary day-to-day lives needed to be made strange by being examined with the supposedly 'impartial' eye of the social scientist.

Mass Observation recruited many respondents who, through the use of diaries and formal reports, would scrutinise and record their own day-to-day actions and behaviour, together with that of other people. The organisation was particularly interested in examining what happened on buses, in pubs, at the seaside and other places where collective behaviour in public places could be observed. And their respondents were expected to distance themselves from ordinary life in order to observe and record those things that might otherwise escape notice as being uninterestingly ordinary. The diaries and notes were sent to a central place where they were analysed and edited in order to provide material for the production of books describing how people behaved in everyday life. Clearly, in all this there was an assumption that 'we' had no adequate sense of our social selves; that we needed to survey the very taken-for-granted parts of our lives that constituted ordinary existence. The apparent fragmentation of the society, the political instability, the vast desire for change, the desolation of many working-class communities – all this might be resolved if only we could get a clear idea of who 'we' were.

Picturing ourselves

Mass Observation used respondents, editors, painters and photographers in its attempt to build up an accurate picture of everyday life. Photographers adopted a range of techniques in order to capture their subjects; while some sought cooperation, most were concerned not to be observed and to work without the knowledge of the photographed.

One characteristic response of photographers to the political and moral debates of the time was to see themselves as part of the camera, merely recording what was in front of them. Bert Hardy, who worked his way up from being a delivery boy to becoming a major photographer on *Picture Post*, described his practice in *Camerawork*: 'I didn't think of it politically. I was never a political animal. I mean the journalists had that sort of job to do. I think I just photographed what I saw. I never angled anything' (Hardy 1977: 9).

However, Humphrey Spender (in a later issue of the same journal) comments on the work he did in Bolton for *Mass Observation* and makes clear his desire to work voyeuristically:

> My main anxiety, purpose, was to become invisible and to make my equipment invisible, which is one of the reasons I carried around an absolute minimum of equipment. . . . Summing up the relics of feelings toward *Mass Observation* I think I can remember the main enemy being boredom and tedium and embarrassment.
>
> (Spender 1978: 7)

Working for a number of magazines and newspapers as well as for *Mass Observation*, Humphrey Spender brought back many of the pictures of working-class life which were later thought to be exemplary images of the time. In one account of this work he described his procedure as allowing 'things to speak for themselves and not to impose any kind of theory'. The difficulty of his journey was that:

> I had to be an invisible spy – an impossibility which I didn't particularly enjoy trying to achieve . . . I was somebody from another planet intruding on another way of life. . . . A constant feature of taking the kind of photograph we're talking about – even when people were unaware that they were actually being photographed – was a feeling that I was exploiting the people I was photographing, even when . . . the aim explicitly was to help them.
>
> (Spender 1982: 16)

Spender's description of himself as an alien and a spy is a dramatic way of emphasising social distance, and in his account of his own feelings he

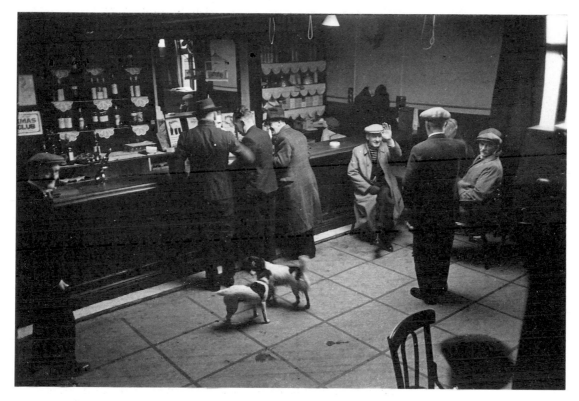

2.8 Humphrey Spender, Men Greeting in a Pub, Worktown Series, 1937
This carefully composed, gentle and humorous photograph reveals the influence of both realist photography and Surrealism on Spender's work

points up the fact that 'our way of life' might also be seen as distinct and separate 'ways of life'. The notion of the workers as productive of useful facts gives way to a consideration of the subjects of representation as potentially exploited by the encounter. Spender worked for *Mass Observation*, but his photographs also appeared in the *Daily Mirror* and in *Picture Post*, and by the 1930s the market for actuality photographs had grown to very large proportions.

Picture Post

The most famous of the British illustrated magazines, *Picture Post* attempted to make visible the whole of society: to show the toffs at Ascot, the clerks in their pin-stripe suits and bowler hats streaming across London Bridge, the housewife out shopping, the unemployed man lounging on the street corner. Its first few issues of 1938 carried stories on 10 Downing Street ('The House from Which the Empire is Governed'), actors in rehearsal, painters in their

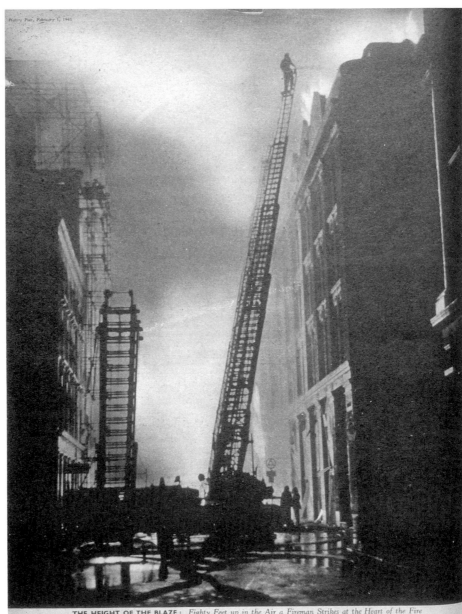

THE HEIGHT OF THE BLAZE: *Eighty Feet up in the Air a Fireman Strikes at the Heart of the Fire*

Stark and grim is the climax of the fire fight. Blazing walls are crumbling. The fire is bursting through. Overhead, guided by the flames, the German bombers are circling. One after another they release their load of death. Unmoved, unflinching, the firemen run out their ladder. One man mounts higher and higher, till he is alone above the flames. There, eighty feet up, he strikes at the very source of the fire.

2.9ab Bert Hardy, Fire-Fighters, 1941
During the Second World War photographs of the Blitz and the aftermath of bombing frequently appeared in *Picture Post* as the magazine played its part in keeping up civilian morale

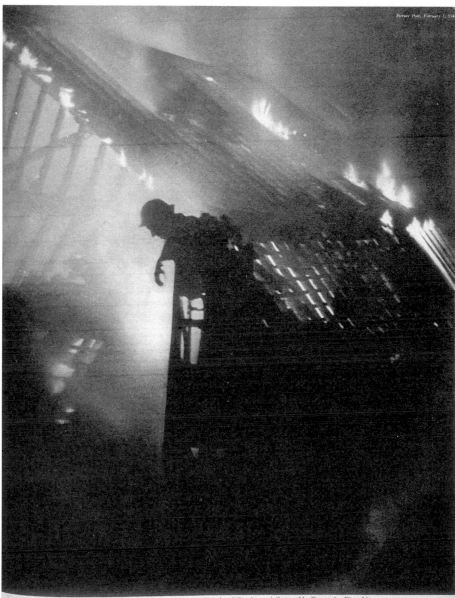

Picture Post, February 1, 194

THE MAN ON THE LADDER: *In Clouds of Smoke and Steam He Faces the Fire Alone*

All night long they have fought the fire. They have fought it in the streets streaming with water. They have fought it within buildings blazing like a furnace. On to the flames they have poured a hundred thousand gallons of water, concentrated at colossal pressure. And still the fight goes on. From our rule of anonymity we except these pictures. They were taken by A. Hardy, one of our own cameramen.

15

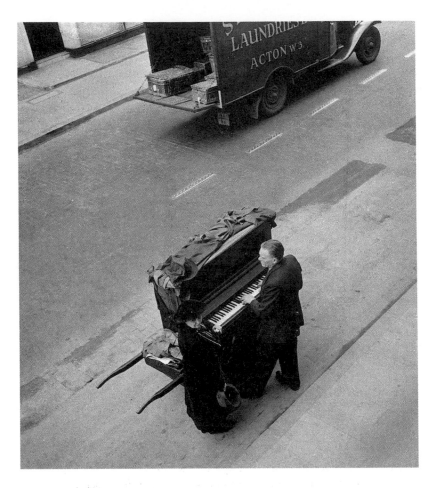

2.10 Edith Tudor Hart, Piano Player in the Street, c. 1934
German-born Edith Tudor Hart photographed workers in London, Tyneside and South Wales in the 1930s. One of
the important documentary photographs of the time, her work is usually direct and concentrated on the subject,
but she sometimes used the tropes of modernism as in this image of a street pianist taken from above

studios, soldiers in training, surgeons in an operating theatre and life on a
lighthouse – together with people in the street, in pubs and on buses, débu-
tantes at a London club, down-and-outs at the Salvation Army, portraits of
the men who built the *Queen Elizabeth*, a history of the corset and images
of an old favourite – London by night. During the Second World War it
helped to articulate a sense of communality within the British people (Hall
1972).

The magazine was determinedly populist and provided readers with a
conspectus of the everyday, inviting them to treat routine and commonplace

aspects of life as worthy of attention. This celebration of ordinary life was intermingled with news stories set in other countries and an attempt to show the extraordinary diversity of human existence. *Picture Post* also used the camera as a kind of character in its own right and recognised that we would be interested in how images were made. It showed us how 'candid camera' shots of the Café Royal were achieved using a camera concealed in a brief-case, explained how a model is made up so as to look beautiful, and gave us a shot of a photographer robing for the operating theatre session. This stress on the capturing of images rendered the camera less awe-inspiring than it might otherwise have been and, together with the conventions of page layouts and picture formats, called up a particular kind of rather quiet, simple photograph – one which sometimes cleverly resembled a snapshot and did not aim to connote complex messages.

The ethics and politics of documentary

Walker Evans was one of the photographers who worked for the FSA for a time. In 1936 he travelled with James Agee to Alabama on an assignment for *Fortune* magazine. They spent six weeks examining the lives of a family of tenant farmers and, although their work was rejected by the magazine, it was published as a book in 1941. In the foreword to that work Agee comments on the nature of the assignment they had been set some years earlier:

> It seems to me curious, not to say obscene and thoroughly
> terrifying, that it could occur to an association of human beings
> drawn together through need and chance and for profit into a
> company, an organ of journalism, to pry intimately into the lives of
> an undefended and appallingly damaged group of human beings, an
> ignorant and helpless rural family, for the purpose of parading the
> nakedness, disadvantage and humiliation of these lives before
> another group of human beings in the name of science of 'honest
> journalism' (whatever that paradox may mean), of humanity, of
> social fearlessness, for money and for a reputation for crusading and
> for unbias which, when skilfully enough qualified, is exchangeable
> at any bank for money . . . and that these people could be capable
> of meditating this prospect without the slightest doubt of their
> qualification to do an 'honest' piece of work, and with a
> conscience better than clear, and in the virtual certitude of almost
> unanimous public approval.
>
> (Agee and Evans 1939: 7)

Agee is here articulating one of the central charges against the documentary project: that in the name of revelation and reform it inevitably preys upon its subjects, aestheticising their suffering or turning them into passive icons of poverty and destitution. Closely associated with this criticism is the charge that the political project implicit in much documentary work is unlikely to succeed given that documentary can, at best, show suffering, degradation, despair, but can do nothing to illuminate the causes of these woes. Power and causality are difficult to express through the camera eye, as are collective struggle and resistance.

We have seen that the documentary movement was part of a reformist political project and we should remember that, politically, the documentary movement was concerned with the promulgation of liberal social values rather than with the revolutionary politics to which so many people in the 1930s subscribed. Martha Rossler has critiqued this political stance in the following terms:

> In contrast to the pure sensationalism of much of the journalistic attention to working-class, immigrant and slum life, the meliorism of Riis, Lewis Hine, and others involved in social work propagandizing argued through the presentation of images combined with other forms of discourse, for the rectification of wrongs. It did not perceive those wrongs as fundamental to the social system that tolerated them – the assumption that they were tolerated rather than *bred* marks a basic fallacy of social work.
>
> (Rossler 1989: 304)

Of course, many people in the 1930s did see those wrongs as a consequence of the prevailing social system and this belief gave rise to a vibrant left oppositional practice of radical theatre, film and photography. Workers' film and photo leagues were established in both Britain and the USA and opened up the medium of photography so that workers could make their own records of their lives and struggles. This was an important principle, but there is little evidence that the results challenged the nature of documentary reportage or established new kinds of image-making. Perhaps more interesting were groups who saw questions of representation as a central part of political struggle and developed an alternative photographic practice. Their intention was not to reveal how things looked in the 'real world', but to disrupt the surface appearance of the image in order to construct new meanings out of the old pictorial elements. This practice was elaborated by Rodchenko in the USSR and by the Berlin Dadaists at the end of the First World War. Working against the central tenets of documentary, these artists argued that, in order to arrive at the meaning that lies below the surface of a photograph, it was necessary to contrive and manipulate the image. John Heartfield's incisive, politically charged **photomontages** are the best-known works of this kind.

Documentary meaning and form

We have so naturalised the idea of documentary as residing within particular texts, forms and traditions (as being *immanent* to texts), that those marginal forms – drama documentary, **staged** reconstructions and the like – are fiercely fought over. It is, perhaps, more useful to pursue questions of the *production* of documentary: the characteristic forms that were used to make 'documents' of this kind. Stott's notion that documentary 'imposes meaning' at a single stroke, before which the spectator is speechless and disarmed, fractures into the examination of particular forms within their institutional and historical settings; clusters of social, cultural, political and technological changes which together create the 'meaning' of documentary. But it is a meaning that is constantly changing, for, while the documentary gaze was anchored in facts and validated particular kinds of enquiry, the practice of documentary was and is problematic. In photography, a series of conventions and practices evolved to mark 'documentary' from other kinds of work. These included, for example, printing the whole of the image with a black border around it to demonstrate that everything the camera recorded was shown to the viewer. At another time, scenes lit by flash were deemed illegitimate, as only the natural light that fell on the scene should be used. A kind of rudimentary technical ethic of documentary work emerged which 'guaranteed' the authenticity of the photograph. Much of the progress of studio-based photography, whether for commercial purposes or as **Art**, was made by suppressing the contingent within the photographic frame and designing the scene so that all aspects of the image were controlled and carefully placed. We have already observed that any attempt to arrange and structure the location by a documentary photographer would be regarded as illegitimate behaviour, yet the aesthetic demand for well-composed shots remained.

Documentary photographers, too, took considerable pains to control the nature of a scene without making any obvious change to it. Thus, the celebrated photographer Henri Cartier-Bresson lay in wait for all the messy contingency of the world to compose itself into an image which he judged to be both productive of visual information and aesthetically pleasing. This he called 'the decisive moment', a formal flash of time when all the right elements were in place before the scene fell back into its quotidian disorder. Increasingly, documentary turned away from attempting to record what would formerly have been seen as its major subjects. Instead, it began to concentrate on exploring cultural life and popular experience and this often led to representations that celebrated the transitory or the fragmentary. The endeavour to make great statements gave way to the recording of little, dislocated moments which merely insinuated that some greater meaning might be at stake (Cartier-Bresson 1952). Cartier-Bresson's work is sometimes regarded as documentary, but often he is seen as working outside the constraints of labels of this kind. As **Alan Sekula** has pointed out, 'Documentary is thought to be art when it transcends its reference to the world, when the work can be regarded, first and foremost, as an act of self-expression on the part of the artist' (Sekula 1978: 236).

ALAN SEKULA (1978) 'Dismantling Modernism, Reinventing Documentary (Notes on the Politics of Representation)' in J. Liebling (ed.) **Photography: Current Perspectives**, Rochester, New York: Light Impressions Co

The problem then becomes how we define 'reference to the world' and how documentary photographers can demonstrate their fidelity to the social world. To have to engage with particular conventions, technical processes and rhetorical forms in order to authenticate documentary undermines the notion of the objective camera and with it, one might imagine, any claim of documentary to be any more truthful to appearances than other forms of representation. But both the test of truth and the nature of documentary photography was changing rapidly in the decades after 1950. The social-democratic political project that underpinned 1930s documentary had lost its radical edge by the 1950s and had, indeed, in Britain, become the ground on which a postwar political consensus was built.

DOCUMENTARY SINCE THE SECOND WORLD WAR

The archetypal documentary project was concerned to draw the attention of an audience to particular subjects, often with a view to changing the existing social or political situation. To achieve this goal, documentary photographs were rarely seen as single, independent images. They were usually accompanied by or incorporated into written texts. Within this context the images functioned both to provide information about the nature of things and to confirm the authenticity of a written account. Individual photographers were rarely credited for their work in magazines, and photographs were treated as though they were anonymous productions. The postwar consumer boom, exemplified in the introduction of television and the growth of car ownership, produced a very different society to that of the 1930s. In commenting on this new social scene some photographers in the United States produced work that was to transform the nature of documentary photography.

In his collection *The Americans*, Robert Frank presented his own version of American life in which he eschewed the usual subjects of documentary investigation and presented us instead with cool and ironic images of the fleeting moments of ordinary life. Significantly enough, the introduction to the book was written by the Beat writer, Jack Kerouac, who said: 'After seeing these pictures you end up finally not knowing any more whether a juke box is sadder than a coffin' (Frank 1959: 5).

Born in Switzerland, Robert Frank brought an outsider's eye to bear on the USA of the 1950s. He went on the road with a camera, an old car and a Guggenheim scholarship and photographed not only juke-boxes and coffins, but cowboys, long empty roads, tract houses on lonely fields, flags and bikers, drive-in movies and barber's chairs. Frank caught America at the point where commonplace life was about to be turned into myth; where even the banal and the prosaic was soon to be commodified into spectacle. People in these photographs were not constituted as 'poor' or 'workers' or, indeed, any kind of active agents. They existed as spectators, gazing out at

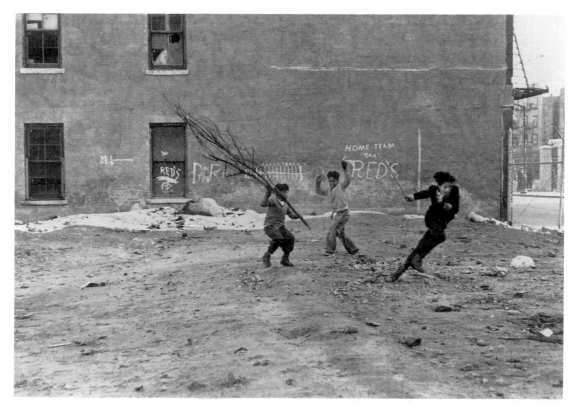

2.11 Helen Levitt, New York, 1942
Levitt photographed New York as a place of community and neighbourhood as in this wartime shot of children playing cheerfully in a setting of urban squalor

some invisible scene: other people, the road ahead, a movie screen, a parade going by. In these closed, watchful faces we could read no significant facts, and if we had a sense of 'being there', it was as a witness to nothing of any great importance. Frank refused a documentary project which saw life as productive of weighty events that the photographer might chronicle and analyse. He seems to be saying that none of the many scenes that happen in the world are invested with any special meaning, although some may be made distinctive by the act of being photographed. Coffins are no sadder than juke-boxes because an old hierarchy of importance has been abolished; hereafter the subject-matter of documentary is both dispersed and expanded to include whatever engages or fascinates the photographer. Facts now matter less than appearances. The old documentary project gives way to a hetero-geneous practice which explores the world in terms of particular subjectivities, identities and pleasures.

Frank was not alone in offering new, less monumental images of America in the 1950s. Around the same time William Klein was photographing New

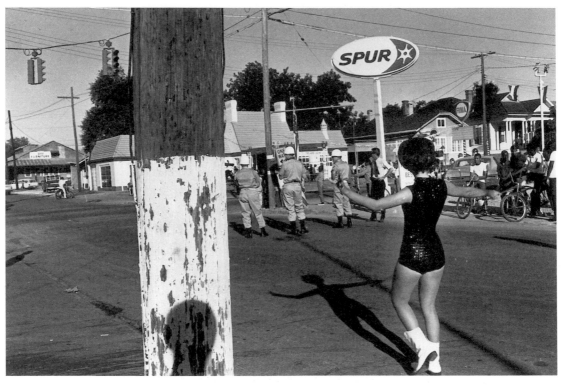

2.12 Lee Friedlander, 1 Lafayette, Louisiana, 1970
In the 1970s, Friedlander was one of the major 'new' documentarists. His images are intricate, ambiguous, sometimes difficult to read, and tell us something about the complexity of modern life

York in a manner that stressed the disorder and randomness of life in great cities. In Klein's crowded streets the point of photographic interest may lie in a half-concealed detail somewhere in the background of a shot. His city is restless, crowded, neurotic and alienating, and was to become one dominant version of how cities were perceived and represented by later commentators. A very different version of life in a big city was offered by the British photographer, Roger Mayne, whose photographs of street life in West London provided a portrait of the lives of people in a particular place that was relaxed, incisive, intimate and very different from earlier British documentary work (Mayne 1986).

Documentary was changing and apparently presenting new subject-matter or old themes treated in new ways. Often called 'subjective' documentary, this work was very influential in both the USA and Britain. It liberated documentary from the political project with which it had formerly been associated, and allowed photographers to move away both from the traditional subjects of documentary and from the conventions of documentary representation. Now, for example, Lee Friedlander could make a series of photographs full of a characteristic ambiguity and allow his own silhouette to fall across his subjects to celebrate his shadowy presence on the scene. Gradually, there was an extension of the subjects which were deemed suitable for documentary. For example, Tony Ray-Jones's *A Day Off: An English Journal* (1974) attempted to cover a spectrum of social class in looking at the English at play, from Glyndebourne and Eton to Butlins and Brighton's Palace Pier. In the 1930s, perhaps the most famous photographer of British life, Bill Brandt, had compared photographs of rich and poor; putting, for example, maids and mistresses into a double-page spread so that we could observe difference and privilege. By the 1960s, however, photographers were concerned to offer more personal versions of the nature of social existence.

Theory and the critique of documentary

Perhaps the single most important influence on British documentary after 1970 came from the new ways in which photography was theorised and the functions it was considered to be able to play in cultural politics. **Semiological** analysis treated films and photographs as *texts* in order to investigate the components of sign systems through which meaning is structured and encoded within a work. The point of concern was not whether the work adequately revealed or reflected a pre-existing reality, but the way particular signifying systems imposed order and created particular sets of meaning. Inscribed within the photograph, then, was not some little likeness to reality, but a complex set of technical and cultural forms which needed to be decoded. Far from being innocent transcriptions of the real, photographs were treated as complex material objects with the ability to create, articulate and sustain meaning. Using theoretical tools which often derived from Film Studies or Literary Studies, critics began to explore the way in which photography functioned as a signifying system. One of the characteristics of photography is, as we have seen, the fact that it appears to have a special relationship to reality. We speak of *taking* photographs rather than *making* them, because the marks of their **construction** are not immediately visible; they have the appearance of having come about as a function of the world itself rather than as carefully fabricated cultural objects. As spectators we are positioned as the eye of the camera and we gaze upon an apparently natural and unmediated scene. Our acts of looking were no longer considered to be disinterestedly innocent, but were analysed in order to distinguish the kinds of psychic pleasure and relations of power that are invested in the process. The concept of power at play in this analysis owes much to the work of the French philosopher, Michel Foucault.

Power is not seen by Foucault as a force held by a particular social group which enables them to coerce another, but is located within all parts of the social system. Power resides in all aspects of a knowledge system: in the construction of archives, the codification of information and the communication chains through which knowledge is disseminated. Nor is 'truth' a special kind of knowledge which allows us to escape the pervasive reach of power: truth and power are also intertwined. Each society has constructed its own 'regime of truth', elaborating frameworks, institutions and discourses which validate particular procedures and permit us to distinguish true from false statements.

JOHN TAGG (1988) **The Burden of Representation: Essays on Photographies and Histories**, London: Macmillan

In his collection of essays *The Burden of Representation* (1988), **John Tagg** analyses the vast increase in the *power* of photography in the latter half of the nineteenth century and traces the 'complicity' of photography in the articulation of particular kinds of surveillance and observation. Documentary is seen as part of the process of examination described by Foucault as 'a procedure of objectification and subjection', in which ordinary lives are turned into accounts – into writing or, for that matter, into photographs. Such an analysis of the function of documentary clearly cast considerable doubts on the reformist social and political project with which it had been identified for so long. Its overt or implicit use as a means of surveillance and control was now being stressed, rather than its ability to reveal the nature of suffering or destitution in the service of social reform. If there was to be a political use for photography, this would not emerge as a function of the technology itself, but would have to be part of a project that took account of the way in which the medium functioned at a number of different levels.

The argument over what the nature of such a project might be signalled a return to earlier debates which questioned the power of documentary to be a form through which radical social and political change might be achieved. In his important essay written in 1931, **Walter Benjamin** quotes Bertolt Brecht:

WALTER BENJAMIN (1972) 'A Short History of Photography', **Screen**, 13(1), Spring. Originally published in **Die Literarische Welt**, 18 and 25 September, and 2 October 1931

> . . . less than at any time does a simple reproduction of reality tell us anything about reality. A photograph of the Krupp works or GEC yields almost nothing about these institutions. Reality proper has slipped into the functional. The reification of human relationships, the factory, let's say, no longer reveals these relationships. Therefore something has actually to be constructed, something artificial, something set up.
>
> (Benjamin 1972: 24)

Brecht is here calling for a photographic practice that would be in sharp contrast to the documentary project, whose practitioners, as we have seen, were often concerned to let things 'speak for themselves' and were confident that things *could* speak for themselves. The dominance of documentary in the 1930s would have obscured any attempt to ground a radical photographic practice in artifice and construction. By the 1970s, however, there was a perception by some groups that the old documentary forms were inadequate to express, let alone help to change, the prevailing conditions of social, political and personal life.

Cultural politics and everyday life

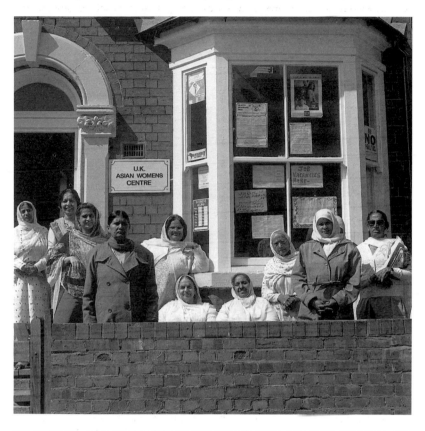

2.13 Roshini Kempadoo, Women of the UK Asian Women's Centre, Handsworth, Birmingham, 1990
In this image, Roshini Kempadoo has used a documentary style that reminds us of a family photograph, in order to portray a group who have not usually been the subject of a public photograph

Documentary was grounded in the recording and delineation of commonplace life, but the idea of 'ordinary, everyday life' was itself now to be problematised. Rather than being seen simply as a method of recording, photography begins to be regarded as a means through which we can express and articulate our own particularity and difference. We can move, as Don Slater has put it, from being consumers of images to becoming active producers:

> the camera as an *active* mass tool of representation is a vehicle for documenting one's conditions (of living working and sociality; for creating alternative representations of oneself and one's sex, class,

age-group, race, etc; of gaining power of analysis and visual
literacy) over one's image; of presenting arguments and demands; of
stimulating action; of experiencing visual pleasure as a producer, not
consumer of images; of relating to, by objectifying, one's personal
and political environment.

(Slater 1983: 246)

If we can actively work on 'representations of ourselves', it seems that
documentary, with its historic weight of practice and ostensible claim to transparency, might not be the perfect photographic form by which this could be
achieved. Documentary began to be deserted in favour of contrivance and
artifice. Work of this kind came from community groups and feminist collec-
tives, and was to be found in certain kinds of gallery practice. For example, the
community group Hackney Flashers used their photographic project to politi-
cise activities and concepts such as motherhood, housework and child-care.
They used a variety of montage techniques, together with text and slogans, to
overcome the perceived limitations of documentary photography, a limitation
that was outlined by Angela Kelly when making her 1979 selection of feminist
photographs:

> The 'analytical' approach sees conventional documentary as prob-
> lematic in the sense that the medium itself is a complex signifying
> process. Photographic images are presented as constructs and the
> viewer is forced to read the system of signs and to become aware
> of being actively involved in the process of the creation of
> meaning. This approach stands in opposition to the notion of the
> photograph as a transparent 'window on the world'.
>
> (Kelly 1979: 42)

Kelly makes it clear that she does not endorse the documentary project,
which she considers to confirm, at least implicitly, photography's claim to
be 'true to appearances'. Similarly, more than a decade later, Tessa Boffin
and Jean Fraser introduced their book of lesbian photography with an explanation that, since sexuality is socially constructed, documentary realism might
be an inappropriate form for its representation:

> Lesbianism exists in a complex relation to many other identities;
> concerns with sexuality intersect with those of race, class and the
> body . . . we looked for work which concentrated on constructed,
> staged or self-consciously manipulated imagery which might mirror
> the socially constructed nature of sexuality. We have not included
> much documentary work as the realism of documentary has often
> been used ideologically to reinforce notions of naturalness. We do
> not want this book to claim a natural status for lesbianism but
> rather to celebrate that there is no natural sexuality at all.
>
> (Boffin and Fraser 1991: 10)

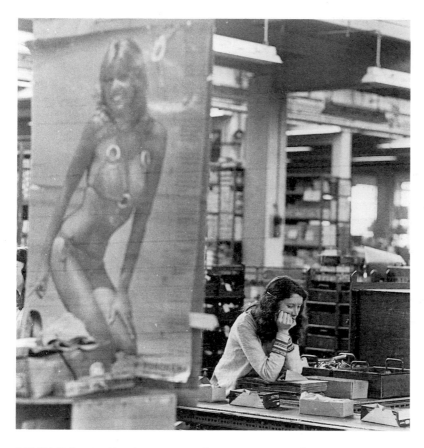

2.14 Nick Hedges, ***Packing department, Lock Factory, Willenhall,*** **from** ***Born to Work,*** **1982**
Nick Hedges made a documentary study of factory life in Britain in the 1980s and many of the images disrupt
our expectations of the image of 'the worker'

Photography is used in projects of this kind in order to explore subjectivity, but, while working-class life has been surveyed through
documentary, it seems that gender, race and sexuality have been analysed
in terms of other kinds of photographic discourses and practices – those
which stress a Brechtian concern with construction and fabrication in
photography. Called into question was the ability of realist practices
adequately to unmask the nature of the prevailing social conditions or to
explore the social and political nature of our subjective lives. John Roberts
has suggested that the movement away from documentary is associated with
the 'downgrading of class within cultural politics' and a retreat from class
politics itself. Rather than simply endorse the documentary movement,
however, he argues:

There can be no representation of class subjectivities without the photographer intervening *in* the process of the production of meaning. Whether you are studio-based or working with conventional documentary images then, work on the representation of class cannot proceed without a recognition of those symbolic processes that shape and determine the construction of class identity.

(Roberts 1993: 13)

Of course, there were documentary photographers who were still concerned to represent the nature of work and the lives of working people in a style that owes a great deal to classic forms of documentary photography. For example, in very different ways, the work of Chris Killip, Nick Hedges and the Exit Photography Group (Nicholas Battye, Chris Steele-Perkins and Paul Trevor) during the 1970s and 1980s were all recognisable in the tradition of documentary, although they were more concerned with exploring class subjectivity than with aspiring to discover the 'facts' of working-class life.

DOCUMENTARY IN THE AGE OF POSTMODERNISM

Documentary photographers are certainly no longer tied to the political project that was espoused by the documentary movement of the 1930s. Nor are the codes that seemed to authenticate documentary photographs necessarily employed. Traditionally, for example, documentary photographs were in black and white. Originally a necessary condition for the reproduction of their photographs it became a guarantor of the integrity of an image for many photographers. The suppression of colour made it possible to control the aesthetic qualities of the picture and helped to structure its connotative meaning. Now colour is freely used by most British documentary photographers for projects from industrial landscapes or new technologies to the social life of teenage girls. Nor are documentary photographs now only to be seen, incorporated with text, as a part of a magazine article, for photographers employ their work in a variety of media from books and television to gallery walls. They take part, in other words, in the endless circulation of images that is a distinguishing feature of **postmodernism**.

Postmodernist movements currently exist at many levels from serious philosophical reflection to particular kinds of surface style and fashions. Linking them all is a concern with the nature of images and their circulation; an elision between high and popular culture; a scepticism about the nature of 'the real' or 'the authentic' (for the 'simulacrum' is held to have taken over from the original); and a suggestion that the discourses that once bounded and structured knowledge (such as history or science) have broken down. Under these conditions, what future might there be for documentary; is it a practice that has run out of history?

In this context it is useful to look at the work of practising photographers whose work is of a kind that would formerly have been labelled 'documentary'. A good example is a recent exhibition and book by Martin Parr, *Small World*, which has a commentary by Simon Winchester (Parr 1995). Parr returns us to the world of travel photography, for his images were taken in several places around the world. Like any good Victorian photographer, he visits Egypt and the Far East, Switzerland and Rome. What he returns with, however, are not carefully composed shots of temples and pyramids, nor artfully posed portraits of picturesque native peoples, but images of other tourists; those who form part of the movement of mass tourism. Photographed in rich colour the tourists struggle with maps, follow the raised umbrellas of guides, buy beads in Goa, take photographs and pose for photographs.

What connects the world in this exhibition is the multiple presence of the camera. Images are intertwined with what would once have been called the 'original' object; signs have broken loose from their former anchorages and float freely around a world that has been constituted as a site of spectacle. Can we consider work of this kind, with its multiple references to other images and its unwillingness to make authoritative statements, to be documentary? Certainly it fulfils the minimal condition of documentary: that it provide an account of events that have their own existence outside the frame of the photograph or the confines of the studio walls. We are no longer asked to accept that such images are impartial or disinterested; instead we inhabit a space between scepticism, pleasure and trust, from which we can read documentary images in more complex ways.

BIBLIOGRAPHY

KEY TEXTS

Benjamin, W. (1972) 'A Short History of Photography', *Screen* 13(1)
Rossler, M. (1989) 'In, Around and Afterthoughts (on Documentary Photography)' in R. Bolton (ed.) *The Contest of Meaning: Critical Histories of Photography*, Cambridge, MA: MIT Press
Sekula, A. (1978) 'Dismantling Modernism, Reinventing Documentary (Notes on the Politics of Representation)' in J. Liebling (ed.) *Photography: Current Perspectives*, Rochester, New York: Light Impressions Co
Solomon-Godeau, A. (1991) 'Who is Speaking Thus?', *Photography at the Dock*, Minneapolis: University of Minnesota Press
Stott, W. (1973) *Documentary Expression and Thirties America*, London: Oxford University Press
Tagg, J. (1988) *The Burden of Representation: Essays on Photographies and Histories*, London: Macmillan
Thomas, A. (1978) *The Expanding Eye: Photography and the Nineteenth Century Mind*, London: Croom Helm
Trachtenberg, A. (1989) *Reading American Photographs*, New York: Hill and Wang

OTHER REFERENCES

Agee, J. and Evans, W. (1939) *Let Us Now Praise Famous Men*, New York: Random House

Boffin, T. and Fraser, J. (1991) *Stolen Glances: Lesbians Take Photographs*, London: Pandora Press

Cartier-Bresson, H. (1952) *The Decisive Moment*, New York: Simon and Schuster

Frank, R. (1959) *The Americans*, New York: Grove Press

Gidal, T.N. (1973) *Modern Photojournalism*, New York: Collier Books

Griffiths, P.J. (1971) *Vietnam Inc.*, New York: Macmillan

Hall, S. (1972) 'The Social Eye of *Picture Post*', *Cultural Studies* 2, CCCS, Birmingham

Hardy, B. (1977) 'Bert Hardy', *Camerawork* 8

Hershkowitz, R. (1980) *The British Photographer Abroad: The First Thirty Years*, London: Robert Hershkowitz Ltd

Hudson, D. (1972) *Munby, Man of Two Worlds*, London: John Murray

Isherwood, C. (1939) *Goodbye to Berlin*, Harmondsworth: Penguin Books

Jameson, S. (1937) 'Writing in Revolt', *Fact* 4

Kelly, A. (1979) 'Feminism and Photography' in P. Hill, A. Kelly and J. Tagg, *Three Perspectives on Photography*, London: ACGB

Lewinski, J. (1978) *The Camera at War*, London: W.H. Allen

Lloyd, J. (1985) 'Old Photographs, Vanished Peoples and Stolen Potatoes', *Art Monthly* 83, February

Mayhew, H. (1861) *London Labour and the London Poor*, reprinted 1967, London: Frank Cass

Mayne, R. (1986) *The Street Photographs of Roger Mayne*, London: Victoria and Albert Museum

Ohrn, K.B. (1980) *Dorothea Lange and the Documentary Tradition*, Baton Rouge: Louisiana State University Press

Parr, M. (1995) *Small World: A Global Photographic Project, 1987–1994*, Stockport: Dewi Lewis Publishing

Powell, R. (1985) *Photography and the Making of History: Brunel's Kingdom*, Bristol: Watershed Media Centre

Quartermaine, P. (1992) 'Johannes Lindt: Photographer of Australia and New Guinea' in M. Gidley (ed.) *Representing Others: White Views of Indigenous Peoples*, Exeter: University of Exeter Press

Ray-Jones, T. (1974) *A Day Off: An English Journal*, London: Thames and Hudson

Riis, J.A. (1918) T*he Making of an American*, New York: Macmillan

Roberts, J. (1993) *Renegotiations: Class, Modernity and Photography*, Norwich: Norwich Gallery, Norfolk Institute of Art and Design

Slater, D. (1983) 'Marketing Mass Photography' in H. Davis and P. Walton (eds) *Language, Image, Media*, Oxford: Blackwell

Spender, H. (1978) 'Humphrey Spender: M. O. Photographer', *Camerawork* 11

Stein, S. (1983) 'Making Connections with the Camera: Photography and Social Mobility in the Career of Jacob Riis', *Afterimage* 10(10)

Trachtenberg, A. (1982) *The Incorporation of America*, New York: Hill and Wang

Treuherz, J. (1987) *Hard Times: Social Realism in Victorian Art*, London: Lund Humphries

Urry, J. (1990) *The Tourist Gaze: Leisure and Travel in Contemporary Societies*, London: Sage

CHAPTER 3

'Sweet it is to scan . . .'

Personal photographs and popular photography

PATRICIA HOLLAND

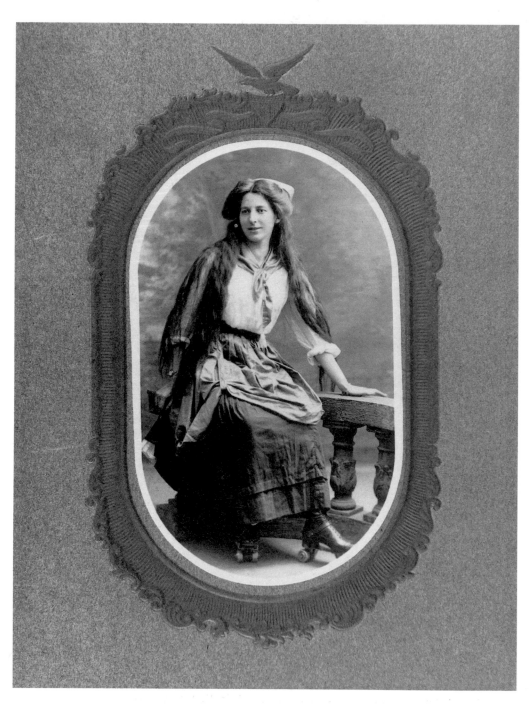

3.1 Studio photograph of Lily Peapell in peasant dress on roller skates, *c.* 1912

'When amid life's surging battle
Reverie its solace lends
Sweet it is to scan the faces –
Picture faces – of old friends
. . .
Some have passed the mystic
    portals
Where the usher Death presides
Some to distant climes have
    wandered
Borne on Time's relentless
    tides;
Some, perchance, to paths
    unholy;
Some to deeds without a name
But the faces in the album
Are for aye and aye the same.
. . .
Picture faces! Oh what volumes
Of unwritten life ye hold:
Youthful faces! pure, sweet
    faces!
Dearly prized as we grow old'

M.C. DUNCAN
Frontispiece to Richard Penlake
*Home Portraits for Amateur
Photographers* (1899)

'Sweet it is to scan . . .'

Personal photographs and popular photography

INTRODUCTION

The doggerel, couched in the language of late Victorian sentiment, with its yearning for purity and sense of the closeness of death, fronted a book of advice for 'amateur photographers' just at the time when home photography was undergoing a dramatic transformation. The crafted work of the 'amateur' or hobbyist, whose proliferating equipment involved tripods, black cloths, glass plate negatives, special backdrops, darkrooms and a cocktail of chemicals, was giving way to an instant push-button affair, in which the film could be sent off for processing and no special skills were required. By 1899 George Eastman had already marketed his revolutionary hand-held Kodak with the slogan 'You press the button, we do the rest' and was about to launch the 'Box Brownie' – the camera he claimed that everyone could afford and was easy enough for children to use.

But the history of personal photography is more than a simple story of technological development. The desire to scan the picture faces of old friends has been expressed in a multitude of different ways over the last century and a half. Social and cultural changes are intertwined with the history of photographic techniques and practices, as are the interpretive meanings we bring to the pictures. This chapter will outline that history, in which taking pictures is both a leisure pursuit and an increasingly flexible medium for the construction of ordinary people's accounts of their lives and **fantasies**. The history of the medium and the separate history of the **discourse** of which photography forms a part, interact with the **social and economic history** of an era. We will begin in the 1840s, imagining how it must have been when, for the first time, people could hold in their hands the marvel of a photographic likeness. The final section of the chapter will start from the other end, as it were, and will look back from where we stand today, finding ways to make sense of personal pictures from the recent and distant past. The meanings brought by the browser in the album both meet up with, and part company, from the external realities of the historical world, particularly when pictures are associated with major trauma or historical displacement.[1]

We have chosen to speak here of 'private' or 'personal' pictures rather than the more usual 'family' pictures, because our private lives cover so much more than our family lives. The equation between 'the family' and private experience is too easily made and excludes too much.[2] The evolution of private photography has indeed been family based but that link is historically contingent, not, as is often assumed, the consequence of 'natural' necessity. Even in 1899 it was the picture faces of 'old friends' that were apostrophised in M.C. Duncan's verse. The point has been made by writers such as Terry Dennett, who compare family albums to other sorts of albums that record the lives of clubs, political groups and other networks of support and obligation (**Spence and Holland 1991: 72**).

That private photography has become *family* photography is itself an indication of the domestication of everyday life and the expansion of 'the family' as the pivot of a century-long shift to a consumer-led, home-based economy. Personal photography has evolved as part of the interleaving of leisure and the domestic, whose development runs parallel to the history of photography itself.

In Britain and the West, the gradual expansion of domesticity from the respectable middle classes through to all but the very poorest, has drawn women, children and finally even men into the 'charmed circle of home'.[3] Such activities as child-care, the preparation of meals and work on improving the house and garden have come to be seen as pleasures rather than duties, and the family has become the main resource for close relationships and

1 Literary theorist Shoshanna Felman and psychoanalyst Dori Laub discuss the significance of certain family photographs for survivors of the Holocaust in *Testimony* (1992), which deals with memory and the possibility of witness.
2 See Michèle Barrett and Mary McIntosh (1982) for a development of this argument.

JO SPENCE AND PATRICIA HOLLAND (eds) (1991) **Family Snaps: The Meanings of Domestic Photography**, London: Virago

3 For an account of the evolution of 'domesticity' as a concept and a way of living, see Catherine Hall (1979) and Davidoff and Hall (1976).

expressive emotion. Now, at the end of the twentieth century, taking snapshots is among a plethora of leisure pursuits that underpin that specific form of family life. However, photography occupies a peculiar place amongst those activities, as pictures are themselves carriers of meanings and interpretations. They record and reflect on daily activities, delicately holding within the innocent-seeming image much that is intimate. Here are M.C. Duncan's 'volumes of unwritten life' for which we must scan beyond the edges of the frame.

Personal photographs are embedded in the lives of those who own or make use of them. Even when they are professionally taken, there is a contract between photographer and subject quite different from other types of photography. Personal pictures are made specifically to portray the individual or the group to which they belong *as they would wish to be seen* and as they have chosen to show themselves to one another. Even so, the conventions of the group inevitably overrule the preferences of individual members. Children, especially, have very little say over how they are pictured, and this discrepancy is the source of many of the conflicting emotions analysed by recent writers on family photography.

The photographs we keep for ourselves – not always in family albums – are treasured less for their quality than for their *context* and for the part they play in confirming and challenging the identity and history of their users. In this discussion it will be useful to distinguish between *users* and *readers* of personal pictures, whether family snaps, school photos or the portraits in the high street photographer's window.[4] Users bring to the images a wealth of surrounding knowledge. Their own private pictures are part of the complex network of memories and meanings with which they make sense of their daily lives. For readers, on the other hand, a hazy snapshot or a smiling portrait from the 1950s is a mysterious text whose meanings must be teased out in an act of decoding or historical detective work. Users of personal pictures have access to the world in which they make sense; readers must translate those private meanings into a more public realm. Private photographs, taken alone, are a 'restricted code' in the sense described by Basil Bernstein, dependent for their specific meanings on knowledge of the rich soil of meanings that holds them in place (Bernstein 1971). Wrenched from that context, they appear thin and ephemeral, offering little in the way of either aesthetic pleasure or historical documentation. But, although such ghostly hints of other lives may tempt the reader to engage in the detective project and to construct stories from these tentative clues, the empirical historian would do well to treat them with extreme caution. The peculiar fascination of personal photographs comes from this contrast between an almost unbearable richness and the inconsequentiality and triviality of the medium. Roland Barthes, writing on photography and memory, could not bear to reproduce the snapshot of his recently deceased mother even though it gave rise to his essay (**Barthes 1982**).

4 The distinction between users and readers derives from Basil Bernstein's analysis of elaborated and restricted codes. A restricted code is one that depends on its context to be understood (see Bernstein 1971: 76–77).

ROLAND BARTHES (1982)
Camera Lucida, London: Jonathan Cape

BRIAN COE AND PAUL GATES (1977) **The Snapshot Photograph: The Rise of Popular Photography 1888–1939**, London: Ash and Grant

COLIN FORD (1989) T**he Story of Popular Photography**, Bradford: Century Hutchinson Ltd/National Museum of Photography, Film and Television

AUDREY LINKMAN AND CAROLINE WARHURST (1982) **Family Albums**, Manchester: Manchester Polytechnic. A fully illustrated exhibition catalogue with an introduction

AUDREY LINKMAN (1993) **The Victorians: Photographic Portraits**, London: Tauris Parke Books

SUE ISHERWOOD (1988) **The Family Album**, London: Broadcasting Support Services

Private pictures, offering up so little to the critic and art historian, have tended to feature in histories of photography chiefly as examples of technological improvement. Historians have noted the increasing lightness of cameras, the invention of roll film and similar developments **Coe and Gates 1977**; **Ford 1989**). Until very recently, twentieth-century snapshots have been ignored, seen as slight and unimportant, of poor quality and of value only to those who make use of them. However, over the last twenty years or so, personal pictures have become the centre of a new sort of interest as the study of history itself has changed, and as working photographers, particularly women, have re-evaluated photographic practice. A concern with local and family histories, women's history, the history of everyday life and history from below has given a new interest to personal pictures as historical documents (**Linkman and Warhurst 1982**; **Linkman 1993**; **Drake and Finnegan 1994**).

When scrutinised under the detective's magnifying glass, private pictures offer up many public meanings, some superficial, some historically illuminating. They tell us about the style of crinoline fashionable in the the 1860s and about the donkeys used by beach photographers in the 1910s. But they also display public **ideologies** – stories and ideas about how things are and how they ought to be (**Isherwood 1988**).

Historically, personal pictures are deeply unreliable, but it is in this very unreliability that their interest lies. It has led to to a new set of questions – for whom are these pictures? who sees them? to whom do they communicate? In making an effort to *reread* private pictures, there has been a move to revalue the undervalued and to bring into public discourse meanings which have hitherto been concealed in the most secret parts of the private sphere. Writers, photographers and curators (Jo Spence, Sue Isherwood and Val Williams among them), while drawing attention to the importance of this most popular of the uses of photography, have insisted that the *privacy* of the meanings should not be dispersed (Spence and Holland 1991; **Spence 1987, 1995**; **Williams 1986**).

JO SPENCE (1987) **Putting Myself in the Picture**, London: Camden Press (1995) **Cultural Sniping**, London: Routledge

VAL WILLIAMS (1986) **Women Photographers: The Other Observers 1900 to the Present**, London: Virago

JOHN TAGG (1988) **The Burden of Representation: Essays on Photographies and Histories**, London: Macmillan (especially chapter 1, 'A Democracy of the Image: Photographic Portraiture and Commodity Production')

The increasing self-consciousness of the modern world has been explored and reworked in many different ways since the mid-nineteenth century. It has been argued that photography is itself a central feature of modernity – not just in its modernist moment, when photographers such as Rodchenko and Moholy-Nagy indulged in formalist abstractions and celebrations of machine culture – but as a *technology*, contributing to the control of the external world with its mechanical eye and potential for scientific neutrality (**Tagg 1988**; Slater 1995a).

Personal photography has played a different but equally important role in the **modernisation** of Western culture. It has developed as a medium through which individuals confirm and explore their **identity**, that sense of self-identity which is an indispensable feature of a modern sensibility – for in Western urban culture it is as *individuals* that people have come to experience themselves, independently of their role as family members or as occupying a recognised social position. The twentieth-century consumer-led economy has shifted these new individuals away from a culture based on work and self-discipline to one based on libidinous gratification which encourages us all to *identify* our pleasures in order to develop and refine them. In a parallel move, the century of Freud has become an age of inwardness and self-scrutiny. These changes are reflected in the images we produce of ourselves and the way we have made use of them. Scanning personal pictures has become part of that act of self-contemplation (Spence and Martin in Spence and Holland 1991; Spence 1987; Spence 1995).

Despite the intensity of such a project, in one of those many paradoxes that makes its study so fascinating, private photography insists on being a *non-serious* practice. Cuthbert Bede, writing in 1855 in the facetiously punning style enjoyed by the mid-nineteenth century, reminded his readers that photography was 'essentially a *light* subject and should be treated in a light manner' (Bede 1855). And so it has continued over its history, seeking the playful and celebrating the trivial. Personal photography sets out to be photography without pretensions and that's how we intend to approach it. In the spirit of much recent work by feminist writers on women's culture (for example, Geraghty 1991), we will not be arguing that these forms of photography should be captured for '**Art**' or 'high culture', but that what is needed is to understand them on their own terms.

IN AND BEYOND THE CHARMED CIRCLE OF HOME

The public and the private in personal photography

From its beginnings in the 1840s, home-based popular photography was balanced by photography that looked outwards. During the nineteenth century, images of the strange and exotic were treated as marvels which enhanced the comfortable home and became part of home entertainment, as television is today. But in some family albums kept by prosperous patriarchs up to the turn of the century, we can see how the middle-class home, even as it became increasingly protected from political and economic life, depended on the world outside. The feminine domesticity of the extended family was visibly sustained by masculine adventure, both military and entre-preneurial. The two sides of popular photography have remained, but the Imperial aspiration of this vision, and the celebration of commerce and military adventure of the Victorian era, have since been replaced by a tamer record of travel and tourism.

The copious albums preserved by Sir Arnold Wilson dramatically illustrate the point. Sir Arnold was a well-connected army officer serving in India and Persia in the early years of the twentieth century. He worked with the Anglo-Persian Oil Company in the 1920s and became a Conservative MP in the 1930s. His family albums cover a period from 1870 to 1920, recording

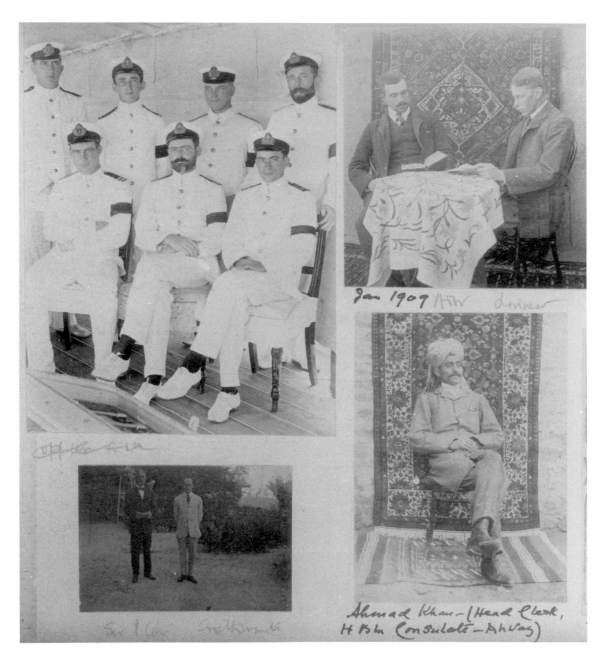

3.2a From the album of Sir Arnold Wilson (No 3 Persian scenes), 1909

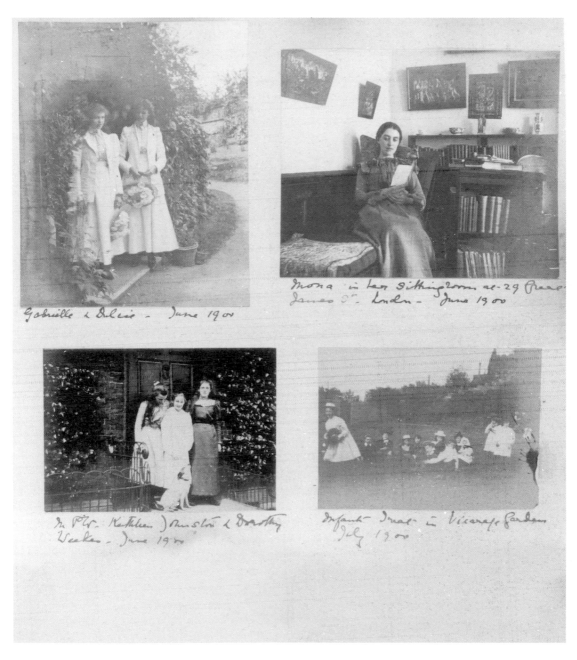

3.2b From the album of Sir Arnold Wilson (No 7), 1900

holiday trips, afternoons in the vicarage garden and regimental postings. Set-piece photographs of India and the Middle East are juxtaposed with gentle family groups and intimate portraits in the gardens and drawing rooms of the family's homes at Leighton Park Estate and in the countryside near Rochdale. In India the regimental tug-of-war team and the local Gurkha regiment present themselves proudly to the camera. In the Middle East, British officers pose one by one with local sheikhs. Tourism overlaps with colonial rule as spectacular views of the Himalayan hill station at Muree are followed by annotated pages showing the complex decoration of local mosques. In the Persian album, alongside the purchased images of silversmiths and weavers at work, Sir Arnold included pictures of executioners and torturers demonstrating their craft.

Discussing the colonialist imagery of advertising at the turn of the century, Anne McClintock argues that 'the cult of domesticity became indispensable to the consolidation of British imperial identity' (Robertson et al. 1994: 133). The starkness of the contrast in Sir Arnold Wilson's albums makes visible the tensions on which domestic photography has continued to be based. They look inwards at an increasingly privatised and protected domestic haven and outwards at a world of political violence, re-presented as spectacular and exotic. The pictures in Sir Arnold's albums present this outside world with great confidence, gazing with the eyes of those who would control it and claim to civilise it. As the twentieth century progressed, and as photography became available to the ruled as well as the rulers, the politics of the world beyond the family group has come to be **repressed** in the domestic image. The *consequences* of colonial domination and the ever possible presence of violence must be read beyond the limits of the frame (S. Hall 1991: 152).

Beyond the domestic

From the very early days to the unflagging popularity of posters and postcards in the twentieth century, popular photography has continued to include purchased pictures of unknown people and places. William Henry Fox Talbot, who first developed a negative/positive **calotype** process in Britain in 1839, hastened to patent his invention and turn it to financial advantage. In 1843 he set up the first printing workshop to reproduce photographs for sale. His book, *The Pencil of Nature*, was the first to be photographically illustrated.

Within twenty years there was a thriving industry in photographic prints, which included impressive landscapes, views and still lives. If Sir Arnold Wilson's turn of the century collection carries the confidence of those who seek to control what they see, these pictures marketed from the 1850s onwards had the more modest aim of entertainment. However, what John Urry described as 'the tourist **gaze**' (Urry 1990) itself ensures a separation between the the one who does the looking, assumed to be familiar and like 'us', and that which is looked at, assumed to be different and strange. A taste for the exotic was already well established in the mid-nineteenth century and photography gave it a new boost. Francis Frith set up a highly profitable company which produced saleable photographs of parts of the world which up till that time had only been seen through the eyes of artists or the imaginative descriptions of travellers. From 1856 he made three expeditions to the bible lands of the Middle East and *The Times* called his resulting photographs 'the most important ever published' (Macdonald 1979). His photographers travelled the length of the British Isles and at the height of his business his firm claimed to have one million available prints, including photographs of every city, town and beauty spot in Britain. By the later years of the nineteenth century, photographs of parts of the world impressive because of their distance, their strangeness or the difficulty experienced in reaching them – from the high Alps to remote areas of China and Japan – were published as prints, lantern slides and stereoscopic views.

The coming of photography gave rise to a new set of dilemmas around the production of the exotic. On the one hand it displayed images of hitherto unknown and remarkable places and people, but at the same time it had to be recognised that these were *real* places and people. The veneer of exoticism may be confirmed or challenged by the photograph itself. We should not forget that photography was also developing in those very places that seemed exotic to the untravelled British. By the end of the nineteenth century in China, Japan and Taiwan, local photographers were making pictures for local use. Pictures which would be seen as exotica in Britain are someone else's family photos.

Popular photography has rarely been a medium of record. Foreign views exaggerated the exotic and the strange, and a fashion developed for the quaint and the traditional (for example, George Washington Wilson's pictures of gnarled old Scottish fishermen and other local types). With hindsight this fashion can be seen as the beginnings of a heritage industry in which the imagery was threaded through with nostalgia brought by photography itself, already capturing a disappearing past. Groups such as the Society for Photographing Relics of Old London set up in 1875 contributed to an archive of the past which itself became part of a tourist view of the world (**Taylor 1994**).

Middle-class artistic travellers came to deplore 'vulgar' sightseers turning up with their cameras, who, they claimed, ruined the very views they had come to discover. From the turn of the century, a new generation of tourists took their cameras in search of natural beauties previously only seen on postcards and in travelogues. At first they went by train or bicycle, but by the 1930s many were travelling by car. Some were satisfied to picnic in the fields, but increasing numbers sought out the famous beauty spots. With each wave of visitors the possibility of an undiscovered rural scene or an unspoilt village seemed to become ever more elusive. A photograph was a nostalgic

JOHN TAYLOR (1994)
A Dream of England: Landscape, Photography and the Tourist's Imagination, Manchester: Manchester University Press

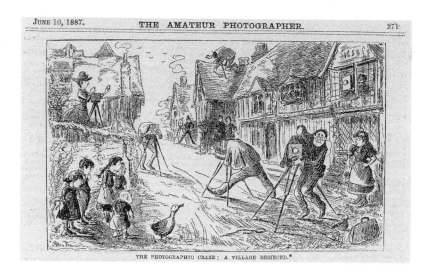

JUNE 10, 1887.   THE AMATEUR PHOTOGRAPHER.   271

THE PHOTOGRAPHIC CRAZE: A VILLAGE BESIEGED.*

3.3 'The photographic craze', *Amateur Photographer*, 10 June 1887

compensation for the loss of a world that appeared to be uncorrupted by industry and urbanisation. In the late twentieth century, that historical world itself has been preserved and packaged. The heritage industry and the tourist trade between them provide renovated antique buildings and tidied up picturesque views that are ready-made photo opportunities. 'Points of view' are now clearly marked on roads and maps. Taking a picture is an intrinsic part of the tourist experience and 'places of interest' dominate the albums of many a modest traveller just as they did those of Sir Arnold Wilson.

Fiction and fantasy

Fiction and fantasy have long been more attractive than the mundanities of everyday life, and this was certainly true of one of the most popular of nineteenth-century domestic media, the stereoscopic view. From 1854 the London Stereoscopic Company produced double pictures which gave a 3D effect when peered at through a binocular viewer. This could be a small hand-held affair or a grand piece of drawing room furniture. By 1858 there were 100,000 different views on offer and the company's slogan was 'no home without a stereoscope'.

Many stereoscopic scenes exploited the Victorians' love of theatrical tableaux and aimed for a style and subject-matter suited to the taste of their middle-brow purchasers. Such 'stereoscopic trash' outraged the proponents of photography as art. The Photographic Society (later to become Royal), founded in 1853 to protect artistic standards, deplored the debasement of the medium. In 1858 its journal fumed,

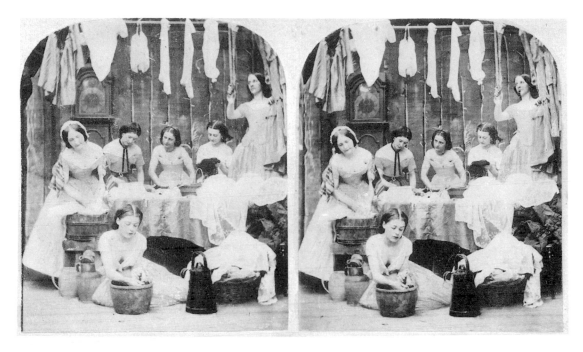

3.4 Stereoscopic slide from the late nineteenth century

> To see that noble instrument prostituted as it is by those sentimental
> 'Weddings', 'Christenings', 'Distressed Sempstresses', 'Crinolines' and
> 'Ghosts' is enough to disgust anyone of refined taste. We are sorry to
> say that recently some slides have been published which are, to say
> the least, questionable in point of view of delicacy.
>
> (Scharf 1974)

Sentiment, jokes, horror, melodrama and material which verged on pornography – this was the stuff of nineteenth-century photographic entertainment.
Some stereoscopes even came with a locked drawer for a gentleman to keep
his risqué pictures away from his family.

In those days before the cinema, magic lantern shows were also popular.
Impressive views could be watched in a darkened room, enhanced by exciting
optical effects – from a sunset over the Alps to lifelike thunderstorms (Chanan
1996). The making of personal portraits was part of this popular aesthetic,
firmly embedded in commercial practices.

Portraits and albums

Louis-Jacques-Mandé Daguerre's invention of positive images on silvered
metal, each one unique, was, from the 1840s, the dominant format for

personal portraits. Enterprising **daguerreotypists** learnt the new skills and tried to interest customers in towns across Europe and the New World. In those very early days, sittings for fifteen to twenty minutes in as bright a sunlight as possible led to extreme discomfort for the sitter and some fairly unflattering pictures which could be difficult to discern on the highly reflective surface. Even so, within a few years, huge numbers of people of middling income wanted their portraits taken and 'daguerreomania' had taken hold.

Photographic 'glasshouses' – so called because of the wide expanse of window needed to maximise daylight – were established in the urban centres across Europe and the United States. In Britain Antoine Claudet had a 'temple of photography' designed by Sir Charles Barry, who built the Houses of Parliament. In Leicester Square there was a 'Panopticon of science and art' with a room 54 feet long (approx 16.5 metres) 'enabling family groups of 18 persons to be taken at once', which also offered lessons in daguerreotyping and studios for hire. Studio portraitists introduced painted backdrops so that the customer, whatever their social standing, could choose to place themselves within dignified parklands, seascapes, conservatories or palm houses. Many were extremely successful: Richard Beard was said to be photography's first millionaire (Macdonald 1979; Ford 1989; Tagg 1988; **Kenyon 1992: 11–12**).

DAVE KENYON (1992) **Inside Amateur Photography**, London: Batsford

The 'cheap and common establishments' in the less fashionable parts of the town got a bad name for aggressive touting for trade. Someone stood outside shouting, 'Have your picture taken', and virtually 'dragging customers in by the collar' (Werge 1890: 202). Most of these early portraits were carefully posed and touched up so as to produce as flattering an image as possible under difficult circumstances. A headrest kept that most important feature, the face, static for the still lengthy exposures needed, or else the posing individual was asked to lean on a table or a mock-classical pillar which also served decorative and symbolic functions. The head resting on the hand achieved the popular Victorian soulful look, as well as helping the sitter to keep still. Smiles were difficult to sustain under such circumstances: the modern ubiquitous snapshot smile should be seen as a technological achievement as well as a change in social mores.

Every innovation was hailed as spreading photography more widely across the classes. 'Such portraits are to be found in everybody's hands', wrote André-Adolphe Disdéri, who had invented the '*carte-de-visite*' in 1854 (Lamagny and Rouille 1987: 38). Named after the leisured classes' 'visiting cards', these were small paper prints mounted on the photographer's own decorated card. Several poses could be produced on a single negative so that the process was speeded up and multiple copies were easily available. This was the first attempt at a form of mass production of popular photographs, and certainly class differences were far less visible in such pictures than they were in everyday life. Shopkeepers, minor officials and small traders all took themselves and their children to pose stiffly in their best clothes in front of one of these early cameras.

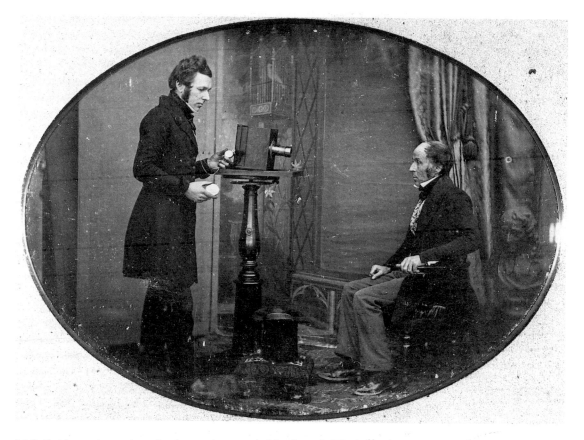

3.5 Earliest known daguerrotype of a photographer at work. Jabez Hogg photographs Mr Johnson, *c.* 1843

A craze for collecting *cartes-de-visite* of the famous developed. Some of the earliest photographic albums were not 'family albums' at all, but handsomely bound volumes filled with pictures of royalty, celebrities and politicians. As pressure increased on middle-class women to make their lives within the confines of the home environment, useless but suitably decorative hobbies such as collecting *cartes-de-visite* fitted in well with other genteel activities such as sketching and pressing flowers (Davidoff and Hall 1976; Warner 1992).

Queen Victoria's family was itself presented as a model of the new respectable domesticity, but published photographs of the Royal Family remained strictly formal. When the celebrated photographer Roger Fenton was invited to photograph the Queen's children dressing up and presenting tableaux, the pictures were felt to lack dignity and were never released to the public (Hannavy 1975). Even so, it was the more relaxed picture of Princess Alexandra giving her daughter Louise a piggyback that became the best-selling *carte-de-visite*. Among their many hobbies and pastimes, women members of the Royal Family took up photography themselves, and Queen Victoria's and later Queen Alexandra's own copious albums were filled with views of family picnics and hunting parties (Williams 1986: 75).

Home photography was not for public display, but for fun amongst friends. In 1855, Cuthbert Bede described, for the benefit of 'all the light-hearted friends of light painting', many such social activities, including 'visiting country houses and calotyping all the eligible daughters' (Bede 1855: 44). The light-hearted uses of photographs, part of the Victorian fascination for fads and fancies, included mounting dainty miniatures into brooches and lockets, decorating jewel cases, or even setting them into the spines of a fan. A Victorian album was itself a series of visual novelties, with the portraits often cut up and arranged in decorative shapes and incorporating drawings and other scrapbook items. Mary Queen of Scots going to her execution was a favourite. And there were the mottoes: 'love me, love my dog' heads a page of pets squatting smugly on their cushions. The interest is not just in the individual pictures but in the arrangement as a decorative collection.[5]

The family-based albums of the nineteenth century are those of prosperous dynasties whose members had both the leisure and the money to take up photography, as well as to buy commercially produced pictures. The life of the Helm family, in their spacious mansion in Walthamstow, elegantly photographed by James Helm and preserved in a set of albums put together in the early 1860s, demonstrates not so much the luxury and overt enjoyment of a free-spending leisure class, but the decency and quiet respectability of the middle-class suburb (H. Cunningham in **Thompson 1990**). The group is large and diverse, with aunts and other relatives and friends as regular members, in striking contrast to today's pictures of tight-knit families in which parents and young children predominate. The leisurely lifestyle included croquet on the lawn, amateur dramatics, young men posing with their musical instruments and dignified ladies in layered crinolines taking tea. These are scenes from everyday life, carefully organised and staged in the tableau manner. In the 1840s, Fox Talbot had written, 'when a group of persons has been artistically arranged and trained by a little practice to maintain an absolute immobility for a few seconds of time, many delightful pictures are easily obtained. I have observed that family groups are especial favourites' (Ford 1989). The tableau was a pleasing artistic picture as much as a family record. Pictures such as these were marking out the evolving domestic sensibility of the nineteenth century, which made the home environment the centre of decent living. It was a model which the lower-middle and working classes were to emulate in the coming century.

If the home was becoming a site of leisure, the creation of the 'hobbyist', and its more elevated relative the 'amateur', meant that leisure time could be used both for scientific experiment and the creation of works of art. Although one aspect of the evolution of domesticity meant that 'the feminine

5 It is relatively new for photographic historians to recognise the album's importance as a complete entity. Collectors have frequently purchased an album simply to remove one or two remarkable prints. Curator Pam Roberts of the Royal Photographic Society is preserving and cataloguing albums in their own right. She makes the point that the way photographs have been selected and put together is an important part of the personal meaning of the pictures in an album.

F.M.L. THOMPSON (ed.) (1990) **The Cambridge Social History of Britain 1750–1850**, Vol. 2, **People and Their Environment**, Cambridge: Cambridge University Press

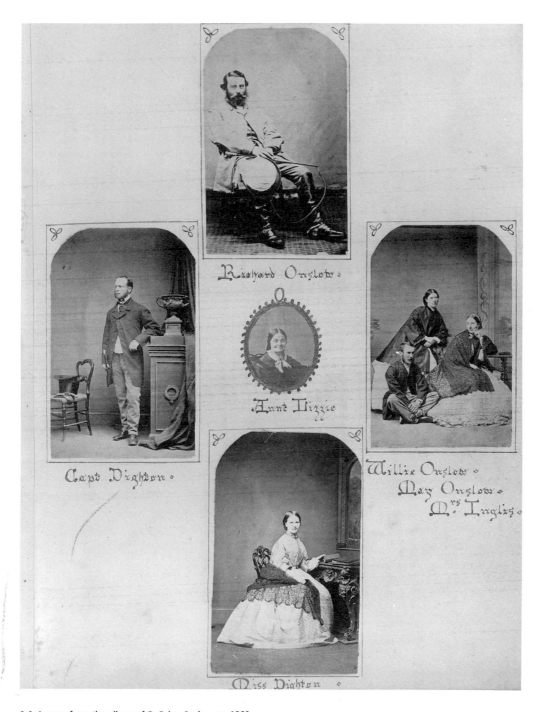

3.6 A page from the album of R. Foley Onslow, *c.* 1860

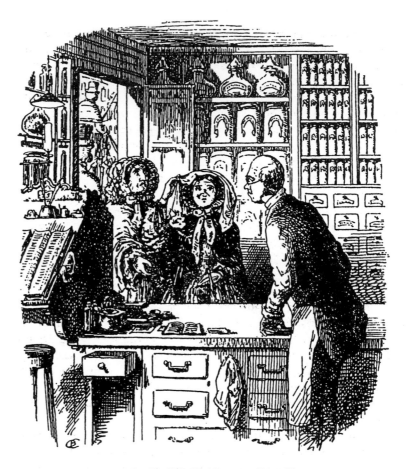

A PHOTOGRAPHIC POSITIVE.

LADY MOTHER (loquitur) "I SHALL FEEL OBLIGED TO YOU, MR. SQUILLS, IF YOU WOULD REMOVE THESE STAINS FROM MY DAUGHTER'S FACE. I CANNOT PERSUADE HER TO BE SUFFICIENTLY CAREFUL WITH HER PHOTOGRAPHIC CHEMICALS AND SHE HAS HAD A MISFOR: ·TUNE WITH HER NITRATE OF SILVER. UNLESS YOU CAN DO SOMETHING FOR HER, SHE WILL NOT BE FIT TO BE SEEN AT LADY MAYFAIR'S TONIGHT."

LONDON. PUBLISHED BY T. MC·LEAN.

3.7 Illustration from Cuthbert Bede, *Photographic Pleasures*, 1855

ideal was to be weak and childlike' (Davidoff in Thompson 1990: 84) women could become home-based hobbyists. 'Photography is the science for amateurs, equally adapted for ladies and gentlemen, which cannot be said of the generality of sciences', wrote Bede. Among the most celebrated photographers of the nineteenth century were comfortably off women with plenty of leisure and domestic help, who made use of their family and their immediate surroundings as raw material for their photographic works, rather than as family record. Julia Margaret Cameron's misty portraits and visions of cupids and angels embraced and transcended Victorian romanticism. Working-class women were needed as servants and helpers to service the middle-class domestic haven. Indeed, Julia Margaret Cameron's own favourite model was her assistant and maid, Mary Hillier. There were women working portraitists, too. John Werge remembers a 'Miss Wigley from London' who came to his home town in the North of England to practise daguerreo-typing as early as the mid-1840s (Werge 1890).

Informality and intimacy

The repertoire of personal imagery was changing. There had been an elegiac tone to much Victorian personal photography, evoked by the solemnity of middle-class portraiture and by the awareness that so many died young. Death was a central part of family life, and memorial pictures of the dead and dying were common. Babies who had died were dressed in their best and photographed in their mother's arms (Williams 1994). By the end of the century the emphasis was changing to a more present celebration of life and a taste for informality.

Photographic portraits had long been valued not only for their likeness to the sitter but also for the apparent escape from convention and the greater naturalness offered by the mechanical process. Bede had written that a calotype is a step beyond a painted portrait, for a painting has 'the artist's conventional face, his conventional attitude, his conventional background' (Bede 1855: 45). In 1899 Richard Penlake advised amateur photographers how to avoid 'perfect' pictures like those of a celebrity, who is so carefully made up and posed as to seem like a wax model, or of royalty, in which the very best pose is selected from many exposures and even then 'so worked up that scarcely a single part of the original negative prints at all' (Penlake 1899: 16).

Penlake also offered advice on tricks and optical effects, such as making double images – so that the sitter magically appears twice in the same picture – and **montaging** photographed heads on to caricatured bodies, but with the coming of hand-held cameras such conceits were on the way out. Albums of the 1880s, compared with those of the 1860s, show a much more relaxed style and closeness to the subjects. The movement and visual interest was now in the picture itself rather than in the decoration and arrangement of the pictures on the page. On one page in Sir Arnold Wilson's album, girls and boys in sailor suits and boaters are trying out a bicycle. They are 'captured' with their back to the camera, in mid-conversation with each other, pointing their own hand-held cameras and playing up to the camera, in a sequence of images which have much in common with the new 'candid' work by photographers Paul Martin and Frank Meadow Sutcliffe. 'Detective cameras' were now all the rage. They were tiny, unobtrusive or concealed so that pictures could be taken without the knowledge of the subject. For the first time there was the opportunity to take a different sort of personal picture, one where the contract between photographer and subject is brought under question. Secret observation was not always welcome to the observed. One local paper wrote in 1893,

> Several decent young men are forming themselves into a Vigilance Association with the purpose of thrashing cads with cameras who go around seaside places taking pictures of ladies emerging from the deep in the mournful garments peculiar to the British female bather ... I wish the new society stout cudgels and much success.
>
> (Coe and Gates 1977)

The working classes picture themselves

From the mid-nineteenth century the middle classes began to move to the new suburbs. Behind their privet hedges they protected themselves from the grime of industry and the potential immorality of the streets. But a large proportion of the working classes remained confined to the inner cities, in areas that were filthy and unhygienic. Their homes were not places of pleasurable relaxation and they could rarely afford the cost of representing themselves through photography. Although we twentieth-century seekers for the past may look at the family of Sir Arnold Wilson and see them as they would like to be seen, the image of the working classes we have inherited has been produced either by those, like Oscar Rejlander, who aestheticised and sentimentalised it, or those, like Thomas Annan, who documented it for the benefit of various official projects. Middle-class concern frequently took the form of outrage at the state of the less salubrious areas, often describing the people who lived there as distasteful, smelly and unhealthy like their dwellings. Photographer Willie Swift, who published *Leeds Slumdom* in 1897, turned his pictures into lantern slides and 'with the help of my daughters who sang suitable solos for us, we went up and down showing the dark places of the city, helping to create that healthy public opinion which eventually demanded clearance of the places shown' (Tagg 1988: 225).

Against this background, middle-class intervention became the context for another kind of personal photograph, often valued by those it represents although not necessarily made for their sake. Following the Education Acts of 1870 and 1893 which introduced universal schooling, some of the earliest photographs kept by working-class families are those depicting their children

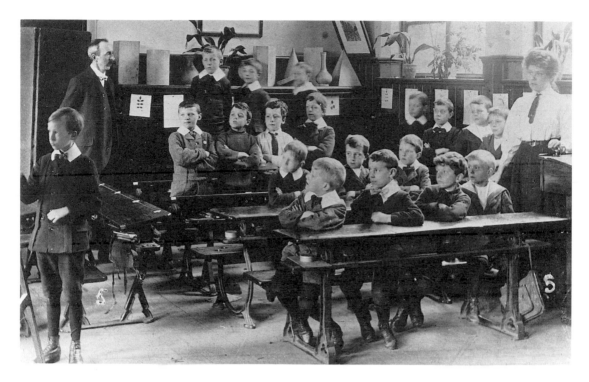

3.8 Pupils at St Mary's School, Moss Lane, Manchester, c. 1910

ranked behind wooden desks. In 1891 and 1893 respectively, the Church Lads' Brigade and the Boys' Brigade were launched to tidy up disorderly youngsters and get them off the streets. Photographs of clubs and bands present a disciplined image, modelled on those produced by the likes of Arnold Wilson and his regiment out in the hill stations of Muree.

However, the shortening of the working week and the coming of the Saturday day off led to new sporting and leisure activities, which working-class people could organise for themselves and which they were beginning to record for their own pleasure. Modest photographs from the 1890s onwards show the cycling group, the football supporters and, above all, the trip to the seaside, made possible by the expanding railway network. Opportunist photographers were now on hand for trippers who wanted their picture taken. Long before the **Polaroid**, the **tintype** could produce an instant metal positive for little boys with buckets and spades, toddlers perched on the photographer's donkey, and young women holding up their voluminous skirts as they paddle in the shallows. Photographers working in the new postcard format were ready with cheeky devices: 'The subject's head would join a monstrously fat body holding countless bottles of beer, or he would sit in a wooden aeroplane among painted stars' (Parr and Stasiak 1986: 13).

123

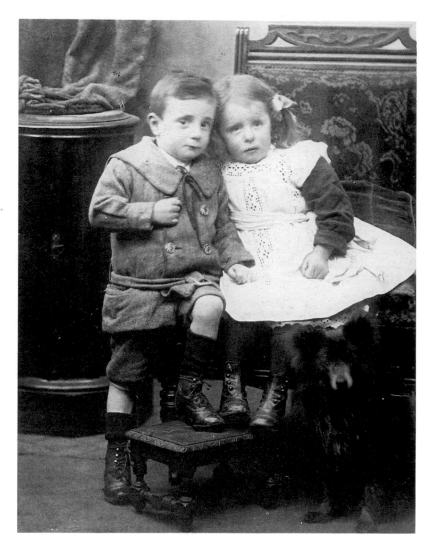

3.9 Studio photograph of Edward and May Bond, c. 1910

Not surprisingly, many of the poorer people continued to choose studio portraits where dignified or exotic backdrops would remove them from their poky homes. However, when the travelling photographer came by to set up his equipment in a local street, all the children of the neighbourhood ran after him to get their picture taken. 'Do not take too much notice of how they are taken', wrote Edward and May Bond's mother when she sent such a picture to her eldest son, 'for they look a bit untidy but I did not know

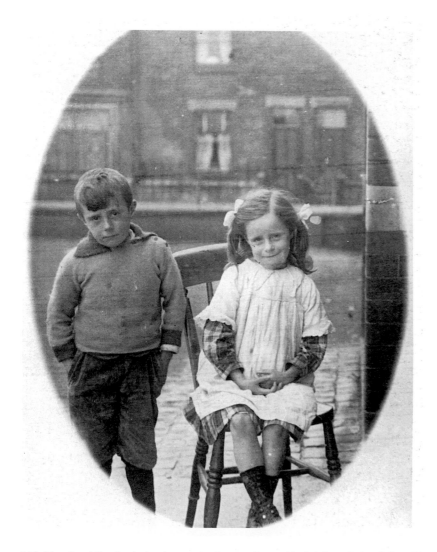

3.10 Edward and May Bond taken by a street photographer outside their home in Manchester, 1910

they were having their likenesses taken, but I thought I would buy one to let you have a look at their dear little faces' (figures 3.9 and 3.10).

By 1910 postcard sales were averaging 860 million per year (Pryce 1994: 143). As well as the usual repertoire of views, royalty, celebrities and tableaux, travelling photographers would set up their stall at a fair or a local beauty spot and offer to put *your* picture on a postcard. When people couldn't afford the threepence (1.5p) or so for a picture, clubs were set up to pay in

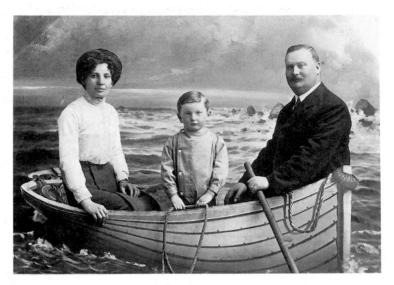

3.11 Holiday postcard from a Blackpool studio, 1910

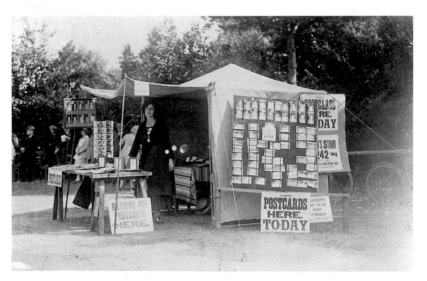

3.12 Mobile sales tent for Bailey's photographers, Bournemouth, _c._ 1910

instalments. These jobbing photographers came from a class background similar to those they served. Photography was fast becoming a medium in which working-class people could present themselves to each other.

Enterprising postcard photographers would visit local collieries, docks or mills, often producing the only photographic record of such workplaces

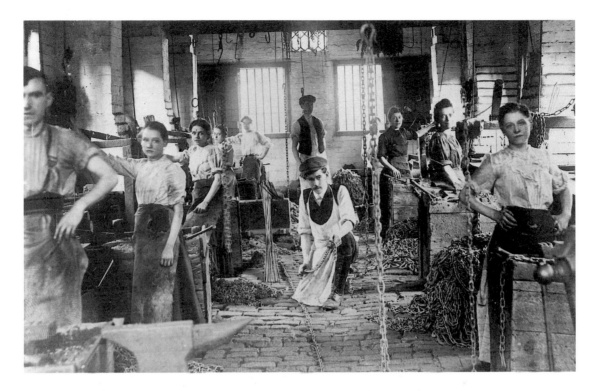

3.13 Black Country chain-makers, postcard, 7 August 1911

that exist. Others specialised in local events, such as strikes, lockouts or disasters. In 1910, John Leach, a local Whitehaven photographer, put together a montage of 124 of those killed in the appalling explosion and fire in the Wellington pit, as a memorial for the traumatised local community (Hiley 1983). Pictures of festivities were especially important to local people. At the Manchester Whit Walks, 'the working class was on display and they knew it' (Linkman and Warhurst 1982). Children who were untidy or had no clean clothes were kept well out of sight by their parents, and such pictures gave a very different impression of life in the inner city from the documentarist's view of picturesque misery. Photographs made for the benefit of the photographer, whether as artist or concerned reporter, stand in striking contrast to those made for the eyes of the people they represent.

Kodak and the mass market

It was not until George Eastman, an American photographic plate manufacturer, successfully produced sensitised paper in 1884, and followed it up with his hand-held camera in 1888, that the paraphernalia of tripods and glass plates could finally be put aside and home photography for all became a possibility. Eastman was an entrepreneur who sought to dominate the world market with a camera simple enough to be used by anyone. His crucial move was the separation of the *taking* of an image from the other stages involved in making a photograph. The smelly and difficult business of processing and printing was placed, conveniently out of sight, in the factory. The leisure activity for the home was supported by mass production and an army of employees – mostly women. Simultaneously, photography was both domesticated and industrialised. The celebrated Kodak camera, marketed in 1888, was a lump-ish wooden box with a hole at one end for the lens. When all the exposures had been made, and they amounted to some 100 on a single film, the whole thing was sent back to the Eastman factory for processing and reloading. The slogan 'you press the button, we do the rest' was to form the basis of personal photography for the next century.

Don Slater has argued that this drastic simplification amounted to depriving the new users of photography both of skills they might have put to more radical effect and a practical understanding of how photography creates meanings: 'Being separated from a knowledge of process, we have no sense of photography as manipulation, as a form of action, as a making sense through the manipulation of tools of representation and meaning' (Slater 1991: 54). However, looking back from the far end of the twentieth century, such an analysis underestimates the scale on which a *new* skill was introduced at the end of the nineteenth. Selecting, framing and achieving the content of a photographic image was now a possibility for those who would not otherwise have had either the time, the money or the inclination to engage in the complex processes of amateur photography. Don Slater's arguments also disregard Bede's reminder that personal photography is a *light* art. Photographic manipulation had long been part of the games people played with their cameras. Producing joke pictures and clowning in front of the lens are activities which have turned taking pictures into a pastime that secures friendship and insists on interaction between photographer and subject. This *is* collaboration in 'manipulating the tools of representation and meaning', even when it's just for fun.

In the twentieth century, the more individualist activities which the full photographic process demands have became part of the 'amateur photo-graphy' movement. Amateur photography has been a more masculine pastime, scornful of the snapshot's cheery refusal to concern itself with the complexities of the medium. Serious amateur practice has retained its fasci-nation with technology and its striving for aesthetic control. It has its own magazines, competitions and standards, and its long-lived aspiration to the sort of pictorialism fashionable amongst artist-photographers at the turn of the century.

Eastman's commercial operations rapidly reached from Rochester, New York to Harrow in Middlesex, and across the world. Developments rapidly followed each other. Daylight loading, where the celluloid film came in light-tight cartons, was an advance that meant there was no longer a need to send the whole camera back to the factory. 'Anybody can use it. Everybody will use it' ran the publicity, listing some of those possible users:

> *Travellers and tourists*: Use it to obtain a picturesque diary of their travels. . . . *Bicyclists and boating men*: Can carry it where a larger camera would be too burdensome. . . . *Ocean travellers*: Use it to photograph their fellow passengers on the steamship deck. . . . *Sportsmen and camping parties:* Use it to recall pleasant times spent in camp and wilderness . . . and *Lovers of fine animals*: use it to photograph their pets.

> (Taylor 1994)

The theme was looking outwards. The new photographer should make the most of new facilities for travelling – the train and the bicycle– and point their camera at the picturesque and the unusual.

Looking inwards towards the domestic and creating an exclusive record of your family was a parallel message, directed largely at the women of the middle classes. The new technology was *gendered*. Its simplicity of operation indicated that the woman of the house could use it, while the chemicals and other technical paraphernalia could be left to the men. And what activity could be more suitable for a woman than to photograph her children. 'Do you think baby will be quiet long enough to take her picture mama?' asks a cartoon-style advertisement from 1889, as a mother lines up her camera on her toddler, 'The Kodak will catch her whether she moves or not. It is as quick as a wink.' The prosperity of those late decades had brought women a new sense of independence. The passive 'angel in the house' was being superseded by the 'new woman', and those who took up their cameras were not just housebound mothers. 'Thousands of Birmingham girls are scattered about the holiday resorts of Britain this month, and a very large percentage of them are armed with cameras', wrote *Photographic News* in September 1905. 'It is as much a feminine as a masculine hobby these days, perhaps more so' (Coe and Gates 1977: 28).

The Kodak girl, her smart but comfortable black and white striped dress always blowing in some breeze or other, was introduced in 1910, and she continued to balance her camera casually in her hand in Kodak advertisements over the next thirty years. Variously drawn by many well-known artists, adapting to changing fashions in skirt length and hairstyle, she was seen perched on a rock pointing out to sea, or on a jetty watching the yachts come in, or picturing the children romping on the beach, always urging purchasers to 'Save your happy memories with a Kodak'. As time went on, even the cameras were feminised. In the late 1920s, Kodaks were produced in fashion colours – pinks, blues and greens – and 'Vanity Kodaks' came with a matching lipstick, mirror and compact holder.

The 'Box Brownie', launched in 1900, cost 5 shillings, a quarter of an average week's wages, which brought it into the reach of all but the poorest.[6] Now the advertisements were directed at children, too. The 'Brownie' was

6 Kenyon (1992) has a detailed discussion of income relative to price of cameras and film

129

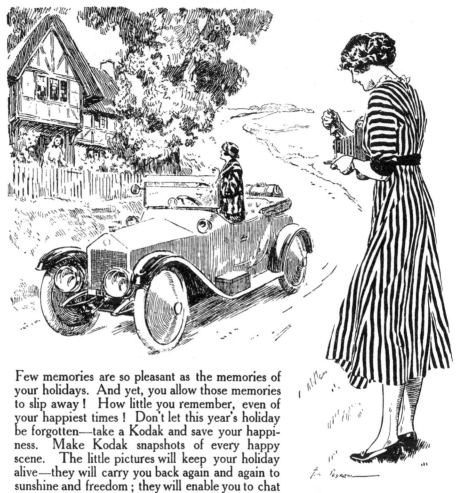

Few memories are so pleasant as the memories of your holidays. And yet, you allow those memories to slip away ! How little you remember, even of your happiest times ! Don't let this year's holiday be forgotten—take a Kodak and save your happiness. Make Kodak snapshots of every happy scene. The little pictures will keep your holiday alive—they will carry you back again and again to sunshine and freedom ; they will enable you to chat once more with your jolly companions, and to enjoy another hearty laugh over the fun you had. Remember, you can learn to use a Kodak in half-an-hour.

The only holiday that lasts forever is the holiday with a
Kodak

Ask your nearest Kodak dealer to show you the latest models.
Kodak Ltd., Kingsway, London, W.C. 2.

3.14 **Kodak** advertisement, 1920

a camera for little folk and could, the advertisements claimed, 'be operated by any school boy or girl'. Like the other Kodaks, it was not only easy to use but was guaranteed to be successful. However inept the operator, its pictures will come out. Brownie albums were provided, with spaces ready prepared for slotting in a sequence of the snapshots.

Photography was not the only medium to shift from small-scale craft production to industrial production for a mass market in the last decades of the nineteenth century. Universal literacy, new printing techniques and the entrepreneurial ambitions of such men as Northcliffe and Rothermere meant that popular newspapers were launched for an unprecedentedly large readership. The advertising industry was rapidly establishing itself, since the mass production of all sorts of goods for domestic consumption required wider and more innovative marketing. Photography was at the centre of these developments and was to become the heart of the intensely visual popular culture of the twentieth century. After the *Daily Illustrated Mirror* (today's *Daily Mirror*) was launched in 1903 as the first newspaper to use photographic illustrations, the popular press came to depend on photography as an indispensable part of *news* reporting, and even more importantly, as central to their *entertainment* role (Holland 1997). Celebrity and royalty pictures, which in the mid-nineteenth century found their way into *carte-de-visite* albums, were now to be found in newspapers and later in the burgeoning consumer magazines. From the latter half of the twentieth century, the coming of full-colour printing first in magazines then in newspapers has meant that the whole range of fashion, gardening, cooking, travel and tourism, celebrities and music have been part of a light-hearted environment of high-quality photographic imagery which we now take for granted. Popular photography is all around us and it exerts its influence on contemporary private photography.

Back in the early years of the century the new domestic photographers had fewer models to imitate. As municipal housing became available for the less well off, the working classes were beginning to follow the familial ideal established – and indeed enforced – by the Victorian middle classes (Davidoff in Thompson 1990: 106). With the coming of gas lighting and piped water, working-class homes were both more comfortable and more consciously 'respectable'. The elaborately furnished and scrupulously protected front parlour was 'not for relaxation, but a controlled and formal social environment' (Daunton in Thompson 1990: 207). As the lifestyles of the different classes grew closer together, the snapshot style could indicate a casual and informal mode which gave a democratic veneer to social divisions. Val Williams describes the relaxed pictures of the little Princesses, Margaret and Elizabeth, taken in the 1930s, as a studied model to which the whole nation could aspire (Williams 1986: 72). The poorer the community, the less directly are their daily activities reflected in the pictures they keep. Those who lived in the inner city tenements remained anxious to record the formality and dignity of their life, not its more distressing moments.

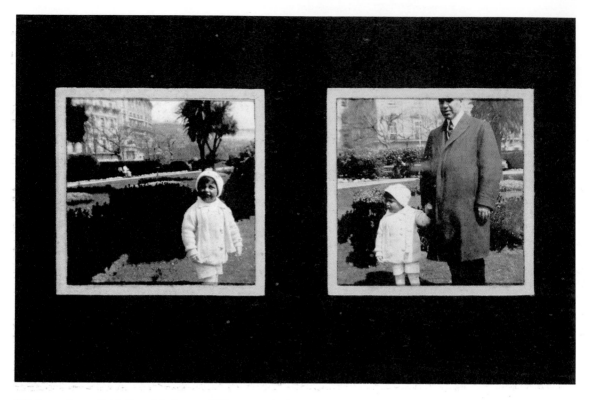

3.15 A page from a Kodak 'Brownie' album, c. 1900

With the coming of the First World War there was a boom in camera sales, reaching its peak in 1917 as families bought cameras to record soldiers leaving for the war (Coe and Gates 1977: 34). Portraits of young men in uniform, many of whom never returned, make a poignant moment in most twentieth-century family collections. The increase in working-class incomes paradoxically brought by the war meant that, by 1916, the *Kodak Trade Circular* could advise retailers that

> the people of the working class could be looked on as a likely buyer . . . it may even be said that they are better able to appreciate the Kodak than some of the people who usually buy it. The craftsman who works a high speed tool and who has to work to very fine measurements is just the right type of man to admire the mechanical excellence of the Kodak- . . . If your shop is near a working class neighbourhood, think this over.

> (Coe 1989: 69)

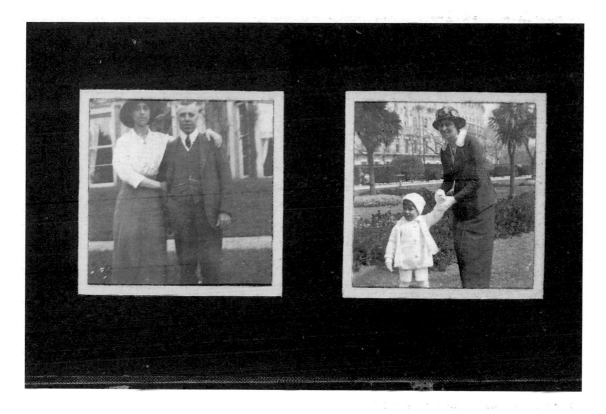

The supersnap in Kodaland

Following each of the major upheavals of the twentieth century, 'the family' was reasserted as a force for reconstruction and social cohesion. During the Second World War, for a brief period, popular photography included high-quality photojournalism developed by *Picture Post*, which concerned itself with the 'home front', with public life and communal responsibility as well as with military campaigns; but in the postwar period, just as in the years following the First World War, a reconstructed economy was based on domestic consumption and the domestic ideal. This required, in particular, women's willing return to the home to become the pivot of family life, relinquishing their public presence in the workplace and revaluing the ideal of a private sphere where political forces appear irrelevant. Twentieth-century family photography, with its resolute insistence on the creation of *happy* memories, has determinedly reflected this mood, in which politics and world affairs, even the most disruptive, are pushed to the background of public consciousness (Taylor 1994: 141).

Despite the depression, it was during the inter-war years of the 1920s and 1930s that a home-based family idyll took hold in the mock Tudor, semidetatched suburbs of English towns. Here the rising working class found for the first time 'such homes of which thousands have only dreamed' (Holland 1991). The stiff front parlour became a living room designed for leisure use and rigid gender and age divisions gave way to companionate marriage and demonstrative parenting (Davidoff in Thompson 1990: 116). The domestic ideal, built up over the nineteenth century as a space that would be calmer and morally superior to the turbulent world outside, was being narrowed down to a much smaller family, made up of two parents and their younger children, who aimed to lead a pleasurable rather than dutiful life. A state of mind was coming about in which the satisfaction of each *individual's* desire for comfort and satisfaction would not seem incompatible with the mutual obligations demanded by family groups. The increasing relaxation and informality appearing in family snapshots echoed that change.

The image of the child became the central icon of family life. By the 1930s the two- or three-child family was the norm, which meant that individual attention could be given to each child and there was more time for birthday celebrations, Christmas trees and the snapshots which accompany these ceremonies. The domestic camera was confirmed as a ritualised element in joint celebrations (Musello 1979). As well as the visible markers for home-centred values, children signified the aspirational optimism of a century dominated by the newly prosperous working and lower-middle classes, whose horizons seemed to be ever widening. The modest pictures of the period between the wars give off a sense of hope, a belief in progress and in the possibility of a comfortable life for all.

Despite the ideology of 'home' as a warm, familial centre, most collections of personal pictures are, in fact, dominated by time spent *away* from the home. As well as becoming closer and more inward-looking, the family was also becoming *mobile* (Slater 1995b: 132). The gradual spread of motor-car ownership meant that holidays and days out could be more private, enjoyed by the couple or the young family or the noisy gregarious group. The domestication of the *un*familiar, by capturing it on film, has remained one of the most important uses of snapshot cameras since Kodak's first appeal to tourists and travellers. A site is not a sight until we've snapped it and made it ours, often by placing a familiar face – whether travelling companion or family member – in an unfamilar place. Many of Kodak's early advertisements addressed themselves to those who set out in search of the impressive and the educational, but these adult activities take second place to trips and holidays which have become an indispensable element of family pleasures. Sightseeing may be for adults alone, but the centre of Kodak's advertising, from the Kodak girl on the windswept British beach to the sun-saturated images from the Costa del Sol, has been the child-centred family holiday.

In the second half of the century, increasing prosperity, together with the introduction of package tours and the establishment of an energetic tourist industry, meant that overseas holidays have gradually become the norm. But,

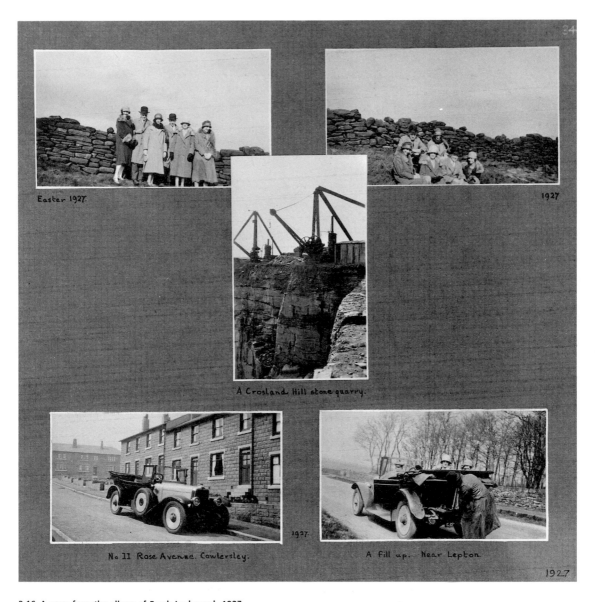

Easter 1927.

1927

A Crosland Hill stone quarry.

No 11 Rose Avenue. Cowlersley.

1927.

A fill up. Near Lepton.

1927

3.16 A page from the album of Frank Lockwood, 1927
Frank Lockwood was a Birmingham watercolourist and designer for Cadbury Brothers

while personal collections became filled with photos of Mum, Dad and the kids in ever more distant locations, pictures of *home*-based daily life emerged in *commercial* imagery. The expansion of packaged foods and branded goods brought new outlets for visual images which showed what a happily consuming family *should* be like. Commercial photographers studied how to create ever more convincing pictures of appetising food consumed by ecstatic and grateful youngsters and of well-groomed mothers delighting in their newly technologised kitchens. Such images, perfected for advertisements and promotional design, were routinely delivered to the breakfast table on corn-flakes packages and baby food jars, and greeted shoppers with their serried ranks on the shelves of the early supermarkets. The 1960s burst into commercial colour as the burgeoning products for domestic use were promoted by advertising-based supplements to the Sunday papers and an expanding range of consumer magazines which drew on the new, high-quality colour printing techniques (Crawley 1989). The lush photography on their feature pages came to cover every aspect of domestic life – from *Home and Garden* to *Mother and Baby* (Holland 1992). Snapshots and consumer imagery were fast becoming two sides of the same coin.

In 1963 Kodak produced 'a complete new system of snapshot photography' when it brought out its 'Instamatic' series of small reliable cameras (Ford 1989: 141). It was the result of ten years of research which sought to make snapshooting even easier. Cheap colour printing and faster film stocks made it increasingly possible for home photographers to emulate the sophisticated images they were seeing all around them. Snapshot photographs now came in 'bright, beautiful colours and subtle shades – like life', in the words of a Kodak advertisement from 1969. Once more, women were the target purchasers. Unlike the 'male jewellery' of massive lenses and proliferating accessories, the 'Instamatic' removed the technological mystique. Cartridge loading and fixed focus made it so simple that 'even Mum could use it'. Advertisements encouraged a wider range of subject-matter and ever more casual and informal pictures, catching 'the moment as it happens'. Automatic built-in flash meant that colour pictures could be taken indoors, in dull weather or in the rain. 'Memories are made of this', was the slogan. Through hundreds of glowing, full-colour pictures, a couple could now confidently record every precious moment, from the birth of their first baby to their grandchildren and beyond. The last quarter of the twentieth century became the age of the 'supersnap in Kodaland'.

Those are the words of Jennifer Ransom Carter, advertising photographer for Kodak Ltd from 1970 to 1984. She produced many of those joyful images which offer themselves in advertisements and on print wallets for snap-shooters to emulate. She 'tried to get pictures which were as close as possible to those that people would have liked to take for themselves'. In Majorca she photographed holiday-makers as well as models. Promotional pictures 'had to have a universal appeal, so that people would say "*I* want to take a picture like that . . ." We aimed to tread a line between reality and unreality as we produced a professional interpretation of the family snap.'[7] And, of course, the pictures people want to keep are those that record the 'happy memories' not the messy reality. It is hardly surprising that family collections include annual pictures of Christmas dinners and birthday teas, but hardly any of the daily meal or the act of peeling the potatoes or washing up. No children's party is complete without snapshots, but crying, bullying or sulky children are definitely not for posterity.

As Leonore Davidoff has pointed out, as the family became more inward-turned, it came to contain 'the most immediate experience of love and hate, power and dependence, interpersonal attention and interpersonal violence that most people would experience in their lifetime' (Davidoff in Thompson 1990: 129). It was that gap between the enrichment and proliferation of ideal images of family life and the complexity of its lived reality which led to the damning critiques of the 1970s, particularly from the youthful and energetic women's movement. Unhappy childhoods, broken families, child abuse, disgruntled teenagers and the persistence of poverty are only a few of the all too common experiences *not* recorded in domestic pictures. The family image came to be seen as riven with fractures and contradictions. Divided, individualised, hypocritical, it was argued that 'the family' itself was coming up against its limits.

Many commentators have stressed the cohesive function of family photography, but the increasing use of snapshots to celebrate time out and time off has meant that fun in Kodaland, seeking individual pleasures, may well be at odds with family obligations. A hint of disruption hovers nervously just below the surface of so many personal pictures. Holidays are a time for throwing off constraints, a time of sexual adventure and illicit indulgence, and in the snapshots many such moments are for ever preserved. Pictures of leisure activities increasingly include the **carnivalesque** – cross-dressing for the last-night party, sidling up to the Greek waiter, the club outing when everyone was impossibly drunk, the risqué nude image. Just as Mediterranean food and street cafés have spilled back on to previously drab British streets, the holiday mood of these snapshots remains as a reproach to dutiful lifestyles. Local pubs now cover their walls with beery pictures which verge on the lewd, where skirts are raised, the wrong husbands kiss the wrong wives, and family values are playfully – and sometimes really– put to the test.

PATHS UNHOLY AND DEEDS WITHOUT A NAME?

Twentieth-century contemplations

Giving an account of twentieth-century personal photography is a complex task. Nineteenth-century pictures are beyond living memory. They can be treated on their own terms – as documents, as aesthetic creations or as someone else's story. Twentieth-century pictures are part of our lived

7 Information from conversations with Jennifer Ransom Carter.

experience and hint at meanings which are tantalisingly within our grasp. Almost everyone has their own collection of pictures – sometimes in albums, sometimes organised in packets or drawers, sometimes just scattered around in a disorderly fashion but impossible to throw away. Every collection is different, every example unique. It is no longer enough to outline a social history of such images, since any history must now include interpretations and contextual information brought by their owners and users.[8] These pictures do not stand alone but are enriched by memory, conversation, anecdote and whispered scandal. They are truly personal because they are part of the accumulated history of people currently alive, who know all too well that memories are not exclusively happy ones. Above all, they include pictures of oneself as a child and at earlier periods of one's life, pictures which carry a burden of significance that only their subjects can comprehend. It is hardly surprising that collections of such photographs hold great personal importance. In an American study of people's 'most cherished objects', many respondents broke down when describing those pictures they felt they could never part with (Csikszentmihalyi and Rochberg-Halton 1992: 68), and yet for writer Teshome Gabriel, a snapshot of himself as a young man, given to him by his mother when he returned to his birthplace in Ethiopia after an absence of thirty-two years, proved to be an 'intolerable gift' (Gabriel 1995).

Because photography in all its forms holds the past before our eyes with unprecedented verisimilitude, a sense of the recent past, including one's own, is more vividly present to those now living than to any previous generation. Yet no photograph can give a clear and straightforward insight into the past. Personal photography, as we have seen, has a history of its own which meets up with and overlaps with social history but needs to be explored on its own terms. While many individuals bring to their personal collection the sort of emotional investment shown by those elderly Americans in the 'cherished objects' study, these are their responses as *users* of the images. To make sense of pictures which are not our own, we must change gear to become *readers* of the pictures and engage in a textual and **semiotic** exploration, paying attention to cultural as well as photographic **codes**. As we will see, many writers have argued that one may become a reader of one's own pictures, too; teasing out meanings that go beyond questions of factual memory and emotional response, giving a different sort of understanding to the history they represent.

Possibly the most frequent – and most important – image in anyone's snapshot collection is the simple shot of a subject presenting themselves to the camera, standing, perhaps in front of a famous monument or beside a car or house, but basically just *being there*. Yet this is the least readable of images, depending heavily on knowledge of the subject, on why the picture was taken and on its context. As Stuart Hall pointed out in relation to portraits of black Britons from the 1950s – dressed in their best and presenting themselves with great dignity – such innocence will always be deceptive,

8 At the Documentary Photography Archive, Manchester, curator Audrey Linkman creates a context for the collection of about 70,000 photographs copied from local family albums by supporting them with detailed information about the subject and the photographer.

subject as it is to pressures from outside the frame (Hall 1991). The calmest portrait may offer evidence of recovery from illness or survival against the odds, and the most conventional of snaps may conceal dreadful abuse (Williams 1994: 31). Discrimination, persecution and social injustice are rarely explicit. 'How will you understand your past when all you have is photographs?' asks Ilan Ziv in his film about memories of the Holocaust.[9]

A rereading and re-viewing of family pictures came with the radical history movements of the 1970s, which brought different ways of understanding history, more sensitive to the type of information carried by everyday documents, including personal snaps. Not only academic historians, but also reminiscence groups, women's groups and local historians, set out to challenge the politics of traditional history writing by looking at the past from a different perspective. There was a desire to write history from below, to listen to ordinary people's accounts and to recapture the texture of ordinary lives. Those who had been hidden from history – women, black people, working-class people and many minorities – insisted on writing their own histories that ran counter to the dominant view of events, and they used personal photographs as part of the process. Arguing that women's stories have been concealed by the conventional ways of recording history, women writers drew on personal pictures to fill those absences. Projects included getting elderly women to recall their times at work, and tracing female ancestors (Stanley 1991; Grey 1991). Radical photographic movements – Camerawork, Hackney Flashers and others – joined in a campaigning attack which took on convention, capitalism and the ideology of the family.

To look back at personal pictures and tease out their meanings has meant that various different approaches to history have been brought into play. First, *community* histories have been recognised; histories of specific groups of many different kinds, say the working class from the Northeast of England or recent immigrants from Bangladesh. Personal photographs expect to be understood within an interpretive community, a group of users who share the same understandings of pictures which record and confirm valued rites of passage and culturally significant moments (Bhabha 1990: 17). Pictures of events such as anniversaries, religious holidays and weddings are symbols of social integration. They have different significations for different cultural groups, who bring an instant recognition to the details by which the meaning of the event 'subtly overwhelms the personal aspect of the picture and fills it with allusions to tribe and ritual' (**Hirsch 1981: 59**).

Even while acknowledging such visible community cues, *family* stories may cut across communal meanings. Julia Hirsch discusses wedding photographs of mixed marriages which must find a way of dealing with two sets of cultural conventions. Family histories often tell of conflict with a community or marginality to it, of migration and mobility across the generations, so that the photographs that accompany family members shift in and out of different contexts of understanding (Solanke 1991). On investigation, many people

9 *Tango of Slaves* written and directed by Ilan Ziv, *TX 31* January 1994, Channel Four Television.

JULIA HIRSCH (1981) **Family Photography: Context, Meaning and Effect**, New York: Oxford University Press

The influence of Hollywood even got to Iran in the 1950s
Serge's Uncle, Haroot in striking pose on the right!

Below, Serge's father Samuel Approx. 1940.
"The adventurer" with rifle and ammunition. Ready to go Tiger hunting in Northern Iran and gold prospecting.
Didn't get a tiger – or any gold!

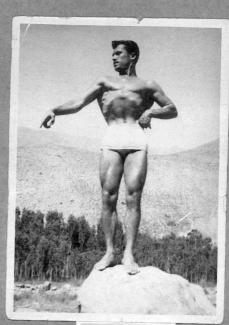

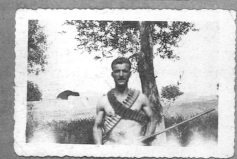

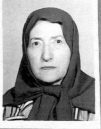

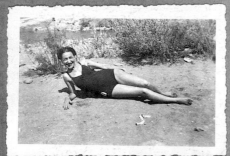

Galipse was, single, educated and a career woman (Matron of a large hospital in the capital Tehran)
How sad that 40 years after the first picture was taken she was forced to wear the Muslim "chador" after Khomeini's Islamic revolution.
Even though, in fairness. they are allowed to remain Christians (Armenian Orthodox) They must conform to the Muslim dress code.

Above and right. Galipse. Serge's aunt on his mothers side.
The influence of Wallis Simpson obviously reached Iran in the 1940's!

3.17 From the album of Ursula Kocharian

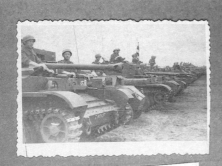

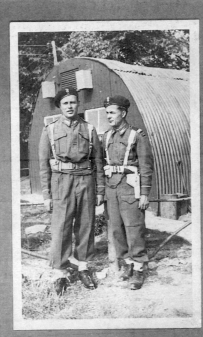

My father (standing, left.) 1942
Fighting with the Brits after
fleeing Poland.
Photo above - one of the many
Army Photos taken by my
father during the war. This
one is the English Cromwell Tanks
1944/45
Afterwards he settled in England
with his Swiss bride and
had Barbara (my sister) in
1951.

And here they are, our children Alex & Joe (both named after
Great Grandfathers) with Serge. Both born in Bradford, W. Yorks
and only here as a result of so many of our family being
uprooted from their countries of origin because of political events.
World War II on my family's side and the 1914 Armenian Massacre
and 1979 Iranian revolution on Serge's

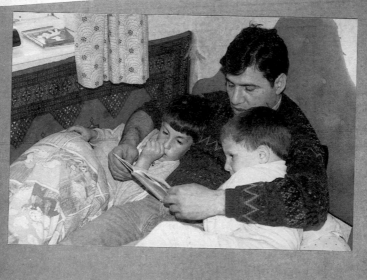

find that their stories tell of hybridity and cultural mixing. Ursula Kocharian put together an album to show the complex ancestry of her sons, born in Bradford because 'so many families were uprooted from their countries of origin due to political events'. By 'reading' the pictures, and referring to influences from popular culture, she produced a document in which cultural, political and family changes are displayed. Ursula's husband, Serge, comes from Iran, where his Armenian family fled from the Turkish massacres of 1918. Her own father came from Poland to fight alongside the British during the Second World War; his album, which he had published at his own cost, was a record of the Polish regiment's campaigns across Germany. The long pressure of political history, invisible in the simplicity of the family photographs of the two boys, has shaped the family's movements, through wars, revolutions and enforced migration.

Just as family histories fit uneasily with histories of communities, *personal* histories remain part of, yet often at odds with, the histories of families. These three different modes rub up against each other, each one important in its own right, but questioned and often invalidated by the others in a recurring dissonance that frequently underlies discussions of personal photographs.

The more ceremonial the occasion, confirming familial and communal rituals, the more important it is that certain rules are followed in the production of the photographs that mark the event. Weddings must provide pictures of the bride and groom together, dressed in the clothes that make the occasion special. 'We do not care whether it was taken, like so many other ceremonial photographs, the day before the wedding or three hours later; we care only that the man and woman look like bride and groom and uphold the decorum of formal weddings,' writes Julia Hirsch (1981: 62). This is one occasion for which a professional photographer (who knows the photographic rules and will abide by them) is usually engaged, for the power of such photographs is precisely in their embrace of convention. Nevertheless, recognising their role in creating cohesion often goes along with resisting that cohesion at a personal level. Pictures which live up to expectations give enormous pleasure precisely *because* their familiar structure is able to contain the tension between an ideal image and the ambivalence of lived experience. They offer a framework within which understandings of the various realities we inhabit may come into play. While the historian is looking for the truths of the past, the user of a personal collection is engaging in acts of recognition, reconstructing their own past and setting a personal narrative against more public accounts (Walkerdine 1991; Watney 1991; Kuhn 1995).

While family pictures may, on the surface, act as social documents, a closer examination reveals the complex of interrelations and scandals that weave through the soap opera of personal life (Spence 1991; Martin 1991; Isherwood 1988). The placing of divorced spouses, children from a previous marriage, disgraced relatives, gay relationships, even awkward and sulky teenagers, poses problems for those who want their pictures to abide by the conventions. The very hints and puzzles they contain have enticed both detectives of family history and those who want to explore the ways in which their present identity carries the weight of the past. Personal pictures may act as an emotional centre for individual self-exploration. Autobiography, 'memory work' and forms of self-expression based on settling accounts with the past have become central to feminist approaches. The disjunction between image and remembered experience, the uncertain borderline between fantasy and memory, the tracing of identity and a sense of self back through one's parents and their sense of *them*selves, the opportunity to relive or re-enact the past – these have all been ways in which family photographs have been used to recapture personal history and make sense of individual lives (Kuhn 1995; Spence 1987).

The work of photographer and writer Jo Spence has shed new light on the construction of complex identities, drawing on personal photographs and family albums for her own, intensely personal work. She began by using the snapshots of her childhood to draw attention to the codes of domestic photography. At the age of five, her mother photographed her with her bubble curls and coy smile to look just like Shirley Temple. When she became a teenager she herself took up the pose of the glamorous pin-ups of 1950s cinema. In her exhibition *Beyond the Family Album* at the Hayward Gallery in London in 1979, she offered her awareness of the sickness, shame and struggles of everyday life as a commentary on the conventional smiles of the snapshots themselves. Annette Kuhn has written that they seemed 'conspicuous by their ordinariness . . . but in aggregate the work felt utterly out of the ordinary' (Spence 1995: 20). It contributed to a revaluation of photographic genres, so that snapshots could no longer be ignored as trivial and irrelevant.

Jo Spence went on to explore her childhood experience in her own photographic work. In collaboration with Rosy Martin she staged possible family pictures in a dramatic performance of concealed relationships and submerged emotion. The work developed into a practice she described as a form of therapy, working through traumatic moments and reliving the intensities of childhood usually accessible only through **psychoanalysis** (Spence 1987). Her work was embattled and engaged, determined to explore the taboos and hidden truths which bedevil family histories. She dealt with class, as she reflected on her working-class upbringing and the half-articulated exclusions that implied; she dealt with gender, approaching the world from an uncompromising feminist perspective with a campaigning edge; and she dealt with subjectivity, always 'putting myself in the picture' in a form of 'politicised exhibitionism' (Spence 1987; Spence 1995: 94). Her most striking images represent her struggles with illness as she faced an operation for breast cancer in 1981. In a series of pictures that were also an ironic commentary on the process of photography itself, she asserted her right to define her own body. Ten years later she faced the ultimate taboo with her approaching death from

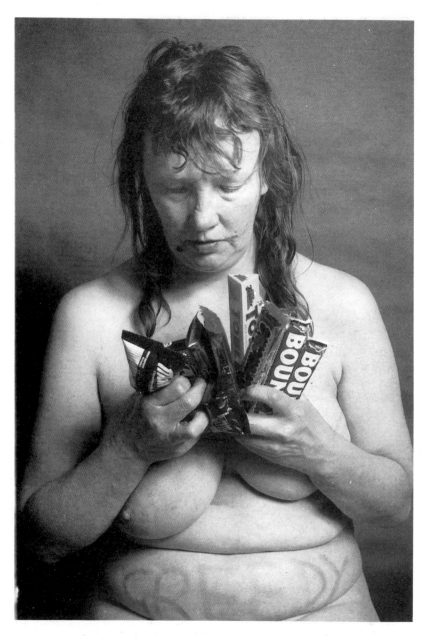

3.18 Jo Spence/Dr Tim Sheard, Greedy – I recreate my journey into emotional eating, a rebellion against parental disapproval, 1989

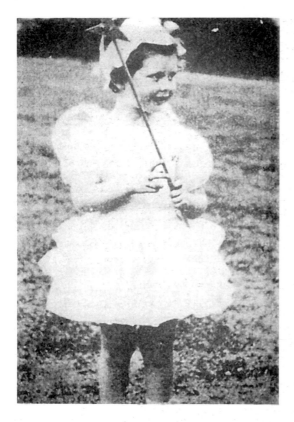

3.19 Valerie Walkerdine as the Bluebell Fairy

leukaemia, but the project of photography remained with her until the last. In one of the few pictures which show her in the hospice where she died, she is lying to one side of the bed, almost pushed off its edge by the dozens of photographic prints spread across it. Her revelation of inner pain and her dialogue with her own body proved an inspiration for many and gave an impetus to a new generation of women photographers.

Other writers, including Annette Kuhn and Valerie Walkerdine, have also used the snapshots of their childhood to tease out the ways in which personal memory and childhood fantasy overlap, and how both interleave with the social and with popular culture. Such memories are rarely comfortable. Looking at pictures of oneself as a child can be a disturbing experience, recognising in the calm exterior of an image the traces of a turbulent inner world. In a series of articles using the insights of psychoanalysis, Valerie Walkerdine writes of an obsession with sickness, death and incestuous sexuality as she repeatedly re-contextualises a snapshot of herself in carnival dress as the 'Bluebell Fairy': 'Even when the images of myself present me as the feminised object of the male gaze, as a pretty little girl who smiles for the camera, there is a terrible rage underneath' (Walkerdine 1991: 40). Critical work like that of Jo Spence and Valerie Walkerdine lays bare the trauma of an ordinary childhood. Revelations about child abuse and family discord indicate that worse horrors may underlie the aspirational surface of the innocent family snap. Family secrecy can give way to family horror story.

Yet late twentieth-century traumas do not only come from within. With the expansion of poverty and the decay of inner city neighbourhoods, the happy memories promised by the Kodak snap are a remote possibility for the disaffected youngsters and struggling single parents living on desolate estates that have been abandoned by a shrinking welfare state. The privatised pleasure-loving family is looking increasingly defensive as the gap widens between the comfortably off and the dispossessed. Family images which have come to epitomise 1990s Britain are the school photos of the 11-year-old boys who murdered toddler James Bulger, and the fuzzy image from a surveillance camera which failed to prevent that atrocity (Kember 1995).

Despite the privacy of family discourse, the public narratives of community, religion, ethnicity and nation cannot be put aside. As the twentieth century collapses, the public media have themselves been looking back on personal upheavals suffered during those years. Millions now watch television programmes that trace the secret histories of ordinary people, often using their personal snaps. In the 1990s it has become common for hitherto unspoken memories to be given public expression, be they of the repressed sexuality of the early years of the century or of global traumas, like those undergone by survivors of the Holocaust or Hiroshima. Often, such dreadful memories can only be given voice many years after the event, and the pictures treasured by those who tell their story have been used not to remember but to forget.

As Ursula Kocharian's snapshots show, for huge numbers of people migration and dispossession are part of recent history. Journeys always disrupt borders, and more journeys are made from economic pressure or are enforced by war or political rupture than they are purely for pleasure. Where do family albums record the memories of atrocities past? Only in sudden disappearances and truncated lives. Violence is only hinted at in the pictures of 'the old country' kept by immigrants and refugees. Whether from Czechoslovakia, Hungary and Poland, or from Somalia, Sri Lanka or Colombia, the previous generations who seem so composed in their portraits have so often perished in wars or concentration camps. And yet, the second generation is often ashamed of its parents: they speak with an accent, their food is different, they cling to the past and their memories are a burden to their children. Their parents look like other people's postcards (Kalogeraki 1991: 40).

Yet, snapshots can be objects which enable the ego to 'bear the difference between now and then',[10] and more comfortable generations are able for

10 Quoted from a lecture given by Mark Cousins at the Architectural Association, London 1994.

the first time to look back at traumas suffered by their relatives. They include middle-aged people like the sole survivor from a cultured Jewish family in Slovakia, who set about making a 'family album' which attempted to piece together obliterated family histories. Andrew Dewdney launched an investigation into hybridity and mixing with a group of teachers and students in Sydney. They were the children of immigrants to Australia from Greece (driven by economic necessity), and Vietnam (driven by war). He himself is from the English port of Bristol, made rich by the slave trade. In the resulting 'extended and shared family albums', the experiences of the native Australians proved as alienating as those first generation white Australians (Dewdney 1991).

Perhaps personal photography has become too knowing. It remains a minor discourse, a knowledge without authority, but we would do well to attend to what it has to tell us. Historians who take note of the details of everyday life and of ordinary people's accounts, feminist writers and photographers, artists of various kinds, are all now making use of personal pictures. Recently many gallery photographers have taken the world of inner experience as their subject-matter, sometimes incorporating snapshots or imitating their style (Williams 1994).

The German artist Joachim Schmidt could, perhaps, have the last word. He collects snapshots, millions of them, sent to him from all over the world. His project is to display them in new contexts; sometimes as multiples of images that have an uncanny resemblance to each other, sometimes compared with the work of prestigious photographers. Here are picture faces of someone's old friends, slight but powerful images whose meanings are for ever lost, because their context has been lost. Personal pictures are also about forgetting.

BIBLIOGRAPHY

KEY TEXTS

Barthes, R. (1982) *Camera Lucida*, London: Jonathan Cape
Coe, B. and Gates, P. (1977) *The Snapshot Photograph: The Rise of Popular Photography 1888–1939*, London: Ash and Grant
Ford, C. (1989) *The Story of Popular Photography*, Bradford: Century Hutchinson Ltd/National Museum of Photography, Film and Television
Hirsch, J. (1981) *Family Photography: Context, Meaning and Effect*, New York: Oxford University Press
Isherwood, S. (1988) *The Family Album*, London: Broadcasting Support Services
Kenyon, D. (1992) *Inside Amateur Photography*, London: Batsford
Linkman, A. (1993) *The Victorians: Photographic Portraits*, London: Tauris Parke Books
Linkman, A. and Warhurst, C. (1982) *Family Albums*, Manchester: Manchester Polytechnic. A fully illustrated exhibition catalogue with an introduction
Parr, M. and Stasiak, J. (1986) *'The Actual Boot': The Photographic Post-card Boom 1900–1920*, Bradford: A.H. Jolly (Editorial) Ltd/National Museum of Photography, Film and Television. Exhibition catalogue and introduction
Slater, D. (1983) 'Marketing Mass Photography' in H. Davis and P. Walton (eds) *Language,*

Image, Media, Oxford: Blackwell

Spence, J. (1987) *Putting Myself in the Picture*, London: Camden Press

—— (1995) *Cultural Sniping*, London: Routledge

Spence, J. and Holland, P. (eds) (1991) *Family Snaps: The Meanings of Domestic Photography*, London: Virago

Tagg, J. (1988) *The Burden of Representation: Essays on Photographies and Histories*, London: Macmillan, especially chapter 1, 'A Democracy of the Image: Photographic Portraiture and Commodity Production'

Taylor, J. (1994) *A Dream of England: Landscape, Photography and the Tourist's Imagination*, Manchester: Manchester University Press

Thompson, F.M.L. (ed.) (1990) *The Cambridge Social History of Britain 1750–1850*, Vol. 2, *People and Their Environment*, Cambridge: Cambridge University Press

Williams, V. (1986) *Women Photographers. The Other Observers 1900 to the Present*, London: Virago

OTHER REFERENCES

Barrett, M. and McIntosh, M. (1982) *The Anti-Social Family*, London: Verso

Bede, C. (1855) *Photographic Pleasures*, London

Bernstein, B. (1971) *Class, Codes and Control*, Vol. 1, *Theoretical Studies Towards a Sociology of Language*, London: Routledge & Kegan Paul

Bhabha, H. (1990) 'Novel Metropolis', *New Statesman and Society*, 9 February

Burgin, V. (1982) *Thinking Photography*, London: Macmillan

Chanan, M. (1996) *The Dream That Kicks*, London: Routledge

Coe, B. (1989) 'Roll Film Revolution' in C. Ford (ed.) *The Story of Popular Photography*, Bradford: Century Hutchinson Ltd/National Museum of Photography, Film and Television

Crawley, G. (1989) 'Colour Comes to All' in C. Ford (ed.) *The Story of Popular Photography*, Bradford: Century Hutchinson Ltd/National Museum of Photography, Film and Television

Csikszentmihalyi, M. and Rochberg-Halton, E. (1992) *The Meaning of Things: Domestic Symbols and the Self*, Cambridge: Cambridge University Press

Davidoff, L. and Hall, C. (1976) 'The Charmed Circle of Home' in J. Mitchell and A. Oakley (eds) *The Rights and Wrongs of Women*, Harmondsworth: Penguin

Dewdney, A. (1991) 'More Than Black and White: The Extended and Shared Family Album' in J. Spence and P. Holland (eds) *Family Snaps: The Meanings of Domestic Photography*, London: Virago

Drake, M. and Finnegan, R. (eds) (1994) *Sources and Methods: A Handbook*, Vol. 4 of *Studying Family and Community History: 19th and 20th Centuries*, Cambridge: Cambridge University Press/Open University

Felman, S. and Laub, D. (1992) *Testimony: Crises of Witnessing in Literature, Psychoanalysis and History*, London: Routledge

Gabriel, T. (1995) *The Intolerable Gift*, unpublished conference paper, London: BFI

Geraghty, C. (1991) *Women and Soap Opera: A Study of Prime Time Soaps*, Cambridge: Polity Press

Grey, C. (1991) 'Theories of relativity' in J. Spence and P. Holland (eds) *Family Snaps: The Meanings of Domestic Photography*, London: Virago

Gupta, S. (ed.) (1993) *Disrupted Borders: An Intervention in Definitions of Boundaries*, London: Rivers Oram Press

Hall, C. (1979) 'Early Formation of Victorian Domestic Ideology' in S. Burman (ed.) *Fit Work for Women*, London: Croom Helm

Hall, S. (1991) 'Reconstruction Work: Images of Post-War Black Settlement' in J. Spence and P. Holland (eds) *Family Snaps: The Meanings of Domestic Photography*, London: Virago

Hannavy, J. (1975) *Roger Fenton of Crimble Hall*, London: Gordon Frazer

Hiley, M. (1983) *Seeing Through Photographs*, London: Gordon Frazer

Holland, P. (1991) 'The Old Order of Things Changed' in J. Spence and P. Holland (eds) *Family Snaps: The Meanings of Domestic Photography*, London: Virago

—— (1992) *What is a Child?* London: Virago

—— (1997) 'Press Photography' in A. Briggs and P. Cobley (eds) *Introduction to Media*, London: Longman

Holland, P. and Dewdney, A. (eds) (1992) *The Child, Seen but Not Heard?* Bristol: Watershed Media Centre. Exhibition catalogue and introduction

Kalogeraki, K. (1991) 'My Father's Land' in J. Spence and P. Holland (eds) *Family Snaps: The Meanings of Domestic Photography*, London: Virago

Kember, S. (1995) 'Surveillance, Technology and Crime: The James Bulger Case' in M. Lister (ed.) *The Photographic Image in Digital Culture*, London: Routledge

Kuhn, A. (1991) 'Remembrance' in J. Spence and P. Holland (eds) *Family Snaps: The Meanings of Domestic Photography*, London: Virago

—— (1995) *Family Secrets: Acts of Memory and Imagination*, London: Verso

Lamagny, J-C. and Rouille, A. (1987) *A History of Photography*, Cambridge: Cambridge University Press

Lewis, B. and Harding, D. (eds) (1992) *Kept in a Shoebox: The Experience of Popular Photography*, Bradford: Yorkshire Art Circus/National Museum of Photography, Film and Television

Macdonald, G. (1979) *Camera: A Victorian Eyewitness*, London: Batsford; based on a Granada television series

Martin, R. (1991) 'Unwind the Ties That Bind' in J. Spence and P. Holland (eds) *Family Snaps: The Meanings of Domestic Photography*, London: Virago

Musello, C. (1979) 'Family Photography' in J. Wagner (ed.) *Images of Information*, London: Sage

Penlake, R. (1899) *Home Portraits for Amateur Photographers*, London

Pryce, W.T.R. (1994) 'Photographs and Picture Postcards' in M. Drake and R. Finnegan (eds) *Sources and Methods: A Handbook*, Vol. 4 of *Studying Family and Community History: 19th and 20th Centuries*, Cambridge: Cambridge University Press/Open University

Robertson, G. *et al.* (1994) *Travellers' Tales: Narratives of Home and Displacement*, London: Routledge

Scharf, A. (1974) *Art and Photography*, Harmondsworth: Pelican

Slater, D. (1991) 'Consuming Kodak' in J. Spence and P. Holland (eds) *Family Snaps: The Meanings of Domestic Photography*, London: Virago

—— (1995a) 'Photography and Modern Vision: The Spectacle of "Natural Magic"' in C. Jenks (ed.) *Visual Culture*, London: Routledge

—— (1995b) 'Domestic Photography and Digital Culture' in M. Lister (ed.) *The Photographic Image in Digital Culture*, London: Routledge

Solanke, A. (1991) 'Complex Not Confused' in J. Spence and P. Holland (eds) *Family Snaps: The Meanings of Domestic Photography*, London: Virago

Soloman, J. (1995) 'Interrogating the Holiday Snap' in J. Spence and J. Soloman, *What Can a Woman do with a Camera?* London: Scarlet Press

Sontag, S. (1978) *On Photography*, Harmondsworth: Penguin

Spence, J. (1991) 'Soap, Family Album Work . . . and Hope' in J. Spence and P. Holland (eds) *Family Snaps: The Meanings of Domestic Photography*, London: Virago

Spence, J. and Soloman, J. (eds) (1995) *What Can a Woman do with a Camera?* London: Scarlet Press

Stanley, J. (1991) 'Well, Who'd Want an Old Picture of me at Work?' in J. Spence and P. Holland (eds) *Family Snaps: The Meanings of Domestic Photography*, London: Virago

Urry, J. (1990) *The Tourists' Gaze: Leisure and Travel in Contemporary Societies*, London: Sage

Walkerdine, V. (1991) 'Behind the Painted Smile' in J. Spence and P. Holland (eds) *Family Snaps: The Meanings of Domestic Photography*, London: Virago

Warner, M. (1992) 'Women in the Victorian Family Album', *Creative Camera*, May

Watney, S. (1991) 'Ordinary Boys' in J. Spence and P. Holland (eds) *Family Snaps: The Meanings of Domestic Photography*, London: Virago

Werge, J. (1890) *The Evolution of Photography*, London

Williams, V. (1994) *Who's Looking at the Family?* London: Barbican Art Gallery. Exhibition catalogue and introduction

CHAPTER 4

Constructions of illusion

Photography and commodity culture

ANANDI RAMAMURTHY

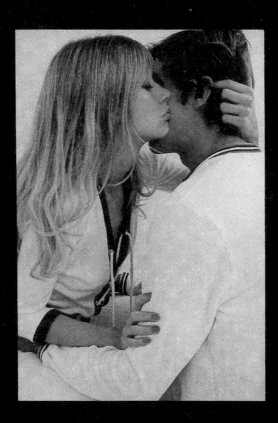

4.1 Victor Burgin, What does Possession mean to you?, 1974

Constructions of illusion
Photography and commodity culture

INTRODUCTION

The photograph as commodity

In the late twentieth century, **commodity** relations rule our lives to such an extent that we are often unaware of them as a specific set of historical, social and economic relations which human beings have constructed. The photograph is both a cultural tool which has been commodified as well as a tool that has been used to express **commodity culture** through advertisements and other marketing material. Tagg has described the development of photography as 'a model of capitalist growth in the nineteenth century' (**Tagg 1988: 37**).

Like any cultural and technical development, the development of photography has been influenced by its social and economic context. The rise of commodity culture in the nineteenth century was a key influence on the way in which this technology was developed and used. John Tagg's essay provides just one example of the way in which photographic genres were affected by capitalism. He discusses the demand for photographic portraits by the rising middle and lower-middle classes, keen for objects symbolic of high social status. The photographic portraits were affordable in price, yet were reminiscent of aristocratic social ascendancy signified by 'having one's portrait done'. Tagg describes how the **daguerreotype** and later the '*cartes-de-visite*' established an industry that had a vast clientele and was ruled by this clientele's 'taste and acceptance of the conventional devices and genres of official art' (Tagg 1988: 50). The commodification of the photograph

JOHN TAGG (1988) 'A Democracy of the Image: Photographic Portraiture and Commodity Production' in **The Burden of Representation: Essays on Photographies and Histories**, Basingstoke, Macmillan

dulled the possible creativity of the new technology, by the desire to reproduce a set of conventions already established within painted portraiture.

If we look at other photographic genres, we can also observe the way in which commodity culture has affected their development. Photojournalism for instance, like other journalism, is primarily concerned with the selling of newspapers, rather than the conveyance of 'news'. For this reason, news photos, as Susan Sontag has noted, have been concerned with the production of 'spectacle' (Sontag 1979). Just as photographic genres have been affected by commerce, so has the development of photographic technology. The 'Instamatic' for instance was clearly developed in order to expand camera use and camera ownership. In turn, this technology limited the kind of photographs people could take (**Slater 1983**).

Were this chapter to discuss the commodification of photography in detail, it would be difficult to limit it, and it would most likely encroach on the subject area of every chapter in this book. Therefore this chapter will concentrate on the way photography has been used in representing commodity culture. In this sense, it will be as much about the decoding of visual commercial messages as about photography. Although the focus is on the specific qualities of photography in the production of commercial messages, photography forms part of a broader system of visual communication including painting, printing, as well as the broadcast media.

DON SLATER (1983) 'Marketing Mass Photography' in P. Davis and H. Walton (eds) **Language, Image, Media**, Oxford: Blackwell

Photographs to represent commodity culture

The use of photography within advertising and marketing does not constitute a particular genre. In fact, this area of photography borrows from all established genres, depending on particular marketing needs. Within the traditional 'history of photography', commercial photography has been ignored, despite the fact that photography produced for advertising and marketing constitutes the largest quantity of photographic production. One possible reason for the lack of documentation and history-writing in this area is that commercial photography has not sought to stretch the medium of photography. One of the key characteristics of photography within advertising and marketing is its parasitism. It borrows and mimics from every genre of photographic and cultural practice to enhance and alter the meaning of lifeless objects – commodities.

Commodities are in fact objects – often inert – that have been imbued with all kinds of social characteristics in the marketplace. Marx called this process the fetishism of commodities, since in the marketplace (which means every place where things have been bought and sold) the social character of people's labour was no longer apparent and it was the products of their labour instead that interacted and were prominent. Advertising, in its turn, imbues these products with meanings which have no relation to the production processes of these objects. Advertising is a cultural form which is integrally linked to capitalism, and constitutes part of the system of production and consumption. Raymond Williams has discussed this relationship and the development of advertising in his essay 'Advertising the Magic System' (Williams 1980). Thomas Richards, in a discussion of Victorian advertisements, describes commodity culture as the 'culture of capitalism' (Richards 1990: 1–16). As Robert Goldman points out, 'ads offer a unique window for observing how commodity interests conceptualise social relations' (**Goldman 1992: 2**). The representation of social relations in advertising has also been discussed in other texts on the history and study of advertising (Leiss et al. 1986; Myers 1986).

Photographs have played an important role in the production of signs, that have invested products with what Marxists have described as false meanings. They have also played an important role in the representation of commodity culture – namely, the culture of capitalism – as natural and eternal. (For a discussion on this, see **Barthes 1977a**.) In this way photographs in advertisements are a key tool for the making of **ideology**.

Breadth of usage

The range of contexts within which photographs are used to sell products or services is so enormous that we are almost unaware of the medium of photography and the language which has been created to convey commercial messages. Photographs for commerce appear on everything from the glossy, high-quality billboard and magazine advertisements, to small, cheap flyers on estate agents' blurbs. Between these two areas there is a breadth of usage, including the mundane images in mail-order information and catalogues, the seemingly matter-of-fact, but high-quality documentary-style images of company annual reports, the varied quality of commodity packaging, and of course the photography on marketing materials such as calendars, produced by companies to enhance their status. While there are a number of critiques on advertising imagery, these tend not to be concerned with the photograph in particular. Other areas of commercial photographic production have received relatively no critical attention from scholars. If any history or literature has been written, it has tended to be commissioned by the companies themselves, or their associates, such as *Thirsty Work: Ten Years of Heineken Advertising* and *Some Examples of Benson Advertising*. These publications have also been unconcerned with the photographic aspect. More recently, articles such as Carol Squiers' 'The Corporate Year in Pictures' have begun to provide an analysis to some of this photography (**Squiers 1992**).

In this chapter, much of the discussion will focus on advertising, partly because it is an area rich for discussion, but also because it will enable us to consider some of the literature which critiques this photography. Through a closer look at ads we can understand the ideological significance of them and other commercial photographs in our lives as well as the **hegemony** of commodity culture. By analysing a run-of-the-mill advertisement, we can understand how advertisements are constructed and act ideologically to

ROBERT GOLDMAN (1992) **Reading Ads Socially**, London: Routledge

ROLAND BARTHES (1977) 'The Rhetoric of the Image' in **Image, Music, Text**, London: Fontana

CAROL SQUIERS 'The Corporate Year in Pictures' in R. Bolton (ed.) **The Contest of Meaning: Critical Histories of Photography**, Cambridge, MA: MIT Press

support commodity culture, and can also see how photographs are employed in the making of ideology.

CASE STUDY: ELIZABETH TAYLOR'S PASSION – THE COMMODIFICATION OF HUMAN RELATIONS

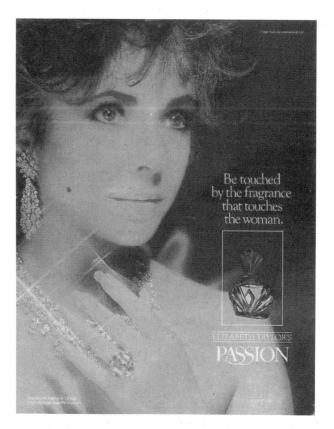

4.2 Elizabeth Taylor's Passion Perfume ad, 1988

The main photograph in the advertisement is a rather soft focus dreamy image of the head and shoulders of Elizabeth Taylor, who appears to be wearing nothing but some diamond studded jewellery. Bright lights (perhaps stage lights) reflect off the jewellery and Taylor herself to present an image which is one of stardom. From our own cultural history we know that Liz Taylor has been associated with heroines such as Cleopatra – a passionate, determined and arresting woman.

156

A crystal clear photograph of the bottle has been inserted into the main photograph on the right-hand side. The juxtaposition of bottle and Elizabeth Taylor's face in the advertisement obviously encourages their association. Purples and pinks within both images also affiliate the two images. The historical and cultural associations which we make with Liz Taylor through her film career are associated here with a bottle of scented liquid. Interestingly, under the bottle of perfume is written 'Elizabeth Taylor's Passion'. This lifeless bottle of liquid appears to have been given a human quality. There is another possibility of meaning too – the bottle is not her passion, despite the use of the possessive, but is the object of her passion. This notion is also enhanced by the glass object which Elizabeth Taylor appears to hold. It is the glass stopper from the perfume bottle. Liz Taylor has obviously opened the bottle and unleashed 'passion', as though it is a quantifiable thing which can be bottled and unleashed in this way! Whether we interpret the perfume as containing Elizabeth Taylor's passion or being the object of her passion, the metamorphosis of the commodity as in some way human is complete. In the first instance it contains a human quality; in the second, passion – a human emotion, which occurs between people – takes place here, between a person and a thing. The photographic **montage** is crucial in this creation of meaning. There is another statement in the advertisement which makes it resonate with further meanings: 'Be touched by the fragrance that touches the woman.' Here, we are invited to join in an experience in which stars have taken part. Yet, we are not simply coaxed into consumption by suggestions of glamour and beauty which Taylor may represent for us. The suggestion is also that she is *the* woman, imbued with qualities of womanliness. The image of Liz Taylor is of course one of standard femininity; she is even looking upwards, suggesting subservience. Her passivity is also increased by the way she holds the bottle stopper. She hardly seems to hold it at all. We cannot imagine those hands actually pulling open the bottle. One easy avenue offered to us in the search to be not just Elizabeth Taylor, but also womanly, is to use Passion. The commodification of human relations is one of the most pervasive influences of modern advertising, and photography plays an important role in creating images expressive of human emotions and relations which are used to give products superficial or 'false' meanings. The pervasive nature of advertisements and the power of the photographic image not only leads us to be unaware of a process, which, when considered rationally, appears absurd, but also enhances these surface meanings above those of other product meanings which may exist through manufacture. What does it cost to produce the perfume? How much were the factory workers who produced and packaged Passion paid? Were they allowed to join a union? What were the health and safety conditions for the workers like? Was Passion tested on animals, and did it lead to animal suffering? Only eight cents out of every dollar in the cosmetics industry goes towards buying ingredients. Even this one piece of information can make us realise how little the advertisement tells us about the products in production. At the same time the ads provide an alluring image, the constructed meanings of which are enhanced by photographic realism, creating a culture in which it appears natural not even to want to know the context of production.

These **constructed** meanings are not simply illusions; rather 'they accurately portray social relations which are illusory' (Goldman 1992: 35).

THE GRAMMAR OF THE AD

The photographic message

The photographic message, as Roland Barthes wrote, is made up of both a denoted message and a connoted message (Barthes 1977b). By the denoted message Barthes meant the literal reality which the photograph portrayed. In the case of the ad for Passion (see case study above), this would be the image of Liz Taylor and the perfume bottle. The second, connoted, message is one which he described as making use of social and historical references. The connoted message is the inferred message. It is symbolic. It is a message with a code – i.e. Liz Taylor signifies beauty, passion, femininity, nobility and mystique. When we look at the documentary photograph, the denoted image appears dominant. We believe the photograph to be 'fact', although, as Tagg has pointed out, it is impossible to have a simple 'denoted' message – all messages are constructed (Tagg 1988: 1–5). All photos are simulations and record moments discontinuous with normal time, and documentary images are highly coded both by the photographer's perspective and the privileging of certain moments, and also by the newspaper captioning of an image. The image for use in advertising, however, is different, in that we know from the start that it is highly structured. In the discussion on Passion, I have already mentioned how the photograph of Elizabeth Taylor does not show her holding the bottle stopper properly. It is obviously a constructed and coded image. The play of light and the soft focus used in her portrait are also constructions, here used to convey romance. The use of soft focus in photography has often been used to signify romance and also femininity, as Pollock has mentioned in her reading of a Levi's advertisement (Pollock 1990: 215–216). The commercial photograph is not therefore perceived as primarily documenting real life. We are therefore unconsciously aware when reading the image that the connoted message is the crucial one.

However, while we know these images to be highly constructed, we are often unaware of the ways in which meaning is framed within them. The framing and structural devices which advertisers use are so well established that we read them unwittingly. Robert Goldman has described the classic advertising format as that of 'the mortise and frame' (Goldman 1992: 61–85). He intends us to understand framing as the process of 'selection, emphasis and presentation', and describes how all photographs are framed in production. In the ad for Passion, the photograph of Liz Taylor, for example, has been framed in such a way as to exclude any clothed part of her body, in order to increase its sexuality. A mortise, as Goldman notes, is a joiners' term for the joining of two pieces of wood together by making a cavity in one, into which a second piece is inserted. In the production of advertisements, the mortise is the small boxed image which usually contains the image of the product (e.g. the bottle of perfume). The photograph of the product is usually in a clear 'showroom' style, which suggests that it is purely documentary, but its frontal angle is one that we would never see in real life. This clear and stark style in itself sets it apart from the larger and usually more atmospheric photographic image, while they are structurally associated in the advertisement. Through this device, advertisers encourage us to combine the meaning of two separate and often seemingly incompatible messages. In the ad for Passion, the image of Liz Taylor and her human qualities of being a passionate woman are transferred to a bottle of perfume; i.e. a material thing is given human value and a human emotion is defined materially. Judith Williamson also discusses the association of two separate images in advertisements in her book *Decoding Advertisements*. She makes the important point that the process of association is one that actively involves the viewer in the production of meaning. She describes the viewer's role in producing meaning as 'advertising work' (**Williamson 1978: 15–19**).

While it is useful to consider the form separately, Judith Williamson has also noted that it is impossible to divide the form and content entirely, since there is content in the form also. Most scholars considering questions of **representation** use methods first discussed in linguistics to decode visual signs (Williamson 1978: 17):

> A sign is quite simply a thing -whether object, word or thing – which has a particular meaning to a person or group of people. It is neither the thing nor the meaning alone, but the two together.
> The sign consists of the signifier, the material object, and the signified, which is its meaning. These are only divided for analytical purposes; in practice a sign is always thing-plus-meaning.

In the ad for Passion, Liz Taylor is the signifier of passion, which is the meaning signified. Through the structure of the ad, the perfume bottle also acts as a signifier of passion, although it does not actually have such a meaning. It is the 'work' we do in reading the grammar of the ad – in reading its structure of form – that leads to the connection between the two signifiers being made.

The transfer of meaning

In his essay 'Encoding/Decoding', Stuart Hall has considered our involvement in the production of meaning in more detail (Hall 1993). He discusses how images are first 'encoded' by the producer, and then 'decoded' by the viewer. The transfer of meaning in this process only works if there are compatible systems of signs and symbols which the encoder and decoder use within their cultural life. However, our background – i.e. our gender, class, ethnic origin, sexuality, religion, etc. – all affect our interpretation of signs and symbols. For this reason, Hall points to the fact that messages are not

JUDITH WILLIAMSON (1978)
Decoding Advertisements: Ideology and Meaning in Advertising, London: Marion Boyars

always read as they were intended to be. He suggests that there are three possible readings of an image: a dominant or preferred reading, a negotiated reading, and an oppositional one. The dominant reading would comply with the meaning intended by the producer of the image. The importance of readers interpreting images as they were intended is obviously crucial for commercial messages, and is one of the reasons why advertisers use the various framing devices which have been discussed above. Hall describes the negotiated reading as one which only partly conforms to the intended, dominant meaning. Finally the oppositional reading is one which is in total conflict with the meaning intended by the image-producer. A feminist interpretation of the advertisement for Passion, which challenged the notion of 'womanliness' presented by the ad, could be viewed as oppositional. Examples of ordinary people producing oppositional readings through graffiti have been collected by Jill Posner in *Spray it Loud* (Posner 1982). In *Reading Ads Socially*, Robert Goldman cites an example of a cigarette advertisement which was misinterpreted by many readers to create an oppositional meaning. In 1986, Kent cigarettes launched an ad campaign which depicted two people flying a kite on a page. In order to involve the viewer in the advertisement, the advertiser emptied the figures of content so that the reader could literally place themselves in the ad. Viewers, however, interpreted the silhouetted figures as ghosts because of the health warnings about smoking to which we have been accustomed (Goldman 1992: 80–81). The question of reception brings in to doubt the notion of global advertising which companies such as Coca-Cola and Benetton have tried to create. Can there really be worldwide advertising campaigns? People across the world will surely find different symbolic meanings in the same signifiers. (This issue will be discussed on pp. 189–96.)

The creation of meaning in photographic styles

All photographs will be viewed by different people in different ways, whether in commercial contexts or not. The same photograph can also mean different things in different contexts. The commercial context, for example, can change the meaning of an image, just as different styles of photography will carry different messages. Let us look at an advertisement which does not use a style of photography normally associated with advertising. Because advertisers have traditionally been concerned with creating glamorous, fantasy worlds of desire for their products, they have tended to shy away from the stark, grainy, black and white type of imagery traditionally associated with documentary images and photojournalism, and have gone instead for glossy, high-colour photography. Yet, at times of company crisis, or when companies have wanted to deliberately foster an image of no-nonsense frankness, they have used black and white imagery. In 1990, a short while after Nelson Mandela was released from jail by the South African authorities, the Anglo-American Corporation of South Africa brought out an advertisement entitled 'Do we sometimes wish we had not fought to have Black trade

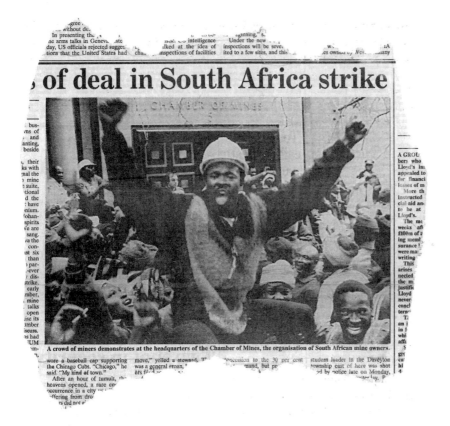

of deal in South Africa strike

A crowd of miners demonstrates at the headquarters of the Chamber of Mines, the organisation of South African mine owners.

4.3 South African miners demonstrating outside the offices of the organisation of South African mine owners. *Independent,* **26 August 1987**
This photograph was used, torn from the newspaper page as it is here, by the Anglo-American Corporation of South Africa in their advertisement DO WE SOMETIMES WISH WE HAD NOT FOUGHT TO HAVE BLACK TRADE UNIONS RECOGNISED?, published in the *Guardian,* 2 April 1990

unions recognised?'. Underneath this title was a documentary photograph of a Black South African miner, in a show of victory (figure 4.3). At a moment when Anglo-American foresaw massive economic and political change, they attempted to distance themselves from the apartheid regime. Yet Anglo-American was by far the largest company in South Africa, 'with a near total grip over large sectors of the apartheid economy'.[1] While presenting this advertisement to the public, De Beers – Anglo's sister company, in which they had a 35 per cent stake – also cancelled their recognition agreement with the NUM at the Premier Diamond Mines, despite 90 per cent of workers belonging to the union. The frank and honest style of address which black and white provided hid the reality for black workers in South Africa. The miner depicted was in fact celebrating his victory against Anglo-American in 1987. Here, at another moment of crisis,

1 As stated in anti-Apartheid campaign literature of the time

Anglo-American have appropriated this image of resistance. The parasitism of advertising enables it to use and discard any style and content for its own ends. Anglo-American are no longer interested in fostering this image (they declined permission to have the advertisement reproduced here). There is an added irony in Anglo-American's use of this image, since it is not strictly speaking a documentary image at all, but a montage of two images to capture the mood of the strike as the *Independent* saw it.

Black and white imagery has been used in other company contexts at moments of crisis. Carol Squiers has discussed the way in which they have been used in annual reports. Black and white, she notes, 'looks more modest and costs less to print'. As Arnold Saks, a corporate designer, said: 'There's an honesty about black and white, a reality. . . . Black and white is the only reality' (Squiers 1992: 208). The symbolic value of using or not using a photograph has also been important for advertisers. Kathy Myers has explored the moments when advertisers have chosen to use and not use photographic images in an attempt to find symbols of ecological awareness (**Myers 1990**).

KATHY MYERS (1990) 'Selling Green' in C. Squiers (ed.) **The Critical Image: Essays on Contemporary Photography**, Seattle: Bay Press

HEGEMONY IN PHOTOGRAPHIC REPRESENTATION

Commercial photography constantly borrows ideas and images from the wider cultural domain. It is clear that when we point the camera we frame it in a thousand and one ways through our own cultural conditioning. Photographs, like other cultural products, have therefore tended to perpetuate ideas which are dominant in society. Commercial photographs, because of their profuse nature and because they have never sought to challenge the status quo within society (since they are only produced to sell products), have also aided in the construction and perpetuation of stereotypes, to the point at which they have appeared natural and eternal (See Barthes 1977a; Williamson 1978, part 2). Through commercial photography we can therefore explore hegemonic constructs of, for example, race, gender and class.

Photomontage – concealing social relations

One of the key ways in which commercial photography has sought to determine particular readings of images and products has been through **photomontage**. Advertisements are in fact simple photomontages produced for commercial purposes, although most books on the technique seem to ignore this expansive area. While left photographers like Heartfield use photomontage to make invisible social relations visible, advertisers have used montage to conceal 'reality'. One of the peculiar advantages of photomontage, as John Berger wrote in his essay 'The Political Uses of Photomontage', is the fact that 'everything which has been cut out keeps its familiar photographic appearance. We are still looking first at things and only afterwards at symbols' (Berger 1972b; 185). This creates a sense of naturalness about an image or message which is in fact constructed. An early example of the photomontage naturalising social relations has been discussed by Sally Stein, who considers 'the reception of photography within the larger matrix of socially organised communication', and looks at the rise of Taylor's ideas of 'scientific management' in the factory, and the way these ideas were also applied to domestic work (**Stein 1981: 42–44**). She also notes how expensive it was to have photomechanical reproductions within a book in the early part of the century.

Yet in Mrs Christine Frederick's 1913 tract, *The New Housekeeping*, there were eight pages of glossy photographic images. This must have impressed the average reader. In her chapter on the new efficiency as applied to cooking, an image was provided which affirmed this ideology as the answer to women's work. The image consisted of a line drawing of an open card file, organised into types of dishes, and an example of a recipe card with a photograph of an elaborate lamb dish (figure 4.4). Despite Frederick's interest in precision, the card, which would logically be delineated by a black rectangular frame, does not match the dimensions of the file, nor does it contain practical information such as cost, number of servings, etc., which Frederick suggests in her text. As Stein points out, however, most readers must have overlooked this point when confronted with this luscious photographic image, which they would have accepted at face value.

SALLY STEIN (1981) 'The Composite Photographic Image and the Composition of Consumer Ideology', **Art Journal** Spring 1981

> Because the page is not clearly divided between the file in one half and the recipe card in the other but instead flows uninterruptedly between drawing below, text of recipe, and photograph of the final dish, the meticulous organisation of the file alone seems responsible for the full flowering of the dish. As a symbolic representation of modern house work, what you have in short order is a strict hierarchy, with an emblem of the family feast at its pinnacle.
>
> (Stein 1981: 43)

The more down-to-earth questions of time and money are ignored and almost banished. In response to those who believed that her reading was too contrived, Stein wrote: 'If it seems that I am reading too much into this composite image, one need only note the title of Frederick's subsequent publication – *Meals that Cook Themselves*' (Stein 1992).

There are two key issues we can draw from Stein's analysis. Firstly, the example highlights the power of the photographic image to foster desire. While a rather ordinary image of a cake may have impressed an early twentieth-century audience, in the late twentieth century we are also mesmerised and impressed by the use of the latest technology, and it is still used to seduce us. Digital image-making is probably the field which is most effectively used today to capture our attention. We can see this clearly within TV commercials, such as the recent advertisements for Guinness and Holsten Pils lager. Spellbinding technology is also used within print advertisements, especially for photographic equipment. Ektakron film, for example, used a

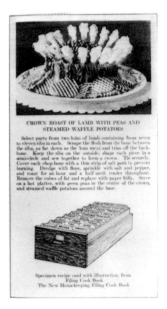

4.4 Illustration from Mrs Christine Frederick's *The New Housekeeping,* **1913**

close-up of a bird's beak in 1989 to stun the viewer with the possible detail that could be achieved by using this film. The impact of the latest tech-nology makes us forget the context of production, and the immediacy of the image makes the surface reality seem more real.

Concealing labour relations

The second issue that Stein's analysis elucidates is the power of photomon-tage in the commercial context to conceal labour relations. Judith Williamson has also discussed this with regard to a Lancia car advertisement from around 1978. The image depicts the Lancia Beta in an Italian vineyard. It shows a man who appears to be the owner, standing on the far side of the car with his back towards us, looking over a vineyard in which a number of peasants are working happily. In the distance, on a hill, is an old castle (this image is illustrated in **Williamson 1979**).

Williamson asks a series of questions:

> Who made this car? Has it just emerged new and gleaming from the soil, its finished form as much a product of nature as the grapes on the vine? . . . Who are these peasants? Have they made the car out in this most Italian field? . . . How can a car even exist in these feudal relations, how can such a contradiction be carried off? . . . What is this, if not a complete slipping over of the capitalist mode of production, as we survey a set of feudal class relations represented by the surveying gaze of possession, the look of the landlord with his back to us?
>
> (Williamson 1979: 53)

Williamson also notes how the feudal Italian owner's gaze does not encom-pass both car (the product of industrial capitalism) and the owner's field of vision (the relations of Italian feudalism). She discusses the structure of the advertisement in order to understand why we don't question the contradictions of the image. The ad uses the traditional grammar of car advertisements with the showroom-effect camera angle, which intersects with the representation of 'Italianness'. The positioning of the car seems so casual that the man leaning against it could have just stopped to have a break and look at this Italian view. Maybe he is not Italian? Perhaps he will drive on and leave the 'most Italian' scene behind. The narrative of chance on the horizontal axis of the photograph naturalises the vertical axis of Italian castle, feudal relations and commodity ownership.

Contemporary advertisements also provide examples of the romanticised and non-industrial working environment. Hovis and other wholemeal bread producers have often used the image of the family bakery. Whisky distillers have also used this image to represent their brand as one which has been produced with special attention and one that has the experience of time behind it. Jack Daniel's whiskey had a series of advertisements in 1995 which

JUDITH WILLIAMSON (1979) 'Great History that Photographs Mislaid' in Photography Workshop (ed.) **Photography/Politics One**, London: Comedia

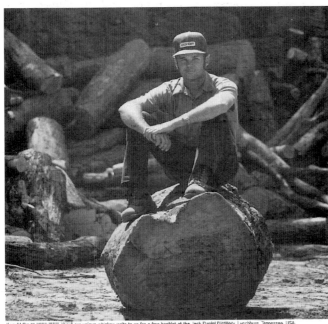

If you'd like to know more about our unique whiskey, write to us for a free booklet at the Jack Daniel Distillery, Lynchburg, Tennessee, USA.

TENNESSEE MEN and Tennessee maple account for the smoothness of Jack Daniel's Tennessee Whiskey.

We get these big chunks of hard maple from the hills around here. They're taken from high ground when the sap is low. Then, men like Billy Durm cut them in strips; stack them in ricks; and burn them to charcoal for smoothing our whiskey. Sometimes we joke about who's more important—the man or the maple? But after a sip of charcoal mellowed Jack Daniel's, you'll know that both are doing good jobs.

JACK DANIEL'S TENNESSEE WHISKEY

4.5 'Billy Durm', Jack Daniel's Tennessee Whiskey
A romanticised labour environment appears more real by its representation as a photograph

presented a labour environment that could not possibly exist today (figure 4.5). The black and white photograph of a romanticised work environment seems to represent both the past and present. There is a reassuring sense of stability. The photograph also seems to illude us into believing that this is a 'real' world, especially since the whisky bottle at the bottom of the ad, which we know to exist, is only engraved.

Gendered representations

Much of the literature which considers racist and sexist imagery, whilst using commercial photography for examples, has tended to discuss broader cultural readings rather than the commercial or photographic context. This section will discuss gendered representations. For explorations of 'race' and racism in commercial photography see case studies on pages 172 and 190).

The stereotypical and highly coded representations of women in popular culture have been given attention by many critics (**Berger 1972a**; **Winship 1987a**, 1987b; Williamson 1978). One of the key criticisms has been the way in which ads always represent women as objects to be surveyed. This has tended to increase the representation of women as both passive and objects of sexual desire. Erving Goffman has explored the body language used to represent men and women in his book *Gender Advertisements* to show how women in particular have been photographed for advertisements in ways that perpetuate gender roles (Goffman 1979). It is important to remember that the photographer always surveys his or her subject and personally selects what is believed to be worth photographing. The photographic process can also, therefore, exacerbate the voyeuristic **gaze**.

To understand the way in which men's and women's bodies are codified, we can look at the representation of hands in advertisements (see Winship 1987a). While male hands are often represented as active in advertising, female hands are usually represented as passive and decorative. In the Passion advertisement described earlier, for example, Liz Taylor did not even seem to be holding the bottle stopper properly; her hands were simply represented decoratively. An advertisement for Ronson Lighters (1951) provides us with a clear example of the different representation of men's and women's hands (figure 4.6). While the male hand plays the active role and activates the lighter, the female hand appears passive, with the cigarette only propped lightly between her fingers. It is also the woman's body – represented by fragments of her body here – that are highlighted as objects of sexual pleasure through the bright red lipstick and the nail polish. Today this **coding** continues, even in advertisements which appear to represent a degree of partnership. An advertisement for Donna Karan perfume shows the male hands still taking the key role in an embrace. The man's arms practically cross the whole double-page spread. In contrast, the woman's hands simply curve upwards to touch his arms gently. Her action and pose do not enable her to play an equally active role in the embrace.

The fragmentation of the body – particularly women's bodies – is a feature of recent commercial photography. It makes the body more easily commodified and, with that, desire is also more easily packaged. In a content analysis of lipstick ads, Robert Goldman has pointed out that while most lipstick ads in 1946 depicted the whole body of a woman, by 1977 most ads only showed a part of the body. A Maxi make-up advertisement from the back cover of the September 1989 issue of *Company* highlights this fragmentation (figure 4.7).

JOHN BERGER (1972a) **Ways of Seeing**, London: BBC
JANICE WINSHIP (1987a) 'Handling Sex' in R. Betterton (ed.) **Looking On: Images of Femininity in the Visual Arts and Media**, London: Pandora

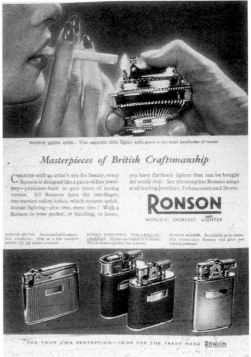

4.6 Ronson Lighters, 1951
Women's hands have traditionally been photographed in ways that make them appear passive and decorative

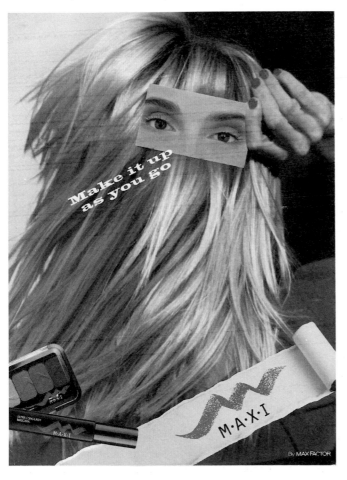

4.7 'Make it up as you go' Maxi make-up ad,
***Cosmopolitan*, October 1989**
The commodification and fragmentation of womens bodies is a common feature of contemporary commercial photography

The face of the woman appears to be a mask whose parts can be altered at will. Here, they not only appear to be divorced from the human being to whom they belong, but are actually separated from the model's face. Each part is like a commodity to be worn and discarded at will. In this way beauty too is fragmented and commodified into ideal 'types' of lips, noses, eyes, etc. One of the most famous examples of this fragmentation is the early 1980s advertisement for Pretty Polly tights, which depicted a woman's legs appearing out of an egg. This objectification and fragmentation of a woman's body received criticism at the time, with graffiti that read 'born kicking'. As Pollock indicates, it was only 'after Picasso had visually hacked up the body, [that] we have been gradually accustomed to the cutting up of specifically feminine bodies: indeed, their cut-up-ness has come to be seen as a sign of that femininity'. Significantly, Pollock adds that this 'came to be naturalised by *photographic* representation in film, advertising, and pornography, all of which are discourses about desire that utilise the dialectic of fantasy and reality effects associated with the hegemonic modes of photographic representation' (Pollock 1990: 218; my emphasis).

FASHION PHOTOGRAPHY

So far I have concentrated on photographs within advertising, yet we cannot allow this area to subsume all discussion on photographs for commerce. Here, it is worth considering the genre of fashion photography, since this area of commercial photography has been particularly targeted with regard to discussions on the construction of femininity and gendered representations.

In *The Face of Fashion*, Jennifer Craik provides an historical account of the techniques of fashion photography from early photographic pictorialism of the nineteenth century, through the gendered constructions of the 1920s and 1930s which increasingly represented women as commodities, to the increasing dominance of the fashion photographer in the 1960s and the influence of filmatic techniques which led to clothes becoming more and more incidental within the fashion photograph. Craik also draws our attention to the increasing eroticism of 1970s and 1980s fashion photography. Most importantly she notes that the conventions of fashion photography are 'neither fixed nor purposeful' (**Craik 1994: 114**). It is perhaps for this reason that critical literature on the genre as a whole is sparse. Most of what has been written does not provide a critique of the genre as a whole, but tends to consider the constructions of gender and sexuality within these images. Femininity, as Craik notes, 'became co-extensive with the fashion photograph' by the 1930s. The heightened sexuality of the fashion image in the 1970s and 1980s, with the work of photographers such as Helmut Newton, has been discussed by Rosetta Brookes (**Brookes 1992: 17–24**).

The way in which women read fashion images of women has also been explored (see **Evans and Thornton 1989: ch. 5**). As Berger commented:

JENNIFER CRAIK (1994) 'Soft Focus: Techniques of Fashion Photography', **The Face of Fashion**, London: Routledge, chapter 5

ROSETTA BROOKES (1992) 'Fashion Photography' in V. Ash and E. Wilson (eds) **Chic Thrills: A Fashion Reader**, London: Pandora

C. EVANS AND M. THORNTON (1989) **Women and Fashion: A New Look**, London: Quartet, especially chapter 5

'Men look at women. Women watch themselves being looked at' (Berger 1972a: 47). As far as the photographic quality of the spreads are concerned, these have tended to be discussed in books, often commissioned by commercial enterprises such as *Vogue*, which eulogise these images and their relationship to '**Art**' photography. In this process the work of individual photographers has been discussed, rather than the genre itself. It is worth noting that even in their discussions of the fashion image and sexuality, that Brookes, as well as Evans and Thornton, discussed the issue through key examples of work by particular photographers. Their essays provide critical case studies of fashion images from the 1960s, 1970s and 1980s by photographers such as Helmut Newton, Guy Bourdin and Deborah Turbeville. In marking out fashion photography as an area for discussion, it seems clear that the glossy images which are mostly discussed contrast to the fashion photographs of the average mail-order catalogue, which could be described as fashion illustration.

Several signs or features of the fashion image which have been pointed out by various writers are worth considering together in order to understand the genre. Firstly, the transitory nature of fashion has impacted on the fashion image. Evans and Thornton have discussed this in terms of the ability of the fashion image to take 'extraordinary liberties' and get away with images which are unduly violent, pornographic or outrageous. Polly Devlin has pointed out the contradictory nature of the fashion image's transitoriness, by their aim to be both timely and timeless: 'Its subject is a product with built-in obsolescence, and the result may be an amusing, ephemeral picture or a monumental statement' (Devlin 1979: 113).

There are other contradictions apparent within the fashion image. Rosetta Brookes has suggested that in fashion photography 'we see the typical instead of the unique moment or event'. Yet, at the same time as producing the typical, fashion photographers have aimed to construct a sense of what is original and unique within a particular fashion. They have also tried to produce images which stand their ground beyond the transitory space of the magazine and the transitory nature of fashion, and for example enter the gallery or the coffee-table book. The *Vogue Book of Fashion Photography* and the major Victoria and Albert Museum exhibition and its accompanying catalogue *Appearances: Fashion Photography since 1945* are testament to this conflict (Devlin 1979: Harrison 1991). Both provide a good collection of images of the classical fashion photograph, although the historical essays tend to be uncritical of the genre. It is clear that there are tensions in the relationship between fashion photography and both advertising photography and 'Art' photography. The fashion image attempts to stand aloof from the undiluted commercial context of advertising, since most fashion spreads are commissioned by magazines which are not directly selling clothes. Yet the undeniable commercial angle has separated it from the 'Art' photograph, despite the inevitable commercial context of the latter.

The relationship of the fashion spread to magazines rather than the manufacturers also emphasises the importance of the images' ability to project 'a
look, an image, a world' (Evans and Thornton 1989: 82). Their aim is not
simply to highlight clothes, but rather to create identities. This construction
has affected all fashion images, including those now produced by
manufacturers. As Steve Edwards wrote, with regards to the *Next Directory*:

> As we flip the pages multiple identities whizz past our eyes.
> Distance and depth collapse into the intricate and exquisite surface
> of the image. What is there now to prevent us switching back and
> forth between these marvellous identities? She: now sipping tea on
> the lawn of the country seat, bathed in golden light, 'well-dressed,
> well-bred,' in that 'endless summer'. Now the belle of the southern
> states, young and raw, perhaps with an illicit negro lover. Now the
> cultured woman, on her travels through Europe in search of
> adventure. He: from the big city gentleman, to the rugged biker, to
> the fictions of Havana. These are the worlds that the photograph
> has to offer. . . . Our only choice is between its choices, we have
> no choice but to consume . . . or so the argument goes.
>
> (Edwards 1989: 5)

In constructing these identities, fashion photography also allows us to view
the social attitudes of a period.

In creating worlds of illusion, fashion photography has been influenced
by all other areas of photographic practice. Early portrait photography and
the *carte-de-visite* had already established ways of photographing people in
fashionable or dramatic clothing, which were adopted by early fashion
photographers (Ewing 1991: 6–10). Fashion photographers such as André
Barre, Irving Penn and Erwin Blumenfield have also been influenced by
Surrealism. The power of photojournalism and documentary photography
in the 1930s also affected fashion images, especially as photographers moved
between the genres. Yet, the concentration on what is contrived and stylised
rather than the 'captured' moment, so revered in documentary, continues to
set it apart. Films have also influenced fashion photography, both in terms
of content and the creation of looks and styles and the way in which we
are able to read what would otherwise appear as fragmentary and disjointed
image sequences in the fashion spread. In creating images and 'looks', the
fashion photograph – in its attempts to always find something new, different,
glamorous and often 'exotic' – has also been influenced by the increasing
experience of international travel. In the following case study we will therefore explore fashion and travel images together. This should indicate the
impossibility of considering various commercial image-making forms in isolation. We live in a world dominated by lifestyle culture, whose conventions
are 'neither fixed nor purposeful'.

CASE STUDY: TOURISM, FASHION AND 'THE OTHER'

In this case study we will consider a particular hegemonic construction from
the nineteenth century – that of the exotic/primitive '**Other**' – and explore
the way in which it has been exploited in the commercial world. Some of
the most dominant ideological and photographic constructs were developed
during the nineteenth century, a period of European imperial expansion. This
history has affected the representation of black people in all forms of
photographic practice (see Gupta 1986; Bailey 1988; *Ten/8* 16; *Ten/8* 2(3).
During the nineteenth century, the camera joined the gun in the process of
colonisation. The camera was used to record and define those who were
colonised according to the interests of the West. This unequal relationship of
power between the white photographer and the colonised subject has been
discussed by many (Bate 1993; Schildkrout 1991; Prochaska 1991; Freedman
1990; Edwards 1992). These early anthropological and geographical photographers were sometimes paid employees of companies who organised
campaigns to explore new markets. Emile Torday, for example – an anthropologist who used photography as a research aid – was paid by the Belgian
Kasai Company to explore the Congo.

This history of photography is integrally linked to colonial and economic
exploitation. A sense of submission, exoticism and the 'primitive' were key
feelings, which these photographers documented and catalogued. Through
these images, the European photographer and viewer could perceive their
own superiority. Europe was defined as 'the norm' upon which all other
cultures should be judged. That which was different was disempowered by
its very 'Otherness'.

During this period, the sense of 'Otherness' and exoticism was not only
captured 'in the field' but was also exploited by photographers working in
commercial enterprises. Malek Alloula has documented the genre of
exotic/erotic colonial postcards which were sent by French colonists back to
France. In his book *The Colonial Harem* he discusses images of Algerian
women taken by French studio photographers in Algeria (**Alloula 1987**).
In the confines of the studio, French photographers constructed visions of
exoticism which suited their own colonial fantasies and those of the European
consumers of these images. The paid Algerian models could only remain silent
to the colonisers' abuse of their bodies (figures 4.8 and 4.13). These images
encapsulate Edward Said's description of Flaubert's Egyptian courtesan:

MALEK ALLOULA (1987) **The
Colonial Harem**, Manchester:
Manchester University Press

> She never spoke of herself, she never represented her emotions, her
> presence or history. He spoke for and represented her. He was foreign,
> comparatively wealthy, male, and these were historical facts of domina-
> tion that allowed him not only to possess Kuchuk Hanem physically but
> to speak for her and tell his readers in what way she was typically
> oriental.

> (Said 1985: 6)

The dominance of photographs of women in these commercial images is not
by chance. Colonial power could be more emphatically represented through

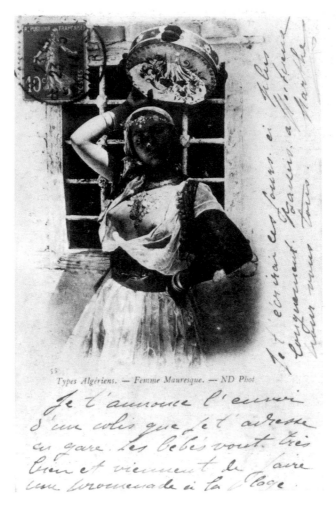

4.8 French colonial postcard, *c.* 1910
White French photographers constructed their own colonial fantasies, which were sent by colonial officers in Algeria to relatives and friends in France

gendered relations – the white, wealthy male photographer versus the non-white, poor female subject. These images, bought and sold in their thousands, reflect the commodification of women's bodies generally in society. They are also part of the development of postcard culture which enabled the consumption of photographs by millions. The production of exotic postcards also brought photographs of the 'Empire' and the non-European world into every European home. It was not only the photographs of non-European women which were sold: landscape photographs, which constructed Europe as developed and the non-European world as under-developed, were also popular (Prochaska 1991). These colonial visions

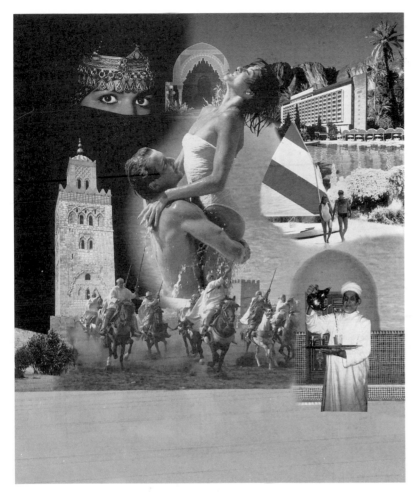

4.9 'Morocco', 1990
The 'East' is still represented as an exotic and erotic playground for the 'West'

continue to pervade contemporary travel photography, not only through postcards, but also in travel brochures and tourist ephemera.

Tourism

Today, many areas of commercial photography exploit exoticism and 'Otherness', along with the ingredient of glamour to invite and entice viewers and consumers. In this way, some of the ideological constructs of colonial domination have become so naturalised that we hardly notice them. In the tourist industry, images of exoticised women and children in tradi-tional garb are used to encourage travel through tourist brochures, posters and TV campaigns. With submissive smiles and half-hidden faces these

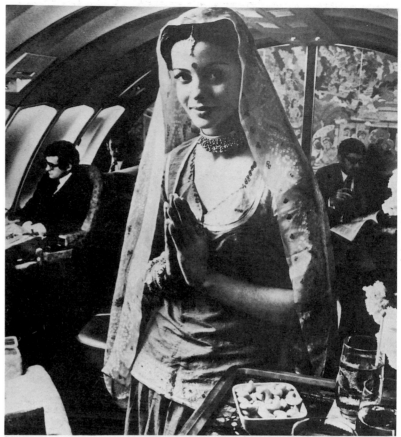

Rajput windows and the ethereal voice of the sitar.
Murals of the legends of Krishna and silks and brocades from Rajasthan.
A glimpse of India on your way to New York.

AIR-INDIA

4.10a

images, echoing those discussed by Alloula, continue to construct the East as the submissive female and the West as the authoritative male (figure 4.9). The non-European world is represented as a playground for the West. The bombardment of these images denies the reality of resourcefulness and intense physical work which actually constitutes most women's lives in the Third World. In the 1970s, Paul Wombell commented on this construct in a photomontage, which contrasted the fantasy tourist world with the reality for many Asian women workers in Britain (figures 4.10a and b). In many tourist advertisements, the image of work is so glamorised that we cannot perceive the reality.

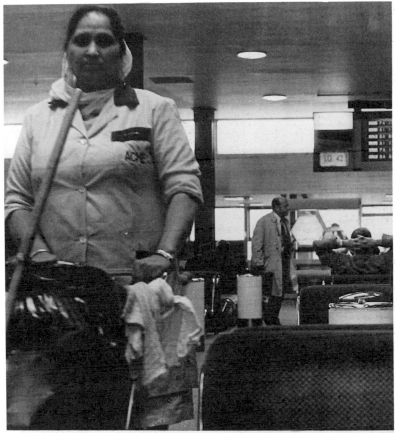

Ash trays and the extensive dirty floors of the airport.
The arrivals and departure board of Heathrow and the overalls from Acme.
A glimpse of exploitation on your way to New York.

IMMIGRANT-LABOUR

4.10b Montage, 1979

The dominant photographic language of the tourist brochure has also affected how tourists construct their own photographs. These snapshots tend to reinforce the constructed and commodified experience of travel: what is photographed is that which is different and out of the ordinary. Most tourist snapshots also use a vocabulary of photographic practice which is embedded in power relations. Let us look at the photographs by Western tourists in the non-Western world. Tourism within Europe produces a slightly different set of relations. In the non-Western world, the majority of tourists who travel abroad are Western. Automatically a relationship of economic power is established, both generally and in terms of camera ownership.

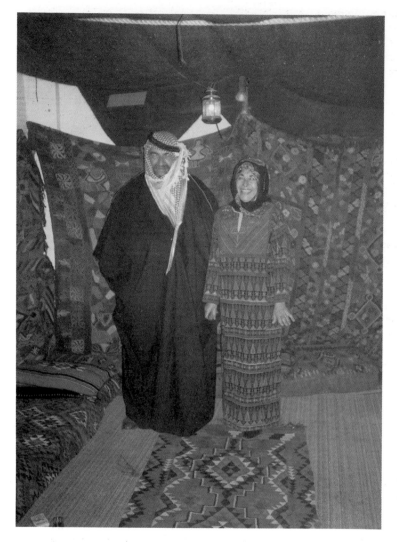

4.11 Tourist photograph
This photograph was taken in a carpet shop where tourists could dress up and role play in a mock bedouin tent

While Don Slater (1983) has discussed the contradictory way in which the expansion of camera ownership has not led to new or challenging photo-graphic practices in the non-Western world, this contradiction between ownership and practice is less evident. Tourists, having already consumed an array of exotic and glamorised photographs of the place before arrival, search out these very images and sites to visit and photograph in order to feel that their trip is complete. While many of the experiences revolve around architec-tural monuments, the desire to consume exotic/anthropological images of people has found a new trade, which has its parallel in the earlier studio-anthropological photography. In many tourist locations – in India, Morocco and Algeria, for example – men and women sit in elaborate garb which the tourist can recognise as traditional and, more importantly, exotic. These people wait for those willing to pay to have their photograph taken with them. Tourism creates its own culture for consumption. Just like the model in the studio, he or she is also paid by the photographer to conform to an image which has already been constructed. Alternatively, at other sites, the tourist can dress up as part of the exotic experience, and photograph themselves (figure 4.11). The trade in these new 'anthropological' images may have expanded to include the unknown snapshooter, but their purpose is not to encourage an understanding of a culture, but rather to commodify and consume yet another aspect of a place through the photographic image – the people.

Fashion

In fashion photography the consumption of 'Other' worlds is domesticated through the familiar context of the fashion magazine and the more-often-than-not white model. In some cases it is hard to know where one genre ends and the other begins. Within fashion, the ordinary is made to appear extraordinary, and vice versa. Fashion photography, as I have already mentioned, is blatantly concerned with the constructed photograph. It is also concerned with what is exotic, dramatic, glamorous and different. Therefore, it is easy to see how some photographers have moved between areas of anthropological and fashion photography. Irving Penn's *Worlds in a Small Room* are a series of constructed images of peoples from around the world, whom Penn photographed while on assignments for *Vogue* (Penn 1974). In these images the genres of fashion and visual anthropology seem to collapse. The images tell us little about the people, but say a lot about Penn's construction of these people as primitive and exotic. As with the fashion shoot, these images are contrived and stylised, and Penn is at pains to find what is extraordinary and to create the dramatic. The isolated space of the studio removes the subjects from their own time and space, in a similar way to the French colonial postcards discussed above (p. 171), and gives the photographer free rein to create every aspect of the image. Interestingly, Penn described this studio space as 'a sort of neutral area' (Penn 1974: 9). Yet, as we look through his book and peruse the photographs of Penn constructing his shots, the unequal relationship of power makes a mockery of the notion of neutrality.

The latent relationship between fashion and popular anthropological photography explains why the fashion magazine *Marie Claire* could include articles about ethnography without losing the tone of the fashion magazine. In their first issue, the article 'Arabia Behind the Veil' represented the jewellery and make-up of Arab women in a series of plates, like fashion ideas (figure 4.12). If we look closely at the images it is clear that the photographer has used just two or three models and dressed them differently to represent a series of styles, just like a fashion shoot.

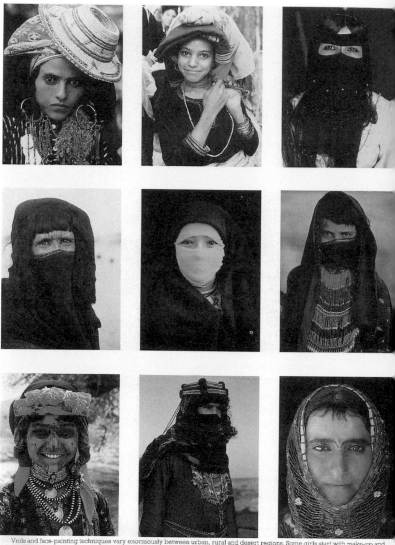

Veils and face-painting techniques vary enormously between urban, rural and desert regions. Some girls start with make-up and 'graduate' to veils; women may combine the two, adding ornate jewellery or beadwork, head rings and, occasionally, hats

14

4.12 'Arabia Behind the Veil', *Marie Claire*, September 1988

In fashion photography we can see the continued use of the 'harem' image, for example, as the site of colonial fantasy and as being oppositional to the white 'norm'. In the November 1988 issue of *Company* magazine, a fashion spread titled 'Arabesque: Rock the Casbah – This is Evening Wear to Smoulder in' features non-white women in brocaded clothes, sitting and lying indoors on heavily ornamented fabrics, while pining over black and white photographs of men. The photographs of the women are bathed in an

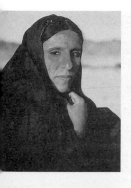
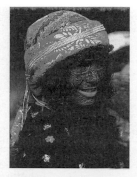
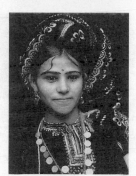
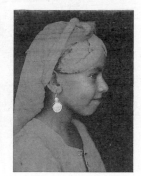

women, then, adopted the veil with the same intention as the Arab women of today: as a shield against the visual aggression and intrusion of men. The most well-documented, archaic function of the veil, therefore, remains simply to protect and preserve.

Sustaining a certain ambiguity of identity is vital in the battle against destructive forces. Moslems often change their names when they enter a strange village or when they fall ill, to avoid tempting fate (understandably making the administration of health centres unduly complicated); and people here do not kiss due to the belief that an open mouth allows bad spirits to enter and the soul to escape. Veiling, make-up and name-changing are all different methods of separating the individual from the malevolent forces, whether human or spiritual, of the outside world.

There is a rigidly drawn division in Arabia between public life, at work, and private life, at home. This is hard for the outward-looking Westerner to grasp, but maintaining the extreme seclusion of the domestic sphere has, particularly in Saudi, developed over the centuries and become a kind of congenital male obsession. A woman who emerges from the confines of the home unveiled goes beyond inviting the advances of strangers: she is in fact, exposing the most vehemently guarded element, prize even, of private life.

Moslems are burdened with an inescapable pressure that comes from constant social surveillance. Each individual is considered responsible for the actions of his neighbours, so a form of sacred citizen's arrest exists whereby people can successfully become their brother's keeper. In Riyadh, even driving through an amber light might lead to the person being followed, detained and denounced by a complete stranger.

It may seem like a distorted view of independence, but the veil can actually serve to release women from the stress of such intense vigilance; behind the thick make-up or black curtain, many Arab women feel liberated by their anonymity.

And the veil does not in itself prevent women from educating themselves or working and can actually co-exist with a surprising amount of freedom. For instance, in a region to the east of Yemen, women – even though they accept the veil – still practise the custom of 'temporary marriage': a woman can, extremely easily, ▷

Maintaining the extreme seclusion of the domestic sphere has developed over the centuries to become a kind of congenital male obsession

15

orangey, rich light. By contrasting colour and black and white photography, the men seem to appear more distant and further unobtainable. The representation of sexuality here is of an unhealthy obsession. In contrast, the fashion spread following it, 'Cold Comfort', features a white couple together, in a relationship of relative equality. Blue and brown predominate, in contrast to the previous spread, and the much more standard photographic lighting contrasts with the previous yellow haze, to present images which

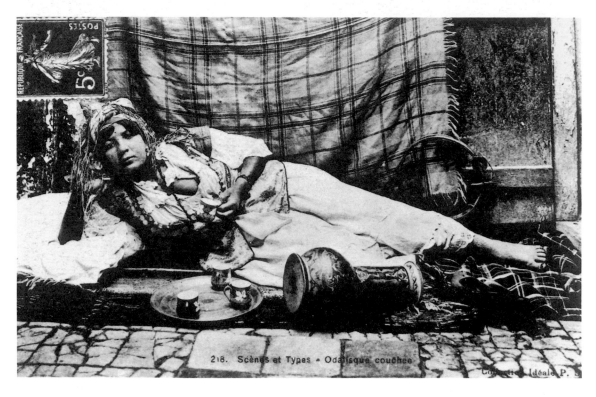

4.13 French colonial postcard, c. 1910
During the ninenteenth century and today, the harem has remained a site for colonial fantasy, and a space which ensures the representation of the 'orient' as oppositional to the 'occident'

seem much more matter-of-fact, like the denim clothing advertised. Here, however, matter-of-factness acts to represent Europe as rational in opposition to the irrational East.

In *Marie Claire*'s June 1994 issue, another pair of fashion spreads also provides an example of the oppositional way in which East and West are presented, not just through content, but also through photographic codes. In 'Indian Summer', the image of an exotic woman in physical and sexual abandon predominates the pages, as in the previous spread and the colonial postcards already discussed (figures 4.13 and 4.14). The pages of this photo-story are almost like a film sequence with rapid cuts. As in the last 'Orientalist' sequence, this woman is alone, but the themes of physical and sexual desire are paramount. Many of the shots use wide angles to enhance their depth and, along with rich oranges and blues, it gives the sequence a heightened sense of physicality. The spread which follows this, entitled 'The Golden Age of Hollywood', contrasts by representing white men and women together, in relative harmony (figure 4.15). This sequence is much more about glamour than 'Cold Comfort', yet here again the notion of rationality

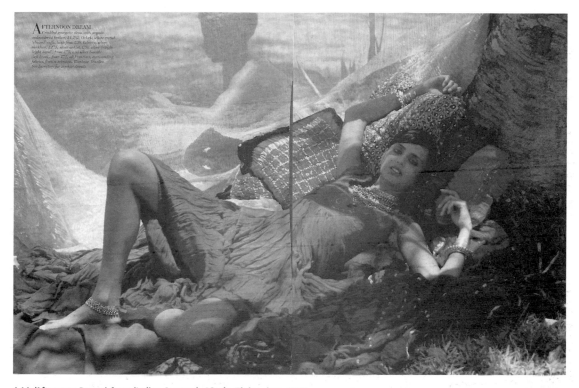

4.14 'Afternoon Dream' from 'Indian Summer', *Marie Claire*, June 1994
Rich reds and oranges dominate this scene in which the mood of sexual abandon that is created is more important than the display of clothes

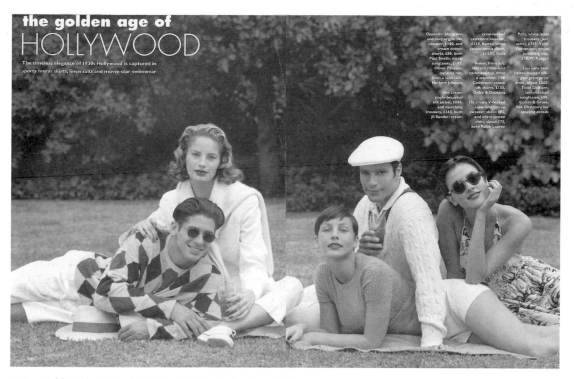

4.15 From 'The Golden Age of Hollywood', *Marie Claire*, June 1994
In contrast to the 'East', Europe is represented as more rational and restrained

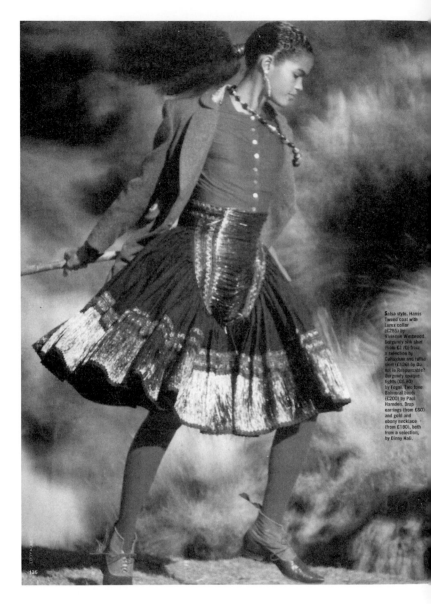

Salsa style. Harris Tweed coat with Lurex collar (£285) by Vivienne Westwood. Burgundy silk shirt (from £170) from a selection by Callaghan and raffia skirt (£126) by Ou est le Responsable? Burgundy opaque tights (£6.80) by Yogal. Two tone Balmoral boots (£200) by Paul Harnden. Drop earrings (from £50) and gold and ebony necklace (from £180), both from a selection, by Dinny Hall.

4.16 Tourism and fashion marketing collide in this feature
Source: British *Elle*, November 1987

is also encouraged by the style of clothing as well as the standard photographic lens used. There is also an almost colonial feel to this fashion spread, through the sepia tones of the photographs and the 1930s styling. The other important difference between the two fashion spreads is that, while the

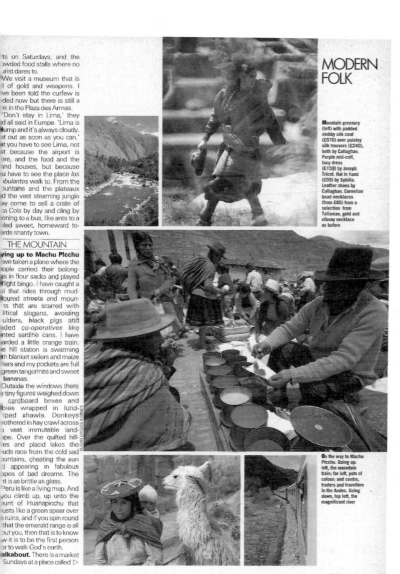

ts on Saturdays, and the
owded food stalls where no
urist dares to.
We visit a museum that is
l of gold and weapons. I
ve been told the curfew is
ded now but there is still a
nk in the Plaza des Armas.
'Don't stay in Lima,' they
all said in Europe. 'Lima is
lump and it's always cloudy.
t out as soon as you can.'
t you have to see Lima, not
st because the airport is
ere, and the food and the
and houses, but because
u have to see the place *los
ibulantes* walk to. From the
ountains and the plateaux
d the vast steaming jungle
ay come to sell a crate of
a Cola by day and cling by
ening to a bus, like ants to a
iled sweet, homeward to-
ards shanty town.

THE MOUNTAIN

ving up to Machu Picchu
ave taken a plane where the
ople carried their belong-
s in flour sacks and played
flight bingo. I have caught a
xi that rides through mud-
loured streets and moun-
s that are scarred with
litical slogans, avoiding
ulders, black pigs and
ded *co-operativos* like
nted sardine cans. I have
arded a little orange train.
e hill station is swarming
th blanket sellers and maize
lers and my pockets are full
green tangerines and sweet
bananas.
Outside the windows there
tiny figures weighed down
cardboard boxes and
bies wrapped in lurid-
iped shawls. Donkeys
othered in hay crawl across
vast immutable land-
ape. Over the quilted hill-
es and placid lakes the
uds race from the cold sad
untains, cheating the sun
appearing in fabulous
apes of bad dreams. The
t is as brittle as glass.
Peru is like a living map. And
you climb up, up unto the
unt of Huanapicchu that
usts like a green spear over
ruins, and if you spin round
that the emerald range is all
out you, then that is to know
w it is to be the first person
r to walk God's earth.
alkabout. There is a market
Sundays at a place called ▷

MODERN
FOLK

Mountain greenery
(left) with padded
slubby silk coat
(£570) over paisley
silk trousers (£240),
both by Callaghan.
Purple mid-calf,
lacy dress
(£159) by Joseph
Tricot. Hat in hand
(£59) by Sybilla.
Leather shoes by
Callaghan. Cornelian
bead necklaces
(from £85) from a
selection from
Talisman, gold and
ebony necklace
as before

On the way to Machu
Picchu. Going up:
left, the mountain
train; far left, pots of
colour; and centre,
traders and travellers
in the Andes. Going
down, top left, the
magnificent river

latter concentrates on the clothing, the former concentrates on atmosphere.
The context of these images within the fashion magazine leaves the predominantly white women as the surveyors of 'Other' women.

While I have discussed the use of colonial and exotic photographic messages in tourist and fashion photography separately, within the recent dominance of lifestyle culture there is little difference between these forms. Sisley's photo 'magazine' from Spring/Summer 1990 makes this clear. The subject of this fashion label's photo magazine was a Moroccan caravan tour. Along with the series of travel photographs of a European man and woman, presumably in Sisley clothes, is the male traveller's diary. There is no written information on the clothes, and they are clearly not the main subject of the photographs, which concentrate on building up an atmosphere of unhindered travel. It is not just the fashion advertiser that has manipulated 'the exotic' into a lifestyle and a fashion statement. Fashion magazines such as *Elle* and *Vogue* have done the same. *Elle*'s fashion spread from November 1987 entitled 'Weave a Winter's Tale of Fashion's Bright New Folklore' was shot in Peru, and combines photographs of the season's clothes with tourist brochure images (figure 4.16). The main text is of a travel diary, with a subtext of photo titles that combine tourist descriptions and clothing details that include prices. Here, Peru is turned into the flavour of the month for fashion influence and tourism, which are not distinguished between in layout and photographic format. In a similar vein, *Vogue* focused on Egypt in their May 1989 issue.

Images and photographs for both these magazines are the key to their commercial success. Here, there is also no distinct line between the advertisement and editorial photograph. What is clear, however, is the dominance of commercial interest in all these photographic images, which are contrived and stylised and are 'positioned on a threshold between two worlds: the consumer public and a mythic elite created in the utopia of the photograph as well as in the reality of a social group maintained by the fashion industry' (Brooks 1992: 18–19).

THE CONTEXT OF THE IMAGE

Don Slater has criticised the **semiotic** critique of advertisements (characterised by writers such as Roland Barthes and Judith Williamson) for taking as assumed precisely what needs to be explained – 'the relations and practices within which discourses are formed and operated' (Slater 1983: 258). Barthes' and Williamson's readings of advertisements have only provided a very limited social and historical context. Often even simple pieces of information, such as the magazine from which the images have been extracted and the date of advertisements, have not been mentioned. Liz Wells has commented on some of the limitations of *Decoding Advertisements*, especially Williamson's lack of consideration of multiple readings (Wells 1992).

While scholars have devoted some space to the understanding of a broad cultural context, the exploration of political and economic contexts is more rare. The vast array of commercial messages has also made their contextualisation increasingly difficult. It would be impossible to contextualise them all. Information about processes of production are not always easily available, and this increases the reality of consumption over that of production:

What commodities fail to communicate to consumers is information about the process of production. Unlike goods in earlier societies, they do not bear the signature of their makers, whose motives and actions we might access because we knew who they were. . . . The real and full meaning of production is hidden beneath the empty appearance in exchange. Only once the real meaning has been systematically emptied out of commodities does advertising then refill this void with its own symbols. Production empties. Advertising fills. The real is hidden by the imaginary.

(Jhally 1990: 50)

To decode photographs and advertising images more effectively, it is essential for us to understand their context. Let us take, for example, Williamson's reading of the Lancia car advertisement (1979). Would a discussion of Lancia manufacturing and car production in the late 1970s reveal more about the image?

Since the founding of the Lancia firm in 1907, Lancia had been known for their production of quality cars for gentlemen, as one writer described it. With increasing conglomeration in all industries throughout the twentieth century, Lancia, as a family firm, ran into trouble and was eventually taken over by Fiat in 1969 (Weernink 1979). The Beta saloon was the first car to be produced by Lancia after the merger, Fiat, which was known for producing smaller, cheaper cars, needed to distinguish the Beta from its own cars. Style and quality needed to be suggested, and 'Lancia – the Most Italian Car' was the slogan used to enhance the sense of stylishness of the Lancia range generally. It is this slogan which has been visualised in the 1979 advertisement discussed by Williamson.

Apart from asserting a sense of style and quality, why has Lancia chosen to represent any form of labour relations in the advertisement? Most car advertisements of this period tended to talk about the car itself and its features – for example, its economical use of petrol or the size of its boot. This advertisement does not discuss the car's actual features at all. In the late 1970s strikes took place in many major industries in Britain and Europe. In September 1978, for example, the Ford car workers at Dagenham went on strike for nine weeks. Car manufacturers generally must have wanted to maintain an image of good industrial relations. The illusion of the contented happy peasant worker in the vineyards depicted by the ad discussed earlier (see page 164) glosses over the general unrest that was present during this period. Finally, the image of the peasant worker could carry another function. During the mid-1970s, the car industry began to introduce microprocessors into production for increased automation. The peasant workers depicted in the ad, outside of industrial production, also acted to represent Lancia as a quality 'hand-crafted', 'gentleman's' car.

Image worlds

Let us look at an example of marketing photography, where an understanding of the context within which images are produced helps us to perceive the extent to which commercial interests affect photographic practice. David Nye, in *Image Worlds*, gives us a detailed exploration of the context of production, dissemination and historical setting of General Electric's photographs between 1900 and 1930 (**Nye 1985**). As Nye notes, commercial photographers do not strive for uniqueness (as does the artist photographer), but rather for a solidity of a predictable character. In spite of their documentary appearance, Nye notes the contrast between the images produced by a socially concerned documentary photographer and a commercial photographer, even when the subject is the same. He compares two photographs of Southern textile mills, one by Lewis Hine, the other by a photographer working for General Electric. While Hine emphasises the people and children in the mills who work in potentially dangerous environments, the commercial photographer's image stresses machinery, electrification and technical progress (Nye 1985: 55–56).

Nye also notes how, by the beginning of the twentieth century, the management of General Electric discovered the need to address four distinct groups – engineers, blue collar workers, managers and consumers. Their desire to say different things to different groups affected the production of images for the company's various publications. While the *General Electric Review* (a company-sponsored scientific journal) used photographs which emphasised the machines, the publications for workers employed images which concentrated on the idea of the corporation as community.

Nye not only notes the varying sorts of photographs for different publications, but also the changing production of images over time. While images from 1880 to 1910 expressed a sense of relationship between workers and managers (they were often photographed together), images after this date present a picture of a workforce which was much more highly controlled by management. Nye details how by the 1920s General Electric had 82,000 workers in their employment, in contrast to 6,000 in 1885. The burgeoning workforce made management's role more important, and the artisanal skills of the previous era had also all but disappeared. Labour unrest began to increase during the 1910s. In 1917, partly in response to these conflicts, General Electric began to publish a magazine called *Works News* which was distributed to all blue collar workers twice a month. The paper did not address the general workforce, but was tailored to each site. The covers of the magazine produced a new kind of photographic image not previously used by the company. They featured individual skilled workers photographed from head to toe and engrossed in a piece of interesting work. This kind of image was repeated on the cover of nearly every issue of *Works News* (figure 4.17), and did not represent the reality for most of General Electric's employees; but, since these workers were individualised and isolated, the

DAVID NYE (1985) **Image Worlds: Corporate Identities at General Electric 1890–1930**, Cambridge, MA: MIT Press

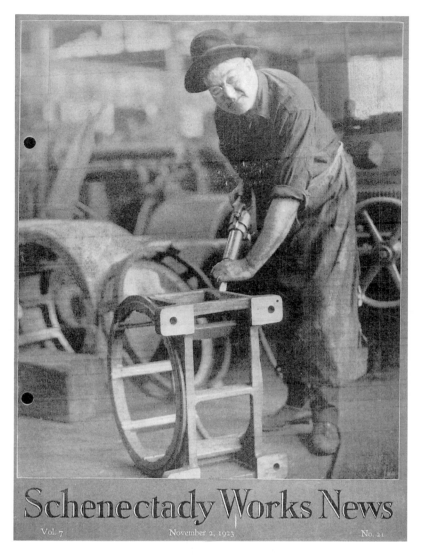

4.17 Schenectady Works News General Electric, 2 November 1923
Images which represented individual workers engrossed in a piece of interesting work dominated the cover of
Works News during the 1920s. It did not represent the reality for most workers, but presented images which
gave a certain dignity and harmony during a period fraught with conflicts

generalisation was only implicit. These kinds of images hardly existed inside
the magazine, which concentrated instead on the workers – as a community
which went on holiday, played in sports teams and participated in other
forms of recreation. The style of the cover photographs had a history in
Lewis Hine's work a decade earlier. He had aimed to represent and give

dignity to 'real men' in difficult work. In adopting this style, the General Electric photographers were simply using it as a representational strategy to define the image world of the General Electric plant. It is only through an appreciation of the context of the image that we can understand the intent in the production of images by Hine and the General Electric photographer as different, and can therefore appreciate the different meanings of the image. The production of meaning is a process. As Marx noted in *Grundrisse*:

> It is not only the object that production creates for consumption . . . [It] also gives consumption its precise nature, its character, its finish. . . . Hunger is hunger, but the hunger that is satisfied by cooked meat eaten with a knife and fork is a different hunger from that which bolts down raw meat with the aid of hand nail and tooth. Production thus produces not only the object but also the manner of consumption, not only objectively but also subjectively.
>
> (Marx quoted in Slater 1983: 247)

CASE STUDY: BENETTON

This final case study will be used to draw together a number of strategies for considering commercial photography which have been suggested above. While giving due importance to economic and social contexts, it will also explore the language of particular ads, as well as their reception. Benetton's advertising photography challenges traditional boundaries and is also a rare

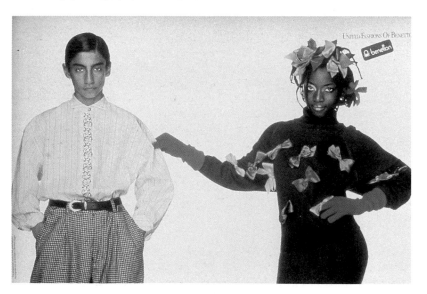

4.18 Benetton advertisement, 1987
Most of the early Benetton advertisements encouraged the notion of racial exclusivity. Europeans were invariably blond-haired and blue-eyed, and Africans were always very dark skinned

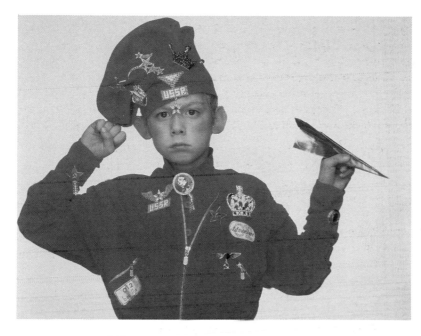

UNITED COLORS OF BENETTON.

4.19 USSR, Benetton, 1987

example of an advertising photographer being constantly named, as one would be in the Art world. It is through his Benetton imagery that Toscani's work has entered the Art gallery and his name has become widely known.[2] In 1984, when Toscani joined Benetton, the United Colors campaign began. Benetton suggests that the genesis of their multicultural image was by chance and that they were originally only concerned with the colour of Benetton jumpers, until somebody pointed out that 'it wasn't just the sweaters that came in different shades' (*The Face* 83, November 1987). Yet what were the economic reasons for using this kind of image? In 1978, Benetton's export market was 26 per cent of its total sales, but by 1981 its export share had increased to 40 per cent of its total output. By 1983 export sales exceeded domestic sales. In 1986 the Benetton Group was finally launched on the stock exchange. During the mid-1980s, therefore, the company changed from being an Italian (and family) company, to becoming an international player for world markets (Belussi 1987: 12–22). The company obviously needed a new image to express their growing importance internationally.

Multicultural multinationalism

Just as Coke had exploited the image of world harmony in the 1970s, so Benetton too decided to foster a 'global' image. David A. Bailey has discussed these early images as a process of 'objectification and fragmentation' (Bailey 1989). By objectification he referred to the usual process of commodification – here of ethnicity – which takes place in advertising. The

2 Benetton imagery was shown in *The Globe* exhibition which toured the UK in 1989. The image of the new-born baby was also shown in an exhibition of images of motherhood at Boymans-van-Beunigen Museum, Rotterdam, Holland.

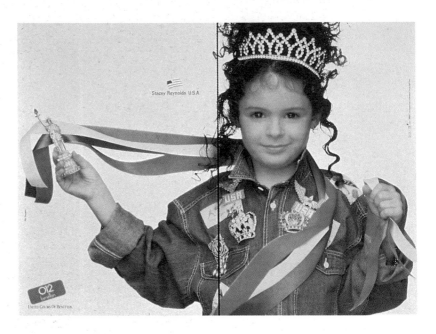

4.20 USA, Benetton, 1987

L. BACK AND V. QUAADE (1993)
'Dream Utopias, Nightmare
Realities: Imagining Race and
Culture within the World of
Benetton', **Third Text** 22

'fragmentation' he referred to was the process whereby national cultures
were reduced to caricatures in the Benetton ads, ignoring the flux within
identities. Benetton's notion of international unity was constructed within a
'grammar of race' (**Back and Quaade 1993: 65**).

It is not the suggestion of unity in difference which was established but
rather the notion of difference as hegemonic. The African children selected
as models are all black – in contrast to the white, blue-eyed Europeans
(figure 4.18).

Benetton's multiculturalism was bound to be hegemonic. Operating through
the confines of a multinational, the most superficial reading of Benetton's
images between 1984 and 1989 suggest that global harmony can be
achieved by wearing Benetton clothes. These images, however, are not
ideologically innocent. All these images were taken in the confines of the
studio, where make-up, lighting, poses, etc. were completely controlled by
Toscani. Let us look at an advertisement made up of two double-page
spreads which depict a young Russian boy, dressed in red Benetton clothing
and sporting Soviet regalia (figure 4.19), and a young American girl called
Stacey Reynolds in denim clothing (figure 4.20) (*The Face*, March 1987).
'Stacey' is obviously a mythic character since two different American girls are
given this name in Benetton advertisements.

Toscani says different things about America and the USSR through the
model's poses and regalia. The Soviet boy stands straight, and salutes us with
a stern expression on his face. In his left hand, he carries a paper rocket in

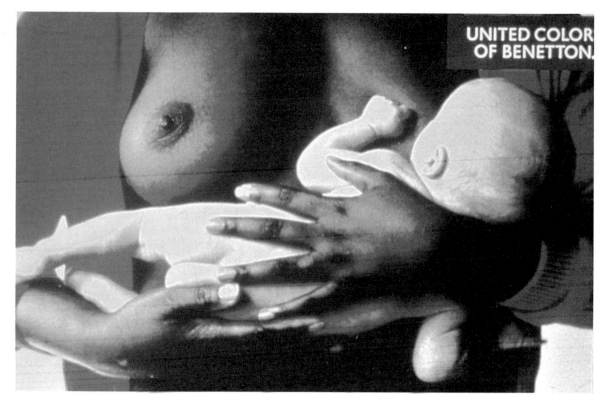

4.21 'Black Mama', Benetton, 1989
Slave relations of black women nursing white children were clearly echoed in this image. The black woman is also dehumanised here into an unidentifiable 'Other'

army, camouflage colours – perhaps a reference to the arms race. In contrast, the American girl smiles at us gently and carries a model of the Statue of Liberty. Symbolically, we have the gentle America presented as the upholder of liberty, contrasting with the stern and uncompromising USSR that is presented as responsible for the build up of arms. In many Benetton photographs there is clear support for capitalist ideology. In another image, a Chinese boy, dressed in blue, carries a copy of Chairman Mao's 'Little Red Book'. The book is upside down.

The Benetton manufacturing model

The stinging contradiction in Benetton's image of global harmony can be seen by exploring their context of production. Benetton's business success rests on their 'flexibility in manufacturing', which allows the company to respond quickly to changes in fashion trends. Through a computerised network that links retailers with the Benetton headquarters, Benetton is immediately made aware of fast-selling items, which can then be reproduced according to demand. This entails a large amount of subcontracting, a system

191

that encourages small workshops with non-unionised labour, and home-
working which is notorious for being badly paid (Phizacklea 1990: 14–16;
Mitter 1986: 112–115). As far as the relationship of this Western company to
Third World workers is concerned, this too is not a picture of world
harmony. Much of Benetton's success in world markets is linked to the
establishment of the multifibre agreement, which limits clothing imports
from the Third World for the benefit of European manufacturers. Secondly,
the system of subcontracting has been used by many companies in the West
to franchise out unskilled 'shell making' to factories in the Third World,
where labour is cheap. It is clear that in 1988, Benetton were looking to
exploit the labour of the Third World. As Luciano Benetton said in the
Channel 4 programme, *How to Survive Lifestyles*, in 1988,

> We want also to analyse the opportunity of manufacturing in Far
> East Asia, because we have solved for the next future the problem of
> the competition coming from those countries and the best way to
> ·face the competition is to combine our technology with very low
> . . . labour cost.

Shock advertising – ahistoricism and ambiguity

Already aware that their advertising campaigns were being read ambiguously, Toscani discarded the slightly sugary image of children smiling sweetly
for a series of bold images which played on contrasts, particularly that of
skin colour. Before 1989, Benetton's images still seemed to relate to the
genre of studio fashion photography. Benetton clothes and other accou-
trements of fashion were worn by the models, who were positioned in a
shallow space. After 1989, this relationship collapsed and the clothes ceased
to be represented at all. Back and Quaade (1993) have described the
1989–1991 phase as that of 'Racialisation and Ambiguity'. The notion of
racial essences continued; but beyond this, racist imagery and history were
evoked. This series included the image of a black woman nursing a white
child, as well as an image of a black and white man handcuffed together.
Both images created an uproar in America, as well as discontent in Britain.
The former image clearly echoed slave relations, where black slave mothers
nursed white children (figure 4.21). The image also dehumanised the black
woman through the way it was cropped – she is a headless unidentifiable
'Other'. This image was not born in isolation. We can even find fashion
quotations for it. The torso of a Dahomey woman was photographed by
Penn in a similar way. Her headless body is totally objectified and dehumanised, and is presented for consumption to the predominantly white viewer
– she cannot even look back (see Penn 1974: 39). Benetton, however,
suggested that their advertisement represented 'racial' harmony, with the
portrayal of black and white together.
Images do change meaning according to their context; yet images, like
everything else, are historically based and cannot avoid the meanings and
symbolisms which the past puts upon them. Benetton, however, with dollars
in their pockets, chose to suggest that they could ignore history and empty

these images of meaning. They insisted that they could not be responsible for how they were decoded by individuals. Historical interpretation was dismissed as individual interpretation. Yet, as Vittoria Rava, Benetton's advertising manager, commented: 'we believe our advertising needs to shock – otherwise people will not remember it' (Graham 1990). Historical referencing was essential for the campaign's effectiveness.

Following the storm over these advertisements in the United States, Benetton's sales figures fell in America. In sneering response, Toscani and Benetton released a series of fluffy animal pictures – a black sheep kissing a white wolf; a black dog and white cat – as though to absolve the previous images of any racist context, and to present Benetton as primarily interested in bold photographs which depicted contrast. The Benetton experience of 'global advertising' clearly indicates the impossibility of globalism. Photographs are read differently in different cultures and countries.

Pseudo-documentary and the courting of controversy

The controversy of Benetton images increased as Benetton discarded the constructed fantasy image of advertising for the seeming realism of photo-documentary. This third phase of advertising has been described as an experimentation with 'pseudo-documentary' whose overriding theme is 'a fetishisation of images of abject catastrophe' (Back and Quaade 1993: 74). The new campaign included the photographs of David Kirby dying from AIDS, an African soldier holding a human femur behind his back, a burning car in an Italian street, an albino Zulu girl being shunned by others and an image of poor black people scrambling in a waste lorry. In using these images, Toscani defied the boundaries of photographic genres, in which the 'reality' of the documentary image stands in stark contrast to the fantasy world of advertising. Luciano Benetton argued that in using these images they were not attempting to be 'eccentric or provocative' but that it was 'an attempt to get away from traditional advertising in the belief that it has no power and no value any more' (Baker, 1991: 29). The collapsing of these genres, however, caused outrage. The photograph of the man dying from AIDS, the Zulu girl and the firebombed car had all been published earlier in documentary contexts, but the context of commodity sales inflamed people's passions and opinions. As has been noted above, the production of meaning is a process, and that process is affected by the photograph's context. The promotion of Benetton has been carried out primarily through the instigation of controversy. It must surely be for this reason that the company has at times refused to recognise or perhaps has exploited the quandaries which editors of magazines have faced. Ambiguity after all has increased the controversiality of images and courted free publicity. *Elle* magazine, for example, accused Benetton of deliberately sending advertisements to magazines just before printing deadlines to make it difficult for magazines to avoid using particular advertisements. On another occasion, Benetton refused to substitute the advertisement representing an Albino Zulu girl being shunned by other girls for the *New Yorker*. The paper was running a piece about Malcolm X and racial tension in the same issue, and they did not want viewers to think that they were mixing advertising and editorial. Benetton argued, 'To ask us to pull

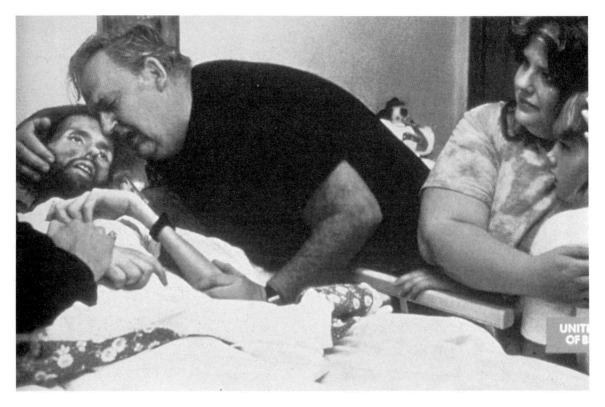

4.22 David Kirby, Benetton, 1992
Documentary images such as this one raised questions about what was morally acceptable within an advertisement. The contrast between the 'realism' of documentary and the fantasy world of advertising also collapsed

this ad because they thought their readers would misconstrue it in the context of the story sets up a dangerous precedent' (Savan 1990).

Yet during the LA riots of 1992, Benetton, of their own accord, withdrew their billboards of a burning firebombed car from the streets of LA. Suddenly Benetton seemed to care about the new meanings which their images could create. They replaced this image with one of people of various ethnic backgrounds smiling broadly. Of course, on this occasion, Benetton again exploited the free publicity of the news cameras. CNN sent a camera crew to document the event. Fred Bacher commented on Benetton's approach: 'What I find offensive about the ads is not their extreme violence; it's their trendy ambiguity. Benetton's ads are not constructed to help their consumers form ideas about social issues' (Bacher 1992: 45–46).

In reading these 'pseudo-documentary' images, we must remember that Benetton has not just added their green logo. These photos have been cropped and touched up, in a similar way to which a commercial photographer might enhance the image of a cake to give it greater visual appeal. The original black and white photo of Kirby was hand-coloured by Benetton

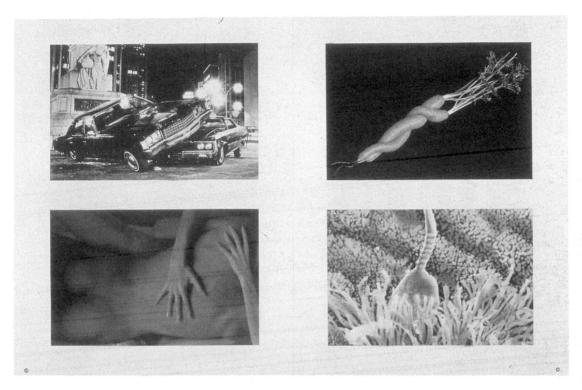

4.23 From *Colors* 13, Benetton, 1995
These photo sequences continue the 'trendy ambiguity' of Benetton advertising

(figure 4.22). One interesting fact about Benetton's use of documentary images is that until 1995 they have always been in fantastic colours, despite the rich black and white documentary tradition. This must be a deliberate decision on the part of Benetton, in order to complement their slogan. The enhanced colouring on some of the images seems to give these photographs a surreality which is disturbing and has added to the distaste which has been felt for their use.

By 1994, Benetton had moved beyond the pseudo-documentary, but continued to refer to conflict situations. Still playing with photographic genres, Toscani photographed the bloodstained clothes of a soldier from former Yugoslavia in catalogue-style photography. The distaste of and for this image and others has led Benetton retailers in Germany, USA and France to take out lawsuits against the company, in the belief that Benetton's ad campaigns have added to their losses.

Colors and the politics of location

In 1992 Benetton launched *Colors*. The magazine has provided Benetton with an avenue to highlight issues, which their advertisements have touched on.

Subtitled 'a magazine about the *rest* of the world' (my emphasis), the centrality of Europe is undeniable. Each issue deals with a subject such as 'race', ecology, immigration, food, etc. The presentation of information is fragmented. What is bizarre and quirky is given importance. 'The rest of the world' remains a space for exoticism and fantasy. In the magazine, form also appears to be as, or more, important than content. Whether dealing with shopping, rubbish or cosmetic surgery, Toscani isolates products or fragments of the human body, photographing them frontally, in a shallow space, in a similar way to the image of a perfume bottle insert in an advertisement. Isolated and often distorted in size, objects are fetishised and appear surreal. Surrealism pervades the magazine and has been enhanced through experimental, digital photography, which has, for example, depicted both Queen Elizabeth and Arnold Schwarzenegger as black and Pope John Paul II as Chinese. Surrealism allows Benetton to highlight issues without taking any particular stance. *Colors* 13 continues the sense of fragmentation and surreality. A page about contact carries a black and white image of two cars which have collided, along with the picture of two entwined carrots, a sperm meeting an egg and two people embracing (figure 4.23). What is different about *Colors* 13 to the previous issues is that there are no words, and many of the photographs are framed in their traditional rectangular shape; it is only at the end of the magazine that we find the written word. The editorial gives us a simple outline about how we read images that could be found in any photography textbook. Here Benetton, targeted for their use of imagery, turns itself into a visual literacy educator. They consider the ambiguity of photographs as well as the way in which editors and photographers crop and retouch images in order to create a 'picture of reality that corresponds with their style or politics'. They make no qualms about adding 'we do that at Colors too', but there is no explanation of what their politics or attitudes to anything may be, and the fragmentation and bizarre juxtapositions of images only mystify further.

Benetton's advertising and photography has become integrally linked to their corporate image-making. It was even their advertisements which furnished the company with a new logo. And Benetton's advertisements have become so divorced from the sales of any particular product that they function much more clearly in the enhancement and creation of their image world-wide. As Luciano Benetton writes in *Global Vision*, a Benetton publication which documents the company's development and marketing and provides a visual catalogue of their advertising, 'Our international image and the substance of our company are the same – a global group open to the world's influences and engaged in a continuing quest for new frontiers' (Benetton 1993). The 'United Colors' campaigns have certainly visualised this imperialist philosophy.

BIBLIOGRAPHY

KEY TEXTS

Alloula, Malek (1987) *The Colonial Harem*, Manchester: Manchester University Press
Back, L. and Quaade, V. (1993) 'Dream Utopias, Nightmare Realities: Imagining Race and

Culture within the World of Benetton', *Third Text* 22

Barthes, Roland (1977a) 'The Rhetoric of the Image' in *Image, Music, Text*, London: Fontana

Berger, John (1972a) *Ways of Seeing*, London: BBC

Brookes, Rosetta (1992) 'Fashion Photography' in J. Ash and E. Wilson (eds) *Chic Thrills: A Fashion Reader*, London: Pandora

Craik, Jennifer (1994) 'Soft Focus: Techniques of Fashion Photography' in *The Face of Fashion*, London: Routledge

Evans, C. and Thornton, M. (1989) *Women and Fashion: A New Look*, London: Quartet

Goldman, Robert (1992) *Reading Ads Socially*, London: Routledge

Myers, Kathy (1990) 'Selling Green' in C. Squiers (ed.) *The Critical Image: Essays on Contemporary Photography*, Seattle: Bay Press

Nye, David (1985) *Image Worlds: Corporate Identities at General Electric 1890–1930*, Cambridge, MA: MIT Press

Slater, Don (1983) 'Marketing Mass Photography' in P. Davis and H. Walton (eds) *Language, Image, Media*, Oxford: Blackwell

Squiers, Carol (1992) 'The Corporate Year in Pictures' in R. Bolton (ed.) *The Contest of Meaning: Critical Histories of Photography*, Cambridge, MA: MIT Press

Stein, Sally (1981) 'The Composite Photographic Image and the Composition of Consumer Ideology', *Art Journal* Spring 1981

Tagg, John (1988) 'A Democracy of the Image: Photographic Portraiture and Commodity Production' in *The Burden of Representation: Essays on Photographies and Histories*, Basingstoke: Macmillan

Williamson, Judith (1978) *Decoding Advertisements: Ideology and Meaning in Advertising*, London: Marion Boyars

—— (1979) 'Great History that Photographs Mislaid' in Photography Workshop (ed.) *Photography/Politics One*, London: Comedia

Winship, Janice (1987a) 'Handling Sex' in R. Betterton (ed.) *Looking On: Images of Femininity in the Visual Arts and Media*, London: Pandora

OTHER REFERENCES

Bacher, Fred (1992) 'The Popular Condition: Fear and Clothing in LA', *The Humanist*, September/October

Bailey, David (1988) 'Re-thinking Black Representations' *Ten/8* 31

—— (1989) 'People of the World' in P. Wombell (ed.) *The Globe: Representing the World* York, Impressions Gallery

Baker, Lindsay (1991) 'Taking Advertising to its Limit', *Times* 22 July, p. 29

Barthes, Roland (1977b) 'The Photographic Message' in S. Heath (ed.) *Image, Music, Text*, London: Fontana

Bate, David (1993) 'Photography and the Colonial Vision', *Third Text* 22

Belussi, Fiorenza (1987) *Benetton: Information Technology in Production and Distribution: A Case Study of the Innovative Potential of Traditional Sectors*, SPRU, University of Sussex

Benetton (1993) *Global Vision: United Colors of Benetton*, Tokyo: Robundo

Benson, S. H. (nd) *Some Examples of Benson Advertising*, S. H. Benson Firm

Berger, John (1972b) 'The Political Uses of Photomontage' in *Selected Essays and Articles, the Look of Things*, Harmondsworth: Penguin

Devlin, Polly (1979) *Vogue Book of Fashion Photography*, London: Condé Nast

Edwards, Elizabeth (ed.) (1992) *Anthropology and Photography 1860–1920*, New Haven: Yale University Press

Edwards, Steve (1989) 'The Snapshooters of History', *Ten/8* 32

Ewing, William (1991) 'Perfect Surface' in *The Idealising Vision: The Art of Fashion Photography*, New York: Aperture

Freedman, Jim (1990) 'Bringing it all Back Home: A Commentary on *Into the Heart of Africa*', Museum Quarterly, February

Goffman, Erving (1979) *Gender Advertisements*, London: Macmillan

Graham, Judith (1989) 'Benetton "Colors" the Race Issue' *Advertising Age*

Gupta, Sunil (1986) 'Northern Media, Southern Lives' in Photography Workshop (ed.) *Photography/Politics*: Two, London: Comedia

Hall, Stuart (1993) 'Encoding/Decoding' in S. Durring (ed.) *The Cultural Studies Reader*, London: Routledge (first published in 1980)

Harrison, Martin (1991) *Appearances: Fashion Photography Since 1945*, London: V & A

Jhally, Sut (1990) *Codes of Advertising*, London: Routledge

Leiss, W., Kline, S. and Jhally, S. (1986) *Social Communication in Advertising*, Toronto: Methuen

Mayle, Peter (1983) *Thirsty Work: Ten Years of Heineken Advertising*, London: Macmillan

Mitter, Swasti (1986) 'Flexibility and Control: The Case of Benetton' in *Common Fate Common Bond; Women in the Global Economy*, London: Pluto

Morris, Roderick C. (1992) 'The Best Possible Taste', *Spectator*, 15 February

Myers, Kathy (1986) *Understains: Sense and Seduction in Advertising*, London: Comedia

Penn, Irving (1974) *Worlds in a Small Room*, London: Studio Vista

Phizacklea, Annie (1990) 'The Benetton Model' in *Unpackaging the Fashion Industry: Gender, Racism and Class in Production*, London: Routledge

Pollock, Griselda (1990) 'Missing Women – Re-Thinking Early Thoughts on Images of Women' in C. Squiers (ed.) *The Critical Image: Essays on Contemporary Photography*, Seattle: Bay Press

Posner, Jill (1982) *Spray it Loud*, London: Routledge

Prochaska, David (1991) 'Fantasia of the Phototheque: French Postcard Views of Senegal', *African Arts*, October

Richards, Thomas (1990) *Commodity Culture in Victorian Britain*, London: Verso

Said, Edward (1985) *Orientalism*, London: Penguin (first published in 1978)

Savan, Leslie (1990) 'Logo-rrhea', *Voice*, 24 November, New York

Schildkrout, Enid (1991) 'The Spectacle of Africa Through the Lens of Herbert Lang', *African Arts*, October

Sontag, Susan (1979) *On Photography*, Harmondsworth: Penguin

Stein, Sally (1992) 'The Graphic Ordering of Desire: Modernisation of a Middle-Class Women's Magazine 1919–1939' in R Bolton (ed.) *The Contest of Meaning: Critical Histories of Photography* Cambridge, MA: MIT Press

Ten/8 16 'Black Image – Staying On'

Ten/8 2(3) 'Critical Decade – Black British Photography in the '80s'

Weernink, Wim (1979) *La Lancia: 70 Years of Excellence*, London: Motor Racing Publications

Wells, Liz (1992) 'Judith Williamson, Decoding Advertisements' in *Reading into Cultural Studies*, London: Routledge

Williams, Raymond (1980) 'Advertising the Magic System' in *Problems in Materialism and Culture*, London: Verso

Winship, Janice (1987b) *Inside Women's Magazines*, London: Pandora

CHAPTER 5

On and beyond the white walls

Photography as art

LIZ WELLS

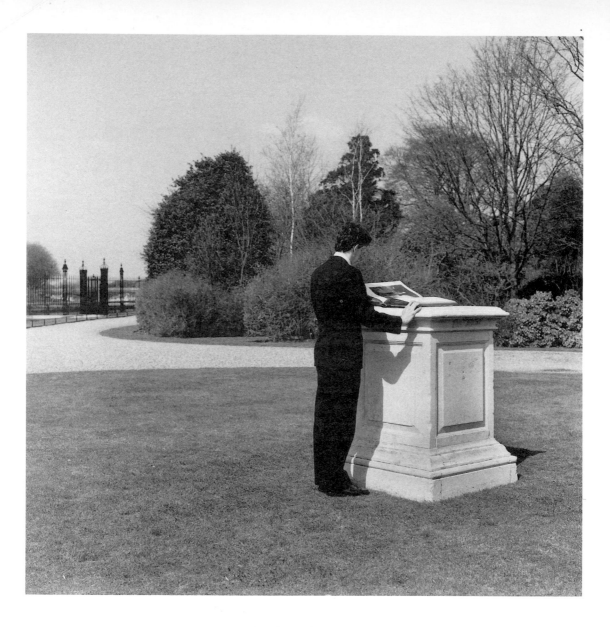

Analytical Inquiry
into the Principles of Taste

5.1 Karen Knorr, from *Country Life*

On and beyond
the white walls
Photography as art

INTRODUCTION

> The history of art photography *is* an extraordinary picture story.
> Individual images, extracted from the larger histories of technology,
> economics, politics, and popular culture, are stripped of their
> context and meaning and then placed in a time line of formal
> invention. And photographs consciously created as art fit right into
> that aesthetic context, all on their own. Photographic images are
> intentionally made into, or are made as, beautiful, prized objects.
>   (Heiferman 1989: 20)

Photography is significant as a means of visual communication. But the
history of photography as **Art** focuses not so much upon photographic
communication as upon photographs as objects, reified for their aesthetic
qualities. It follows that, typically, such histories focus upon pictures, and
the works of specific practitioners. Thus, the story of photography as art
tends to be presented as a history of 'great', or 'master' (sic), photographers.
Such accounts not only divorce photography as fine art from the larger
history of photography with its ubiquity of practices, but also rarely engage
with broader political issues and social contexts.

   This chapter considers debates relating to the status of photography as fine
art. In particular, it discusses photography and the art gallery. The first section

focuses on nineteenth-century debates and practices. The principal focus of the chapter is twentieth-century photography considered in the context of Western modern and post-modern art movements. Finally, there is discussion of funding structures, the gallery system, publishing, and the international context. The chapter is written from a British perspective: obviously Britain cannot be considered in isolation from broader debates and developments, but attention is given to particular British manifestations. For instance, Britain is not unique in providing state finance for the Arts, but, as is indicated in the brief discussion of the Arts Council funding system in the final section of the chapter, particular **ideological** assumptions characterise British provisions.

As with any overview, a word of caution is appropriate: this discussion should be taken as a starting point for fuller exploration of sets of debates, not as a comprehensive compendium. For instance, choice of photographs for illustration has been restricted to landscape. As will be seen in the third case study, focus on a particular genre allows more immediate comparison of form, content and subject-matter than would be the case with a random compilation of images. Landscape also contrasts with the emphasis on people (in personal albums or in the streets) in previous chapters.

The status of the photograph as Art

In 1989, 150 years after Fox Talbot's announcement, the Royal Academy, London, mounted its first ever photography exhibition, *The Art of Photography*. Arguably this represented the acknowledgement by the Arts establishment that has been sought, variously, throughout photography's history.

Photographs have been exhibited right from the inception of photography. They were included in the Great Exhibition of 1851, and the Royal Society of Arts organised its first show of photography in 1852.[1] In the nineteenth century, there were no mass media of the sort taken for granted now, so exhibition was one of the prime ways of communicating information about new technological developments. But, from very early days, critics and practitioners disagreed as to the status of photography as Art.

This debate begs the question as to what is meant by 'Art'. In this chapter we use 'Art' to refer to fine art practices relating to the gallery and the Arts establishment, by contrast with more general understandings of photography as an 'art' or expressive skill. Many claims have been made for photography as Art. Art tends to be acclaimed for its perception on the condition of humankind. The artist is characterised as a special sort of 'seer', or visionary of 'truth', poetically expressed. In the case of photography, the artist is viewed as transcending 'mere recording' of events, offering a unique perspective on or insight into people, places, objects, relationships, circumstances.

Photography impacted on the role and status of painting. Writing in the 1930s, Walter Benjamin argued that the 'aura' associated with the uniqueness of the work of fine art such as a painting would wither in favour of

MIKE WEAVER (1989a) **The Art of Photography**, London: Royal Academy of Arts

1 The 1851 exhibition, a celebration of British achievements, was held at the purpose-built Crystal Palace, London. The Royal Society of Arts is also London-based.

the photograph, which he welcomed as a more democratic – or less exclusive – medium because of its potential for mass reproduction (Benjamin 1992b). Here it is the anti-elitist potential of photography which is being stressed. Other critics, including curator and historian, Beaumont Newhall, have based claims for photography on its formal and expressive qualities which accord with the Western, post-Renaissance tradition. Such claims stem from connoisseurship; that is, valuation of the sensitive and the precious within photography. They are not necessarily intended to assert parity of status with older Art forms.

Since the 1970s the question of the status of photography as fine art has become increasingly complex – or increasingly irrelevant (depending on your viewpoint) – as lens-based media, including photography, video, slide projection and installation have increasingly featured within the gallery. Furthermore, subject-matter has · shifted in consequence, in particular of feminist critiques, and of the influence of popular media.

In considering the status of nineteenth-century photography it is important to remember that art and technology, the expressive and the mechanical, were viewed as distinct. Given video, and multimedia, this conceptual opposition is obviously outdated, even supposing it was ever valid. But, historically, this distinction characterised the reception of photography and attitudes towards it. The status of photography is related to this. To take an example: historian Margaret Harker notes that combination printing, using two or more 'negatives' (glass plates) in order to achieve particular pre-visualised results, was common from the 1850s. This could be viewed as an artist's approach to using the medium. But she argues that the first attempt to promote photography as *fine art* was not made until a Camera Club exhibition in Vienna in 1981 (Harker 1979). Yet Aaron Scharf, in relation to the Paris photography exhibition of 1855, describes photographers including Durieu, Nadar and Bayard as '"immigrants" to the Fine Arts' (Scharf 1974: 140). For many photographers, it was artistic potential in association with its apparent accuracy of transcription which was the source of fascination, but they did not necessarily see themselves as fine artists. For instance, British photographers such as Julia Margaret Cameron or Lady Clementina Hawarden, whose work might now be viewed as Art, did not themselves make this claim.

Thus, we should distinguish between claims made by photographers for themselves, or for particular movements, and claims made at a later stage by historians, critics and curators. For instance, Soviet revolutionary artists aimed to take work out from the gallery into everyday social life, viewing art both as an essential tool in the re-education of the mass of the Russian people and also as 'art for the people'. Nowadays, retrospectives of this work are curated for Art galleries, spaces which the Soviet artists would surely have viewed as bourgeois and elitist! Likewise, early twentieth-century documentary, originally destined for publications in social surveys, magazines or books, now takes pride of place within the gallery and the archive. Peter Galassi, as curator of the 1995–1996 touring exhibition of highlights from the photography archive at the Museum of Modern Art in New York, distinguishes between photography intended as Art and 'vernacular' photography, noting the differing lineages of work now included within the same collection (Galassi 1995). This distinction over-simplifies a complex history primarily as a means of classification for museums and archives which, in the late twentieth century, has become increasingly prominent – with curators increasingly influential – in both the conservation of history, and its interpretation.

EARLY DEBATES AND PRACTICES

The complex relations between photography and Art

Understanding the relationship between photography and painting in the nineteenth century involves a number of interconnected considerations. Photography in Britain and France was initially heralded for its technical recording abilities. With few exceptions, the emphasis was upon *picture-taking* rather than *picture-making* – to echo a distinction made by Margaret Harker (Harker 1979). She suggests that the development of the art of photography in the late 1850s can partly be accounted for through the increasing involvement of people trained as artists. They brought with them a concern for form and composition and, in particular, the use of light. She notes that the use of photographs as illustrations for poetry or literature, or as picture narrative and allegory, also dates from the late 1850s. In this section we consider first the influence of the transcriptive qualities of photography within changing nineteenth-century fine art practices; second, photography democratising Art; and third, photography, aesthetics and Western Art. In the following section we discuss pictorialism, and claims for the photograph as fine art made by photographers at the turn of the century.

Writing on *Art and Photography* **Aaron Scharf** (1974) emphasises uses of photographs by artists; for example, as reference notes. Only in the later chapters on twentieth-century Art movements does he acknowledge the photograph as art in its own right. As both Van Deren Coke and Aaron Scharf have indicated, a number of artists used photographs as study devices, eliminating the need to pay for models or to spend long periods of time sketching. For some, these photographic 'sketches' ultimately took over as works in their own right. For example, the French caricaturist, Nadar, first used photography as the basis for satirical portraiture, later acknowledging the photographs themselves.[2] But the use of photography also allowed artists to extend their range of references, returning from both urban 'public' spaces and rural 'open' spaces with photographic notes to support paintings made in the studio. Photographs could be used as research notes, or as models for painting. For instance, Aaron Scharf notes that Manet used photographs of the Mexican emperor, and of soldiers, when working on his paintings

AARON SCHARF (1974) **Art and Photography**, London: Allen Lane, Pelican Books, revised edition

VAN DEREN COKE (1972) The **Painter and the Photograph**, New Mexico: University of New Mexico Press

2 This was clearly indicated in sketches, photographs and tear sheets from the collection at the Paris *Bibliothèque Nationale* exhibited at the *Maison de Balzac* as part of *Mois de la Photo*, 1990

of the emperor's execution. Scharf also includes two examples, a riverscape and a seascape, by the French realist painter, Gustave Courbet, which seem to be based directly upon contemporary photographs (Scharf 1974: 127).

Realism and systems of representation

Photography was implicated within nineteenth-century Realism as an aid to painting. Discussing the implications of Realism as an historical movement in painting and in literature, in France and elsewhere, Linda Nochlin has suggested that the degree of social change experienced during the Industrial Revolution in Britain from the late eighteenth century, and the political revolutions in France, induced artists to explore everyday social experience (Nochlin 1978). Noting the dominance of Realism as a radical movement from about 1840 until 1870–1880, she suggests that there are a number of associated ambiguities including, crucially, the issue of the relation between **representation** and 'reality', itself a problematic concept. She argues that:

> The commonplace notion that Realism is a 'styleless' or transparent style, a mere simulacrum or mirror image of visual reality, is another barrier to its understanding as an historical and stylistic phenomenon. . . . Realism was no more a mere mirror of reality than any other style and its relation *qua* style to phenomenal data . . . is as complex and difficult as that of Romanticism, the Baroque or Mannerism. So far as Realism is concerned, however, the issue is greatly confused by the assertions of both its supporters and opponents, that Realists were doing no more than mirroring everyday reality. . . . These statements derived from the belief that perception could be 'pure' and unconditioned by time or place.
>
> (Nochlin 1978: 14)

Central to her approach is the contention that perception is culturally conditioned.

Aesthetic conventions reflect broader sets of ideas. Western Art since the Renaissance has used perspective as the principal system of visual organisation. Perspective is organised around a single, central viewing point and it has been argued by some critics that this system, in prioritising one central viewing position, reaffirms individualism, that is, the emphasis on the individual which emerged within entrepreneurial capitalism.

That camera optics conform to the rules of perspective has meant that photographic notes could support composition in painting. As Bill Nichols has suggested, 'Renaissance painters fabricated textual systems approximating the cues relating to normal perception better than any other strategy until the emergence of photography' (Nichols 1981: 52). Indeed, as has been noted, one of the claims made was that the photograph had the technical ability to reproduce from actuality with more accuracy than any other form

Key Archive: The National Gallery, London for a collection of nineteenth-century French paintings (including one version of Manet's *The Execution of the Emperor Maximilian*)

of representation. As such, photography, itself a part of scientific and technological development, seemed to fit within the spirit of modernity, as well as offering realist possibilities for representing aspects of modern life.

Paris underwent massive architectural and cultural change in the first half of the nineteenth century; becoming, in effect, the first modern city. Writing at that time, French poet and philosopher, Baudelaire, argued that the painter of 'modern life' should focus on the contemporary, upon the movement and change which had revolutionised everyday experience. He was among the first critics to support Realist painters, including Courbet and Manet, who challenged previous aesthetic convention through the introduction of everyday subjects and ordinary people into their work, and through the use of less 'finished' styles of painting than those expected or in keeping with the conventions of the French Academy of Art. Yet he made no particular connection between Realism and photography, dismissing the latter as an inferior form of artistic expression due to its mechanical nature. Thus, his view of the potential and limitations of the camera seems in line with that, for instance, of critics who dismissed Courbet's series of large-scale pictures of the rural community in Ornans on a number of grounds, including not only the everyday content of the image but also, as one critic put it, its appearance as 'a faulty daguerreotype'.

Photography extending Art

Photography supported painting. It also encroached very directly upon genres of painting such as portraiture, not only taking over some of the work of painters, but also extending the compass of the work. For instance, while few could afford the time and the cost of sitting for a painted portrait, the studio photographer could offer a similar service much more cheaply. As such, portraiture became more democratically available. Both high-street studios, and the touring 'jobbing' photographer became common from the mid-nineteenth century (see chapter 3). This did not prevent a continuing hierarchy; the painted portrait was still commissioned by the wealthy and the aristocracy. But it did allow a greater number of people the status of seeing themselves pictured.

Furthermore, photography provoked artists to re-examine the nature and potential of paint as a particular medium. Photography appeared more successful than painting in capturing likenesses. It also had a sense of instantaneity which painting lacked. It has been suggested that photography encouraged the Impressionist painters to experiment with manners of painting which also could capture a sense of the moment, and the passage of light. It is a truism that photography 'released' painting from its responsibility for literal depiction, allowing it to become more experimental. The developing relationship between the two media was considerably more symbiotic.

The other respect in which photography may be said to have extended Art was in its role as the re-presenter of art objects. It was no longer necessary to travel to Florence to see paintings commissioned by the Medicis, or to

Key galleries:
National Portrait Gallery,
London
Scottish National Portrait
Gallery, Edinburgh

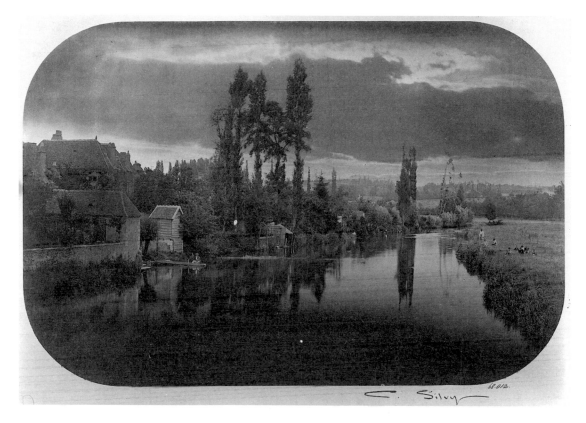

5.2 Camille Silvy, River Scene, France, 1858
Two exposures combined to create the idealised rural scenario

Egypt to contemplate classical architecture and artefacts; you could attend slide talks, or visit an exhibition, and see reproductions. Virtual reality, with its possibilities of seemingly travelling around a painting or sculpture, viewing it from every possible angle, now makes the 2D black and white photograph appear highly limited as a means of showing an art object. But, at the time, the possibility of seeing photographs of art objects was highly radical. Among the first illustrated art histories was an 1847 limited edition book of Spanish Art which included sixty-six **calotypes** by Fox Talbot (Scharf 1974: 160).

Photographs not only reproduced Art, they also mirrored Art in making pictures in accordance with established fine art conventions. *Before Photography*, **Peter Galassi**'s comparative study of photographs and paintings within the same genres, draws our attention to continuities in aesthetic convention including compositional similarities. Likewise, in a more detailed manner, **Mark Haworth-Booth** has examined the construction of 'River Scene, France' by Camille Silvy, which was a combination print involving staging people within the rural setting (figure 5.2). Not only does its composition

PETER GALASSI (1981) **Before Photography**, New York: MOMA

MARK HAWORTH-BOOTH (1992) **River Scene, France**, California: The J. Paul Getty Museum

echo traditional aesthetics, but the image romanticises the pastoral (in line with many examples of landscape paintings).

Indeed, staged photographs depicting idealised or mythical scenes became common from the 1850s onwards. Among earlier examples is the work of Julia Margaret Cameron. She invited friends, family and servants to pose for her, either for portraits or as actors within her dramatic scenarios. Since she moved in Victorian middle-class circles, this legacy includes portraits of well-known artists, writers and intellectuals, including Alfred Lord Tennyson and Charles Darwin. But it is her tableaux which have significance in relation to Art. Cameron's photography coincided with Pre-Raphaelite Art in Britain. Through mythologising the past, the Pre-Raphaelites arguably represented a conservative response to modernity. Cameron likewise staged mythical scenes, using costumes and titles to indicate the poetic.

Julia Margaret Cameron was one of a number of serious 'amateurs' who figure prominently in the history of photography in Britain. Others were more professional, in the sense that photography was their source of income. For instance, Swedish painter-photographer, Oscar Rejlander, set up a commercial studio in Victoria, London. But he became known for his allegorical compositions, in some cases of a scale equivalent to paintings. For example, 'The Two Ways of Life', involving a number of models playing roles ranging from the religious (charity) to the debauched (gambling), was nearly three feet (a metre) long. It was made from thirty separate photographs, entailing pre-visualisation on a grand scale. Such work reflected Victorian preoccupations, including religion, class and morality. This particular picture must have accorded with social concerns acceptable to the Establishment – it was purchased by Queen Victoria in 1857.

Thus pictures made by Victorian photographers reflected conventions and tensions in other areas of Victorian Art. Indeed, photography itself impacted on such tensions and aesthetic developments, with emphasis upon interpretation rather than upon accuracy of recording. In line with other areas of the Arts there was an emerging schism between those preoccupied with the realist concerns of nineteenth-century industrialisation and those with more romantic aspirations.

Photography claiming a place in the gallery

In 1892 a number of photographers seceded from the Photographic Society of Great Britain – which in the 1870s and 1880s had emphasised the science and technology of photography, and offered no support for the progress of photography as Art. Led by Henry Peach Robinson, they formed the Linked Ring Brotherhood (which did include a few women). Robinson suggested:

It must be admitted by the most determined opponent of photography as a fine art that the same object represented by different

MIKE WEAVER (ed.) (1989b) **British Photography in the Nineteenth Century: The Fine Art Tradition**, Cambridge: Cambridge University Press. A collection of essays on major photographers of the Victorian era

MARGARET HARKER (1979) **The Linked Ring: The Secession Movement in Photography in Britain, 1892–1910**, London: Heinemann

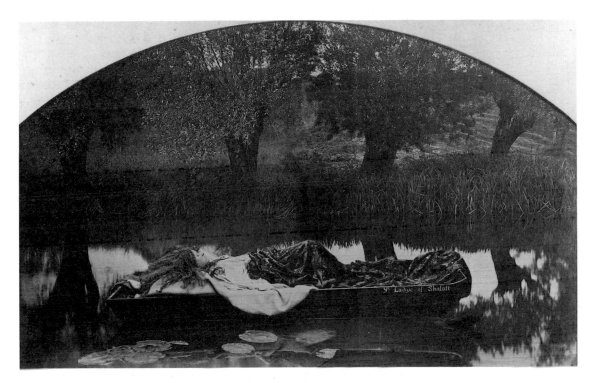

5.3 Henry Peach Robinson, *The Lady of Shallot*, 1860–1861
A Medieval Tale interpreted allegorically

photographers will produce different pictorial results and this invariably not only because the one man uses different lenses and chemicals than the other but because there is something different in each man's mind which somehow gets communicated to his fingers' ends and thence to his pictures.

(Harker 1988: 46)

Retrospectively labelled 'pictorialist', typically their imagery was soft focus, with metaphoric connotations, often drawing upon traditional fable and allegory (figure 5.3). Again, the Pre-Raphaelites may have been one source of influence. Defining pictorial photography, Mike Weaver notes the aim:

to make a picture in which the sensuous beauty of the fine print is consonant with the moral beauty of the fine image, without particular reference to documentary or design values, and without specific regard to personal or topographical identity.

(Weaver 1986: preface)

Membership of the Linked Ring was international, with photographers in other secessionist movements in Europe and the USA joining by invitation. In France the first exhibition of the newly formed Photo-Club of Paris was held in 1894; in Germany Hamburg became the centre for art photography. The Photo-Secession in New York — founded by Alfred Stieglitz, a member of the Linked Ring — was not established until 1902. Its objectives echoed the emphasis on the impressive potential of the medium which characterised the European movements. However, membership was restricted to Americans. Margaret Harker suggests that this was to facilitate the raising of standards within American photography to exceed those in Europe. Stieglitz, who had previously organised a number of exhibitions of work by European painters, introducing the Impressionists to New York and bringing what he considered to be the best in art to America, also founded and edited *Camera Work*, published from 1903 to 1917, described by Aaron Scharf as 'undoubtedly one of the most influential journals ever published to be concerned equally with art and photography' (Scharf 1974: 240).

Given the complexity of the relation between photography and painting, and the exent to which photographers since the mid-century had sought 'artistic results', why such emphasis on photography as Art at the end of the century? One factor is that secessionism coincided with the development of technologies such as roll film and the box camera, which allowed the casual amateur to take photographs. Serious amateurs, in claiming artistic status, were also claiming a distinction between themselves and the newly emerging mass market.

Furthermore, dissent within photography, represented by the various secessionist groups, echoed dissent more generally within the Arts. The end of the nineteenth century witnessed the challenge posed by the Impressionists in painting, Naturalism in theatre and, indeed, the birth of cinema. It also witnessed the development of lithographic techniques necessary for the mass reproduction of photographs in print. It was an era of considerable change. The pictorialists claimed the photograph as Art, but this claim was made at a time of challenge to dominant aesthetics. With revolutions in European painting effected by the Impressionists and, later, the Fauvists, the authority of the Academy was in decline. Traditional aesthetics, to which the Pictorialists subscribed, came to seem increasingly conservative. Pictorialism not only seems reactionary now, it probably seemed so to many then.

Indeed, tension, debate and dissent characterised the era. Peter Henry Emerson is known for his picturesque renderings of life in East Anglia. Defining picturesque, Harker notes 'emphasis on acute observation and appreciation of scenery; an understanding of proportion and perspective in landscape; and the conception of architecture at one with its natural environment (not to be considered in isolation)' (Harker 1979: 27). Emerson's emphasis was upon what he termed 'Naturalistic Photography', which was the title of his book published in 1889. He advocated realism and 'truth-to-nature' as opposed to the impressionist or the idealistic. For this reason he has been viewed by some critics as a forerunner of modern photography. But his concern with composition and differential focusing, including soft focus where appropriate, would have allowed him a place within Pictorialist circles had he so desired.

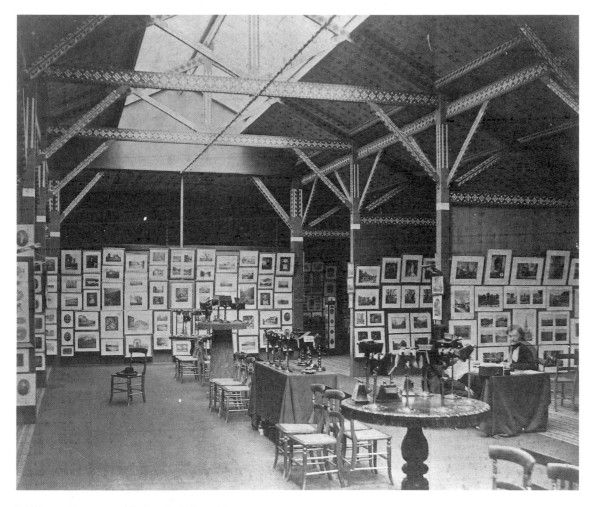

5.4 Thurston Thompson, Exhibition Installation, 1858
Installation shot of the fifth exhibition of the Photographic Society of London, 1858. Photographs were framed and matted but crowded in blocks, some so high or low as to render them difficult to see

Well-documented disputes with H.P. Robinson were probably the main cause of his exclusion. He remained in the Photographic Society and is credited

3 The RPS remains a major photographic institution to this day. Paradoxically, perhaps, it is now the major archive for nineteenth-century British Pictorialism, holding work by many of those who led the secessionist challenge to the Photographic Society. It remains a centre for exhibitions, with up to four shows at any time

4 Books of photographs date from the very early days with Henry Fox Talbot's *The Pencil of Nature* or Anna Atkins' use of photographic illustrations in her studies of flora. But each image had to be hand printed. Therefore books could only be produced in limited editions

with responsibility for Royal acclaim, hence the change of title to the Royal Photographic Society (RPS).[3]

Aside from illustrated talks, the exhibition was the principal space for public display of photographs.[4] Claiming photography as Art did not mean seeking different forms of display so much as claiming different cultural significance. Relevant historical research to date is limited, but it should not be assumed that the Victorian gallery operated quite like the contemporary gallery. For instance, gallery display conventions emphasised quantity of work, rather than the singularity of the specific image. Paintings, prints and photographs were hung floor to ceiling, with little regard to size or frames (figure 5.4). Since it would be almost impossible to view those hung at floor or ceiling level, certain parts of the wall were, in effect, pride of place. An example of this may be found in the Round Room at Birmingham Museum and Art Gallery, England, which has been hung to demonstrate the style of the gallery in 1885 (although with only about fifty paintings rather than nearly ninety, as originally). The legacy – and difficulties – of this style of hanging may also be seen annually, particularly in the print sections of the Royal Academy Summer Show. Galleries were not painted white, and lighting was limited, in contrast to the visibility standards of the late twentieth century. Just seeing monochrome images must have been difficult, let alone discerning the detail of resolution and tonal contrast for which the Pictorialists strived.

Indeed, the Linked Ring were instrumental in introducing changes to the gallery, emphasising the presentation of the picture. Photographer Frederick Evans is credited with the introduction of mounts in more muted colours in order not to distract from the delicacy of detail and imagery achieved through the various photographic printing and toning processes. Photographs were framed more uniformly and less heavily than previously; more wall space was allocated to each picture, and the hanging space restricted to the central area of the wall, not too high or too low. Although the concentration of photographs would surprise viewers accustomed to late twentieth-century gallery conventions, the Pictorialists did set new standards of display at the time.

THE MODERN ERA

Modernism and Modern Art

The Modern Movement in the twentieth century has often involved painters and sculptors in an exploration of the idea that art has a purely formal language in which meaning is conveyed by shape, texture, colour and size. This exploration has been in a shifting dialogue with the traditional subjects of art, such as landscape, the figure and still life.

(Tate Gallery, St Ives, Cornwall, 1995)

In his essay 'When Was Modernism', Raymond Williams notes that the idea of the Modern began to take on what he terms 'a favourable and

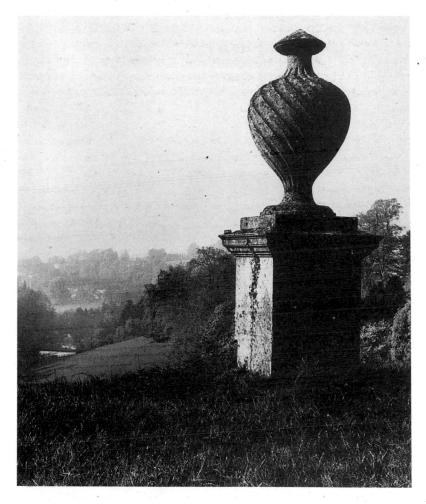

5.5 Bill Brandt, Prior Park, near Bath, 1936
Straight photography used with great compositional effect to describe the contours of the park, and of the sculptural urn in the foreground

progressive ring' in the mid-nineteenth century (Williams 1989). He adds that, in its more specific use, 'Modern' soon developed into a categorisation of a number of art movements broadly located between the 1890s and the 1940s, so that by 1950 it was possible to contrast 'Modern Art' with 'contemporary Art'. 'Modernism' increasingly came to refer to avant-garde art movements within which the emphasis was on the specific medium and experiments in forms of expression, rather than on subject-matter. Williams notes a number of social factors which contributed to making the early twentieth century the key era of artistic change. These included

Key galleries: The Tate,
Liverpool and London.
The Tate, St Ives, is largely
devoted to English Modernism

the dislocation of artists caused by war and revolution, which contributed a sense both of art movements as international and of the artist as somehow outside of modern society and therefore in a position to offer a particular perspective on it. He also cites the growth of publishing, noting that the Futurists, Surrealists, Cubists, Constructivists, and others, announced the birth of their new Art movement through manifestos published in magazines or journals.

American critic Clement Greenberg wrote extensively on the subject of Modernism, taking the position that Art is autonomous from its social context of production. He emphasised the *medium*, and method of expression, arguing that 'the essence of Modernism lies ... in the use of the characteristic methods of a discipline to criticize the discipline itself, not in order to subvert it but in order to entrench it more firmly in its area of competence' (Greenberg 1961: 308). His influence as a critic, and his unequivocal support for abstract Art, contributed to the international respect accorded to American Abstract Expressionism (including painters such as Mark Rothko and Jackson Pollock).

Earlier, in 1939, Greenberg had distinguished between avant-garde art, and 'kitsch', by which he meant the popular and the commercial 'product of the industrial revolution which urbanised the masses of Western Europe and America and established what is called universal literacy' (Greenberg 1939: 533). For him the avant-garde was the historical agency which functioned to keep culture alive in the face of capitalism. At this point in his development as a critic, Greenberg acknowledged the social and historical contexts in which the experience of Art occurs, asserting that the avant-garde was a type of political engagement.

Modern Art came to occupy a relatively autonomous, arguably elitist, position which remained unchallenged until the 1960s. The internationalism of Modern Art rests on this notion of autonomy. If art is viewed as *not* context-specific it can be assumed that it communicates regardless of national and cultural differences. Artist-critic Victor Burgin has commented sardonically on such assumptions:

> *Art* is an activity characteristic of humanity since the dawn of civilization. In any epoch the *Artist*, by virtue of special gifts, expresses that which is finest in humanity. ... The visual artist achieves this through modes of understanding and expression which are 'purely visual' – radically distinct from, for example, verbalization. This special characteristic of art necessarily makes it an autonomous sphere of activity, completely separate from the everyday world of social and political life. The autonomous nature of visual art means that questions asked of it may only be properly put, and answered, in its own terms – all other forms of interrogation are irrelevant. In the modern world the function of art is to

preserve and enhance its own special sphere of civilizing human values in an increasingly dehumanizing technological environment.

If these beliefs sound familiar – perhaps even self-evident – it is because they long-ago became part of the received common-sense we in the West learn at our mother's knee.

(Burgin 1986: 30)

Modern photography

In America, Greenberg condemned the literal in painting. By contrast, he welcomed it in photography:

The art in photography is literary art before it is anything else: its triumphs and monuments are historical, anecdotal, reportorial, observational before they are purely pictorial . . . The photograph has to tell a story if it is to work as art.

(Greenberg 1991: 131)

In his view the photograph was transparent, documentary, and marked by speed and ease (relative to painting): 'All visible reality, unposed, unaltered, unrehearsed, is open to instantaneous photography' (Greenberg 1991). This view clearly prioritised **straight photography**, by then well-established in American documentary, over American photographic **Formalism** which, in its mid-century heyday, was experimental and more gallery oriented.

Photography figured extensively within European radical movements of the first half of the twentieth century, but in ways which did not pose it as Art or lead to gallery exhibition. In order to examine developments in slightly more detail, this section offers two case studies. First, we focus on ways in which art and design were implicated politically in social reconstruction in both Soviet Constructivism and the German Bauhaus. These movements show artists reaching out beyond the gallery system. Second, we consider photography in relation to a specific art movement – namely Surrealism – noting, in particular, the intellectual currencies which informed Surrealism, its multidisciplinary nature, and subsequent comments and reappraisals. Each case study is intended to offer an example of ways in which photography, caught within specific broader movements, might be analysed and contextualised. Each also draws attention to the emphasis upon aesthetic radicalism which typified Modern movements.

CASE STUDY: ART, DESIGN, POLITICS: SOVIET CONSTRUCTIVISM AND THE BAUHAUS

A brief background

Discussing experimentation in Russian art from the 1860s to the early 1920s, Camilla Gray traces a number of strands within Russian Modern Art, ranging from spiritual interest in medieval icon painting to a realism which mirrored developments in other parts of Europe (Gray 1962). In the mid-nineteenth

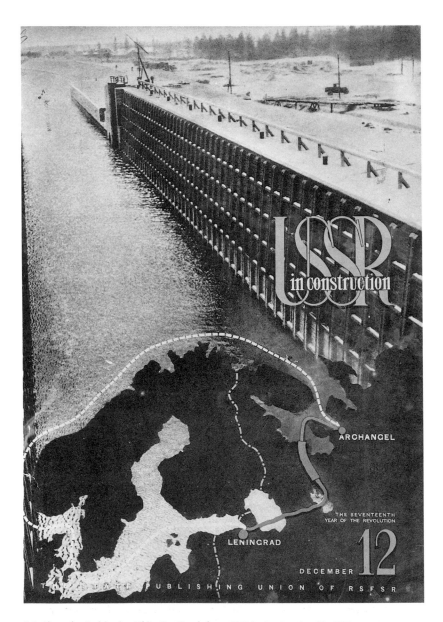

5.6 Alexander Rodchenko, White Sea Canal, from USSR in Construction 12, 1933
One example of the geometric style and the commitment to a new angle of vision, literally and metaphorically, which characterised both the Bauhaus and Constructivism

century, 'The Wanderers' – a group of Russian painters who, like their contemporaries in France, had broken from the Russian Art Academy – committed themselves to developing art which was about the everyday. Links with Paris, Munich and Vienna, especially immediately after the failure of the 1905 Revolution, led to a number of major exhibitions in Moscow and St Petersburg wherein Russian artists showed alongside their Western European contemporaries. By the time of the 1917 Revolution there was an identifiable avant-garde which, in the paintings of Malevich, Popova, El Lissitzky, paralleled Cubism in France in exploring the surface of the canvas and the nature of artistic language.

Experiments in the social role of art

The success of the 1917 Revolution led to a new political context, one in which the nature and social role of art was hotly debated. A number of artists, led by Malevich, stressed the formal and spiritual supremacy of art in itself. A Russian form of Modernism. Others emphasised proletarian culture advocating a social role for artist-workers in the vanguard of Revolutionary change. The new situation encouraged a radical aesthetics. Painter-photographer Alexander Rodchenko asserted that

> Art has no place in modern life. It will continue to exist as long as there is a mania for the romantic and so long as there are people who love beautiful lies and deception. . . . Every modern cultured man must wage war against art, as against opium. . . . Photograph and be photographed.
> (Rodchenko 1928)

For Rodchenko and the other Constructivists, new art involved first, the depersonalisation of practice, that is, taking art out of the realm of individual artistic expression; second, logical laboratory study of form and composition; third, analysis of rules governing the nature of artistic communication. That photography was technological made it particularly appropriate. Art set out to renegotiate itself as a type of practice which was utilitarian in foregrounding design and function, and selfless from the point of view of the artist. As such it represented the socialist ideals of the Revolution. Soviet Constructivism flourished for about a decade, before being superseded by Socialist Realism with its focus on glorification of the worker, the peasant and 'heroes' of the Revolution.

Constructivist photography

For the Constructivists, photography was a popular form which, through its usage in posters, magazines and publishing, could be at the forefront of taking new ideas to the people. Emphasising art's post-Revolutionary responsibilities, Rodchenko stated that he was fed up with 'belly button' shots, by which he meant photographs composed conventionally shot from waist level through cameras with their viewfinder on top. He argued for full exploration of the geometry of the image which would, literally and metaphorically, engineer a new angle of vision. Indeed, for Rodchenko photography was the true modern art. He argued that, unlike painting and sculpture which he viewed as outdated, photography could express the reality of post-Revolutionary society. Thus, in the case of Soviet Constructivism, the issue was not one of photography attempting to claim status as Art, but rather a democratisation of artistic practices in the service of social and cultural revolution within which photography, by its enquiring nature and its ubiquity, could play a leading role.

The integration of art and design

Shifting political circumstances are also reflected in the fortunes of the German Bauhaus (1919–1933), which was founded in Weimar under the leadership of Walter Gropius. It moved to Dessau in 1925, by which time Herbert Bayer, photographer and typographer, was a key influence: and to Berlin in 1932, before disbanding in consequence of the election of Hitler's National Socialists. (Many Bauhaus theorists were exiled to the United States where they formed The Chicago Art Institute.) The Bauhaus was a clear response to the destruction and dereliction witnessed during the First World War. 'Bauhaus' literally means 'house for building'. Like Soviet Constructivism, the Bauhaus was multi-disciplinery, although architecture came to be the central concern. Taking the notion of reconstruction as the central tenet, Bauhaus theorists emphasised the relation between form and function, and stressed what they saw as a potential unity of art, design and the everyday (see Rowland 1990). Their radical approach was not uncontroversial. For instance, Frankfurt School theorist, Walter Benjamin, expressed impatience with such experimentation, accusing the 'new objectivity' photographers of the Bauhaus of making the world artistic rather than making Art mundane. For Benjamin, emphasis on form detracted from the democratic characteristics of photography which, in his view, should be a comprehensible means of communication for everyone. He opposed formalism and abstraction because, he argued, experimentation in visual languages tends to be exclusive, and therefore elitist.

A new instrument of vision

The Bauhaus viewed radicalism in photography in different terms. László and Lucia Moholy-Nagy were perhaps the best-known photographers associated with the Bauhaus. They stressed ways in which use of light, mechanical reproduction and the possibility of sensitive printing expressed the machine aesthetic of the Modern Age. In parallel with the Soviet emphasis upon photo-eye as the modern method of communication, Moholy-Nagy empha-sised the relation between the mechanical nature of the camera, form, the use of light, and visual perception, arguing that photography enhances sight in relation to time and space (Moholy-Nagy 1932). Like Benjamin, their writings opposed the reification of the individual artist. Unlike Benjamin, they stressed the compositional qualities of the image, viewing this as central to the means of expression.

Photographers move geographically and aesthetically over a lifetime, chang-ing their style and subject-matter, their work reflecting differing political con-texts. The most obvious contrast between America and Europe was the

CHRISTOPHER PHILLIPS (ed.) (1989) **Photography in the Modern Era: European Documents and Critical Writings 1913–1940**, New York: MOMA

JOHN WILLETT (1978) **The New Sobriety, Art and Politics in the Weimar Period**, London: Thames and Hudson

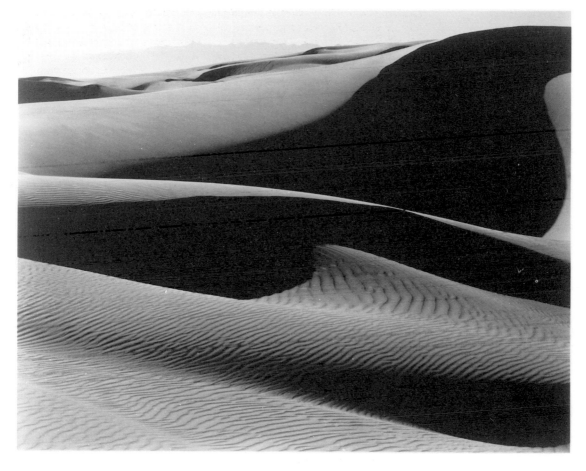

5.7 Edward Weston, Dunes, Oceano
Photographic seeing with emphasis on the rhythm of form

emphasis on reconstruction in Europe subsequent to the First World War and the Russian Revolution. Discussing photography and architecture in Europe between the wars, Ian Jeffrey describes 1920s photographic modernism in Europe as engaged with social totalities and worthy of respect, 'premised on selflessness, transcending local and even national affiliations' (Jeffrey 1991: 60). By contrast, he notes more archaic subject-matter in the 1930s, with its more romantic focus on secret worlds and marginalised people within the city. The imagery of Krull, Atget, Brassai can be viewed as more conversational, in a classic documentary manner, less experimental and less inclined to celebrate the promise of a new social order so eagerly supported in the first half of the 1920s. In effect, reminding us of the changing European political circumstances, Jeffrey proposes that optimism in the 1920s was superseded by a retreat into romanticism in the 1930s and, crucially, that this can be discerned in the shifting subject-matter and style of the image.

Nonetheless, broadly speaking Modern photography sought to offer new perceptions, literally and metaphorically, using light, form, composition and tonal contrast as the central vocabulary of the image. In this respect photographers such as Florence Henri (France) or Paul Strand (USA) seem to have echoed the Cubists in their concern with form. This can be seen at its extreme in American Formalism, for example, in the work of Edward Weston and Tina Modotti, whose abstract visual poetics concentrated on tone and shape rather than on the subject of the image. Edward Weston defined his approach as both abstract and realist, emphasising the observational basis of the photograph. Beaumont Newhall has stressed the interdependence of the technological and the aesthetic in Weston's work, noting his insistence upon pre-visualisation of the image. Weston sought clarity of form and extolled the camera for its depth of focus and its ability to see more than the human eye. The f/64 Group, founded in 1932 by a number of American photographers, including Weston, Imogen Cunningham and Ansel Adams, was so-named precisely to reflect the emphasis upon sharpness of image. Their approach emphasised photography as a specific type of medium with its own optical, chemical and consequent aesthetic properties. Unlike other photographic movements of the time, Formalism sought gallery exhibition.[5]

H.H. ARNASON (1988) **A History of Modern Art**, London: Thames and Hudson. This revised and updated third edition includes photography

5 Curiously, Stieglitz never showed Edward Weston's work in New York in his Madison Avenue gallery, named An American Place, which he ran from 1929 to 1946

CASE STUDY: ART MOVEMENTS AND INTELLECTUAL CURRENCIES: SURREALISM

What was Surrealism?

It is always relevant and, in academic terms, interesting, to trace links between the general intellectual climate of any era and aesthetic developments. Surrealism took the idea of the individual psyche as its theoretical starting point, thus particularly reflecting the **psychoanalytic** work of Sigmund Freud. Surrealism emphasised artistic processes whereby the imaginary can be recorded through automatic writing or drawing which would thus offer insights into the world of thought and therefore disrupt taken-for-granted perceptions and frames of reference. For the Surrealists, the artist was the starting point or material source of what was to be expressed. Freud distinguished between the Id, the **unconscious** instinctual self, and the Ego, the largely conscious socialised self. Likewise, Surrealism distinguished between 'thought' and 'reason', and aimed to bypass what they saw as the **repressive** nature of reason in order to express what they viewed as natural desires.

Surrealism has been regarded as attempting to replicate the world of dreams. This is premised directly on Freud's dream theory wherein he argued that analysis of the manifest content of dreams offers perception on subjective responses to experience. However, this is to oversimplify, as the aims of Surrealism were complex and, to some extent, changed over time, and included a direct attack on the nature of Art. Many of the early Surrealists were also involved in the First World War anti-Art movement,

Dada (Ades 1974). Both Dada and Surrealism were interventionist in challenging what was happening in the gallery, rather than ignoring it. For instance, Marcel Duchamp placed a urinal in the gallery claiming that the location made it 'Art'.

French poet André Breton described 'A desire to deepen the foundations of the real; to bring about an ever clearer and at the same time ever more passionate consciousness of the world perceived by the senses' (Breton 1978: 115). In the late 1920s, Surrealists, led by Breton, called for adherence to Marxist dialectical materialism and to the ideal of revolution. This caused splits in the Paris-based group (including the expulsion of Salvador Dali because of his support for Fascism in Spain). Fundamentally, Surrealism was premised on challenging philosophical distinctions between interior experience and exterior realities. The radicalism of Surrealism lay in its aims: to disorient the spectator; to push towards the destruction of conventional ways of seeing; and to challenge rationalist frameworks.

Fine art movements transcend national boundaries, albeit reflecting particular national features. In exploring photography as Art, it is necessary to take account of the interplay between that which characterises specific social and political circumstances, and more general international contexts. For instance, the first Surrealist Manifesto was published in Paris in 1924, but the first International Surrealist Exhibition in Britain did not take place until 1936, by which time, arguably, the movement had lost its more experimental edge.[6] Furthermore, a number of the original Paris-based group became members of the Communist Party. In Britain, with Roland Penrose as the key Surrealist artist and exponent, the emphasis lay more on visual form and psychoanalytic references than on political revolution.

6 Held in London at the New Burlington Galleries in Burlington Gardens; that is, in a modern gallery

Surrealist photography

How does lens-based imagery, including photography, fit within Surrealism? For Dali, the mechanical nature of the camera was liberating: 'photography sets imagination free', he claimed. Breton stated:

> The invention of photography has dealt a mortal blow to the old modes of expression, in painting as well as in poetry, where automatic writing, which appeared at the end of the nineteenth century, is a true photography of thought'.

(Breton 1978: 7)

He also noted approvingly that 'belief in an absolute time and space seems to be vanishing', a reference to the photograph's ability to picture the past, or the geographically distant, and welcomed the fact that 'today, thanks to the cinema, we know how to make a locomotive *arrive* in a picture' (1978: 7). Despite the involvement of artists such as Herbert Bayer, previously associated with the Bauhaus, Surrealist photography clearly differed both in principle and in vision from the Formalist 'new objectivity' of the Bauhaus. Stressing the imagination as the source of insight on experience, the Surrealists used **photomontage**, double exposure, **rayographs**, or **solarisation**, in order to produce disorienting imagery.

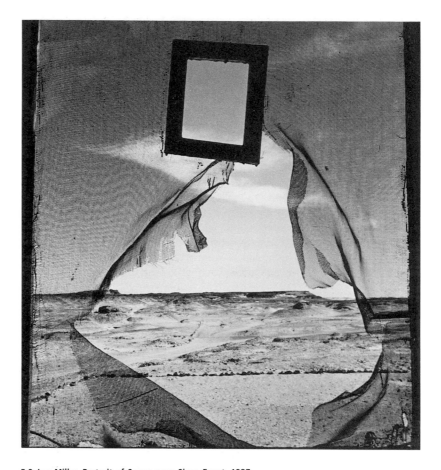

5.8 Lee Miller, Portrait of Space, near Siwa, Egypt, 1937
An example of a Surreal juxtaposition of interior/exterior to achive a dreamlike effect. Mirrors frequently feature, referencing reflection. Possibly the inspiration for Magritte's *Le Baiser*

Critical reappraisals

Feminism has provoked reappraisal of Surrealism in recent years, both through debates about patriarchal attitudes in psychoanalysis and, more specifically, through new art history. Women figured in Surrealism as artists but, until recently, their position and contribution has been largely ignored (see Chadwick 1985). Reinstatement has focused attention on the work of many women Surrealists, including photographers Lee Miller and Claude Cahun. Indeed, allegedly Lee Miller 'discovered' solarisation by turning on a darkroom light, not realising that Man Ray was printing.

The feminist critique has also drawn attention to the role of woman as muse. Considered from a feminist perspective, the expression of unconscious desires, central to Surrealist imagery, seems merely an excuse for male heterosexual fantasy. 'Woman' is objectified. The distorted or fragmented female figure is a common motif. Hans Bellmers' female dolls most obviously degrade and violate woman through her disfiguration or dismembering. Surrealists viewed such imagery as an expression of innate, but repressed, desire, and no doubt welcomed the challenge to bourgeois boundaries of permissibility. With hindsight, and in the light of feminism, the misogyny is clear.

Reappraisal has also focused upon the relation between photographic representation of the real, and the surreal effect, for instance, of doubling a particular motif within the image or of distortion. The taken-for-granted realism of the photographic became the source of the *coup d'oeil* effect which often operated to disorient the spectator. Rosalind Krauss notes metaphoric effects: 'we see with a shock of recognition the simultaneous effect of displacement and condensation, the very operations of symbol formation, hard at work on the flesh of the real' (**Krauss and Livingston 1986: 19**). The shock emanates from the refusal of the transcriptive realism expected of photography.

ROSALIND KRAUSS AND JANE LIVINGSTON (1986) **L'Amour Fou**, London: Arts Council of Great Britain

RUDOLF E KUENZLI (1991) 'Surrealism and Misogyny' in Mary Ann Caws, Rudolf Kuenzli and Owen Raaberg **Surrealism and Women**, Cambridge, MA: MIT Press

Modern photography, the Gallery and the Archive

Nowadays Modern photography is central to the archive. Historical connoisseurship has created a canon of photographers whose imagery is now highly regarded. This was not always the case. In Britain, the main impetus in photography for most of this century was in documentary and photojournalism, studio portraiture and commercial art. From about 1905 (towards the end of Pictorialism) photography had little visibility in the art gallery. The work of British photographers – such as Bill Brandt and George Rodgers, whom we now celebrate – was not made initially for gallery exhibition, nor was it necessarily widely known. Bill Brandt's now famous collection *Perspective of Nudes* was not published until 1961.

Developments can be mapped through a number of exhibitions. A major retrospective of photographs by Bill Brandt, curated in 1969 for MOMA, New York, arrived at the Hayward Gallery on London's South Bank in 1970. *The Land: 20th Century Landscape Photographs*, also by Bill Brandt, was exhibited at the Victoria and Albert Museum in 1975. A now forgotten show, *Spectrum*, at the Institute of Contemporary Arts (ICA), London, in 1969, included four British-based photographers – Tony Ray Jones, Enzo Ragazzini, Dorothy Bohm, Don McCullin – and encompassed straight photography, optical experiments, photojournalism and portraiture. In 1975 the Arts Council organised a touring exhibition, *The Real Thing, An Anthology of British Photographs 1840–1950*. Thus, a diversity of work was brought into focus.

Key collection: The Print Room, Victoria and Albert Museum, London

Conceptual art and the photographic

Photography in the 1960s was centrally implicated in the expansion of the mass media, including fashion shots, album covers for long playing (33⅓) records, photojournalism (the *Sunday Times* colour supplement was launched in 1962). In the Art gallery, two parallel developments in the 1960s and 1970s contributed to shifting the position of photography. First, Pop Artists such as Andy Warhol (USA), Roy Lichtenstein (USA), David Hockney and Richard Hamilton (both British) started to use the photographic in order to reference and comment on lifestyles and consumerism. To echo Roland Barthes, many elements within their pictures were *déjà-lu* ('already read'). This was the whole point. Raymond Williams has suggested that in the 1960s the two dimensions of the modern, radical aesthetics and technological change came together in the pictures of artists whose work engaged with the revolution in mass culture consequent upon developments in technology and communications such as television (Williams 1989). Indeed, arguably photography contributed to creating a more visually sophisticated audience than had previously obtained: 'that painters have used photographs does not legitimize photography; on the contrary, such cross-pollination has primarily helped *painting* remain a vital and effective medium' (Coleman 1979: 121). Through Pop Art the photographic gained a presence in the gallery (see Alloway 1966 for an account of British Pop Art).

Second, in Conceptual Art the photographic became accepted as a valid medium of artistic expression. It was in the 1970s that American Art magazines, including *Artforum* and *Art in America*, took photography into their remit. Conceptual Art stressed the concept which was the starting point for any piece of work. Modernist theory had focused on the medium. By contrast, Conceptual Art stressed ideas. Artists were concerned to draw attention to the manner or vocabulary of expression; also, to contexts of interpretation, that is, the influence of the situation within which the spectator responds to the image or art object. Indeed, in a number of instances artists placed a statement about an art object in the gallery, thereby focusing attention on the idea, rather than the object (which might never have been actually made). From the postmodern theoretical perspectives of the 1990s the notion of explicitly requiring spectator interpretation comes as no surprise. But, at the time, Conceptual Art, especially in its more critical or political forms, constituted a challenge to the Art establishment (see Harrison and Wood 1993). In conceptual photography the characteristics of the medium could be used as a part of the means of expression of an idea. Thus, for instance, Keith Arnatt's sequence of digging himself into a hole in the ground (figure 5.9) is obviously, at one level, a metaphoric reference to the well-known phrase. But the documentary idiom secures a sense that this event literally did take place through demonstrating the sequence of moments in time.

Conceptualism challenged the dominance of abstract Formalism. It was not that it denied the significance of form. Rather, form was brought into play differently with a view to social, political, metaphysical, or simply humorous, comment. This challenge took a number of guises; for instance, the 'new topographics', photographers, including Lewis Baltz (USA) and

JONATHAN GREEN (1984) 'The Painter as Photographer', **American Photography**, New York: Harry N. Abrams, chapter 9

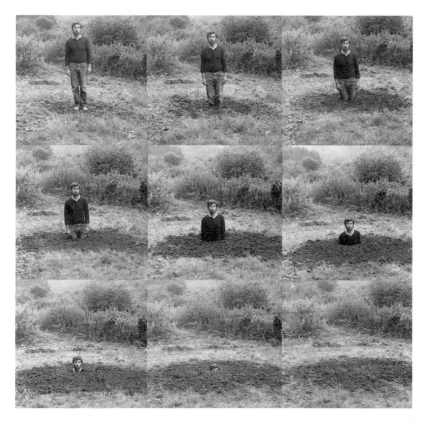

5.9 Keith Arnatt, Self Burial, TV Interference Project, 1969
Photograph on paper, 467 × 467cm. The humour of the piece of work emanates from the realism attributed to photography. One way of testing the implication of choice of specific medium and, therefore, the implied comment on the nature of the medium, is to imagine what interpretational shift might occur if the sequence had been, say, painted

Bernd and Hilla Becher (Germany), explored the act of looking through the detailed mapping of industrial edifices or locations. (The term 'new topographics' references nineteenth-century topographical work, especially the photographic charting of the American West.) Similar images are blocked next to one another, thereby bringing into question the degree of detailed discrimination involved in day-to-day perceptions. Clearly this work drew on the emphasis upon detailed seeing typical of, for instance, the f/64 group. But the new topographics, in charting the industrial landscape, implied a social and environmental questioning which did not figure in American Formalism.

Land Art also dates from this period. Here, the photograph is the record, and the final product, of an intervention within the rural. Work by British artists, including Richard Long and Andy Goldsworthy, has become well-known not through direct experience of the results of their investigations and interventions, but through their photographs. The sculptural intervention ameliorates, deteriorates, and becomes reabsorbed within the environment. Ultimately only the picture remains. Unlike the new topographics, Land Art persists as a strand within landscape. Both might be said to have their roots in the conceptual investigations of the 1970s. Furthermore, as photography became accepted within Conceptual Art, so attention came to be paid to straight photography, both the historical and the contemporary. In effect, Conceptual Art offered photography a bridge into the gallery.

CONTEMPORARY PERSPECTIVES

The American and European Avant-garde art movements of the 1960s emphasised idea and process over the conventions of painting and sculpture. The war in Vietnam, the civil rights movement in America, the development of feminist politics and theory, and the student protests of 1968, were reflected in works that were challenging to the status quo, to ideas about the artist as apolitical and working alone, and to art institutions.

Comment and Commitment: Art and Society 1975–1990
Tate Gallery, London 1995

Photography and the post-Modern

Since the 1970s there have been significant developments in Art practices founded in the new centrality of critical ideas to the visual arts, and in what was often referred to as the 'return to the figurative'. Of course the figurative had never entirely disappeared. The 'return' was more a question of a regeneration of interest in the representational on the part of curators and critics, now moving beyond Modernist preoccupations with the specificity of each medium. For example, as noted, Conceptual artists referenced the media and used 'found' images and materials not previously associated with fine art. Parody and pastiche featured in postmodern Art practices. New Art also posited questions of representation. By the 1980s Art had ceased to be self-obsessed, was looking outward beyond the boundaries of the gallery, taking on contemporary issues and making a range of references that ruptured Modernist assertions of the autonomy of Art.

Critical theorist, Douglas Crimp, suggested that photography contributed centrally within this challenge to the museum and gallery:

From the parochial perspective of the late-1970s art world, photography appeared as a watershed. Radically reevaluated, photography took up residence in the museum on a par with the visual arts' traditional mediums and according to the very same art-historical

tenets. New principles of photographic connoisseurship were
devised; the canon of master photographers was vastly expanded;
prices on the photography market skyrocketed. Counterposed against
this reevaluation were two coincident developments: a materialist
history of photography and dissident photographic practices . . .
taken together and brought into relation, they could tell us somehing
about postmodernism, a term coming into wide use at just that time.

(Crimp 1993: 2)

Thus, from the 1970s on, emphasis upon conceptual ideas and critical
practices contributed to creating a place for the photographic within the Art
gallery. Furthermore, photography contributed to the regeneration of art
practices. The sources of this shift are complex. First, the radicalism of 1968
in Europe heralded a Left cultural agenda in the 1970s. This underpinned
critical interrogation of dominant cultural practices. Examples may be found
in the work of British-based artists Victor Burgin and Mary Kelly, both of
whom, notably, wrote about photographic practices as well as making photographic work. Second, and as a part of this, Modern theory had begun to
be questioned across many realms of academic enterprise, from the scientific
to the aesthetic. In the fine arts this questioning took off earlier in North
America than it did in Europe. Thus, in Britain, the third influence was
new American Art, including photographically based work by artists such as
Cindy Sherman and Barbara Kruger.

Art education reflected the changes. In England there was a move to
consolidate art schools within the newly established polytechnics in the 1970s
and to upgrade courses from diploma to degree status. This involved
changing the erstwhile 'liberal studies' agenda to more purposeful critical
appraisal of art history. Art school graduates, who subsequently formed the
new generation of gallery curators, were increasingly well-informed and
interested in exhibiting a greater range of ideas-based work. Not only had
photography moved into the art gallery but, more broadly, critical ideas
moved on to the agenda in photography education; an agenda that was
increasingly influenced by feminist perspectives and critiques. A number of
new degrees in photography became established wherein 'theory' meant
thinking about photography **semiotically**, and in relation to questions of
identity, gender and representation.[7] By the 1990s, digital imaging was adding
its voice to the claims (see chapter 6).

Developments do not proceed in an orderly and coherent fashion. Whilst
digitally produced work takes its place alongside the straight photograph and
constructed imagery, the relative lack of photographs in a number of major
museum collections indicates that photography is still seen by some as a lesser
Art. The corollary of the new emphasis upon ideas and critiques was that,
from the mid-1980s, modern photography – abstract Formalism as well as
documentary-based imagery – found it more difficult to retain the space

7 The most prominent
example was at the
Polytechnic of Central
London in the 1980s.
Tutors then included Victor
Burgin and Simon Watney

227

within the gallery. The foothold established in the 1970s came to seem precarious. This was partly a consequence of fashion and the focus on the postmodern. But it was expressed in the more practical issue of scale. Photography galleries had been designed to accommodate the standard-format image. A number of the newer photo-media galleries, which were larger-scale, became key institutions within the new debates. The standard photograph became harder to show. For instance, Watershed Media Centre, Bristol, includes the original high warehouse roof in its main gallery space, thereby dwarfing smaller pictures.

It is no accident that a key exhibition of contemporary British photography at the Victoria and Albert Museum in 1988 was titled *Towards a Bigger Picture*. The *double entendre* of the title refers particularly to the extension of photography within Art practices and to diversity of subject-matter. But it also relates to conceptual understanding of ways in which scale contributes to the claim for place within the Art gallery. For example, very small-scale work, carefully mounted and framed, inherits the sense of the precious associated with miniature painting. It demands close-up and detailed looking. Preciousness is emphasised if individual works are hung with space between them. By contrast, large-scale photographic works claim the status traditionally accorded to academic painting and other Art made for public spaces. They also assert their presence and, therefore, the significance of their theme or subject-matter. Such pictures engage with contemporary myth in ways which echo the ideological and political involvements typical of classical painting.

New constructions

Discussing pluralism in American Art in the 1970s, critic Corinne Robins comments on the increasing eclecticism of photography, noting:

> Photographers concentrated on making up or creating scenes for the camera in terms of their own inner vision. To them, reportage as such had become the job of the video artist, who had the heritage of *cinéma vérité* behind him [*sic*]. To the 1970s camera people, realism belonged to the earlier history of photography and, as seventies artists, they were embarked on a different kind of aesthetic quest. It was not, however, the romantic symbolism of photography of the 1920s and 1930s, with its emphasis on the abstract beauty of the object, that had caught their attention, but rather a new kind of concentration on narrative drama, on the depiction of time changes in the camera's fictional moment. The photograph, instead of being presented as a depiction of reality, was now something created to show us things that were felt rather than necessarily seen.
>
> (Robins 1984: 213)

Central to the postmodern is an emphasis on **construction**, the forging, **staging** or **fabrication** of images. Pictures are preconceived by the artist. Constructed photography includes photomontage, **staged imagery**, **image-text** works, slide-tape installations, photographs derived from Land Art; indeed, any photographic imagery wherein the conceptual engineering of the artist is clearly evident. Contemporary photographers as divergent in concerns as Bernard Faucon, Mary Kelly, Peter Kennard, Barbara Kruger, Richard Long, Mari Mahr, Cindy Sherman, Susan Trangmar and Joel-Peter Witkin all fall within this broad category. The notion of construction derives from two sources: first, the idea that art can intervene politically, as in the example of the Soviet Constructivists or of the German *monteurs*. Second, in postmodern terms, 'construction' directly relates to **deconstruction** theory and practices. Both approaches refuse to take the world at face value. Constructed imagery in effect *critiques* what Grundberg has defined as 'concentration on the literal surfaces of things and on subject matter that seems to speak for itself' (Grundberg 1991: 82).

For example, in the example of Karen Knorr's series 'Country Life', countryside becomes a setting for reflections upon bourgeois taste and lifestyle (figure 5.1, page 200). Likewise, Patricia Townsend uses double exposure techniques to provoke a sense of dislocation which reminds us that we are objects of the look, as well as lookers, and that walls conceal metaphorically as well as literally (see book frontispiece). Zarina Bhimji uses photography within installations, creating a tension between the pleasurable textures and colour of the materials used and the questions of identity provoked (see book front cover). In each case, the images use the **indexical** qualities of the photographic – that is, the way in which the photograph draws upon actuality – as part of their vocabulary of expression, but only a part of it. Each invites the spectator to actively *read* the image, and all, variously, implicate questions of subjectivity and **identity**.

There are a number of methods whereby the interpretive latitude of an image may be limited, including photomontage, sequencing and image-text techniques. We also have to take account of factors beyond the image itself. The mounting and framing of pictures – whether single images, or series, or sequences – is not neutral. Framing contributes to the rhetoric of the image through delineating the edge of the picture, that which is put into the frame. It also acts as a margin between the work and the wall on which it hangs. The established convention in post-Renaissance Art of framing paintings means that the frame also signifies the special status of a picture. However, the meaning of the frame is ambiguous: from the point of view of the gallery wall, it is a part of the picture, but from the point of view of the picture it dissolves into the wall. In relation to the single image, this ambiguity is relatively clearly comprehended. Within sequences, or blocks of images, the play of the frame is more complex: the frame not only plays between the setting and the image, but also interacts with other frames within the grouping of pictures.

Written text commonly accompanies both single pictures, and series, groups or sequences. Written text includes titles, captions, artists' statements, poetry, or forewords which accompany an exhibition or book publication. Titling, and the signature of the artist, contribute to the claim for the status of the image as Art. Titles may be cryptic, or metaphoric, operating to extend resonances, or they may be primarily descriptive. For instance, a title such as 'Rome, 1975' or 'Waiting Room' specifies place or type of location. However, the caption does not simply anchor; writing constitutes a further signifier within the complex interaction of discourses with which the spectator engages. For instance, the title 'Rome' at the very minimum means something different to an Italian than to someone of another nationality. Titles, or captions, simultaneously anchor, and become implicated in, play of meaning. The refusal of a title, as in 'Untitled', is, likewise, not neutral. That something is not captioned implies that the image is to 'speak for itself'.

Writing operates complexly. This is often particularly so in constructed imagery within which text is montaged as an integral element. Here the verbal is articulated not only as a poetic reference but also as a visual element. Colour, handwritten or typographic style, placing, scale, prominence – all contribute to how we read the overall piece. Likewise, artists' statements do not simply contextualise, or determine a position from which the work is to be read, although, of course, they do offer this. If an artist is viewed as a special sort of seer, offering particular insights into the world of experience, then his or her statement contributes to this claim for authority.

Towards the postmodern

Any attempt to overview recent thematic developments is fraught with difficulty, not only because of diversity but also because of the lack of the benefit of hindsight. Nonetheless, concentrating on developments in Britain, we have selected some examples of group exhibitions from the late 1970s through to the early 1990s as a focus for discussion.[8]

A note of caution: gallery administrators and curators are caught up in the fashionable. An overview of exhibitions does not necessarily tell everything about contemporary developments – although it might say quite a lot about the politics of the gallery. For instance, as **Brett Rogers** suggests in her introduction to *Documentary Dilemmas*,

> Ignored by the art world which favours big pictures and high prices, and outstripped by technology that gives the edge to television and digital developments, documentary photography has also come under harsh scrutiny from post-modern critics, who question its tendency to separate and exploit certain groups of people, serving up the poor as exotic fare for voyeuristic consumers.

(Rogers 1994: 5)

8 Space does not allow discussion of all group shows, let alone the many single-person shows which have attracted attention during this period, but they are traceable through *Creative Camera* and *Portfolio*

BRETT ROGERS (ed.) (1994) **Documentary Dilemmas: Aspects of British Documentary Photography 1983–1993**, London: British Council. This exhibition was curated for an international tour, and included work by John Davies, Anna Fox, Julian Germain, Paul Graham, Anthony Haughey, Chris Killip, John Kippin, Karen Knorr, Martin Parr, Ingrid Pollard, Paul Reas, Paul Seawright and Jem Southam

She goes on to suggest that this has led to the ignoring of new rhetorical strategies in use within documentary, including fill-in flash, colour, scale, captioning, sequencing, and the use of text within the image. Trends within curatorship, criticism and, indeed, the international Art market, marginalise some areas of practice. Any attempt to define trends and developments should acknowledge this.

Furthermore, as Mary Kelly has noted, there is a sense in which the gallery itself, although of central symbolic significance, is less important in the history of artistic production than catalogues, books, reviews, and other accompanying, more permanent, forms of reproduction of work (Kelly 1981). Exhibitions are ephemeral. It is published reviews, catalogues or books, rather than the shows themselves, which reach the wider audience. In this section, discussion is based upon catalogues and reviews, so no account is taken of how each show was hung within the particular gallery space.[9]

In 1979 The Arts Council mounted 'Three Perspectives on Photography', a show of recent British photography, at the Hayward Gallery, on London's South Bank. This exhibition makes an interesting contrast to the 1991 Arts Council show, 'Shocks to the System'.

'Three Perspectives on Photography' was organised as three different groups of work, each separately curated, thus acknowledging diversity of approaches. In so doing it appeared a radical initiative at the time. Section One, on 'Photographic Truth, Metaphor, and Individual Expression' included series of photographs – each captioned – by six (male) photographers. Stylistically the images reflected a modernist emphasis on photographic seeing. But Paul Hill, in his introduction to the section, stressed the expressive and metaphoric dimensions of the photograph, opposing any simple equation of believability with truth. Indeed, suggesting that the photograph should be understood as a *symbol* for that which is depicted, he drew attention to what would now be termed the **semiotics** of the image.

Of even more significance retrospectively are the two following sections: 'Feminism and Photography' and 'A Socialist Perspective on Photographic Practice'. Neither of these topics would figure in so blunt a way in the 1990s. Feminist perspectives have, on the whole, been taken on board, some might say diluted through incorporation. By contrast, socialism has been marginalised, and would be a distinctly unfashionable exhibition title! A decade later, in 1991, nothing so succinct as three perspectives could be claimed. The imagery included in 'Shocks to the System' was largely made during, and influenced by, the Thatcher decade. Here it is not Left art which is emphasised so much as a range of different visual methods of drawing attention to subjective and political issues and complexities, often employing humour or parody. The show was multicultural, and reflected the diversity which now obtains in gallery photographic practices.

9 In viewing exhibitions, you should take into account particular relations set up between the work of different photographers and consider how this contributes to interpretation. To take the most obvious question: What work is hung at the entrance point? Does this indicate a central theme or preoccupation?

Three Perspectives on Photography, London: Arts Council, 1979; **Shocks to the System**, London: The South Bank Centre, 1991. The latter catalogue includes thirty-seven photographers represented by one photograph, and a mini-biography. Two further shows – **About 70 Photographs**, ed. CHRIS STEELE-PERKINS, curated from the Arts Council collection in 1980, and GERRY BADGER and JOHN BENTON-HARRIS, **Through the Looking Glass**, London: Barbican Art Gallery, 1989 – also demonstrate something of the diversity of practices within mainstream gallery photography in the 1980s. Both include straight photography alongside more conceptual works

Women's photography

The mere mention of the phrase 'women's art' sends shivers down the art establishment spine – more radical feminists on the warpath! Feminism, advocacy of women's rights on the ground of equality, is usually misinterpreted to mean exclusively female, probably radical and, more than likely, shaven-headedly lesbian. It's curious how this misconception perpetuates!

(Libby Anson
Untitled #7, Winter 1994/1995)

Question: Do women have to be naked to get into the Metropolitan Museum of Art?
Answer: Less than 5% of the artists in the Modern Art are women, but 85% of the nudes are female – Guerilla Girls

Key resource:
Women's Art Library and Magazine, London. Established 1982 as a slide library, publication archive and national/ international membership network

VAL WILLIAMS (1986) **Women Photographers: The Other Observers 1900 to the Present**, London: Virago. This was researched and curated for the National Museum of Photography, Film and Television in Bradford, Yorkshire as a touring show with accompanying book, although it is the text which has become the classic introduction to the recuperation of a range of types of work by women

The resurgence of feminism in the 1970s challenged the patriarchal establishment. This challenge included a set of questions about women, representation and Art, which led to critical work on three key fronts. First, examination of ways in which women have been represented in Western Art. Within patriarchy, active looking has been accorded to the male spectator. 'Woman' becomes the object of his **gaze**. Although this does not only concern 'the nude', the representation of naked women for visual consumption formed one obvious focus for accusations of sexism in visual culture. Fundamentally it was argued that the term 'nude', central to the visual arts tradition, lent a guise of respectability to the practice of naked women being objectified for **fantasy** libidinous gratification. Second, feminist art historians pursued the archaeological project of rediscovering and drawing attention to the work of women artists, previously ignored or marginalised. Third, women in art schools, galleries and publishing asserted a right for space devoted to contemporary women artists. The revolution took several forms. In art education the art history curriculum was brought under scrutiny, and various guises whereby sexism figured in the studio were challenged. Alongside this, the demand was made that galleries and publishers should examine their record in exposing the work of women artists – and set out to rectify it! Protests were mounted against exhibitions showing work deemed offensive to women.

This revolution obviously influenced photography, itself forging space in the Art gallery. Three projects stand as key examples. They relate, respectively, to the diverse history of photography, modern aesthetics and postmodern gallery-based practices. First, in *Women Photographers: The Other Observers 1900 to the Present* writer-curator **Val Williams** traced and surveyed a range of work, from high-street studio portraiture to fashion photography, from the documentary and photojournalistic to the snapshot, and to contemporary feminist practices. The purpose was to expose the names and work of women photographers, previously hidden from history, and to demonstrate the diversity of practices within which they had been active. This exhibition, with its broad remit, opened at the National Museum of Photography, Film and Television; significantly, a photography organisation (as opposed to an Art gallery). It contrasts with the second example, **Constance Sullivan**'s selection, also entitled *Women Photographers*, which more specifically recuperates women as artists in terms of the precepts and principles of modern photography. From the point of view of considering photography and the Art gallery in the context of contemporary, postmodern practices, the third example, *Shifting Focus*, curated by **Susan Butler**, was of central import both for its focus upon contemporary work made for the gallery and for its internationalism. Most significantly, *Shifting Focus* posited the question, what happens when women look? If, traditionally, women have been the object of the gaze, the viewed rather than the viewer, the represented rather than the author of representation, what happens when she takes a more active role? Butler was concerned to explore ways in which, in exercising the right to look, women alter the terms of visual culture which, as feminist art historians have argued, was premised upon unequal viewing relations.

The 1994 (British) Signals Festival of Women's Photography continued the overall aim to draw attention to, encourage and celebrate work by women, both within and without the gallery. Indeed, now it is commonplace for exhibitions to include work by women artists. But perhaps the strength and confidence of women's work is best testified by the shift to more specifically themed exhibitions, for example, self-portraiture, war, the family, lesbian identity. The presence of women photographers in the gallery is now taken for granted. Furthermore, the shift in focus has influenced new themes within the work of male photographers.[10]

The influence of women's photography within the gallery thus goes beyond simply securing a rightful place for work by women. Feminist theory posed a more fundamental critique of aesthetic conventions and practices. This has led to determined retrieval of the terms of visualisation. As American artist, Barbara Kruger, asserted in one of her renowned photomontages, 'we will not play nature to your culture'. Women's photography now has moved beyond critiques of representation to exploration of relations of looking. The terms posed are increasingly diverse: for example, in relation to the body, Della Grace's work overtly acknowledges and invites a lesbian gaze. Katrina Lithgow depicts naked pregnant women in a matter-of-fact manner which both asserts woman's right to represent herself and refuses romanticisation. More experimentally, in both aesthetic and technological terms, Mona Hatoum revealed internal organs of the body normally only subjected to the medical gaze. Each, variously, poses questions of identity using the body as a focus. This has been critiqued or dismissed as a retreat into the personal. (It may, indeed, reflect a sense of the limited influence of the artist within contemporary global politics.) However, it also reflects the

CONSTANCE SULLIVAN (ed.) (1990) **Women Photographers**, London: Virago. This book concentrates on high-quality reproduction of photographs by women historically. with a view to reclaiming their work for the canon

SUSAN BUTLER (1989) **Shifting Focus**, Bristol/London: Arnolfini/Serpentine. The catalogue comments internationally on contemporary work by women

10 Examples include John Coplan's imaging of the male body (Tate collection), Paul Rhys' exploration of his relationship with his father (included in *Who's Looking at the Family*, Barbican Gallery, London, 1994) and David Lewis' appraisal of the black body within anthropology (*The Impossible Science of Being*, The Photographers' Gallery, 1995)

influence of the central tenet of psychoanalysis, namely, that the individual subject is formed through cultural experience. As subject-matter within photography, 'the body' implicates broader cultural concerns.

Questions of identity

> Post structuralist thinking opposes the notion that a person is born with a fixed identity. . . . It suggests instead that identities are floating, that meaning is not fixed and universally true at all times for all people, and that the subject is constructed through the unconscious in desire, fantasy and memory.
>
> (Bailey and Hall 1992: 20)

From the perspective of the present, contemporary art practices appear to be marked by diversity, if not incoherence. Arguably this diversity variously reflects issues of identity. Psychoanalytic theory suggests that images, through offering points of identification, offer fantasy resolutions for subjective angst. Identification, in this context, refers to processes whereby the individual subject assimilates an aspect, property or attribute of that which is seen, and is transformed, wholly or partially, after the model the other – in this instance, the image – provides. Personality is constituted through such imaginary identifications. Thus, Art may be seen as feeding our need for a clear sense of identity and of cultural belonging. This is a continuous process of reassurance, since identity is neither uniform, nor fixed, and is subject to continuing processes of challenge, shift and reaffirmation. In other words, any sense of self-location through the contemplation of the photographic image is temporary. Indeed, desire for reassurance may be one of the factors propelling us to keep on looking at images.

Black and British

Curator Sunil Gupta has noted that the history of black photography in Britain is brief. As a movement, he ascribes its early development to funding initiatives taken by Labour-controlled local city councils in the early 1980s context of Thatcherism, and of inner-city racial tension (Gupta 1990). Key exhibitions and initiatives included *Reflections of the Black Experience* (curator, Monika Baker, Brixton Art Gallery, 1986), which, as a primarily documentary show, offered evidence not only of the diversity of black experience in Britain but also of the presence of good black photographers. The Association of Black Photographers, later Autograph, was formed soon after this to promote the work of black photographers across a range of fields. Meanwhile, *D-Max* (curator, Eddie Chambers) toured work for the gallery by British Afro-Caribbean photographers.

Racism, the post-colonial context and the desire to explore ethnic difference, mean that questions of identity figure centrally in black Art. Obvious avenues of exploration include the dislocated family, diaspora, internationalism, and media representation of the '**Other**' of British culture. Exhibitions which have explored these themes include *Disrupted Borders*, which connected work from widespread parts of the world – including Finland, India, North America – all of which in some way treated questions of cultural integration or marginality (**Gupta 1993**), and *Mirage* which included work, in a range of media, by black artists from Europe and North America (Bailey, ICA, 1995). A number of British-based photographers are prominent within new black Art practices. These include Ingrid Pollard (figure 5.10) whose work regularly poses questions of history and heritage, and David A. Bailey, whose 1987 series on the family album was the subject of the following evocative description:

> Against the background of a 'Made in England' clock and a montage of snapshots, a family album is displaced by a Black magazine which in turn is displaced by the screaming headlines of a tabloid newspaper. As the clock ticks on, marking the shifting historical context, the changing assemblages of images address the contradictions between private and public representations of race.
>
> (Gilane Tawadros in Haworth-Booth 1988)

Explorations of post-colonial identity typically interlink the political and personal. Two themes predominate: first the legacy of colonialism; and second what it is to be British, regardless of ethnic identity, given 'New Europe'. Post-colonial preoccupations are clearly marked in Black Art, but likewise figure within Scottish and Irish Art. To take an example: black artist David Lewis has pictured the map of Africa as a chess board for a game played by European players (*D-Max*). Scottish artist Ron O'Donnell depicted a map of Scotland with a noose round the Highlands (*I-D Nationale*, Portfolio Gallery, Edinburgh, 1993). The point is similar! Questions of lineage and heritage within European Britain, conceptualised subjectively and socially, are central to the contemporary cultural agenda. As will be argued, this is not only reflected in art practices but also in the centrality of the Art gallery and museum within the burgeoning British heritage industry.

CASE STUDY: LANDSCAPE AS GENRE

Genre

Developed within film studies to reference clusters of movies of a similar sort (such as the Western, melodrama, film noir), the term 'genre' refers to types of cultural product. But genre is not simply a classification. Genres carry with them specific sets of histories, practices, ideological assumptions and expectations, which shift over time to take account of changing cultural formations. We have chosen the example of landscape, but the principal point about change and continuity can be examined in relation to any chosen genre.

DAVID A. BAILEY and STUART HALL (eds) (1992) **Critical Decade** *Ten/8* 2(3)
SUNIL GUPTA (ed.) (1993) **Disrupted Borders**, London: Rivers Oram Press

Key resource:
Institute of International Visual Arts (INIVA), London, an umbrella organisation coordinating initiatives (African and Asian Artists Slide Library, Bristol)

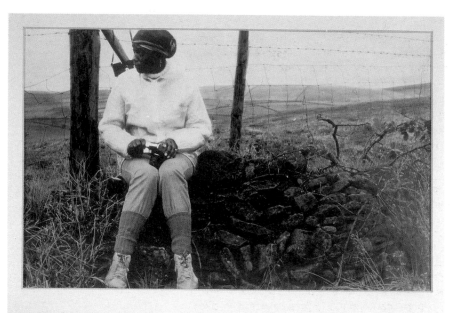

"pastoral interlude"
... it's as if the Black experience is only lived within an urban environment.
I thought I liked the Lake District; where I wandered lonely as a Black face in
a sea of white. A visit to the countryside is always accompanied by a feeling
of unease; dread ...

5.10 Ingrid Pollard, from *Pastoral Interludes*, 1987 (original in colour)

Landscape as genre

There is a key distinction between 'land' and 'landscape'. In principle, land is
a natural phenomenon, although most land, certainly in Britain, has been
subjected to extensive human intervention (creating fields, planting crops,
shoring up the coastline, and so on). 'Landscape' is a cultural construct. It
dates from seventeenth-century Dutch painterly practices, but became central
to English painting. The eighteenth-century English landscape painting did
not simply echo the Dutch, but re-articulated the genre to incorporate the
increasing emphasis on technological achievement (Bright 1990) – A clear
example of accommodation to particular cultural circumstances!
Landscape can be defined as vistas which encompass both nature and the
changes which humans have effected in the natural. Broadly interpreted, this
includes sea, fields, rivers, gardens, buildings, canals, and so on. It thus
encompasses emblems of property ownership (such as fences), or of industrialisation (such as mines or factories). Typically, English landscape pictures
rarely depict work or, on occasion, romanticise the rural labourer. For the

236

aristocracy, landed gentry and nineteenth-century industrialist, land ownership symbolised hereditary status or entrepreneurial success. As John Berger
has argued, landscape paintings operated to reassure this status (Berger
1972).

Landscape photography

In considering landscape as an example of a genre within photography, we
are concerned first to identify typical aesthetic and sociopolitical characteristics of landscape imagery; and second to explore ways in which the genre
has accommodated change, reinvented and reinvigorated itself over time.
Landscape photography has largely inherited the compositional conventions
of landscape painting. Typically landscape photographs are a lateral rectangle
– it is no accident that 'landscape format' has come to describe photographs
where the width is greater than the height. Compositionally, the 'golden
rule' of one-third/two-third horizontal proportions is usually obeyed.
British landscape photography is founded as much in the documentary
endeavours of travelling photographers, at home and abroad, as in the
gallery. Thus there are two lines of inheritance within landscape photography: on the one hand, straight photographs, topographical in intent,
although on the whole echoing the composition of the classic landscape
painting, and, on the other hand, images constructed in accordance with a
preconceived idea, be it poetic, mythological or critical import. These two
strands, in effect, constitute the twin poles of the genre. Landscape also
reflects new aesthetic ideas, for instance, Surrealist dreamlike states (figure
5.8, page 222) or the Constructivist compositional radicalism based on the
ideal of a new angle of vision. (figure 5.6, page 216).

Historical development and change

By the nineteenth century 'landscape' also stood as an antidote for the visual
and social consequences of industrialisation, offering a view of nature as
therapeutic, a pastoral release from commerce and industry. Art movements
such as Romanticism and Pictorialism reflected such changing attitudes:
ignoring ways in which the industrial actually impacted on the visual
environment, Romanticism in painting reified the rural idyll. This reification is
reflected in photographs of the time. For instance, Camille Silvy's 'River
Scene, France' (figure 5.2, page 207) is a carefully staged myth about the
calm, leisure and pleasure of the countryside. There are several examples of
seascapes, for instance, by Gustave le Grey (also French) wherein combination
printing has, similarly, been used to effect pleasing scenes; for instance,
clouds above the serene waters.

As we have seen, such stagings are taken further in Pictorialism, within
which people were frequently depicted in close relation to what was
perceived as 'natural' environment, with no stated documentary or topographical location. Thus, for instance, the Lady of Shallot is re-presented by
Henry Peach Robinson as a picturesque tale (figure 5.3, page 209). Here
landscape becomes the background against which a story is staged.

New aesthetics

Modern landscape photography has been particularly associated with American photographers, including Ansel Adams, Minor White and Edward Weston, who subscribed to the notion of pure photographic seeing. Unlike most of Britain, the American West is characterised by vast open spaces. Nineteenth-century pioneers, such as Carleton Watkins, whose work is now central to the photography archive, were employed to chart land prior to its opening up by, in his case, the laying of the Pacific Railroad. Modern photographers laid more stress upon the aesthetics and spiritual dimensions of landscape, producing elegant and elegiac abstract imagery. Edward Weston's images, in which the sharpness of the realisation of the photograph is tempered with the rhythm of form, offer prototypical examples (figure 5.7, page 219).

Genres typically are characterised by continuity through change, by an ability to reform in order to incorporate new aesthetics and circumstances. Landscape is no exception. Now fences, the railway, brick walls, motorways, pylons, signs and hoardings have all, variously, become rendered as a part of traditional imagery and myth. Of course, 'translations' are involved: landscape photographs are often monochrome, the countryside represented in terms of shape and tonal gradings. The fundamental point is that the photograph reinflects subject-matter in terms which reflect current cultural currencies. In this sense, the Modernist landscape, with its emphasis on aesthetics, was one moment in the regeneration of the genre. The focus upon more obviously intrusive cultural elements, or industrial legacies, in the work of Ray Moore or John Davies, for instance, offers another.[11]

11 Work by each of these photographers can be found in monographs published under their name

The modern and the postmodern

Analysis of aesthetic and ideological change involves engagement with broad socio-economic and political circumstances as well as with aesthetics. But genre analysis is always best pursued through comparison of specific examples. For instance, in this chapter there are two compositionally somewhat similar square-format photographs, by Bill Brandt (figure 5.5, page 213) and Karen Knorr (figure 5.1, page 200). Both use photographic techniques and conventions to effect a sense of harmony. Yet they are different in import. Brandt's image is a documentary statement, the location is given. Knorr's, through the presence of the man and the book, and the caption, offers a conceptual comment upon English culture, one which provokes critical interpretation. The difference between the Modern aesthetic, and the postmodern critique, is marked.

The politics of landscape

A number of contemporary photographers, including Keith Arnatt, John Davies, John Kippin, Ingrid Pollard and Jem Southam, engage in critical terms with notions of landscape, commenting, for example, on the legacy of industrialisation whether it be rural industry such as tin-mining (Southam) or the Northern industrial landscape (Davies). Fay Godwin's work on land, access and property rights offers a further significant example. Landscape imagery reflects and

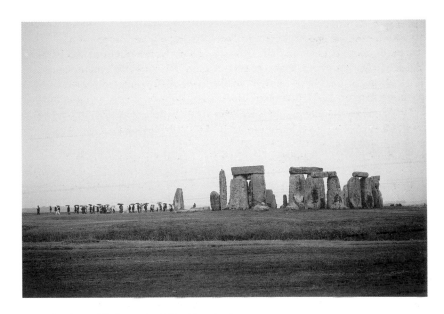

5.11 John Kippin, Pilgrims, 1994 (original in colour)

reinforces particular ideas about class, gender, race and heritage in relation to property rights, accumulation and control (see Taylor 1994; Wells 1994). A number of contemporary photographers have made it their business to question this. John Kippin's work on the commodification of heritage (figure 5.11) is one such example. The contrast between this type of contemporary emphasis and the nineteenth century idyllic image is obvious from a comparison of the work of Kippin, or Pollard, with Silvy or Peach Robinson.
Yet all these pictures 'fit' within landscape as a genre, and contribute to its regeneration, typifying the attitudes and discourses characteristic of their respective eras.

PHOTOGRAPHY WITHIN THE INSTITUTION

In 1939, the Victoria and Albert Museum, London (V&A), home of the National Collection of the Art of Photography, mounted a small centenary exhibition. In 1972, the museum hosted a major exhibition of nineteenth-century photography including over 800 pictures, entitled 'From Today Painting is Dead': The Beginnings of Photography (a quote from artist Paul Delaroche in the 1840s) organised by the Arts Council in conjunction with the National Portrait Gallery and the Science Museum. This coincided with other developments in Britain, including the opening of The Photographers' Gallery in London, 1971, and of Impressions Gallery, York, in 1972. Stills Gallery, Edinburgh, was set up in 1977, and the Association of Welsh Photographers, later Ffotogallery, Cardiff, in 1978. Plans to establish the National Museum of Photography, Film and Television (NMPFT) in Bradford, as a branch of the Science Museum, were announced in 1980. Also in 1980 the Royal Photographic Society (RPS) moved their library and archive from London to Bath. The Scottish Photography Archive, part of the National Galleries of Scotland, was established in 1984 and, by 1995, included over 20,000 photographs. Thus, the 1970s and 1980s were characterised not only by the extension of provision for photography collections and exhibitions, but also by an increase in major institutions located away from London.

This echoes a general expansion whereby by the mid-1980s there were over 2000 museums and galleries in the United Kingdom, with new ones opening at the rate of one a fortnight. Discussing *The Heritage Industry*, Robert Hewison argues that 'in the twentieth century museums have taken over the function once exercised by church and ruler, they provide the symbols through which a nation and a culture understands itself' (Hewison 1987: 84). Museums have become key patrons of Art, influencing priorities and pricing within the Art market. Given the monumental dimensions of some new centres (for instance, the Pompidou Centre, Paris, or the planned Bankside extension to the Tate in London) galleries also influence the conceptual scale of imagery. The photograph has been used extensively within the expanding museum both to document and to celebrate the history. It has also been implicated in critiquing this 'heritage industry' (Taylor 1994: 240ff.).

Funding for the Arts in Britain involves private, commercial and public sources; it is essentially a mixed economy. Typically, exhibition organisers seek private or commercial sponsorship as well as revenue from admission tickets and sales such as postcards and catalogues. Many public galleries are partly funded by local authorities, regional arts boards or the Arts Council of England. (Wales, Scotland and Northern Ireland each have their own provisions.) Alongside this is the network of national, regional and local museums and art galleries, often Victorian in origin which, again, are funded both by the national government (the Department of Heritage) and by local authorities.

The Arts Council

Central to the subsidy system is the Arts Council of England (ACE) which is appointed by government as an independent or 'arms-length' organisation, financed and monitored through the Department of Heritage. Its officers enact decisions within a policy framework established by the Council members and their specialist arts advisers (for a critical discussion of history and priorities, see Hutchison 1982). ACE works in liaison with a network of regional arts boards in England and Wales. Photography became an identifiable concern in 1967, when a committee was set up to advise the Council's visual arts panel on photography exhibitions. A full-time officer responsible for photography was appointed in 1973.

The degree of actual autonomy of the Arts Council as a Quasi Autonomous Non Governmental Organisation (QUANGO) has been much debated. Writing in 1979, Raymond Williams described the system as more 'wrist's length', noting the extent to which the public funding system is tied into government interests through the appointment to intermediate bodies of 'the great and the good' as decision makers – a system which he defined as 'Administered Consensus by Co-option' (Williams 1979). In effect, the government trusts appointees to take decisions which do not contravene government interests. The Arts Council has included architects, critics, academics, business people, as well as established artists and writers. The set-up both perpetuates the notion that the arts are outside politics and leaves the arts in a marginal position in terms of financial and cultural policy debates in Parliament. Of course, this is not the same thing as saying that the arts are apolitical.

There is tension between those who support Art *per se*, and those who view the fine arts as intrinsically elitist since, historically, these have been the leisure activities of the aristocracy and the bourgeoisie. To simplify: conservatives wish to encourage interest in the established Arts. This has been criticised as attempting to use the Arts to assert **hegemonic** influence. This is not just a question of social class, nor of history and heritage. The Arts Council, and interrelated systems of influence such as arts criticism, have been accused of metropolitan myopia; that is, failing to acknowledge that which occurs outside of major cities, particularly London. The community arts movement of the late 1960s and 1970s posed a challenge to static notions of what constitutes Art and demanded democratisation not only in terms of education and access to the Arts but in the definition of Arts activities acknowledged (Braden 1978). Furthermore, past policy priorities often failed to take account of diverse ethnicity. The Greater London Council (dissolved by the Conservative Government in 1985) took a lead in supporting multicultural initiatives.

Since the 1980s, the idea that the Arts could and should be kept at a distance from political control has lost credence. The Conservative Government, elected in 1979, has been committed to reductions in public expenditure and the fostering of initiatives for business sponsorship for the Arts. This is the new 'partnership' in Arts patronage. Preservation of artworks from the past for museums has always been the subject of direct political intervention, so two systems operate in parallel: direct finance via the Department of Heritage through museums and major galleries, and indirect finance through the Arts Council for living artists (Hewison 1987). But this is to oversimplify: for instance, museums, including the V&A and NMPFT, not only maintain archives but also collect contemporary work, thereby, in effect, supporting photographers.

Barry Lane, photography officer at the Arts Council 1973–1995, attributes the burgeoning of interest in photography in the 1970s to three key factors.[12] First, developments including community arts, performance art and 'happenings' signified a broadening of definitions of 'Art'. As already noted, photography breached the gallery around this time. Second, developments in America lent impetus and contacts for fostering photography in Britain. Third, there were energetic claims from within the British documentary movement for the artistic integrity of the medium, and such claims were further fuelled by the commercial success of leading British 1960s photographers.

The range and diversity of photography organisations and practices listed poses a problem for the Arts Council, more accustomed to developing artistic and financial policies for established arts organisations and practices:

> With its base in modern technology and its place in the contemporary communications media, photography is an art form that goes beyond the traditional arts. While one small sector may be found within fine art institutions, most independent photography belongs in a far broader range of cultural, community and educational institutions. 'Independent', rather than 'creative' or 'art', is rapidly becoming the accepted term used to distinguish this work from the dominant forms of commercial and amateur practice. It covers cultural work for publishers, archives, picture agencies, galleries, art centres, local authorities, educational institutions, trade unions, voluntary sector organisations, community and community arts groups.
>
> (Arts Council 1987)

In practice the Arts Council and the regional arts boards have financed publishing and marketing of photography books and magazines, commissions for photographers, major exhibitions including touring exhibitions, initiatives in training and education, provision of research, information and advice services, and a network of regional centres for photography which typically include a gallery and darkroom facilities, and provide a local or regional focus for education and training.

There is a key distinction to be made between photography galleries, and art galleries such as the Tate, which include photographically produced work within their collection as Modern Art, but have no particular policy towards photography. Photography galleries have a narrower remit in terms of focus upon the particular medium (whether chemically or digitally based), but a much broader cultural remit in, potentially, displaying and interrogating all aspects of photography as visual communication, historically and now. Photography is situated both within the fine art gallery system and beyond it. This inevitably poses problems when it comes to determining the scope of public subsidy within a system which, in the case of the Arts Council, has its origins in fine art practices.

Curators and exhibition contexts

Photography exhibitions tour nationally and internationally. Museums and galleries commission exhibitions which are 'hired' by other galleries; it is not uncommon for exhibitions to be 'on the road' for two years. They are curated by one or more people, whose role includes researching the exhibition concept, the selection (or commissioning) of work, planning how the work will be hung within the exhibition space, and writing a significant part of any accompanying book or catalogue. The power of the curator, operating regionally, nationally or, increasingly, internationally, has come up for question in recent years. Of course curators take initiatives which contribute to the exposure of work. But they may also regularly favour certain artists, or types of work, at the expense of others. For example, until recently, historians and curators have tended to ignore the work of women artists or artists from ethnic minority groups (in Britain and elsewhere). Furthermore, it has been suggested that curators often act more as 'creators', putting together theme exhibitions which, however relevant and interesting, serve as much to advance themselves as to showcase the work of artists.

The archive, the critic and the curator interact with the international market for both contemporary and historic photographic work. International auction houses, such as Christie's or Sotheby's, note the influence of exhibitions (and events, such as the death of an artist) on auction prices.[13] Considering places in which the validation and valuation of art occurs, **Sandy Nairne** notes the key influence of the private gallery, the private collector, the public museum and the art magazine (Nairne 1987).

Commercial art dealers scrutinise trends in order to maintain their position in a competitive market. In Britain, the market for both old and contemporary photography is a relatively new phenomenon; a response, perhaps, to both the renewal of interest in the photograph in the 1970s and 1980s and the increasing emphasis upon private commercial practices which characterised 1980s Thatcherism. But 'collection' as a commitment on the part of particular individuals or businesses is not new. Indeed, royal patronage for artists, since the Renaissance, has taken precisely this form. The key purchasers may now be entrepreneurs, rather than the Royal Family, but patronage through payment for ownership of the art object persists. As Walter Benjamin suggested in 1931, 'The most profound enchantment for the collector is the locking of individual items within a magic circle in which they are fixed as the final thrill, the thrill of acquisition, passes over them' (Benjamin 1992a: 62).

Outside the mainstream

Photography has also challenged dominent aesthetics, in a range of contexts, usually with some commitment to political empowerment. Central to the politics of representation is the question of whose experience is validated. This

13 For example, in 1995, prior to auction, a collection of paintings and photographs by Man Ray was exhibited at the Serpentine, one of London's higher profile public galleries for contemporary art.

SANDY NAIRNE (1987) 'Value, Commodity and Criticism', **State of the Art, Ideas and Images in the 1980s**, London: Chatto & Windus

motivates the work of many contemporary women and black artists. In this respect the gallery is sometimes overtly a site of political engagement. In community arts, the emphasis is not so much on Art as exhibition or publication, as on the darkroom as workshop and on ways in which photographic seeing can contribute to self-esteem and the fostering of social and political perceptions. Community workshops and schools-based initiatives have offered a number of opportunities for photographers to run a range of projects. Among the best known was the Cockpit in London in the 1980s. Projects often operate through workshops for teachers or community workers, who then take ideas back into their schools or local areas. Some of these projects owe their roots to higher profile initiatives such as international festivals concerned not to overlook the locality in which they are based.

Internationalism: festivals and publishing

The 1980s also saw a burgeoning of international photography festivals. The first such international festival was established as an annual meeting place and showcase for photography at Arles, France, in 1970. Others, such as Houston (biennial since 1986) and Rotterdam (biennial since 1988), have been more or less based upon the same model involving some thematic focus, a number of lectures and events, opportunities for less-experienced or less-established photographers to show their portfolio to known photographers, critics and curators and, in certain instances, some form of schools- and community-based spin-off. The other major European festival is the biennial Paris *Mois de la Photo* which, since 1980, has taken place throughout the city. *Fotofeis*, the biennial Scottish International Festival of Photography, was established in 1993. England has no regular, large-scale international festival, although there have been a number of one-off themed festivals; for instance, the 1994 Signals Festival of Women's Photography.

The purpose of festivals is to offer a focus, meeting place and showcase for photography. As such they contribute to raising the profile of photography nationally and internationally. Along with gallery exhibitions, photography magazines and books, they profile trends in photography and the work of particular photographers. But festivals require attendance and participation. This contrasts with photography publishing which, in principle, can attain widespread distribution through bookshops (although few bookshops stock much other than a few more popular titles by 'household name' photographers). Furthermore, as has been noted, publications outlive festivals and exhibitions. It is photography magazines such as the two-monthly *Creative Camera*, based in London, or the biannual *Portfolio*, based in Edinburgh, which trace debates and developments, and shape history, through featuring the work of particular photographers, discussing contemporary issues, reviewing shows and books.

The Gallery as context

Galleries are particular sorts of meeting places, often including coffee bars and/or bookshops. Arguably, the gallery network not only offers visual pleasures but also operates to reassure a certain sense of intellectual and cultural elitism. Part of the pleasure of looking at pictures lies in discussing images, in sharing responses. This assumes and reaffirms biographical and cultural similarities in terms of class, gender, ethnicity, education and interest or involvement in the Arts. Sociologist Terry Lovell has suggested that 'the discerning of aesthetic form itself must be seen as a major source of pleasure in the text – the identification of the "rules of the game", and pleasure in seeing them obeyed, varied and even flouted' (Lovell 1980: 95). Galleries have specific profiles within this. For instance, organisations such as Camera Work in East London and Side Gallery, Newcastle, were founded in socialist commitment.

The political significance of the contemporary gallery is complex. There is a sense in which curator, critic, audience and artist are all complicit in perpetuating an exclusive system which functions hegemonically in ways which seem relatively detached from economic imperatives. On the other hand, the private collector and the public museum and Art gallery, along with the public subsidy system, exercise a significant degree of economic influence on developments within the Arts, not only in relation to the past and the present but also in terms of the heritage for the future. The increasing significance of the museum and gallery within the ever-expanding heritage industry perhaps accounts for the extent to which, since the 1980s, a presence in the gallery has seemed so crucial to photographers.

BIBLIOGRAPHY

KEY READING

Arnason, H.H. (1988) *A History of Modern Art*, London: Thames and Hudson, third edition (updated and revised to include photography)

Arts Council (1979) *Three Perspectives on Photography*, London: Arts Council

—— (1991) *Shocks to the System*, London: The South Bank Centre

Badger, Gerry and Benton-Harris, John (eds) (1989) *Through the Looking Glass*, London: Barbican Art Gallery

Bailey, David A. and Hall, Stuart (eds) (1992) *Critical Decade*, Ten/8 2(3)

Bright, Deborah (1990) 'Of Mother Nature and Marlboro Men: An Inquiry into the Cultural Meanings of Landscape Photography' in Richard Boston (ed.) *The Context of Meaning*, Cambridge, MA: MIT Press

Butler, Susan (1989) *Shifting Focus*, Bristol/London: Arnolfini/Serpentine

Coke, Van Deren (1972) *The Painter and the Photograph*, New Mexico: University of New Mexico Press

Galassi, Peter (1981) *Before Photography*, New York: MOMA

Green, Jonathan (1984) 'The Painter as Photographer', *American Photography*, New York: Harry N. Abrams

Gupta, Sunil (ed.) (1993) *Disrupted Borders*, London: Rivers Oram Press

Harker, Margaret (1979) *The Linked Ring: The Secession Movement in Photography in Britain 1892–1910*, London: Heinemann

Haworth-Booth, Mark (1992) *River Scene, France*, California: J. Paul Getty Museum

Krauss, Rosalind and Livingston, Jane (1986) *L'Amour Fou*, London: Arts Council of Great Britain

Kuenzli, Rudolf E. (1991) 'Surrealism and Misogyny' in Mary Ann Caws, Rudolf Kuenzli and Owen Raaberg *Surrealism and Women*, Cambridge, MA: MIT Press

Nairne, Sandy (1987) *State of the Art, Ideas and Images in the 1980s*, London: Chatto & Windus

Phillips, Christopher (ed.) (1989) *Photography in the Modern Era: European Documents and Critical Writings 1913–1940*, New York: MOMA

Rogers, Brett (ed.) (1994) *Documentary Dilemmas: Aspects of British Documentary Photography 1983–1993*, London: British Council

Scharf, Aaron (1974) *Art and Photography*, London: Allen Lane, Pelican Books, revised edition

Steele-Perkins, Chris (ed.) (1980) *About 70 Photographs*, London: Arts Council of Great Britain

Sullivan, Constance (ed.) (1990) *Women Photographers*, London: Virago

Weaver, Mike (1989a) *The Art of Photography*, London: Royal Academy of Arts

—— (ed.). (1989b) *British Photography in the Nineteenth Century: The Fine Art Tradition*, Cambridge: Cambridge University Press

Willett, John (1978) *The New Sobriety, Art and Politics in the Weimar Period*, London: Thames and Hudson

Williams, Val (1986) *Women Photographers: The Other Observers 1900 to the Present*, London: Virago (new edition titled *The Other Observers*)

OTHER REFERENCES

Ades, Dawn (1974) *Dada and Surrealism*, London: Thames and Hudson

Alloway, Lawrence (1966) 'The Development of British Pop' in Lucy R. Lippard (ed.) *Pop Art*, London: Thames and Hudson

Arts Council (1972) From Today Painting is Dead, London: Arts Council

—— (1975) *The Real Thing, An Anthology of British Photographs 1840–1950*, London: Arts Council

—— (1987) *Independent Photography and Photography in Education*

Benjamin, Walter (1992a) 'Unpacking My Library' in *Illuminations*, London: Jonathan Cape, 1970; Fontana, 1973/1992. Originally published in *Literarische Welt*, 1931

—— (1992b) 'The Work of Art in the Age of Mechanical Reproduction' in *Illuminations*, London: Jonathan Cape, 1970; Fontana, 1973/1992. Originally published in *Zeitschrift fur Sozialforchung* 5(1), 1936

Berger, John (1972) *Ways of Seeing*, London: BBC/Penguin Books

Braden, Su (1978) *Artists and People*, London: Routledge & Kegan Paul

Brandt, Bill (1961 *Perspective of Nudes*, London: Bodley Head

Breton, André (1978) *What is Surrealism*, London: Pluto Press

Bright, Deborah (1990) 'Of Mother Nature and Marlboro Men: An Inquiry into the Cultural Meanings of Landscape Photography' in Richard Boston (ed.) *The Context of Meaning*, Cambridge, MA: MIT Press

Burgin, Victor (1986) *The End of Art Theory*, London: Macmillan

Chadwick, Whitney (1985) *Women Artists and the Surrealist Movement*, London: Thames and Hudson

Coleman, A. D. (1979) *Light Readings*, New York: Oxford University Press

Crimp, Douglas (1993) *On the Museum's Ruins*, Cambridge, MA: MIT Press

Galassi, Peter (1995) *American Photography 1890–1965*, New York: MOMA

Gray, Camilla (1962) *The Russian Experiment in Art*, London: Thames and Hudson

Greenberg, Clement (1939) 'Avant-Garde and Kitsch' reprinted in C. Harrison and
P. Wood (eds) (1992) *Art in Theory 1900–1990*, Oxford: Basil Blackwell
—— (1961) 'Modernist Painting' reprinted in F. Frascina and J. Harris (eds) (1992) *Art in Modern Culture*, London: Phaidon
—— (1991) 'Four Photographers', first published 1964, reprinted in *History of Photography*, 15/2 Summer 1991
Grundberg, Andy (1990) 'On the Dissecting Table' in Carol Squiers *The Critical Image*, London: Lawrence and Wishart
Gupta, Sunil (1990) 'Photography, Sexuality and Cultural Difference', *Camerawork Quarterly* 17(3)
Harrison, Charles and Wood, Paul (1993) 'Modernity and Modernism Reconsidered' chapter 3 of Paul Wood, Francis Frascina, Jonathan Harris and Charles Harrison *Modernism in Dispute*, Yale/OU 1993
Haworth-Booth, Mark (ed.) (1975) *The Land: Twentieth Century Landscape Photographs*, selected by Bill Brandt. London: Gordon Fraser Gallery
—— (ed.) (1988) *British Photography: Towards a Bigger Picture*, New York: Aperture
Heiferman, Marvin (1989) 'Everywhere, All the Time, for Everybody' in Marvin Heiferman and Lisa Phillips (eds) *Image World*, New York: Whitney Museum of Art
Hewison, Robert (1987) *The Heritage Industry*, London: Methuen
Hutchison, Robert (1982) *The Politics of the Arts Council*, London: Sinclair Browne
Jeffrey, Ian (1991) 'Morality, Darkness and Light: The Metropolis in Pictures' in Martin Caiger-Smith *Site Work*, London: The Photographers' Gallery
Kelly, Mary (1981) 'Reviewing Modernist Criticism', *Screen* 22(3)
Lovell, Terry (1980) *Pictures of Reality*, ch 5.3, London: BFI
Bill, Nichols (1981) *Image and Ideology*, Bloomington: University of Indiana
Nochlin, Linda (1978) *Realism*, Harmondsworth: Penguin
Pollock, Griselda (1977) 'What's wrong with "Images of Women"?', reprinted in R. Parker and G. Pollock (eds) (1987) *Framing Feminism*, London: Pandora Press
Robins, Corinne (1984) *The Pluralist Era: American Art 1968–1981*, New York: Harper and Row
Rodchenko, Alexandr (1928) 'Against the Synthetic Portrait, for the Snapshot', published in the Moscow journal *Novy LEF: New Left Front of the Arts* in C. Phillips (ed.) *Photography in the Modern Era: European Documents and Critical Writings 1913–1940*, New York: MOMA (1989)
Rowland, Anna (1990 *The Bauhaus Source Book*, Oxford: Phaidon, chapter 6 'Graphics'
Taylor, John (1994) *A Dream of England*, Manchester: Manchester University Press
Weaver, Mike (1982) *Photography as Fine Art*, London: Thames and Hudson
—— (1986) *The Photographic Art*, London: Herbert
Wells, Liz (ed.) (1994) *Viewfindings, Women Photographers: 'Landscape' and Environment*, Tiverton, Devon: Available Light
Williams, Raymond (1976) *Keywords*, London: Fontana
—— (1979) 'The Arts Council' *Political Quarterly* Spring 1979
—— (1989) 'When Was Modernism' in *The Politics of Modernism*, London: Verso

CHAPTER 6

Photography in the age of electronic imaging

MARTIN LISTER

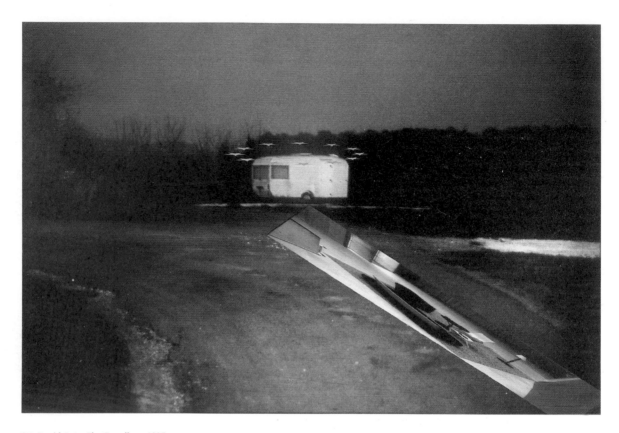

6.1 David Bate, The Travellers, 1995

Photography in the age of electronic imaging

INTRODUCTION

> Until recently, at least, it was possible to define photography as a process
> involving optics, light-sensitive material and the chemical processing
> of this material to produce prints or slides. Today, though, that defini-
> tion is subject to change. Technological innovations . . . are shifting
> photography from its original chemical basis towards electronics. . . .
> It is not overstating it to say that the advent of this new technology is
> changing the very nature of photography as we have known it.
>
> (Bode and Wombell 1991)

In 1991 an exhibition called *PhotoVideo: Photography in the Age of the Computer* was held at The Photographers' Gallery, London. The exhibition and a book of the same title, set out to consider the impact of new electronic and digital technologies on the 150-year-old practice of photography. The authors pointed directly to the process which was at the centre of the technical devel- opments in question – the process of digitisation – and they sketched out the implications of encoding photographs as 'units of electronic information':

PAUL WOMBELL (ed.) (1991)
PhotoVideo: Photography in the Age of the Computer, London: Rivers Oram Press

- A shift in the location of photographic production: from the chemical darkroom to the 'electronic darkroom' of the computer
- The outputting of single photographic originals in an expanded range of ways, from 'hardcopy' through transparencies and varying forms of print, to the TV screen

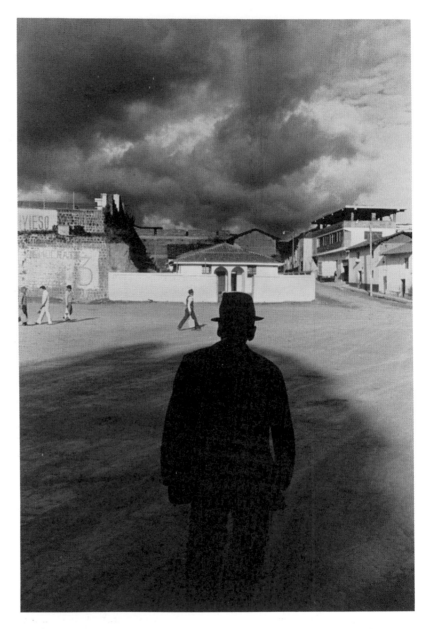

6.2 Pedro Meyer's image El Asombrado. The title of this photograph, shown at the Photovideo Exhibition in 1991, contains a play on words. Sombrero – hat, asombro – astonishment, sombra – shadow. This was an image that the photographer valued but the exposure was the last on a roll of film and was badly damaged. Each chemical print that he made from the negative took 'countless hours' and the traces of the manual restoration were always visible. This image, as was the one shown in Photovideo, has been electronically restored. The image now exists as a file of digital information, a perfect original from which thousands of perfect prints can be made. It was transmitted for publication in this book in digital form. Some might mourn the loss of the traces of the 'artist's hand' in the process (the preservation of the paradoxical idea of a photographic original). A more progressive view would see that the new technology facilitates the reproduction and circulation of the photographer's vision.

- An unprecedented ease, sophistication and invisibility of enhancing and manipulating photographic images
- The entry of photographic images into a global information and communications system as they become instantaneously transmissible in the form of electronic pulses passing along telephone lines and via satellite links
- The high-speed transmission of news images which are no longer containable within territorial and political boundaries
- The conversion of existing photographs and historical archives into digital storage banks which can be accessed at the screens of remote computer terminals
- The potential of the new information and image networks for greatly extending the practices of military and civil surveillance
- The unprecedented convergence of the still photographic image with other, previously distinct, media: digital audio, video, graphics, animation and other kinds of data in new forms of interactive multimedia.

However, as the authors stressed, probably more significant than these capacities of the new technologies to change *how* images are produced, distributed and used, are the *ideas* to which the changes are giving rise: 'Perhaps the most profound effect of these new technologies is their capacity to challenge categories and assumptions that have been at the heart of traditional ways of seeing and thinking' (Wombell 1991: 5).

The directions that such changes would take were broadly signalled in *Photo Video*. 'With the arrival of new and increasingly seamless ways of editing and changing images, our traditional belief that the "camera never lies" is brought into question. "Who", they ask, "stands to lose when the 'truth' of the photographic image stops being accepted?"'[1] In other quarters there was a sense of a growing excitement about the developments, as 'these new forms of electronic image-making are providing artists and photographers with new ways of representing this changing visual and cultural landscape'.

Two other sets of issues were raised in *Photo Video*: the use of new image and information networks for the surveillance of Europe's black population (Piper 1991) and the question of what motivations and discourses are driving these developments in new image technologies (**Robins 1991**).

In *Photo Video* we see the beginnings of something like a critical agenda for what was soon to be called the 'post-photographic era'. Since 1991 debates about the significance of new image technologies have continued and deepened. It is the aim of this chapter to review some of them and the main directions that they have taken.

First, it will look at the claims that a new era in visual culture is coming about with the advent of new image technology and then it will consider some challenges to this view. These come from critics who stress elements of cultural continuity which run across the technological change; continuities of social and cultural use which are common to photographic and digital

1 The authors' use of scare quotes in relation to the 'camera [that] never lies' and the concept of photographic 'truth' already signal the direction in which qualifications to these fears was to come

K. ROBINS (1991) 'Into the Image: Visual Technologies and Vision Cultures' in P. Wombell (ed.) **Photovideo: Photography in the Age of the Computer**, London: Rivers Oram Press

technologies. Third, it will outline the terms of a debate about the perceived threat that digital technology poses for a faith in the special truth value of photographs; especially those of documentary photography and photojournalism. Finally, it looks at the way in which digital image technologies are being seen to be an element within a larger scenario, the transition from **modernity** to **postmodernity**, and the implications of such a view.

Thinking about digital images: some initial points

What are we looking at?

There are images which are visibly marked by the electronic means of their transmission, such as the breaking down of a 'photographic' image into horizontal lines (a 'video effect'). Such features have now come to connote immediacy or authenticity much in the same way as the grainy black and white news photograph did in contrast to the high-resolution, full colour feature or advertising photograph (Becker 1991). In much the same way, the electronically produced 'transitions' between still images, which are a feature of multimedia authoring software such as Macromedia Director, have rapidly become conventions. As the image on a computer monitor breaks up and fades through a veil of simulated grain, 'the photographic' is signified.

For the most part, however, the significant differences between the purely photographic and the digitally registered photograph lie in the way it was 'taken' or transmitted, not simply the way it looks. Hence, in thinking about 'pre-' and 'post-' electronic 'photography' we are not always faced with evident and visible differences in the images themselves. This is because it is precisely the capacity of the new image technologies to carry, mimic or simulate photographic images in increasingly undetectable ways. It is this factor that has given rise to ethical debates in many areas of photographic practice, especially in the case of documentary photography and photojournalism.

Similarly, in the case of the impact of digitisation on archive images, picture libraries and image banks, the issues are ones of access, transmission and the use of images which *continue to look like photographs* but which have been stored in an immaterial and malleable digital form.

FROM ANALOGUE TO DIGITAL

Traditionally, images have been analogue in nature. That is, they consist of physical marks and signs of some kind (whether brush marks, ink rubbed into scored lines, or the silver salts of the photographic print) carried by material surfaces. The marks and signs are virtually inseparable from these surfaces. They are also continuously related to some perceivable features of the object which they represent. The light, for instance, cast across a rough wooden table top, becomes an anal-

ogous set of tonal differences in the emulsion of the photograph. A digital medium, on the other hand, is not a transcription but a conversion of information. In short, information is lodged as numbers in electronic circuits. It is this feature of digitisation which has meant that images can now be thought to exist as electronic data and not as tangible, physical stuff. Some of the key differences can be set out as follows:

Analogue	Digital
transcription: the transfer of one set of physical properties into another, analogous, set	*conversion*: physical properties symbolised by an arbitrary numerical code
continuous: representation occurs through variations in a continuous field of tone, sound, etc.	*unitised*: qualities divided into discrete, measurable and exactly reproducible elements
material inscription: signs inseparable from the surface that carries them	*abstract signals*: numbers or electronic pulses detachable from material source
medium specific: each analogue medium bounded by its materials and its specific techniques	*generic*: one binary code for all media, enabling convergence and conversion between them

Digitisation is also the effective precondition for the entry of photographic images into the flow of information which circulates within the contemporary global communications network. It is their translation into a numerical code that now enables them to be electronically transmitted. For the above reasons, questions have arisen about the place of images in time and space, where they can be said to actually exist, how and where they are stored when in electronic form, how and by whom they can be accessed, used, owned and controlled.

TIMOTHY BINKLEY (1993)
'Refiguring Culture' in P. Hayward and T. Wollen (eds)
Future Visions: New Technologies of the Screen, London: BFI

'Photographs' and 'photographic images'

In the growing critical literature about photography and new image technologies, two related sets of questions are currently being asked. Which set is asked depends, to a great extent, on the scope of the critic's or author's interest in photography. One set of questions tends to be of a philosophical kind. They are about the **epistemological** and **ontological** status of visual images. The epistemological questions ask what kind of *knowledge* a digital rather than a photographic image provides us with and *how* it does it. The ontological questions are asked about what kind of thing an image is (or is now coming to be) and *in what form or material does it exist*? These questions most often arise in connection with discussions about 'photographic truth' and the part that visual perception plays in gaining knowledge of the world.

At other times the questions are framed differently. Traditionally, the main way of understanding images has been to think of them as referring to, or depending upon, objects in the real world. They represent, or are caused by, these objects. With the application of electronic and digital technologies to image production, can we still understand the 'image world' in which we live as continuing to refer beyond itself to a prior reality? Has it become autonomous; a 'virtual' realm of illusion and spectacle, effectively challenging older ideas about photographic **representation**? What kind of power are images coming to have: is their power magnified by the new means of production and transmission, or is it being devalued? With what effects and under whose control?

These latter sorts of question lead us more directly to a major issue which requires a more historical and sociological approach. How do current developments relate to an earlier 'age of mechanical reproduction' in which the photographic image has been so important? Is the use of digital image and other new communications technologies bringing about a further expansion and intensification of the age of mass reproduction? If so, are we looking at more of the same; at differences and transformations within larger processes of continuity? Or, is the new digital and electronic culture qualitatively different from the photographic one; is a new language and a new way of seeing being born? Are the established media and art institutions involved, or are new networks and opportunities for communication and creativity opened up?

These two sets of questions – the philosophical or the historical and sociological – can be usefully thought of as arising from different ways of thinking about photography. On the one hand, there is a primary interest in understanding the impact of digital technology on the *specific properties of original chemical photographs* (fine, framed prints or the individual snaps collected from Quick Print) and, on the other, there is an emphasis on the wider implications of new technology for the more generic 'photographic image' of *mass reproduction and 'mass' culture.*

This latter image culture is based upon photographic originals, but ones which are processed by other graphic and reprographic technologies, and are a key element in a range of other media forms: newspapers, magazines, books, supersite posters, educational and publicity material. The term 'photographic image' is often used to denote this broader range, and also the constituent images of film and cinema (while we have to be careful to remember other factors such as time, narrative and the different kinds of exhibition and institution that are involved). And finally, by one more extension, the term can include the images of video, which share some of the lens-based and analogue features of the chemical photographic process, although these images are registered electromagnetically.

A. M. WILLIS (1990) 'Digitisation and the Living Death of Photography', in P. Hayward (ed.) **Culture, Technology and Creativity in the Late Twentieth Century**, London: John Libbey and Co Ltd

A 'POST-PHOTOGRAPHIC' ERA?

With the adoption of the term 'post-photographic era', a more decisively historical and epochal dimension was given to the thinking about current developments. The term was probably given its currency in the title of a book by **William Mitchell**, although the term was earlier used in *Photo Video* (Wombell 1991: 150).

Mitchell sees the emergence of digital image technology as one of a number of historical moments in which we can identify 'the sudden crystallisation of a new technology [which] provides the nucleus for new forms of social and cultural practice and marks the beginning of a new era of artistic exploration' (1992: 20). For Mitchell, the 1990s, which finally saw the effective and widespread application of computers to image-making, is just such a historical moment; one which is comparable to the 1830s and the revolutionary birth of photography itself.

In an equally dramatic tone, the art historian Jonathan Crary sees 'the rapid development in little more than a decade of a vast array of computer graphics techniques' as bringing about 'a transformation in the nature of visuality probably more profound than the break that separates mediaeval imagery from Renaissance perspective' (Crary 1993: 1). While Crary himself has questions to ask about the completeness of this 'break', this is a bold claim and one which, in other contexts, has been contested (**Lister 1995A**; Virilio et al. 1988; **Robins 1995**).

Such claims have done more than encourage a wave of speculation about what such digital futures may hold. They have also led to a renewed interest in the emergence of earlier image and communication technologies and the claims that accompanied them (Marvin 1988; Boddy 1994). They have brought about a new kind of interest in the early histories of photography, film, radio and television as a way of researching the historical grounds for such speculation (Punt 1995; Slater 1995). In a parallel development there is now much interest in the history of the computer as the machine which is credited with this epochal transformation (**Darley 1990, 1991**).

PHOTOGRAPHY AND DIGITISATION

Digitisation has more than one kind of relationship to photography. Three main kinds can be distinguished:

- the *encoding* of the 'message without a code' (Barthes 1977a: 17, 1977b: 36) – the conversion of original analogue photographs to digital images
- the *simulation* of photographs: the production of images which have the appearance of a chemical photograph but which are constructed from information which is processed within the computer
- the *dematerialisation* of the photograph and its convergence with other media as multimedia or virtual environment

WILLIAM J. MITCHELL (1992) **The Reconfigured Eye: Visual Truth in the Post – Photographic Era**, Cambridge, MA: MIT Press.

K. ROBINS (1995) 'Will Images Move Us Still?', In M. Lister (ed.) **The Photographic Image in Digital Culture**, London and New York: Routledge

A. DARLEY (1991) 'Big Screen, Little Screen, The Archaeology of Technology', *Ten.8* 2(2), 'Digital Dialogues' (1990). 'From Abstraction to Simulation: Notes on the History of Computer Imaging' in P. Hayward (ed.) **Culture, Technology and Creativity in the Late Twentieth Century**, London: John Libbey and Co Ltd

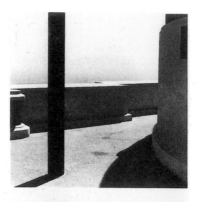

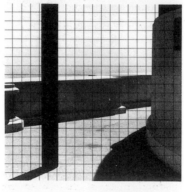

0	1	2	3	4	5	6	7	8	9	10	11

1	1	1	1	10	11	1	1	1	1	1	1	1	1	1	1	1	1	9	8
1	1	1	1	10	11	1	1	1	1	1	1	1	1	1	1	1	2	8	9
1	1	1	1	10	11	1	1	1	1	1	1	1	1	1	1	1	4	8	10
1	1	1	1	10	11	1	1	1	1	1	1	1	1	1	1	1	4	8	10
1	1	1	1	10	11	1	1	1	1	1	1	1	1	1	1	1	5	8	10
1	1	1	1	10	11	1	1	1	1	1	1	1	1	1	1	1	5	8	8
1	0	0	0	10	11	0	0	0	0	0	1	1	0	0	0	5	8	8	
0	2	2	2	10	11	2	3	3	4	4	5	7	7	7	6	8	8		
3	5	9	8	10	11	7	7	7	7	8	8	8	7	6	6	6	6	8	8
11	9	9	6	10	11	7	7	8	8	8	8	6	5	5	5	6	8	8	
10	9	9	6	10	11	7	8	8	8	8	3	5	6	4	6	8	8		
10	7	6	6	10	11	6	7	7	6	6	6	4	3	2	2	5	8	8	
4	3	8	7	10	11	5	4	3	2	2	2	2	2	4	8	8	8		
6	4	2	2	10	11	2	2	2	2	3	2	2	2	7	9	8	8	8	
2	2	2	2	10	11	2	2	2	2	2	5	7	9	9	7	8	8		
2	2	2	2	10	11	2	2	2	4	2	8	9	9	10	9	8	7	8	
2	2	2	2	10	11	2	2	2	2	5	7	9	10	11	9	10	9	7	
2	2	2	2	10	11	2	2	2	2	7	9	9	9	10	11	10	9	7	
2	2	5	7	9	8	2	2	2	2	7	9	9	10	11	11	11	11	10	7
7	9	7	5	2	2	2	2	2	2	8	9	9	10	11	11	11	11	11	10

6.3 A three-stage illustration of the principle of digitising a photograph.
The tones or colours of the chemical photograph which are represented by a seamless and random grain are divided into a grid of small picture elements (pixels). Each area of the grid is then assigned a number which corresponds to the brightness of a grey scale or to the three primary colours. Changes in resolution, definition and contrast can be achieved by changing the value of these pixels, and even the configuration of the image can be invisibly altered by removing or adding pixels

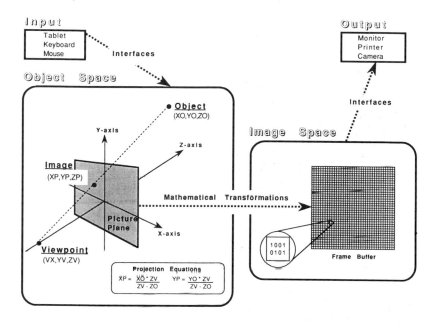

6.4 Diagrammatic representation of the concept of a 'virtual camera'

Digital encoding

Digital technology facilitates the introduction of a matrix of tiny manipulable elements at the physical base of the photographic image. This amounts to an 'infection' of the stable analogue photographic image by an intrinsically fluid and malleable digital code.

The material basis of the chemical photograph, the photographic emulsion, is a granular structure of silver halides dissolved in gelatin and spread on a plastic or acetate base. This emulsion holds the nearest thing there is to a photographic 'mark' – the tiny light-sensitive grains of silver, the constituent bits out of which an image is configured. This material basis of the photograph has long been industrially produced. It is put in place by workers in the factories of Kodak, Ilford, Fuji or Agfa. The individual photographer has never had access to this level of signification, except to control the degrees of contrast which various intensities of light reflected from an object in the real world bring about within this granular field. It is this sense, that something pre-exists the photographer's intervention in the forming of an image, that underpins our belief in the chemical photograph's special claim to veracity.

The computer, with its immaterial field of binary switches, has unlocked this inaccessible level of signification. Chemical grain can be scanned by a set of linked Charge Coupled Devices to become digital

259

pixel. Digital pixel can also be made to mimic chemical grain. In short, a code has been imported into, has translated and reconfigured, the granular field of the chemical photograph. With this code in place the photographic image (now strictly speaking the 'photographic' image) becomes manipulable to a fine degree.

Digital simulation

A second use of computers represents an even more dramatic assault on the notion of photographic causality – the sense that photographs are caused by the objects and the light that make those objects visible. This is the manner in which digital technology is being used to generate images, which have a photographic appearance, from pure data. The images which are constructed in this way have no traditional photographic referent. Such a 'photograph' may be based on knowledge of, but not caused by, the action of light reflected by a particular object. But what it does refer to is *other photographs*. In fact the whole motivation in the generation of many such images is that they carry the authority and information of a photographic image (and the way that a photograph carries such information). Given this aim, the continuity of photographic codes between chemical and digital photographic production is strong.

Such 'object-based' systems work by using the computer to define the geometry of objects and then to render its surfaces by the application of algorithms which simulate the objects' constructed surface according to information about viewpoint, location, illumination, reflection, etc. This ability of the computer to construct objects in space is in direct line with the perspectival geometry of the Western pictorial tradition. This has its roots in the work of fifteenth-century painter-mathematicians and art theorists of the early Italian Renaissance, such as Leon Battista Alberti, Piero della Francesca and Paolo Uccello.

In this sense, the computer's simulation of photographic images shares much with the constructed perspectival views of early Renaissance painters. They both construct views of the physical world which are centred on the eye of a spectator in a given position, and they do so by organising information about objects, spaces and the behaviour of light which is the result of observation, data and its rigorous conceptual systematisation. The greatest challenge to both is the representation of the human figure and, to date, it seems reasonable to judge that the computer-generated image has some way to go to match the achievements of the painter. But, in other ways, the computer has been used to produce images which precisely mimic the look of the world as seen by a camera.

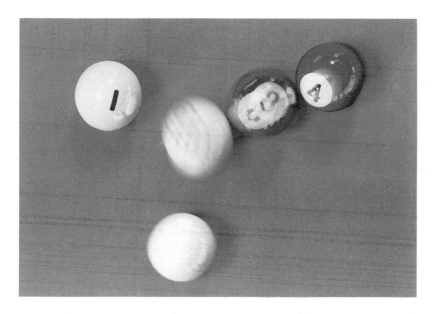

6.5 Computer-generated image of billiard balls
This image of impacting billiard balls is a computer simulation of 'photographic seeing'. These particular balls do not exist and neither does the room which is reflected on their surfaces. They are constructed mathematically and their surfaces are rendered according to the computer's 'knowledge' of the action of light upon specified kinds of surface, over a given distance and from a certain position and source, etc. The balls are represented in movement as if photographed with a shutter speed of 1/250 of a second. The realism to which this computer-generated image aspires is the 'look' of a photograph; realism equals the signifying means of the photographic image

Multimedia: digital editing, interactivity and media convergence

> . . . you can take a video-tape or a laser disc of a film, and you can send the signal to the computer and watch the film on the screen. You can stop it, reverse it, put it in slow motion, and so on. And you can behave like a photographer in the street. You can grab that Cartier–Bresson-inspired moment, and save it. . . . The computer gives you the power to shift everything around in the film. I can take a character from one scene, store the character in the attitude that I've selected, and then I can move that character into any of the other scenes.
>
> (Burgin 1991)

Another use of digital technologies, which strikes at historical certainties concerning photography, is the manner in which digital code can be used as a common denominator for effecting translations between the range of older and previously separate analogue media. In this way digital technologies are being used to bring about a convergence of the still and moving image with sound. Such a converging of previously discrete media (print, photography, film, video, recorded sound and speech) in new interactive audiovisual architectures is currently developing in the form of 'multimedia' interactive CD-Rom.

What this basically enables is an unprecedented kind of editing, within and across previously distinct media, to build new kinds of audiovisual structures or 'architecture'. In common with traditional film editing this involves the practice of selecting, cutting, combining, juxtaposing and narrative reorganisation of material from diverse places and times. Crucially, in this form, digital technology also extends the producer's selecting and editing function (the choice of what to view and when), through mouse, keyboard or touch screen, to the consumer. This offer of *choice and non-linear* access to content has come to be described as 'interactivity'.

'Convergence' is again a striking feature of the form. In everyday life, the activities of reading a book, looking at still images in a magazine, watching a film, TV or video tape, are temporally sequenced and spatially distributed; we are likely to do them in different places at different times, and each engages our attention differently. In using a multimedia programme these different modes of attention to a range of specific media are simultaneously drawn together; they converge. If we add activities like listening to a lecture and asking questions at a tutorial to the above list, we can see how the multi-mode, distance-learning packages of institutions like the Open University seem to prefigure the educational use of interactive multimedia.

The concept of convergence, together with that of interactivity, signals some actual changes in the relationship between a viewer and an image or a sequence of images and text. Multimedia audiences or users cannot, for instance, be thought of as gazing distractedly, as 'delegating their look' as the TV viewer has been observed to do (Ellis 1991: 112). They do not experience sound and image as it weaves in and out of other domestic activities and relationships, in the manner of TV viewing. Nor, in comparison to the 'viewing subject' of cinema, can they be thought of as being swept along by a narrative's tensions and resolutions; secretly aligning their own looking with that of the camera and the actors with which they identify (Ellis 1991; Mulvey 1981). The replacement of the term 'viewer' with that of multimedia 'user' is intended to signify the way attention is differently engaged. Nothing 'happens' or proceeds without their initiation. Any sustained involvement requires concentration and motivation, whether the programme in question is a game, pornography or an educational or database package.

Virtual realities

Systems of sensors which respond to the body's actions and shifting positions in physical space can be related to simulated visual projections of other bodies, objects and spaces. The resulting images are relayed to binocular screens mounted close to the eye and are seen to become both physically and conceptually interactive with the viewer, now rethought as 'user' or even 'author' of the 'virtual' environments which they perceive visually and sense kinaesthetically.

It is with such developments that ideas about a post-photographic era meet the scenarios of 'virtual reality'. This is where the techno-dreaming starts. It is important to stress that, beyond research laboratories and 'shoot-em-up' arcades, 'virtual realities' are not socially available in any way that matches the concept. At this time, the apparatus is presently more of a 'discursive' than a material object. That is, it is something that is reported rather than seen. It is something that is talked and speculated about, and represented in other media – cinema, TV, novels, comics – rather than used (Hayward 1993). In this way contemporary VR technology has much in common with the status of the camera obscura throughout the eighteenth century. Then, according to the research of Crary, the main use of the apparatus was not to produce images but as an object which stimulated philosophical reflection and speculation on the nature of perception and knowledge (Crary 1993: 29). It was a model for thinking about the nature of knowledge and reality.

Virtual reality technologies have given rise to a speculative, quasi-philosophical set of ideas; a cluster of speculative propositions about the future and the nature of change in visual culture. It is being argued that Virtual Reality technologies will usher in a culture beyond representation; a culture in which images do not in some way refer to and mediate a socially given reality, but are, virtually (that is, 'for all intents and purposes'), reality itself. Or, in a somewhat more measured formulation, the promise is that the whole human sensorium will be engaged in an electronic environment that will become 'virtually' indistinguishable from the social and material realities which people inhabit or may wish to inhabit. It will make the Renaissance use of pictorial perspective to render the imaged world continuous with the spectator's physical space seem like a primitive form of hieroglyphics. Here, the speculation is that the very sense of the viewer being before a material image, of reading a text, will cease. The notion of a viewer will become redundant as we actually inhabit constructed sensory worlds.

Virtual Reality stands ultimately for the aspiration to dissolve material images altogether; the removal of any material interface between vision and image. While being quite remote from the practical production of photographic images, a relationship is frequently proposed by seeing VR as a new stage in a teleology of the cinema. It is seen as a progressive technological fulfilment of the cinema's illusionistic power, which, on this view, was itself an heir to still photography, the camera obscura, and the centred eye of the perspectival tradition of image-making.

The end of the 'Cartesian dream' and new ways of seeing?

For William J. Mitchell the application of the computer and digitisation to image-making has brought an age of ('false') innocence to an end. This was the 150-year period during which chemical photographs provided us with images that we could comfortably regard as 'causally generated truthful reports about things in the real world', which could be confidently distinguished from 'more traditionally crafted images, which seemed notoriously ambiguous and uncertain human constructions' (Mitchell 1992: 225).

Mitchell argues that the once fixed and stable images of photography 'served the purposes of an era dominated by science, exploration, and industrialisation'. It is this historical period that he sees as passing 'as we enter the post-photographic era' and have to face again 'the ineradicable fragility of our ontological distinctions between the imaginary and the real, and the tragic elusiveness of the Cartesian dream' (Mitchell 1992: 225). In his view, the new image technologies have unsettled older and established attitudes and beliefs in the status of images. He sees digital technology as taking us beyond the historically specific and temporary limits of photographic 'seeing' in a progressive movement which is in tune with a postmodern age (see 'the postmodern connection' later in the chapter).

In calling up the name of the seventeenth-century philosopher René Descartes, Mitchell is pointing to the 'Cartesian' tradition in Western philosophy which bears his name. In broad and simplified terms, this has generally come to stand for a search for certain and objective knowledge through the exercise of scientific reason; for a disinterested and rational method of enquiry untainted by the feelings and subjectivity of the observer. The attainment of such certain knowledge by an abstract reason exercised by a 'disembodied' mind is the 'Cartesian dream' to which Mitchell refers.

By the early nineteenth century such a search for scientific knowledge had taken a fiercely empirical turn and had been extended to the study of the social as well as the natural world within the social philosophical framework known as positivism. This was characterised by an exclusive concern for empirically verifiable and measurable facts. A connection between this 'positivist' method and the birth of photography has been frequently noted. As John Berger (1982) has put it,

> The camera was invented in 1839. Auguste Comte was just
> finishing his Cours de Philosophie Positive. Positivism and the

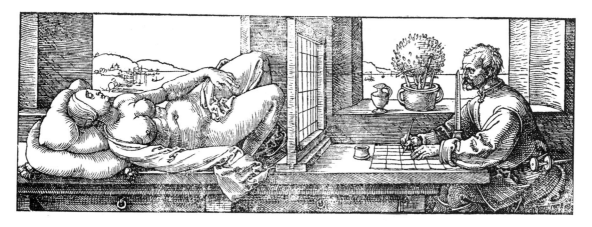

6.6 Albrecht Dürer, Draughtsman Drawing a Nude, 1538
Dürer depicts one of many apparatuses in the history of art through which the appearance of the world was organised in relation to the position of the observer. It is an apparatus and a way of seeing which is later embodied in the camera. It also, as Lynda Nead observes, already positions the female as the object of the male gaze (*The Female Nude: Art, Obscenity and Sexuality*, London: Routledge, p. 11)

> camera and sociology grew up together. What sustained them all as practices was the belief that quantifiable facts, recorded by scientists and experts, would one day offer man such total knowledge about nature and society that he would be able to order them both.
>
> (Berger and Mohr 1982: 99)

As real as this historical link with positivist social science may have been, photography has never been exclusively contained within positivism's framework or limited to such uses. It is, however, an aspect of photography's history which is being thrown into sharp relief by theorists of post-photography like Mitchell, who stress the mechanical process and optical realism of analogue photography as a radical contrast to a new digital 'age of **electrobricolage**'.

For Jonathan Crary, the constructed or 'virtual' visual 'spaces' of computer-generated imagery are radically different from the 'mimetic capacities of film, photography, and television'. The latter depended upon 'a point of view static, or mobile, located in real space' while the techniques of computer imaging 'are relocating vision to a plane severed from a human observer'. As the new image technologies become 'the dominant models of visualisation', Crary believes that 'Most of the historically important functions of the human eye are being supplanted by practices in which visual images no longer have any reference to the position of an observer in a "real" optically perceived world' (Crary 1993: 2).

Both Mitchell and Crary sketch out a scenario in which seeing and representing the world through a camera lens, from a definite position in space, are giving way to new forms of vision and image.

This is a vision in which older lens-based images are either converted into electronic data or new images are constructed directly from data which simulate the appearance of a photograph. These images can be infinitely changeable, as they continually circulate within global telecommunication networks, available for convergence with one another and other 'abstract visual and linguistic elements' (Crary 1993). Further, these images do not necessarily refer to anything that is empirically verifiable as 'real' but to ensembles of concepts, other images and data.

It is not difficult to see how, on this way of thinking, that the traditional hand-me-down, Cartesian framework for thinking about how we observe the external world is deemed to have become hopelessly inadequate. Faced with Crary's vision of the new image technologies, the question no longer seems to be 'can an observer see clearly from their position?', but whether we, as observers, have any fixed or secure position from which to see anything that is material and stable! New possibilities for vision and visualisation are opening up, as the computer extends the realm of what the visual sense. On the one hand we (or perhaps – given the globally locally uneven distribution of technologies and information circuits – 'some of us' would be more accurate) can 'see' distant planets, the inside of a beating heart, a molecule that is a concept, we can move through buildings which have not been built, we can window-shop in cyberspace. On the other hand, the qualities and formal means of images are undergoing certain kinds of change; this is probably most remarkable in terms of the spectacular extremes of scale and detail, of focus and viewpoint, of subtle and dramatic kinds of juxtaposition, in the degree of fragmentation and fusion, and in the transformation and mutation of images that we are coming to see regularly in the advertisements on our television screens. There is a scrambling, to an unprecedented degree, of the real and the imagined.

We will not, however, as Crary argues, get far in understanding our newly 'precarious' position within this shifting scenario of images and imaging technologies if we fail to see it in an historical context (for there are precedents of sorts) and take account of the forms of social and cultural power which drive and shape such developments (Crary 1993: 2).

WALTER BENJAMIN AND THE PRECEDENT OF THE AGE OF MECHANICAL REPRODUCTION

WALTER BENJAMIN (1973a) 'The Work of Art in the Age of Mechanical Reproduction' in H. Arendt (ed.) **Illuminations**, Glasgow: Fontana Collins

As many art and photographic historians have been quick to see, current developments echo **Walter Benjamin**'s classic account of the impact of photography upon the handmade image in his 1936 essay 'The Work of Art in the Age of Mechanical Reproduction'.

The parallel has been so compelling that a good deal of the writing which deals with current developments explicitly plays with Benjamin's original title (including the title of this chapter itself). Articles and scholarly papers with titles which echo Benjamin's abound; transposing the 'Mechanical Age' to the Electronic, the Cybernetic, the Digital, the Post-Photographic Age, Era or Culture. The newspaper pastiche 'Mute' sports the banner, 'The Work of Art in the Age of Post-Mechanical Reconstruction!' (Grundberg 1990; Jukes 1992; Malina 1990; Nichols 1988; Virilio et al. 1988).

Why is this so? Benjamin, writing sixty years ago, offered two basic sets of propositions about the epochal significance of film and photography as means of mechanically reproducing images.

The first concerned the power of a new image technology – photography – to reproduce **autographic** images. A second set concerned the particular ways that the camera – still and moving – represented the contemporary world itself. These two sets of propositions are now being transposed in efforts to think about the impact of digital technology upon photography.

Benjamin pointed out that mechanical reproduction substituted 'a plurality of copies for a unique existence' (Benjamin 1973a: 223). These were not copies in the sense of fakes (they could not be passed off for the original) or imperfect handmade copies, but were the outcome of an independent technical process. Through this process, images which had previously existed in one place at one time could now be seen simultaneously by a variety of new audiences in a diverse range of situations. Knowledge of the work was no longer restricted to being in the presence of the original. The images were no longer dependent upon their original contexts for their meaning and became open to multiple interpretations and readings. They could also be put to new uses. It became, for instance, possible to compare and connect images that were previously separated in space and time. Reproduction created a new kind of portable cultural object (Lury 1992: 396) which was free from the controlled environments and rituals of the church, the civic state, and the aristocratic cultures in which the unique handpainted image had been predominantly produced and used.

Now, it is the photographic image itself which is subject to a similar process as it is converted, reproduced or simulated in digital form, stored electronically, and transmitted by telecommunications networks. Hence, the question arises as to whether there is a second 'electronic' or 'digital' revolution in visual culture which is usurping the role of photography in the 'age of mechanical reproduction' which Benjamin first described.

Benjamin's second set of propositions concerned the camera itself. He sees that photography developed as a part of the scientific and technological endeavours of nineteenth- and early twentieth-century industrial capitalism. The physical context of this development was the nineteenth-century city. He stressed the way that urban experience was newly characterised by speed, rapid change and a fragmentation of everyday experience. This was brought about by new transport and communications systems, by the industrial division of labour on the production line, and by the separation of leisure and work in a wage labour economy. Benjamin argued that a rapid succession and juxtaposition of shifting viewpoints and experiences confronted the city dweller, who was bombarded with an unprecedented level of physical and psychological shocks by the new industrial and urban environment (Benjamin 1973b: 177).

Benjamin sees the camera and its images as making this bewildering environment possible to contemplate, and points to the way that still photography renders faithfully the plethora of everyday detail that would normally be overlooked. He points to factors such as the way in which the photographic camera can put the 'eye' in places that it could not otherwise be, or the way in which the shutter freezes action not perceivable by the eye alone. With movie film the speed of human and mechanised action was slowed down. Through editing, a range of shots, frames and actions – matching the bewildering viewpoints of the city dweller – could be put together in a coherent narrative. Benjamin suggests that, in this period, a kind of 'optical unconscious' was revealed by the camera, just as, through **psychoanalysis**, 'the instinctual **unconscious**' was discovered.

So, in Benjamin's view, photography, and then cinematography, were particularly suited to depict the changed environment of industrial societies and, moreover, they could reach mass urban audiences rather than small elites. They represented a new way of organising perceptions within the dramatically changed environments of early twentieth-century cities. In his 1993 essay, 'Postmodernism and Consumer Society', Frederick Jameson proposed that our perceptual skills and habits are again lagging behind our apprehension of a new kind of urban environment, represented most clearly in the new forms and spaces of postmodern hotels and shopping centres.

> My implication is that we ourselves, the human subjects who happen into this new space, have not kept pace with that evolution . . . [of postmodern architectural space] . . . we do not yet possess the perceptual equipment to match this new hyperspace . . . in part because our perceptual habits were formed in that older kind of space I have called the space of high modernism.
>
> (Jameson 1993: 198)

Jameson makes it clear that he sees himself as following in Benjamin's footsteps when making this point (Jameson 1993: 202). Similarly, albeit in the sphere of visual representation rather than architectural space, it is now being argued, by theorists like Mitchell and Crary, that we are moving rapidly into a time where the new means of digital and electronic imaging are coming to supersede those of the age of mechanical reproduction. As they do, they suggest that new kinds of perception are being born, which are adjusted to a world in which significant global economic, technological and cultural change is again taking place on a scale that is likened to that of industrialisation itself.

B. NICHOLS (1988) 'The Work of Culture in the Age of Cybernetic Systems', **Screen** 29(1), Winter

Although he is interested in film rather than still photography, **Bill Nichols** investigated the idea of such a parallel in his essay, 'The Work of Culture in the Age of Cybernetic Systems' (1988).

Here, following Jameson (1984), he drew up three parallel lists of the technological, legal and cultural features of three stages of capitalism – the entrepreneurial, monopoly and multinational. With more emphasis on social and economic processes, David Harvey (1989: 174–179) has also reproduced a number of charts which represent the changes which have been seen to take place in the transition from industrial capitalism to present conditions, variously described as 'late capitalist', 'disorganised capitalist', 'postmodern', 'post industrial' and 'post Fordist'. In a much reduced form, the kinds of change pointed to in this way of thinking are as follows:

the mechanical camera	the electronic computer
the photograph	the digital image
industrialism	a 'post-industrial age'
the modern era	postmodernity
modernism	'postmodernism'
rationalism/positivism	structuralism/poststructuralism

TECHNOLOGICAL CHANGE AND CULTURAL CONTINUITY

We have seen that much thought about the place of photography in an age of electronic imaging has been based upon ideas of ruptures, breaks and radical change, not only in the means of producing images, but also in the culture itself. However, alongside these propositions, other media theorists and historians have argued that such a view fails to take enough account of photography's history in particular, and the kind of relationship that new technologies have to cultural change in general. They argue that such claims place too much emphasis on the evident technological difference between photographic and digital processes. A preoccupation and fascination with technological difference obscures important elements of continuity in the cultural meaning and uses of technologies.

Rather than simply see a break between the 'old' chemical technology and the 'new' electronic and digital one, these critics argue that we have also to see how both are shaped and developed by powerful social and cultural forces which run through nineteenth- and twentieth-century western culture. The *difference* between analogue and digital image technologies is only one factor within a much larger context of *continuities and transformations*. In short, in order to assess the significance of new image technologies we have also to look at how images are *used*, by whom, and for what purposes.

For instance, a major use of new image technologies is to be found within medicine, where they are being used to make the interior of the living body visible. Some writers have stressed the way in which such new, non-invasive, medical imaging techniques can be seen as liberating and wholly benign (Stafford 1991). However, in her study of the way in which these technologies are being used to produce and construct images of the body within medical science, Sarah Kember (1995) argues that the highly mediated images of CAT scans and Magnetic Resonance Imaging have their antecedents in nineteenth-century medical photography. For Kember, 'there is in fact no clear separation between photo-mechanical and electronic imaging in the context of the surveillance and classification of the body' (1995: 95–96). Both, she argues, participate in the gendered power relations of (an increasingly technologised) masculine medical science which seeks to dominate the female body with its connotations of the 'natural' and 'maternal'.

In order to see the kinds of cultural continuity which run through technological change, we have to pay attention to the institutions and social sites in which new image technologies are being applied, and at the established cultural forms and practices which are being extended and transformed through such use. These sites are predominantly ones in which the photographic image has long been put to work: in the production of news, in the making of art, in advertising, in military and civil surveillance, in the production of spectacle and entertainment, education, pornography, to name only the more obvious ones.

Before looking more closely at two examples of such sites and uses, we can note a number of more general ways in which the use of digital technology can be seen as an acceleration or intensification of photographic processes which have a lengthy history. These aspects of photographic culture also lead us to see the way in which the use of digital image technologies continues or builds upon photographic forms.

Photography's promiscuity: its historical interface with other technologies, sign systems and images

> Throughout its history, photography has always enjoyed a complex relationship with other text-based or visual information media.
>
> (Bode and Wombell 1991: 4–5)

The new digital media, especially in its interactive, multimedia forms, are being celebrated for their capacity to generate **polysemic** meanings which involve the viewer's active participation. The two main bases for this are the capacity of digitisation to bring about first, a convergence of previously separate media, and second, an 'interactive' relationship between the viewer and the text (see discussion, 'Multimedia: digital editing, interactivity and media convergence' p. 261).

The first wave of critical responses to digital image technology have overwhelmingly valued this capacity to produce layered and open-ended images which are always in creative process. By being included within digital multimedia programmes, it can seem that photographic images are newly exposed to multiple contexts of sound, other images, speech and text, etc.

Multiple, alternative, radical and unexpected meanings are then seen to be the result of this new kind of complex of messages. Moreover, such meanings can now be discovered or created by the viewer (or 'user') of multimedia, as they interact with material which is structured with their participation in mind.

In the very celebration of this real capacity of 'new' media, an opposition is often made, or implied, with an idea of an older 'pure' photography which was an 'automatic' source of fixed, singular and stable meaning (Robins 1991: 56–60; **Lister 1995b: 8–11**). The evident technological difference between photographic, camera-based, processes on the one hand, and digital, computer-based processes on the other also becomes the basis for constructing different intellectual and creative conceptions of practice, production and, especially, of what is involved in viewing or using images. There are, indeed, such differences to be thought about, as there are between the traditional practices of working with still or moving images, or as there were between making 'silent' and 'talking' movies. However, this is not the same as mistaking the increased possibilities for bringing about a creative convergence of older forms of media as if it were an entirely new situation. Also, convergence is assumed to be an inevitable achievement *of the technology*, rather than how it is used, what it is used for, and whether, in any particular case, it is of value to use it.

MARTIN LISTER (1995b)
Introductory essay in M. Lister (ed.) **The Photographic Image in Digital Culture**, London/New York: Routledge

The degree to which these factors of convergence and interactivity can be seen as entirely new features of 'digital' art, media and communications is dependent on failing to take into account a number of factors. When such factors are included in our thinking, the frequently made opposition between the photographic and the digital turns instead into a picture of the latter extending and building upon some key aspects of the former. This is important to remember; otherwise, two difficulties arise.

First, the degree to which digital image production draws upon the received conventions and codes of older media (as, for example, those discussed in chapter 4) is lost to sight. 'Codes' are not just a matter of routine practice or 'know-how', but have ideological weight. This means that there is a danger that a rich resource can, in fact, be drawn upon, but without an informed, critical awareness of the politics of representation which have been developed around these practices. Second, the euphoric over-evaluation of digital 'culture', which is achieved by means of simple and ahistorical oppositions, casts photographic culture in a poor light and obscures its continuing power and complexity (Robins 1991: 56–57).

Three features of photographic culture will indicate how the meanings and uses of photographs, in a pre-digital period, have involved issues of convergence and relationships with other media. (For a discussion of the limits of the current opposition between ideas of the 'passive' viewer of photographs and the 'interactive' user of digital multimedia, see Lister, 1995b.)

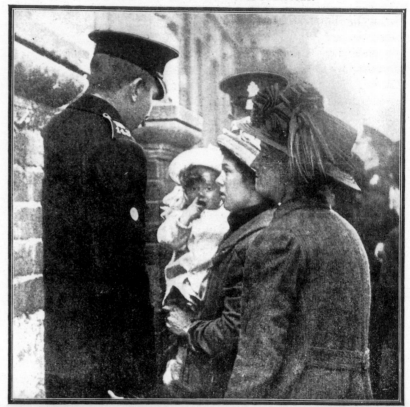

The Daily Mirror

THE MORNING JOURNAL WITH THE SECOND LARGEST NET SALE.

No. 2,649.   Registered at the G.P.O. as a Newspaper.   SATURDAY, APRIL 20, 1912   One Halfpenny.

ONE OF THE THOUSANDS OF TRAGEDIES WHICH MADE THE TITANIC WRECK THE MOST HORRIBLE IN THE WORLD'S HISTORY.

Of the 903 members of the crew of the Titanic, only 210 have been saved. This means tragedy upon tragedy for Southampton, where the majority of the men lived, for by this appalling disaster mothers have been robbed of sons, wives of husbands and young girls of sweethearts. Yesterday was a terrible day in the history of the town, though it put an end to all suspense. A list of the saved was posted outside the White Star offices, and mothers and wives who had been hoping against hope eagerly read the names, only to find that their worst fears were realised. For some, of course, the list contained glorious news, but they hushed their joy in the presence of the terrible grief of their friends and neighbours. The photograph illustrates one of the many tragedies, and shows two women anxiously awaiting the posting of the list, and what happened in Southampton yesterday has been happening in New York and London for five days. *Daily Mirror* photograph.

6.7 Front page of the *Daily Mirror*, 22 April 1912. An early use of a screened photograph printed with text

● Mass produced, mediated and hybrid 'photographic images' have circulated throughout the twentieth century. This has depended upon a convergence of photography with print, graphic, electronic and telegraphic technologies. As John Tagg put it, 'the era of throwaway images' began in the 1880s with the introduction of the half-tone plate. It was this interface of the chemical photograph with print technology which 'enabled the economical and limitless reproduction of photographs in books, magazines and advertisements, and especially newspapers' (Tagg 1988: 56). In 1903 the telegraphic transmission of half-tone images became possible and the *Daily Mirror* launched a photo-telegraphy service as early as 1907 (Harvie et al. 1970).

- Photographic images have seldom been met in isolation. They are embedded and contexted in other signifying systems. Primarily, those of the written or spoken word, graphic design and the institutional connotations of power, authority, neutrality or glamour. As Barthes (1977: 15) puts it, the photograph is at the centre of 'a complex of concurrent messages'. In a newspaper these are the text, the title, the caption, the layout, and even the title of the newspaper or publication itself: a photograph can change its meaning as it passes from the page of the conservative to the radical press. Photography as an element in 'a complex of concurrent messages' predates the technological convergence of the new hybrid media.

- The sheer number of photographs circulating in the world, and the frequency with which we meet them, is also a basis of their intertextuality. None is free standing. Each one is a small element in a history of image production and a contemporary 'image world'. Within this environment, the photographic image gains its meaning by a continual borrowing and cross-referencing of meanings between images. The still photograph quotes a movie, the cinematographer adopts the style of an advertising photographer, the music video mimics an early silent movie.

CASE STUDIES

We can now consider this argument for continuities of use and cultural meaning between pre- and post-digital photography by looking at two brief case studies, chosen from many possible ones. While not discussed here, equally strong examples can be found in the production of erotica and pornography (Graham 1995), and the relationship of digital image culture to domestic snapshots (Slater 1995).

WAR AND SURVEILLANCE

> From the original watchtower through the anchored balloon to the reconnaissance aircraft and remote sensing-satellites, one and the same function has been indefinitely repeated, the eye's function being the function of a weapon.
>
> (Virilio et al. 1988)

The remote digital video cameras, sensors and image processors used in modern warfare have taken over and extended an historic role of

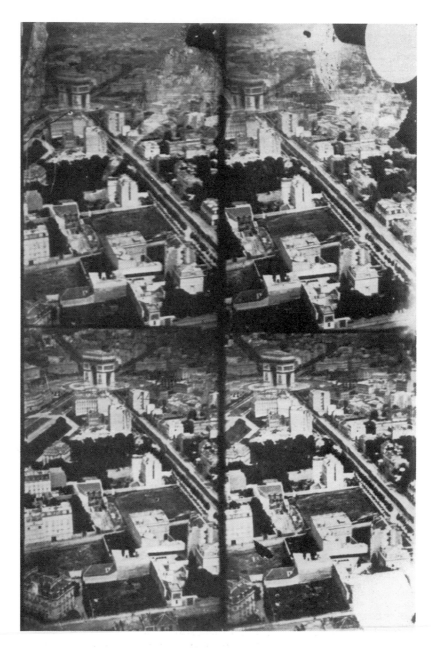

6.8 The Arc de Triomphe and the Grand Boulevards, Paris, from a Balloon, 1868, by Nadar (Gaspard Felix Tournachon). A (civil) example of how, within twenty years of its invention, the camera was airborne and pointing to its usefulness as a tool of intelligence gathering and surveillance

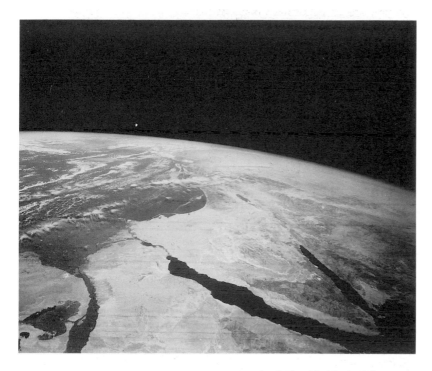

6.9 NASA, Johnson Space Center, Houston, Texas. STS-052. 'Earth View (Sinai Peninsula)'

photography. Paul Virilio clearly has in mind that an early use of photography was the mounting of a camera in a balloon for the purpose of aerial reconnaissance. In this way vision and its record were placed in the service of military intelligence; it was given a new vantage point and power. This has been built upon ever since, as a sequence of new image technologies has been harnessed to, and often developed for, military surveillance purposes. With the contemporary use of satellites, remote sensing technology, digital enhancement of images and the establishment of global information networks, this early means of lifting a mechanical eye above the enemy has continued to develop. A point has been reached where the entire planet is 'becoming encapsulated by whole networks of orbital devices whose eyes, ears, and silicon brains gather information in endless streams' which produce a kind of 'portrait of what is happening on planet earth painted electronically in real time' (Robins 1991: 72).

In the nineteenth century portable, if cumbersome, darkrooms were trundled out to war. As early as the 1850s Fenton was commissioned by the British government to photograph the Crimean War, and Brady worked the battlefields of the American Civil War. By the First World War, photography played a key part in reporting war and providing propaganda for the public at home. In 1991 the Gulf War revealed the scale and depth to which technologies of surveillance and so-called 'information' technologies had reached. The

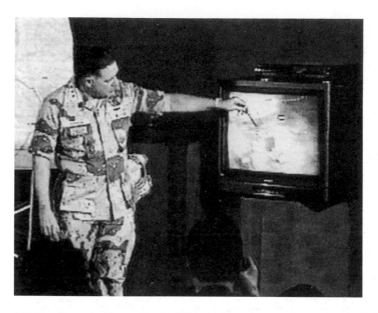

6.10 Press photographer photographing the Gulf War in progress. Access to the war action is confined to a video screen at a military briefing

domestic television set became the mesmerising end point of an electronic image chain which started with a digital camera travelling on the nose of a smart bomb (Druckery 1991). Immersed in real-time simulations, pilots attacked by computer and video, functioning 'as components in the virtual domain of the military technological system', disembodied and dislocated from material reality. Visual surveillance systems have become simulation systems. The gathering of data and intelligence was converted into a real-time digital image of war which paralleled an awful reality which few of us in the West could know or, mercifully, experience.

A highly selective and orchestrated spectacle of this war, at least partly derived from the same material, was relayed to the domestic television set. When Paul Virilio called this war 'the first totally electronic war', we can, as Ian Walker (1995) has pointed out, take this phrase 'in two ways, to describe how the war was fought *and* how it was represented'. At many points these two aspects came together, as 'the most potent images were those taken by the military themselves' which were then relayed on through the world's media. The journalists and war correspondents, like the rest of us, saw the war mainly on television. Photographers were reduced to taking pictures of military personnel pointing to video monitors at prearranged press briefings. However, the 'invisibility' of the Gulf War and the highly mediated nature of the images received is squarely in the tradition of 'self censor-ship [imposed] in the name of social cohesion' which has been part of war reporting and photojournalism from the Great War to the Falklands (Taylor in Walker 1995).

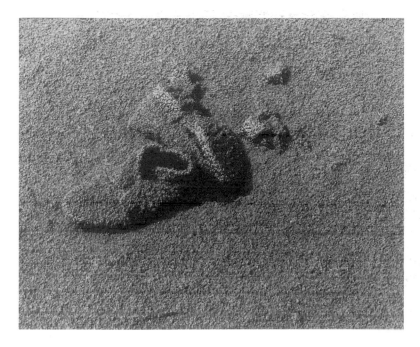

6.11 Sophie Ristelhueber, Fait. Photograph from the exhibition and book *Aftermath*. Still photography was practically and officially made almost impossible during the 1991 Gulf War, but Sophie Ristelhueber's camera offers an alternative and critical view of the aftermath of the events 'in considered retrospect' (Walker 1995)

Ian Walker has also argued that in this new context, where the photographer is removed from the scene of cybernetic warfare and its electronic reporting, that photography continues to play a role in offering us a view of events 'in considered retrospect' (Walker 1995). Considering Sophie Ristelhueber's photographs of the aftermath of the Gulf War, Walker agrees with Taylor that it is ill-informed simply to oppose photography's old role as reportage to its recent displacement and deconstruction by digital image technology. He points instead to the range of political and aesthetic strategies which an artist like Ristelhueber brings to their use of photography. He then suggests that the future of the medium may lie in such critical-artistic interventions and not in the traditional genre of documentary photography and photo-reportage.

POPULAR ENTERTAINMENT

Photography was . . . only one of many instruments, institutions, and practices designed to engage, astonish and entertain the eye; only one of a vast array of machines for the production of spectacle.

(Neale 1985: 23–24)

277

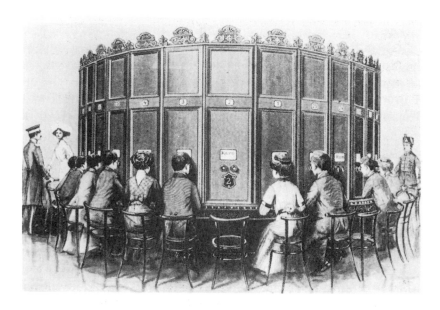

6.12 Viewers at a Panorama (1991), *The Dialectics of Seeing; Walter Benjamin and the Arcades Project*, Cambridge, Massachusetts, MIT Press, p. 82

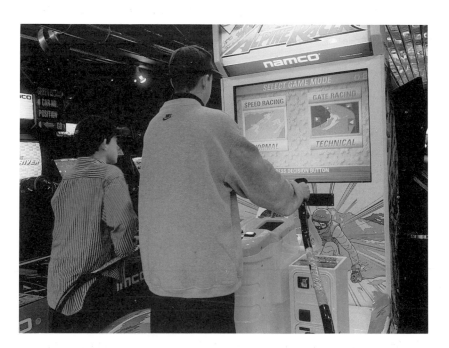

6.13 A contemporary games arcade

While we may not associate the still photograph with spectacular effect, Steve Neale reminds us that the stereoscope was one of the most popular ways of viewing photographs in the nineteenth century. Projected images for entertainment (both painted and photographic) as in the Phantasmagoria, and other environments in which transparent and backlit images were presented to audiences (the Diorama, the Eidophusikon), were very much part of the culture in which photography emerged.

All of these machines were united by their '"astonishing" capacity for realism and painstakingly detailed representation'. With their use of light and movement, they lured and manipulated the spectator's gaze. With the coming of electricity and mechanical music towards the end of the nine-teenth century these luminous photographic entertainments became the technical and cultural antecedents of cinema which, in one of its earliest forms – Edison's Kinetoscope – was an arcade machine designed to be used by individual viewers (Neale 1985).

Currently, two major popular forms which digital image technology has taken are those of the console-based interactive computer game, for domestic use, and the 'coin-op' arcade game (Haddon 1993). The magazine *CD Rom Today* reports that the gross US turnover for computer games now equals that of the Hollywood movie industry (Dewdney and Boyd 1995). The interactivity which is central to the design and use of personal computers has major roots in the arcade game, the 'earliest form of interactive software to find a mass market' (Haddon 1993). The imagery of interactive CD-Rom also strives for the high resolution of the photographic image in combination with full motion video and stereo sound. These are held in audiovisual structures, exhibited on luminous screens, which invite the individual viewer to navigate in and out of parallel or forking narrative paths which frequently draw upon a range of traditional narrative genres borrowed from cinema or television.

In these ways digital CD-Rom can be understood as a developed electronic version of many preceding forms of visual entertainment which has, as one of its roots, these nineteenth-century forms of photographic entertainment and spectacle (Dewdney and Boyd 1995).

DIGITISATION AND THE QUESTION OF PHOTOGRAPHIC TRUTH: THE ISSUES FOR PHOTOJOURNALISM

As was noted at the beginning of this chapter, a fear for the demise of photographic truth was one of the initial responses to digital image technology. We have also seen how the fervour raised by the prospect of a new 'techno–culture' has led to this issue being frequently raised in over–simple terms; terms which suffer from an ignorance of theories of photographic representation.

Theories of photographic realism

Traditional claims about photography's truth value have rested upon the causal relationship the photographic image has to the real world. In realist theories, photography was primarily defined by its technical basis – the way in which light reflected by an object or event in the real world is registered on the film emulsion (or, in the case of video, on electromagnetic tape). The photograph was understood as an index or trace of what had caused it. But, it has long been clear that this aspect of the photo-mechanical process has only a small part to play in the meanings that a photograph has. (For discussions of realist theories of photography and their fallacies, see Snyder and Allen 1975; Snyder 1980). Subsequently, the ambiguously complex meanings of photographs have been understood to be the result of complex technological, cultural, ideological and psychological processes in which indexicality is but one element.

Despite this recognition, it is currently this **indexical** quality which is stressed, above all others, in the polarised debates of the 'photography equals old, bad and limited' versus 'the digital equals new, good, and open-ended' kind. Such positions and debates short-circuit much of what has been understood about photographic representation. They divert attention from the whole range of decisions, conventions, codes, operations and contexts which constitute photographic meaning. However, even where ill-informed oppositions are avoided, there is still a sense in which many practitioners feel that the ethics and politics of photographic representation are under threat.

This is the position taken by Fred Ritchin, a photographer and teacher of photojournalism, who has claimed that '. . . the new malleability of the image may eventually lead to a profound undermining of photography's status as an *inherently truthful* pictorial form' (**Ritchin 1990b: 28**; my emphasis). This, however, is not the only way in which the issues are being conceived. **Martha Rosler**, an artist and critical theorist, argues that they cannot be posed in terms of photography's essential or inherent truth value. Her thinking on the matter proceeds by stressing that 'Any familiarity with photographic history shows that *manipulation is integral* to photography' (1991: 53; my emphasis). In the face of what she sees as 'slightly hysterical' pronouncements that 'photography as evidence of anything is dead', Rosler wants to remember a more complex history of photography in which contradictions abound and its objective realism is not an essential quality of the medium. Instead, as we shall see, she argues that photographic truth is based upon a set of historically and culturally specific beliefs about photographs as documents.

We will first attend to Ritchin's thoughts on the issue, which express some widespread concerns which are close to the professions of documentary and photojournalistic practice. Rosler's different perspective on the issues will be more fully outlined in the following section, as they properly belong within the wider debates about the status and meaning of images in a 'postmodern' world.

F. RITCHIN (1990a) **In Our Own Image: The Coming Revolution in Photography**, New York: Aperture (1990b); 'Photojournalism in the Age of Computers', in C. Squiers (ed.) **The Critical Image**, Seattle: Bay Press, pp. 28–37
MARTHA ROSLER (1991) 'Image Simulations, Computer Manipulations, Some Considerations' in *Ten/8* 2(2) 'Digital Dialogues'

Ritchin and 'the end of photography as we know it'

For Ritchin, the choices which the photographer makes at the point of exposure (which can now be digitally altered in retrospect), together with subsequent editorial and post-production manipulations, have been so greatly extended by the use of computers that ethical problems now arise 'with the greatest urgency' (1990a: 29). He believes that traditional manipulations of photographs were somehow held in ethical check and were usually undertaken without 'damaging the image's integrity'. New digital image technologies, however, mean that an 'editor has the ability to reach into the guts of a photograph and manipulate any aspect of it', much in the way that texts can be edited and the writer's meanings subtly but effectively altered.

Ritchin, whose thinking is haunted by an Orwellian nightmare of a future digital dystopia (1990a: 3), searches for strategies which will enable photojournalists to ward off the digital undermining of their vocation. He is too keenly aware of the **semiotic** complexities and the politics of photojournalism to be able to seek reassurance in any simple idea of photographic realism. He recognises that the genre of documentary photography has long been the subject of critical debate and that naive reflection theories have for some time ceased to inform most documentary photographic education and practice (1990b: 28). And, given this history of critical debate, Ritchin then sees 'the application of computer technology to photography' as a second challenge to what he calls 'photography's putative capacity for reliable transcription'.

Ritchin entertains two responses to this second challenge. First, he plays with the idea of securing a protected category of stable, verifiable, images, whose epistemological and ethical status would, in some way, be officially accredited. One can imagine some kind of 'kite mark' or official caption stating that this is a 'certificated' chemical photograph or an 'ethically manipulated' digital photograph (1990b: 28–37). With this suggestion Ritchin comes close to occupying a defensive, rearguard position that William Mitchell foresees for photojournalists:

> Protagonists of the institution of journalism, with their interest in being trusted, of the legal system, with their need for provably reliable evidence, and of science, with their foundational faith in the recording instrument, may well fight hard to maintain the hegemony of the standard photographic image . . . .
>
> (Mitchell 1993)

Second, Ritchin (1990b) avoids basing his defence of photojournalism on any form of technological veracity and shifts it to the ground of authorship. In fact, Ritchin's best argument is based upon a claim for some parity between the photojournalist and the journalist who writes, where the authority of the writer's report is based upon the reputation of the author and the institutions for which they work. Finally then, Ritchin, seems to accept that the value of the photographic image in a digital age will not be secured by tracing its truthfulness to its origins in a photo-chemical process. Rather, it must rest on the conscience and the reputation of the photographer who made the image. In this one respect, he comes close, as we shall see, to Martha Rosler's argument.

Overall, Ritchin casts the difficulty for photojournalism in a digital age as a largely personal and ethical problem – a problem for individual photographers and picture editors as they are pitched into a situation in which truth and integrity are ever harder to defend against what he sees as an inherently unscrupulous and deceitful digital technology.

THE POSTMODERN CONNECTION

In this section we will revisit a number of ideas that we have met so far. This is in order to see how accounts of postphotography form part of a larger analysis or story about the distinctive features of the culture of late capitalist societies; what has come to be described as the condition of postmodernity (Harvey 1989). Three sets of ideas are particularly relevant in this respect:

- Rosler's views on photography's inherent manipulability and her argument that we have to see present developments as part of a longer history of nineteenth- and twentieth-century mass media: a history of the mass production and consumption of images as commodities
- The kind of view that Mitchell advances about the emergence of a new 'post-photographic era', together with a current interest in reapplying Benjamin's ideas to current developments in visual culture, which proposes that digital image technology represents a new way of seeing within changed cultural and economic conditions
- a popular and widespread excitement about the birth of a new 'techno-culture' based upon digital technology, virtual realities, interactive media and the Internet, in which the production and transmission of visual images plays a central part. This has led to a devaluation and a rapid **historicisation** of photographic culture. It is seen, suddenly, as an outmoded culture which is finally limited to a recording function and a naive desire to gain an objective view of the world, while digital image technology restores and extends the creative and imaginative possibilities of the image.

Rosler and the commodification of images

We saw in the previous section how Fred Ritchin argued that a kind of photographic integrity was at stake as digital image technology dramatically increased the possibilities of image manipulation. We can now return to this issue by looking more closely at the arguments of Martha Rosler. By reminding us of the part that photography itself has played in creating a market in images, appearances and illusions throughout the twentieth century, she offers us a view of the fragility and partialness of the 'modern' idea of photographic truth. In doing so, she sketches a tradition of critical thought which long precedes the advent of digital images and which points to a longer historical process, in which the photographic image has served to bring about a condition where we 'prefer the sign to the thing signified, the copy to the original, fancy to reality, the appearance to the essence' (Rosler 1991: 61).

Rosler has no time for the opposition between photographic truth and digital manipulation which has become central to much discussion about 'post-photography'. She warns that 'critical considerations of the possibilities of photographic manipulation tend to end with the tolling of the death knell of *truth*. This discussion will not end that way'. The manipulation which Rosler sees as integral to photography itself is shown by any familiarity with photographic history from the very earliest uses of multiple negatives by photographers like Oscar Rejlander.

In Rosler's thinking, any sense of there being a crisis of photography's truth value is fundamentally to mistake what is going on. She agrees that we may no longer look at photographs 'as ways of communicating *facticity*, but that doesn't amount to asserting either that "truth is dead" or that "photography is used up"'. Rosler argues that we are mistaken if we think that the changes taking place are simply or primarily caused by the new technologies, or that some kind of essential 'nature of photography' is now undergoing change. Rather we need to look at wider cultural factors and recognise that our ideas and beliefs about photographs, as well as many other things, are changing.

Rosler stresses the importance of understanding that the **straight photography** of documentary and journalism is a genre. It has its own history, a politics, and institutional frameworks (of the press and broadcasting) which lend it its special, if contestable, authority. The term 'straight photography' points us to a way of making photographs in which evident artifice, construction and manipulation are avoided as a matter of principle. It does not, and cannot, mean an unmediated, uncrafted photograph or an image which is not the result of intention and shaping by the photographer. The very choice to work in this way, to avoid dramatic and rhetorical artificial lighting for example, to resist any setting up and orchestration of the subject, or the many manipulations and devices of the darkroom, is itself the outcome of working with ideas and making choices within a wider set of possibilities.

For Rosler, the question is not how accurately or objectively photographs represent the appearance of reality but whether they, or any other kinds of image, can be used to 'tell the truth' about a reality whose appearance can itself be an illusion. In seeing the issue this way Rosler points to the openly manipulative, alternative traditions of photography, represented by the **photomontages** of the Dadaists and John Heartfield. This was a way of

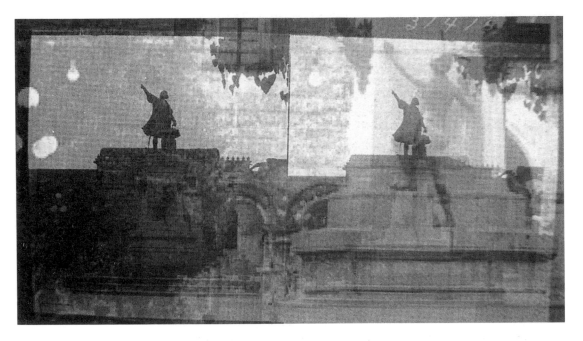

6.14 Esther Parada, 2–3–4–D: Digital Revisions in Time and Space, 1991–1992, At the Margin
In Esther Parada's work the qualities of layering, displacing, overlap and juxtaposition are highly evident. Such operations are facilitated by computer-based, image manipulation software. It is arguable, however, that these qualities are chosen by the artist and are not essential or necessary outcomes of using a digital medium

using photography that sought to prise open and dismantle appearances in order to point to the social realities that their surfaces do not reveal. Rosler sees these political photomontages as sharing with the early practitioners of photography – those who used multiple negatives to overcome the limitations of orthochromatic film – a search for a '*truer truth*, one closer to conceptual adequacy'. If, then, manipulation is recognised as integral to photography, it is best embraced and consciously directed.

> If we want to call up more hopeful or positive uses of manipulated images, we must choose images in which manipulation is itself apparent, not just as a form of artistic reflexivity but to make a larger point about the truth value of photographs and the illusionistic elements in the surface of (and even definition of) *reality*. . . . Here we must make the requisite bow to Brecht's remark about the photo of the exterior of the Krupp works not attesting to the conditions of slavery within.
>
> (Rosler 1991: 58)

Rosler argues that the 'identification of photographs with objectivity is a modern idea' and it is one that may be passing together with many other certainties of the modern age, such as a belief in progress. The meanings that images carry, whether photographic or digital, are not 'fully determined by the technologies used in their production', but they are shaped by the ideas and beliefs that are invested in and brought to them.

Rosler sees 'the questioning of photographic truth' as part of a 'more general cultural delegitimisation [that] is at work in industrial societies'. Rosler has in mind Guy Debord's theory of a 'society of the spectacle', in which the cultural industries of capitalist societies, which centrally included photography, have turned the very look of the world, its appearance, into a type of marketable commodity (Debord 1970). This, Rosler argues, was the material basis for a far-reaching change in the status of images and it is one that substantially takes place across the late nineteenth century and the first half of the twentieth century, prior to the emergence of digital image technologies.

Images, then, had already been severed from any simple equation with 'truth' in the earlier history of the mass production of images, advertising, cinema, propaganda, popular visual culture and spectacular entertainment. The question of the truth value of images or the reliability of the evidence which they provide does not simply rest on the kind of technology which was used to produce them, whether mechanical, electronic or digital. The use of photographs for propaganda purposes, argues Rosler, 'neither began nor will end with the electronic manipulation of photographic imagery'.

The postmodern image

It is William Mitchell who has made the connection between 'post-photography' and 'postmodernity' most explicitly when he states that 'The tools of digital imaging are felicitously adapted to the diverse projects of our postmodern era'. This is because, argues Mitchell, the digital medium 'privileges fragmentation, indeterminacy, and heterogeneity' and 'emphasises process or performance' rather than 'a kind of objective truth' which has previously been assured by traditional photography's 'quasi-scientific procedure and closed, finished perfection'.

The 'felicitous' link that Mitchell sees between such images and our diverse postmodern projects is largely a metaphorical one. In describing digital images with words like 'fragmentation', 'indeterminacy' and 'heterogeneity', Mitchell echoes closely the language of postmodern social and cultural theory. Steven Best and Douglas Kellner, for example, characterise postmodern patterns of thought as rejecting 'modern assumptions of social coherence and notions of causality in favour of multiplicity, *plurality, fragmentation, and indeterminacy*' (Best and Kellner 1991: 4).

This analogy, as there is no inherent reason for a particular technology to always be used in the same way, is a little slim. An instructive example is the CD-Rom 'I Photograph to Remember' (1993), in which the photographer Pedro Meyer uses the digital medium in a way that does not foreground its technical capacity for producing fragmentation or indeterminacy. On the contrary, he presents a narrative sequence of traditional photographs at high resolution, through which the viewer is able to move at a contemplative pace, reflecting upon each one and its relationship to a thoughtful and economic voiceover.

The point here is not that one of two competing forms or styles – that of 'fragmentation and indeterminacy' – is somehow necessarily superior to the other – that of a supposed photographic unity – but that *neither* is the necessary outcome of the technologies employed. Both technologies can be used either way, given the intention and the skill to do so. The fact that they may not be used in one way or another is a cultural, and not a technological, matter.

Digital deconstruction and theories of language

In an interview, the artist Esther Parada has suggested that the application of the computer to photographic representation will result in more 'overt recognition and discussion' of the manipulation that is inherent in the practice (Ziff 1991: 132). In holding this view she is clearly on similar ground to Martha Rosler, in that they both choose to stress the manipulability of the photographic process. However, it is William Mitchell – whom we have met, so far, as the theorist of the difference between photographic and the digital image processes – who pursues this point furthest. In difficult language, he proposes that the emergence of digital imaging can be seen as a means to 'expose the aporias in photography's construction of the visual world, to deconstruct the very ideas of photographic objectivity and closure, and to resist what has become an increasingly sclerotic tradition' (Mitchell 1991: 8).

By this, Mitchell seems to mean two things. First, that a software application, such as Adobe Photoshop, can be an **heuristic** tool for *understanding* photographic representation. Within a few hours' use, such a program allows the user to run through many of the manipulations and conventions which can be part of the practice of photography. Seen this way, digital image technology becomes a critical tool which can demonstrate in practice what has been argued in theory for some three decades; that photographic images are themselves special kinds of constructions. This 'deconstructive' project is itself fully in line with aspects of postmodern cultural practice, which is frequently concerned with a self-conscious and playful use of language – whether visual, literary or architectural – or sets out to reveal its operation.

Mitchell proceeds from this statement to draw an analogy between digital imaging and some contemporary theories of language. He suggests that an analogy can be drawn between the open-endedness of the digitised image and **poststructuralist** theories of language and meaning. The emphasis in such theories is on the polysemic nature of signs (their capacity to mean more than one fixed thing) and their indeterminacy (the way that language and sign systems are always 'in process' because they are being continually modified and nuanced as they are written and spoken in differing social contexts).

They never reach a final destination of fixed, settled meaning; that is, any kind of 'closure'. Mitchell suggests that we should understand digital imaging in this way. He proposes that, in the realm of visual images, digital technology is deconstructing the singular, fixed images of photography (their objectivity and closure). In this process, we are released from the grips of a worn-out and ailing photographic tradition and its outmoded mission.

These are suggestive analogies and Mitchell draws on many insights and ideas in making them. His ideas, however, must be criticised on a number of grounds. First, as was pointed out above, they are based on a very selective view of photography and a rather predetermined view of digital imaging. He cites the work of Paul Strand and Edward Weston, whom he sees as two modernist heroes of photography, and whose work he sees as exemplifying the aesthetic characteristics of photography (Mitchell 1992: 6–9). This hardly does justice to the range and variety of photographies which have been practised for a century and a half. It does, however, allow him to juxtapose a kind of stereotypical icon of photography: an image of the carefully framed and finely resolved photographic print, with another image; the pixelled, layered, montaged and, possibly, interactive digital image. Second, Mitchell largely ignores the many historical and social continuities of use to which the photograph and the digital image is put. Third, Mitchell's arguments tend to sail very close to a kind of **technological determinism**, a way of seeing technology as an autonomous force having definite outcomes which are independent of the culture which conceived and developed them, and of the uses to which they are put.

Finally, it has also been argued that, behind Mitchell's proclamation of a digital revolution in image culture, there is a deeper sense in which he believes there is a logical and progressive, technological evolution at work in the replacement of the camera by the computer (Robins 1995).

The limits of critical thought about post-photography

Robins accepts Mitchell's claim that 'The "image revolution" is significant in terms of a further and massive expansion of vision and visual techniques, allowing us to see new things and to see in new ways'. This involves a 'logic of development which is about a shift from a perceptual approach to images (seen as quotations from appearances), to one more concerned with the relation of imaging to conceptualisation'. In short, 'post-photography' displaces chemical photography's basis in the representation of appearances with a more sophisticated way of knowing; one that is based upon theories, algorithms and data. These are now used to simulate or to image *concepts about* objects and processes. In an age when our ideas about science, fact, truth and reality have become increasingly complex and problematic, 'post-photography' turns out to be a continuation, on a higher plane, of just one historical aspect of photography. This is the positivist project to collect facts, to measure and to record as a means of gaining objective knowledge of the world (see chapter 2). Seen this way, talk of digital images as revolutionary becomes 'hype'; they are simply a more sophisticated technology which continues to be harnessed to the task of 'getting at the real truth' (Robins 1995).

We have seen a number of times in this chapter how much thinking about photography and digital imaging tends to work through constructing binary oppositions between them. Robins warns of similar problems in the 'technological progressivism' which he detects in this emerging **discourse** on 'post-photography'. This is because it constructs a false polarisation between past and future, between photography and digital culture, and unthinkingly conflates new technology with good technology:

> From such a deterministic perspective, it is no longer relevant to take seriously the virtues of photographic culture, nor is it meaningful to question the virtues of post-photographic culture. Should we not be challenging this affirmative logic? Is not the whole process more complex. . .?
>
> (Robins 1995: 33)

This new 'post-photographic' discourse tends to limit the breadth of the ways in which we have been used to thinking about the culture of images. Our sense of the complexity and imaginative richness of images and visual culture is reduced to the terms of rational logic and progressive development. There is a danger that this discourse ignores other ways of thinking about images and their relation to the world: their emotional and subversive power, the awkward questions they can pose, and the alternative worlds they can help us imagine.

IN SUMMARY

A great deal of what has been considered in this chapter suggests that developments in digital image technology build upon the forms, uses and practices of photographic culture. They are accelerating many of the cultural processes in which photography has been involved and are in the process of transforming others. Yet, at the same time, a good deal of the critical attention given to photography in an age of electronic imaging is preoccupied with exploring – whether to deplore (Ritchin) or to celebrate (Mitchell) – the idea of a radical break – a momentous rupture – in visual culture.

There is clearly a real tension here; one which may be characteristic of moments of such change involving 'genuinely new technologies' (Williams 1974) and the different locations and levels on which change is experienced. Many a darkroom and enlarger has been replaced with an Apple Mac, a range of peripheral technologies, and the rapid acquisition of the 'know-how' to use them. Courses in photography increasingly add multimedia and digital imaging to their curricula. The everyday landscape of 'photographic' images – on TV, at the cinema, and in magazines and newspapers – change in both subtle and sensational ways, and these changes to traditional media have been joined by media forms, the domestic PC running multimedia CD-Roms for entertainment, education, publicity and communication.

For some, particularly a generation of photographers trained before the mid-1980s, these changes may be experienced on a scale that can be likened to that which photography brought about for the portrait painters of the mid-nineteenth century (Freud 1980), although such a comparison has to be tempered by several things. Digital technology impacted upon a photographic practice which had already been changed by analogue electronic and video technologies. Digital technology arrived in a technologically sophisticated world which cannot be directly likened to the nineteenth-century impact of photography on a handmade image culture. And finally, at the time of writing, the first generations of 'Photography' students who have grown up with the computer as a familiar object are now entering colleges and universities; for them, digital technology and the images it produces were always already there.

It is at the level of ideas and critical responses to these changes that the tension seems to be greatest. Thinking through the implications of technological change and conceiving of ways in which it may be creatively used is not simply an abstract and academic task. It will need to be undertaken in close relationship to the practical use of the new image technologies as their possibilities are selectively invested in, and explored. This may well call for new frameworks of understanding as other genuinely new media and communications technologies have called forth in the past. Yet, there is a clear danger that premature generalisations and simplifications are likely to be rife – and mystifying – if the historical and cultural context of technological change is not taken fully into account.

BIBLIOGRAPHY

KEY TEXTS

Benjamin, W. (1973a) 'The Work of Art in the Age of Mechanical Reproduction' in H. Arendt (ed.) *Illuminations*, Glasgow: Fontana/Collins
Binkley, T. (1993) 'Refiguring Culture' in P. Hayward and T. Wollen (eds) *Future Visions: New Technologies of the Screen*, London: BFI
Darley, A. (1990) 'From Abstraction to Simulation: Notes on the History of Computer Imaging' in P. Hayward (ed.) *Culture, Technology, and Creativity in the Late 20th Century*, London: John Libbey and Co Ltd
—— (1991) 'Big Screen, Little Screen: The Archaeology of Technology', Ten/8 2(2), Autumn, 'Digital Dialogues'
Lister, M. (ed.) (1995a) *The Photographic Image in Digital Culture*, London/New York: Routledge

—— (1995b) Introductory essay in M. Lister (ed.) *The Photographic Image in Digital Culture*, London/New York: Routledge

Mitchell, W. J. (1992) *The Reconfigured Eye: Visual Truth in the Post-Photographic Era*, Cambridge, MA: MIT Press

Nichols, B. (1988) 'The Work of Culture in the Age of Cybernetic Systems', *Screen* 29(1), Winter

Ritchin, F. (1990a) *In Our Own Image: The Coming Revolution in Photography*, New York; Aperture

—— (1990b) 'Photojournalism in the Age of Computers' in C. Squiers (ed.) *The Critical Image*, Seattle: Bay Press, pp. 28–37

Robins, K. (1991) 'Into the Image: Visual Technologies and Vision Cultures', in P. Wombell (ed.) *PhotoVideo: Photography in the Age of the Computer*, London: Rivers Oram Press

—— (1995) 'Will Images Move Us Still?' in M. Lister (ed.) *The Photographic Image in Digital Culture*, London/New York; Routledge

Rosler, M. (1991) 'Image Simulations, Computer Manipulations: Some Considerations', *Ten/8* 2(2), 'Digital Dialogues'

Willis, A.-M. (1990) 'Digitisation and the Living Death of Photography' in (ed.) Hayward, P, *Culture, Technology, and Creativity in the Late 20th Century*, London: John Libbey

Wombell, P. (ed.) (1991) *PhotoVideo: Photography in the Age of the Computer*, London: Rivers Oram Press

OTHER REFERENCES

Barthes, R. (1977a) 'The Photographic Message' in *Image-Music-Text*, London: Fontana

—— (1977b) 'The Rhetoric of the Image' in *Image-Music-Text*, London: Fontana

Becker, K. (1991) 'To Control our Image: Photojournalists Meeting New Technology', in P. Wombell (ed.) *PhotoVideo: Photography in the Age of the Computer*, London: Rivers Oram Press

Benjamin, W. (1973b) 'Some Motifs in Baudelaire' in H. Arendt (ed.) *Illuminations*, Glasgow: Fontana/Collins

Berger, J. and Mohr, Jean (1982) *Another Way of Telling*, London/New York: Writers and Readers Publishing Co-op Ltd

Best, Steven and Kellner, Douglas (1991) *Postmodern Theory: Critical Interrogations*, London: Macmillan

Boddy, William (1994) 'Archeologies of Electronic Vision and the Gendered Spectator', *Screen* 35(2): 105–122

Bode, S. and Wombell, P. (1991) 'Introduction: In a New Light' in P. Wombell (ed.) *PhotoVideo: Photography in the Age of the Computer*, London: Rivers Oram Press

Burgin, V. (1991) 'Realising the Reverie', 'Digital Dialogues', *Ten/8* 2(2)

Crary, J. (1993) *Techniques of the Observer*, Cambridge, MA: MIT Press

Debord, G. (1970) *The Society of the Spectacle*, Detroit: Black and Red

Dewdney, A. and Boyd, F. (1995). 'Television, Computers, Technology and Cultural Form' in M. Lister (ed.) *The Photographic Image in Digital Culture*, London/New York: Routledge

Druckery, Timothy (1991) 'Deadly Representations or Apocalypse Now', 'Digital Dialogues' *Ten/8* 2(2): 16–27

Ellis, John (1991) *Visible Fictions: Cinema, Television, Video*, London/New York: Routledge

Graham, B. (1995) 'the panic button (in which our heroine goes back to the future of pornography)' in M. Lister (ed.) *The Photographic Image in Digital Culture*, London/New York: Routledge

Grundberg, A. (1990) 'Photography in the Age of Electronic Simulation' in *Crisis of the Real*, New York: Aperture

Haddon, Leslie (1993) 'Interactive Games' in P. Hayward and T. Wollen (eds) *Future Visions: New Technologies of the Screen*, London: BFI

Hall, S. (1988) 'The Work of Art in The Age of Electronic Age', *Block* 14

Harvey, David (1989) *The Condition of Postmodernity*, Cambridge, MA: Blackwell

Harvie, C. et al. (1970) *Industrialisation and Culture 1830–1914*, London: Macmillan/Oxford University Press

Hayward, Philip (1993) 'Situating Cyberspace: The Popularisation of Virtual Reality' in P. Hayward and T. Walker (eds) *Future Visions: New Technologies of the Screen*, London: BFI

Jameson, F. (1984) 'Postmodernism or the Cultural Logic of Late Capitalism', *New Left Review* 146, July/August

—— (1993) 'Postmodernism and Consumer Society' in A. Gray and J. McGuigan (eds) *Studying Culture*, London/New York/Melbourne/Auckland: Edward Arnold

Jukes, Peter (1992) 'The Work of Art in the Domain of Digital Production' *New Statesman and Society*, 17 July 40–41

Kember, S. (1995) 'Medicine's New Vision' in M. Lister (ed.) *The Photographic Image in Digital Culture*, London/New York: Routledge

Lury, C. (1992) 'Popular Culture and the Mass Media' in R. Bocock and K. Thompson (eds) *Social and Cultural Forms of Modernity*, Cambridge: Polity Press

McGrath, R. (1984) 'Medical Police', *Ten/8* 14: 13–18

Malina, R. F. (1990) 'Digital Image – Digital Cinema: The Work of Art in the Age of Post-Mechanical Reproduction', *Leonardo*, Supplemental Issue: 33–38

Marvin, Carolyn (1988) *When Old Technologies Were New*, New York: Oxford University Press

Mulvey, Laura (1981) 'Visual Pleasure and Narrative Cinema' in Tony Bennett et al. (eds) *Popular Television and Film*, London: BFI/OU

Nead, L. (1992) *The Female Nude: Art, Obscenity and Sexuality*, London/New York: Routledge

Neale, Steve (1985) *Cinema and Technology: Images, Sound, Colour*, London: Macmillan

Piper, K. (1991) 'Fortress Europe: Tagging the Other' in P. Wombell (ed.) *PhotoVideo: Photography in the Age of the Computer*, London: Rivers Oram Press

Punt, M. (1995) 'The Elephant, the Spaceship and the White Cockatoo: an Archaeology of Digital Photography' in M. Lister (ed.) *The Photographic Image in Digital Culture*, London/New York: Routledge

Robins, K. (1992) 'The Virtual Unconscious in Post-Photography', *Science as Culture* 14

Slater, D. R. (1991) 'Consuming Kodak' in J. Spence and P. Holland (eds) *Family Snaps: The Meanings of Domestic Photography*, London: Virago Press

—— (1995) 'Domestic Photography and Digital Culture' in M. Lister (ed.) *The Photographic Image in Digital Culture*, London/New York: Routledge

Snyder, J. and Allen, N. W. (1975) 'Photography, Vision, and Representation', *Critical Enquiry* 2, Autumn: 143–169

Snyder, J. (1980) 'Picturing Vision', *Critical Enquiry* 6, Spring: 499–526

Stafford, B. M. (1991) *Body Criticism, Imaging the Unseen in Enlightenment, Art and Medicine*, Cambridge, MA; MIT Press

Tagg, J. (1988) *The Burden of Representation*, London: Macmillan

Virilio, P., Baudrillard, J. and Hall, S. (1988) 'The Work of Art in the Electronic Age', *Block* 14

Walker, Ian (1995) 'Desert Stones or Faith in Facts' in M. Lister (ed.) *The Photographic Image in Digital Culture*, London/New York: Routledge

Williams, R. (1974) *Television: Technology and Cultural Form*, London: Fontana

Ziff, T. (1991) 'Taking New Ideas Back to the Old World', in P. Wombell (ed.) *PhotoVideo: Photography in the Age of the Computer*, London: Rivers Oram Press

GLOSSARY

Key terms

analogue A form of representation, such as a painting, a chemical photograph or video tape, in which the image is composed of a continuous variation of tone, light or some other signal. Similarly, a gramophone record is an analogue medium for reproducing sound or music. Analogue **representation** is based upon an unsegmented **code** while a digital medium is based upon a segmented one in which information is divided into discrete elements. The hands of a traditional (analogue) clock which continuously sweep its face, in contrast to a digital clock which announces each second in isolation, is a common example of the difference.

art In this book we distinguish between 'Art', referring to high art and related gallery and funding institutions, and 'art' as creative skill.

autographic A generic term applied to all of those processes – drawing and painting being the main ones – in which images are made by the action and coordination of the eye and hand, and without mechanical or electronic intervention. Autographic images are authored wholly by physical and intellectual skill, or as a general field of (artistic) practices.

carnivalesque A concept developed by the Russian theorist Bakhtin to describe the taste for crude laughter, bad taste, excessiveness (particularly of bodily functions) and offensiveness. It celebrates a temporary liberation from recognised rules and hierarchies and is tolerated because, once people have been allowed to let off steam, those norms can be re-established.

code Used here in the **semiotic** sense to refer to the way in which signs are systematically organised to create meaning – the Morse code is one simple example. Cultural codes determine the meanings conveyed by various cultural practices, say, the way people dress or eat their meals; photographic codes control the way meanings are conveyed in a photograph – for example, the details that give a news photograph its sense of authenticity, or a wedding photograph the right sort of dignity. In chapter 3 the discussion of Jo Spence's work elaborates on the use of photographic codes. Cultural codes are centrally examined in chapter 4.
See **semiotics**

commodity Something which is bought and sold. The most commonly understood forms of commodity are goods which have been manufactured for the marketplace, but within capitalism other things have also been commodified. Natural resources and human labour have also been metamorphosed into commodities.

commodity culture A term increasingly used to describe the culture of industrial capitalism. Within today's culture everything, even the water we drink, has become a product to be bought and sold in the marketplace. Commodity culture also infers the naturalisation of this system to the extent that we cannot imagine another way of living.

construction This refers to the creating or forging of images and artefacts. In photography this particularly draws attention to the deliberate building of an image, rather than its taking from actuality, through **staging**, **fabrication**, **montage** and **image-text**. The term also reminds us of Soviet Constructivism, which emphasised the role of Art in the building of a new social order and used industrial elements, putting them together as work. It also draws upon theories of **deconstruction**.

deconstruction A radical poststructuralist theory, centred upon the work of French literary theorist, Jacques Derrida, which investigates the complexity and, ultimately indeterminable, play of meaning in texts. Derrida's focus is literary, but the analysis may be extended to the visual.

discourse The circulation of an idea or set of ideas. Photography is one the many media – including newspapers, books, conversation, television programmes, and so on – which constitute contemporary discourses.
See **ideology**.

epistemological A branch of philosophy concerned to establish by what means knowledge is derived. It is concerned with questions such as what it is possible to know and how reliable is knowledge. In the present context, questions can be asked about what kind of knowledge images provide, and how they do It.

fantasies The term 'fantasy' usually refers to stories, daydreams and other fictions. It is sometimes distinguished from 'phantasy', which is a more technical term from **psychoanalysis** referring to **unconscious** processes. This book draws on both meanings, especially when discussing writers and photographers influenced by psychoanalytic thought.
See **psychoanalysis**, **unconscious**

formalism The prioritisation of concern with form; that is, composition and the material nature of any specific medium, rather than content.

gaze This has become a familiar term to describe a particular way of looking at, perceiving and understanding the world. It was brought into currency by writers on cinema, concerned to analyse the response of the audience as voyeurs of the action on the screen. The voyeuristic gaze is used to describe the way in which men often look at women, as well as the way in which tourists look at the non-Western world. More recently, discussions have focused on the implications of a 'female gaze'.

hegemony Dominance maintained through the continuous negotiation of consent by those in power in respect of their right to rule. Such consent is underpinned by the possibility of coercion.
See **ideology**

heuristic An educational strategy in which students (or researchers) are trained to find things out for themselves.

historicisation Used (in chapter 6) to refer to the process by which events or other phenomena are given a place in an historical narrative. Photography may be defined by the position that it occupies in a larger historical schema or an unfolding over time of technologies and practices.

identity A person's identity is their sense of self and the different contexts within which that selfhood is constructed. It can never be given one simple, coherent description. For example, the national identity into which one is born may well clash with the cultural identity of the community in which one chooses to live; or a gay identity, based on sexuality, may clash with a religious identity based on strict rules governing sexual behaviour.

ideology This term is commonly used in two differing but interconnected ways. In this book it is used primarily to refer to a system or bodies of ideas which may be abstract, but which arise from a particular set of class interests. The term is also commonly used to refer to ideas which are illusory, whose purpose is to mask social and economic relations which actually obtain. For instance, the idea that children need their mother at home (which was common in the 1950s) masked the economic relations of patriarchy whereby married women were rendered financially dependent upon their husbands.

index One of three kinds of sign defined by American semiotician, C. S. Pierce. The indexical sign is based in cause and effect, for example, the footprint in wet sand indicates or traces a recent presence. The other two types of sign are the iconic (that which is based in resemblance), and the symbolic, or sign proper (that which is entirely conventional).
See **semiotics**

mimetic representation based upon imitation, upon showing rather than telling, a concept central to traditional post-Renaissance art theory.
See **representation**

modernism In everyday terms 'modern' is often used to refer to contemporary design, media or forms of social organisation (as in 'the modern family'). But, 'modern' also frequently refers to the emphasis upon modernisation from the mid-nineteenth century onwards, and, more particularly, to Modern movements in art and design from the turn of the twentieth century. It is essentially a relative concept (modern by contrast with . . .); its precise usage depends upon particular contexts. In this book we distinguish between three terms: *modernism*, sets of progressive ideas in which the modern is emphasised and welcomed; and *modernity*, social, technological and cultural develop-ments. The term '*Modernism*' is used in chapter 5 to refer to particular emphasis on form and materiality in modern art. Throughout the book a distinction is made between the modern, and the postmodern or contemporary. The modern refers to the era after the Age of Enlightenment wherein the world became conceptualised as human-centred, rather than, as in medieval times, god-centred.
See **postmodern**

ontological Ontology is a branch of philosophy. It concerns the study of how things exist and the nature of various kinds of existence. It involves the logical investigation of the different ways in which things of different types (physical objects, numbers, abstract concepts, etc.) are thought to exist.

the Other A concept used within **psychoanalysis** and **identity** theory, and within post-colonial theory, to signify ways in which members of dominant groups derive a sense of self-location partly through defining other groups as different or 'Other'. Thus, within patriarchy, the male is taken as the norm, and woman as 'Other'; that is, not male. Similarly, in racist ideologies, whiteness is taken for granted, therefore blackness is seen as Other.

polysemic A property of signs is that they can have many meanings, depending on their context and the interests of their readers. Hence the frequent use of captions, or words within the image, to help anchor meaning.

postmodern Literally 'after the modern', the postmodern represents a critique of the limitations of modernism with its emphasis upon progress and, in the case of the Arts, upon the materiality of the medium of communication. Philosophically, postmodernism has been defined as marking the collapse of certainty, a loss of faith in explanatory systems, and a sense of dislocation consequent on the global nature of communication systems and the loss of a clear relation between signs and their referents.

poststructuralist At its most simple, this means 'after Structuralism', also implying critical thinking that contests and goes beyond Structuralist theory and method, rejecting the idea that all

meaning is fundamentally systematic. In this book it is used to refer to a group of theories which stress the way that the human 'self' and the meaning made of the world is constructed through the languages (including visual languages) which we use. Poststructuralist thinking challenges the idea that there is a fixed and stable human subject who can have certain knowledge.
See **identity**, **structuralism**

private and public spheres We lead our lives within two distinct modes, a 'private ' sphere, which is made up of personal and kinship relations and domestic life, and a 'public' sphere, made up of economic relations, work, money-making and politics. The 'private' sphere tends to be controlled by moral and emotional constraints, the 'public' sphere by public laws and regulations. This distinction, although contested by feminist writers, underlies the way the terms 'private' and 'public' are used in this book, especially in chapter 3.

psychoanalysis The therapeutic method established by Sigmund Freud, which involves seeking access to traumatic experiences held in the **unconscious** mind.
See **repression**, **unconscious**

representation This refers to ways in which individuals, groups or ideas are depicted. Although this seems obvious, the use of the term usually signals acknowledgement that images are never 'innocent', but always have their own history, cultural contexts and specificity and, therefore, carry **ideological** implications.

repression Unpleasant or unwelcome thoughts, emotions, sensation are 'repressed' when they are forced into the **unconscious**. The phrase 'the return of the repressed' means that such emotions surface into the conscious world in different form.
See **psychoanalysis**, **unconscious**

semiology see **semiotics**

semiotics The science of signs, first proposed in 1916 by linguist, Ferdinand de Saussure, but developed in particular in the work of Roland Barthes (France) and C. S. Pierce (USA). Semiotics – also referred to as semiology – is premised upon the contention that all human communication is founded in an assemblage of signs, verbal, aural and visual, which is essentially systematic. Such sign systems are viewed as largely – or entirely – conventional; that is, consequent not upon 'natural' relations between words or images and that to which they refer, but upon arbitrary relations established through cultural convention. The sign proper has two aspects, signifier and signified. The signifier is the material manifestation, the word, or pictorial elements. The signified is the associated mental concept; that is, conventionally associated with the specific signifier. Whilst separable for analytic purposes, in practice the signifier and the signified always go together.
See **code**

social and economic history History may be written in many ways. Economic history deals with changes in work patterns and the ways in which human societies have sustained themselves. Social history deals with the organisation of societies – marriage, education, child-rearing and the like. A history of photography is normally seen as part of art history or, more broadly, of cultural history. In chapter 3 it is suggested that we can understand personal photography better if we consider it within a social and economic context. Chapter 4 takes the social and the economic as the primary context for understanding commercial uses of photography.

structuralism Twentieth-century theoretical movement within which stress is laid upon analysis of objects, cultural artefacts and communication processes, in terms of systems of relations rather than as entities in themselves.

technological determinism This refers to the proposition that technological invention alone determines new cultural formations. The notion has been criticised primarily on the grounds that new technologies arise from research enterprises driven largely by economic imperatives and perceived social or political needs. Technological developments may be seen as an effect of cultural desires as well as a major influence within cultural change.

teleology Arguments and explanations in which the nature of something is explained by the purpose or 'end' which it appears to have. In this view photography, and then cinema, may be understood as being caused by a human desire to achieve ever more comprehensive illusions of reality and are seen as striving towards a future achievement.

unconscious In **psychoanalysis**, that which is **repressed** from the individual's conscious awareness yet gives rise to impulses which influence our behaviour. Freud insisted that human action always derives from mental processes of which we cannot be aware.
See **repression**, **psychoanalysis**

Photographic terms

bricolage A process of improvisation in which various elements and 'bits and pieces' are joined together to make something. In French a *bricoleur* is a handyman, and *bricolage* refers to DIY. The term has been adapted for use within digital imaging by adding the prefix 'electro'.

calotype Photographic print made by the process launched by William Henry Fox Talbot in England in 1840. It involved the exposure of sensitised paper in the camera from which, after processing, positive paper prints could be made. Not much used in England in the early days, because it was protected by Fox Talbot's own patents, but its use was developed in Scotland, especially by David Octavius Hill and Robert Adamson.

carte-de-visite A small paper print (2½ × 4⅛") mounted on a card with the photographer's details on the reverse. This way of producing photographs for sale was developed by André-Adolphe Disdéri in France in 1854. Eight or more images were made on the same glass negative by a special camera with several lenses and a moving plate-holder. The prints were then cut up to size. Such prints could be produced in very large numbers.

daguerreotype Photographic image made by the process launched by Louis-Jacques-Mande Daguerre in France in 1839. It is a positive image on a metal plate with a mirror-like silvered surface, characterised by very fine detail. Each one is unique and fragile and needs to be protected by a padded case. It became the dominant portrait mode for the first decades of photography, especially in the United States.

electrobricolage See **bricolage**

fabrication The crafting of images which have been **staged** or appropriated and adjusted for the camera. The term is more common within American photography than European, referencing the craft base of the medium. It stands by contrast with '**constructed**' imagery, which inflects the directorial approach in more political terms through referencing both Soviet Constructivism and theories of **deconstruction**.
See **construction**, **deconstruction**, **staged images**

image-text Pictures within which visual imagery and written text are integrated in order to effect a play of meaning between them.

montage See **photomontage**

photomontage The use of two or more originals, perhaps also including written text, to make a combined image. A montaged image may be imaginative, artistic, comic or deliberately satirical.

polaroid The Polaroid land camera, producing instant black and white positives, was first marketed in 1947, but produced poor-quality images. Polaroid instant colour prints and slides were launched in 1963.

staged images Described by American critic A. D. Coleman as 'falsified documents', this refers to the creating of a scene for the camera (as in staging within theatre).

straight photography Emphasis upon direct documentary typical of the Modern period in American photography.

tintype Tintypes, instant positive images on enamelled iron plates, were produced from 1852 to around 1946. As one of the cheapest methods, they were especially favoured by seaside photographers.

KEY PUBLIC ARCHIVES

The Documentary Photography Archive, GO 11, Tylecote Building, Cavendish Street, Manchester M15 6BG, tel: (0161) 247 1765
Jo Spence Memorial Archive, 152 Upper Street, London N1 1RA, tel: (0171) 359 9064
National Museum of Photography, Film and Television, Pictureville, Prince's View, Bradford BD5 0TR, tel: (01274) 727488
National Portrait Gallery, Charing Cross Road, London WC1. For photographic portraiture archives and exhibitions
Royal Photographic Society, The Octagon, 46 Milsom Street, Bath BA1 1DN, tel: (01225) 462841
Scottish National Portrait Gallery, 1 Queen Street, Edinburgh. For portraiture archives
Victoria and Albert Museum, South Kensington, London SW7. Holds the National Collection of the Art of Photography

Note: Many organisations, including newspapers and commercial companies, maintain their own archives. However, access to these may be limited, by appointment only or based on payment of search fees

KEY BRITISH MAGAZINES

British Journal of Photography, London
Camerawork, London (until 1985)
Creative Camera, London, published six times a year
History of Photography, Oxford
Portfolio, Portfolio Gallery, Edinburgh, published twice yearly
Ten/8, Birmingham (until 1992; titled *Ten.8* in the two most recent issues)

Index